SCHOOL COUNSELING AND COUNSELOR INTERVENTION

SCHOOL COUNSELING AND COUNSELOR INTERVENTION

Edited by Delila Owens

cognella® | ACADEMIC PUBLISHING

Bassim Hamadeh, CEO and Publisher
Jennifer Codner, Acquisitions Editor
Michelle Piehl, Senior Project Editor
Alia Bales, Production Editor
Emely Villavicencio, Senior Graphic Designer
Stephanie Kohl, Licensing Coordinator
Natalie Piccotti, Director of Marketing
Kassie Graves, Vice President of Editorial
Jamie Giganti, Director of Academic Publishing

Printed in the United States of America.

ISBN: 978-1-5165-2796-0 (pbk) / 978-1-5165-2797-7 (br)

cognella® | ACADEMIC PUBLISHING

For all the educators who work tirelessly
to improve the lives of children.

CONTENTS

PREFACE

> The classroom, with all its limitations, remains a location of possibility. In that field of possibility we have the opportunity to labor for freedom, to demand of ourselves and our comrades, an openness of mind and heart that allows us to face reality even as we collectively imagine ways to move beyond boundaries, to transgress. This is education as the practice of freedom.—bell hooks[1]

The purpose of this book is to provide a multifaceted approach to issues impacting the academic success of students. It is specifically designed for training school counselors. I have often heard individuals say that schools are a microcosm of our communities. This means that the same issues that are prevalent in communities will be manifested in the schools. If educators continue to harbor low expectations and provide below standard education to our children, we will continue to have impoverished communities. Schools cannot build a foundation in children. However, caring and committed adults, coupled with useful interventions can bring out the best in children.

If we, as scholars and school counselors, are serious about moving away from the deficit perspective and giving all children *equal access,* we must build on their strengths. As such, a review of school policies, instructional practices and resources for optimal student development is warranted. Students of color outnumber White students in public schools in the United States (Carr, 2014). However, most training programs still train educators using theories developed from a Euocentric perspective and do not address key developmental concerns that can impede academic success.

Training using Eurocentric theories leave educators with the assumption that children should be radically individualistic. This stance goes against the norm of many communities of color. For example, elders are held in the highest regard

1 hooks, bell. (1994). *Teaching to transgress.* New York: Routledge.

in the Native American community. In many instances, it is impossible to work with the children or young adults in the community without gaining the consent of an elder. Many people of color have historically survived using a more collective framework. Ethnocentric monocultural bias in educational institutions unfairly penalizes children who are culturally diverse. Yet, counselor education training is still very intrinsic. We must guard against ethnocentrism. School counselors must consider developmental concerns that impede academic success and become culturally responsive in addressing these concerns. A comprehensive assessment of a child (race, culture, and environmental forces) will produce the best outcomes.

Empathetic school counselors, who assist without bias, is what brings out the best in children. I choose to believe this because of a school counselor who was instrumental in my life (Mr. Green). Mr. Green is the school counselor that I aim to produce: one who is nonjudgmental and holds high expectations for every student encountered. A true soldier of justice.

PART I

Foundations of Counseling

CHAPTER 1
History of School Counseling

Delila Owens and Tanya Middleton

INTRODUCTION

The school counseling profession has its roots in the vocational guidance movement. Jesse B. Davis was the first to begin systematic guidance in public schools. He began this work at Central High School in Detroit, MI. He later became a principal in Grand Rapids, MI. During his time as a principal he began training English teachers in how to prepare students for vocational careers, develop moral character, and avoid behavioral concerns (Coy, 1999; Gladdings, 2004). He is credited for being the first person to start the moral guidance movement.

Educational historians have credited Davis for his implementation of a systematic guidance system as having laid the foundation for future career and school counseling programs (Aubrey, 1977; Pope, 2000). Through his own personal journey, Davis was able to utilize the basic Parsonian career development process (Parsons, 1909). This process included incorporating self-knowledge, information gathering, and ability to understand the relationship between these to make an effective decision. This method was further chronicled in his work titled *Vocational and Moral Guidance* published in 1956. It highlighted the need for individuals to focus attention on comprehension skills and abilities as well as moral conscious (Davis, 1956).

Throughout his travels in the early 20th century, Davis toured the United States promoting this new plan. He became involved in various professional organizations such as the National Vocational Guidance Association in 1913 (currently known as the National Career Development Association) and the National Association of Secondary School Principals where he served as the founder and second president. These among other professional organizations served to further advance the field and shed light on the need to implement guidance services in all schools.

The general goals of counseling can be described as a process of helping individuals by assisting them with making decisions and changing behavior (Chesapeake Public School, 2013; Schmidt, 2010, 2014). Professional school counselors are certified/licensed trained mental health professionals. They address the needs of students in three core areas. These areas include academic, career, and social personal development (Schmidt, 2010, 2014). Professional school counseling is distinguished from clinical mental health counseling in that school counselors are charged with removing personal/social issues that impede academic success. They are also charged with ensuring that the school counseling program is comprehensive in nature. Comprehensive school counseling programs must be holistic, systemic, balanced, reflective, proactive, and infused into the academic curriculum (Dollarhide & Saginak, 2017).

In 1997, the American School Counseling Association implemented the scope of responsibilities that detailed the evolution of the school counseling profession. School counselors along with students, school staff, families, and members of the community all work together to play an integral part of the education program by promoting school success while focusing not only on academic achievement, but also prevention and intervention activities, advocacy, and social-emotional and career development (Chesapeake Public Schools, 2013, p. 16).

EVOLUTION OF SCHOOL COUNSELING AND SOCIAL REFORM

School counseling emerged in the late 19th century to respond to the evolving workforce and assistance with job placement. Historians such as Brewer (1942) and Pope (2000) have described the emergence as a response to "progressive social reform aimed at eradicating poverty and substandard living conditions spawned by the rapid industrialization and consequent migration of people to major urban centers at the turn of the 20th century" (Pope, 2000, p. 196). The designation, "school counselor" is one that has transcended over time and was first termed *vocational guidance* by Frank Parsons during the early guidance movement in 1908 (Parsons, 1909). Brewer (1942) described vocation guidance as "assisting young people in planning and carrying out their working careers, with primary emphasis on choosing a vocation." Vocational guidance eventually spawned into career development. These noted transitions were to attest for the increased industrialization and urbanization occurring in the United States. The initial intention of guidance was aimed to assist with vocational aspirations and academics. It was identified in later years (Bauman et al., 2003) that the original process included counseling as a tool or technique to aide specialists rather than a single entity to alleviate emotional concerns. Many theorists including Brewer (1942) and Pope (2000) concluded that "the birth and development of career counseling in the United States occurred during times of major societal change." School counseling also transitioned over the 20th and 21st centuries in response to the demand of the climate. Brewer summarizes the field of school/vocational guidance as weaving social work, psychology, and counseling into an education format.

The initial phase of guidance was noted to be quite simplistic and ingrained in an existing curriculum often led by teachers versus trained professionals (Aubrey, 1977). This period was controversial because it lacked theoretical foundations and was based on simple and logical thinking. Jesse B. Davis's work encompassed a foundation built on the principles of understanding self, knowledge of the requirements and conditions for success, and ultimately reasoning between the two. His method was correlated to the work of Frank Parsons (1909) often called the parent of career counseling.

Parsons' work was guided by the earlier work of Jane Adams who was a philanthropist in Chicago. She and colleague Ellen Gates Starr founded the Hull House on the south side of Chicago. Parsons was the most visible in the guidance movement, Parsons was employed as a social worker in Boston at a settlement house for young people identified as unemployed or displaced. It was from this experience that he established the Vocation Bureau at Civic Service House in Boston in 1908. The Vocation Bureau is credited as the first institutionalization of career counseling in the United States (Aubrey, 1977). Self-assessment and psychological testing were major factors of this stage, factors that many theorists (Super & Crites, 1962) believe provided career counseling with respectability and validity in the United States. The Smith-Hughes Act of 1917 and the George Reed Act of 1929 further added esteem while supporting the need for trained professionals. The act established secondary school and vocational educational training (Rojewski, 2002). This progression also paved the way for endeavors such as *The Vocational Guidance Bulletin* in 1915 (currently *The Vocational Guidance Journal*) and conferences on vocational guidance, both of which led to expansions to the field (Aubrey, 1977).

Parsons is also credited for being the first to attempt to establish education for teachers desiring to learn skills necessary for vocational guidance (Savickas, 1993). He joined with the local Young Men's Christian Association (YMCA) in Boston to implement an informal training program. He died a short time after its induction. However, the plan he established set the blueprint for formal education to follow. Following Parsons' death a new director, Meyer Bloomfield, expanded the Vocation Bureau and its services. Bloomfield, a noted preeminent leader of the vocational guidance movement in the early 20th century, added the component of placement and follow-up with students to the Parsons model (understanding of self, information gathering, and combining the two) (Savickas, 1993). Initial reports from the Vocational Bureau were also that guidance should be a part of school systems and performed by trained professionals (Stickel & Yang, 1993). Following the success of Parsons' informal training, Bloomfield was able to teach a group of volunteer teachers known as Boston School Vocational Counselors. As a result, the first "vocational counselors" were placed in many elementary schools within the Boston area in 1910 (Savickas, 1993). Bloomfield has the distinction of having instructed the first credited course on vocational guidance at Harvard College in 1911 (Aubrey, 1977). Of importance was the urging of the vocational counselors to study the home, community, and other vocational influences of their students. This was an effort to identify barriers of success and provide efficient job placement. By 1910, 35 cities in the United States such as Boston, Des Moines, Cincinnati, and Grand Rapids were cited either to have implemented or to be planning to have vocational guidance in their schools (Aubrey, 1977).

It was during this period that attention was increased in the area of social reform and protection of human beings from unjust treatment. This was a driving force with vocation building due to the unlawful exploitation of children. Although legislation was not passed until 1938, Parsons was at the forefront of this issue (Aubrey, 1977).

The progression of educational counseling at the elementary and secondary school levels was prominent in the 1920s and 1930s. This focus shifted in part because of the economic depression of 1930s and the rising population of elementary school children born following World War I (Super & Crites, 1962). The social reform movement and the merging of guidance, testing, and social work was forged and the need for job creation and services was further amplified by President Franklin D. Roosevelt's New Deal. His deal was a plan that fought to combat the strengthening of unions and job decline (Super, 1955). The year 1933 witnessed the creation of the Civilian Conservation Corps (CCC), designed to provide training and education for unemployed youth. Guidance conventions also continued to grow, urging a need to address the lack of vocational guidance within the schools promoting career counseling for students (Pope, 2000).

The 1940s through the 1960s experienced renewed interest in career readiness and were in part rejuvenated by World War II and the USSR's launching of the Sputnik that orbited Earth (Pope, 2000; Schmidt, 2010, 2014). These two events illuminated the fact that the United States was no longer superior in developing new technology. The U.S. government sought to address this concern by altering the course of guidance counseling. The creation of the National Defense Act in 1958 served to offset this hierarchy (Herr, 2001) and overcome the loss of superiority by forming counseling and guidance training institutes aimed at identifying and encouraging students to pursue science and math majors at the collegiate level. Because of the increased attention on higher education, the National Defense Act was in part responsible for the rise in training of school counselors and increased funding. The direct effect was an increase in the number of school counselors from 6,780 in 1951 to more than 30,000 in 1965 (Aubrey, 1977). Truman's Fair Deal and the G.I. Bill also served to provide training and employment for returning home soldiers and displaced veterans, who benefited from the increase in counselors for proper placement. This era also produced more identification for vocational counselors in the area of professional development and organization (Herr, 2001). While the National Vocational Guidance Association (NVGA) had grown to approximately 6,000 members, the recognition of joining with others led to NVGA being one of the founding divisions of the American Personal and Guidance Association (APGA), later named American Association for Counseling & Development (AACD) and in 1951 American Counseling Association (ACA) (Lambie & Williamson, 2004; Schmidt, 2014).

Another factor that impacted the direction of the guidance movement was a shift from a more authoritarian approach where the counselor took the lead to one that was more client-centered. Carl Rogers is credited for the new wave of collaboration and counseling that was more of an "adjunct tool" and integral in the actualization of self through a life span journey of career (Aubrey, 1977). With this new direction came more emphasis on techniques, goals, and objectives to assist with self-discovery and decision making.

Meaningfulness was the ideology for students and adults entering the workforce starting in the 1960s. The idea was for this population to secure employment that was meaningful and world changing. This movement was spearheaded by the election of President John F. Kennedy and the civil rights movement (Pope, 2000). With a population that was comprised of more people of color and war veterans, President Kennedy worked to alleviate the unemployment rate of 8.1%, the highest since the days of the Great Depression. In his quest, he placed higher emphasis on school counselors. He passed the Vocational Education Act of 1963 along with the Economic Opportunity Act that created other social historic programs including Job Corps, Neighborhood Youth Corps, VISTA, Youth Opportunity Centers, and Head Start (Herr, 2013). The Elementary and Secondary Education Act was amended in 1969 to assist with providing resources to disadvantaged children in schools without proper guidance or library sources.

Accountability for counselors was also key during this process. It was determined that the effectiveness of its counselors could only be measured by the impact on the students (Gysbers, 2004). Following a series of seminars held by the U.S. Department of Education, direct objectives and process models in the domains of educational, vocational, and social development were created.

The 1980s witnessed yet another shift in the field of career counseling in the United States. The changing landscape of the country led to economic hardship and a loss of jobs as careers shifted to more technological advances and qualified applicants to meet the demand were less available (Pope, 2000). Also of notice was the fluctuating demographics that forecasted a workforce that would be have a large number of people of color (Sue & Sue, 2012). Legislation that was most prominent during this time was the Carl D. Perkins Vocational Act of 1984. This act replaced the Vocational Education Act of 1963 and has been viewed as integral to authorizing career counseling in the schools.

Guidance in the schools continued to unfold working to redefine the roles and purpose in the 1960s, 1970s, 1980s, and 1990s. The efforts were in response to social problems such as mental health concerns, substance abuse, family issues, and violence in schools (Gysbers, 2001). Stripling and Lane (1966) also introduced the notion of pupil services and working to strategize not only with the students but also with parents and teachers. As the decades progressed there was an apparent need to further define the role and developmental programs. They were structured moving away from a set of services to a more well-rounded approach aimed to uphold the need of the ever-changing environment (Gysbers, 2004). Examples such as Myrick's developmental model (Myrick, 1997) that emphasized "a focus on provision of programs for all students, the recognition that the guidance curriculum must be organized, planned, sequential, yet flexible, and the need for an integrated approach involving all school personnel." Gysbers and Henderson (2000) further expanded other models focusing on results while emphasizing "an organizational structure consisting of content (competencies), organizational framework (structural components and program components), and resources (human, financial, and political)." Ultimately, the school counselor is charged with boosting academic achievement.

CONCLUSION

Scholastic development is contingent on a number of factors, namely the interconnection of schools, families, and communities. The learning experiences gained from all are equally vital. Teaching styles and instructional approaches all play important roles in a child's motivation and achievement. Parental involvement is also important. Given the growing diversity among school-age children, school counselors must be culturally aware. School counselors must pay careful attention to ethnocentric monoculturalism and how it can be manifested in systems (Sue & Sue, 2012; Sue, 2015). School counselors must always guard against viewing children from a single lens. School counselors are instrumental in the life of school-age children.

REFERENCES

American School Counselor Association. (1997). *Definition of school counseling.* Alexandria, VA: Author.

Aubrey, R. F. (1977). Historical development of guidance and counseling and implications for the future. *Journal of Counseling & Development, 55*(6), 288–295.

Bauman, S., Siegel, J., Falco, L., Szymanski, G., Davis, A., & Seabolt, K. (2003). Trends in school counseling journals: The first fifty years. *Professional School Counseling, 7*(2), 79–90.

Brewer, J. M. (1942). *History of vocational guidance: Origins and early development.* New York: Harper and Brothers.

Chesapeake Public Schools. (2013). *2013 Secondary Student Catalog—A Student Handbook & A Course of Study Guide.* Retrieved from http://docplayer.net/13553790-Secondary-chesapeake-public-schools-catalog-a-studenthandbook-course-of-study-guide-secondary-student-catalog-1.html

Coy, D. R. (1999). The role and training of the school counselor: Background and purpose. *NASSP Bulletin, 83*(603), 2–8.

Davis, J. B. (1956). The problem of vocational guidance stated. *Journal of Counseling & Development, 34*(7), 420–422.

Dollarhide, C. T., & Saginak, K. A. (2017). *Comprehensive school counseling programs: K-12 delivery systems in action* (3rd ed.). Boston: Pearson Education.

Herr, E. L. (2001). The impact of national policies, economics, and school reform on comprehensive guidance programs. *Professional School Counseling, 4*(4), 236.

Herr, E. L. (2013). Trends in the history of vocational guidance. *Career Development Quarterly, 61*(3), 277–282.

Gladdings, S. T. (2004). *Counseling: A comprehensive profession* (5th ed.). Columbus, OH: Pearson.

Gysbers, N. C. (2001). School guidance and counseling in the 21st century: Remember the past into the future. *Professional School Counseling, 5*(2), 96.

Gysbers, N. C. (2004). Comprehensive guidance and counseling programs: The evolution of accountability. *Professional School Counseling, 8*(1), 1–14.

Gysbers, N. C., & Henderson, P. (2000). *Developing and managing your school guidance program.* Alexandria, VA: American Counseling Association.

Lambie, G. W., & Williamson, L. L. (2004). The challenge to change from guidance Counseling to professional school counseling: A historical proposition. *Professional School Counseling,* 8(2), 124–131.

Myrick, R. D. (1997). *Developmental guidance and counseling: A practical approach* (3rd ed.). Minneapolis, MN: Educational Media.

Parsons, F. (1909). *Choosing a vocation.* Boston: Houghton Mifflin.

Pope, M. (2000). A brief history of career counseling in the United States. *Career Development Quarterly, 48*(3), 194–211.

Rojewski, J. (2002). Preparing the workforce of tomorrow: A conceptual framework for career and technical education. *Journal of Vocational Education Research, 27*(1), 7–35.

Savickas, M. L. (1993). Career counseling in the postmodern era. *Journal of Cognitive Psychotherapy, 7*(3), 205–215.

Schmidt, J. J. (2010). *The elementary/middle school counselor's survival guide* (3rd ed.). San Francisco: Jossey-Bass.

Schmidt, J. J. (2014). Counseling in schools: Comprehensive programs of responsive services for all students (6th ed.). Boston: Pearson.

Stickel, S. A., & Yang, J. (1993). School guidance and counselling in the United States and Taiwan: Parallels and beyond. *International Journal for the Advancement of Counselling, 16*(3), 229–244.

Stripling, R. O., & Lane, D. (1966). Guidance services. Scope of pupil personnel services, 25–35.

Sue, D. W. (2015). *Race talk and the conspiracy of silence.* Hoboken, NJ: John Wiley & Sons.

Sue, D. W., & Sue, D. (2012). *Counseling the culturally diverse. Theory and practice* (6th ed.). Hoboken, NJ: John Wiley & Sons.

Super, D. E. (1955). Transition: from vocational guidance to counseling psychology. *Journal of Counseling Psychology,* 2(1), 3–9. doi:10.1037/h0041630

Super, D. E., & Crites, J. O. (1962). Appraising vocational fitness. Oxford, England: Harper.

CHAPTER 2

The Voices of School Counselors

Essential Characteristics of School Counselor Leaders

Anita Young, Colette T. Dollarhide and Amber Baughman

ABSTRACT

The majority of school counselor leadership studies focus on quantitative data. The current study contributes to the limited qualitative research surrounding school counselor leadership. The analysis of an open-ended statement from a national study gives voice to school counselor perceptions about leadership characteristics pertinent to the profession. Five themes emerged from the findings: leadership attributes, relationship attributes, communication and collaboration, exemplary program design, and advocacy. The themes align with characteristics previously identified in the school counseling literature.

Defining the how and why of effective school leadership is complex. Yet, mobilizing a vision and impacting change is considered a key skill set in educational settings. Leadership is about commitment to goals and a foundational belief that goals are achievable (Marzano, Waters, & McNulty, 2005). Educator effectiveness, particularly administrator effectiveness, has been equated with the ability to demonstrate leadership characteristics and

Anita Young, Colette T. Dollarhide, and Amber Baughman, "The Voices of School Counselors: Essential Characteristics of School Counselor Leaders," *Professional School Counseling*, vol. 19, no. 1, pp. 36-45.

practices that result in positive student outcomes (Marzano, 2010). Practices such as articulating a strong vision, demonstrating knowledge about instructional curriculum, promoting a positive school climate, and partnering with community members to develop student strengths are often considered core competencies for school leaders (Dufour, Dufour, Eaker, & Many, 2010; Finnigan & Stewart, 2009). Leithwood, Day, Sammons, Harris, and Hopkins' (2006) meta-analysis of literature on the meaning and definition of leadership identified 14 core behaviors: setting goals, vision, individualized support/consideration, emotional understanding, intellectual stimulation, modeling, building a collaborative culture, structuring the organization to facilitate work, creating productive relations with family and communities, connecting the school to wider environment, managing staffing, providing teaching support, monitoring progress, and buffering staff from distractions to their core work. Examples of these core leadership behaviors are frequently present in school vision statements, identifiable in the goals of School Improvement Plans (SIPs), or observable daily in instructional settings.

Another common behavior among school leaders such as principals is the ability to recognize and embrace the evolving leadership potential of others to move schools toward rigorous academic achievement for all students (Clark & Stone, 2001). Although the number of studies focused exclusively on school counselor leadership may not be as abundant as principal leadership, researchers agree that leadership is important to the principal–school counselor relationship, and to the ability to impact the quality of the school counseling program (Armstrong, McDonald, & Stillo, 2010). The purpose of the present study was to illuminate the voices of practicing school counselors and capture their beliefs about essential school counselor leadership characteristics. Qualitative analysis of an open-ended statement from a national school counselor leadership instrument was the impetus for the study (Young & Bryan, 2015).

SCHOOL COUNSELOR LEADERSHIP

The literature provides evidence of the importance of school counselor leadership through studies using existing leadership surveys. For example, Kouzes and Posner's (2011) Leadership Practices Inventory (LPI) has been used as a platform to study how school counselors demonstrate leadership practices. McMahon, Mason, and Paisley (2009) and Shillingford and Lambie (2010) used the LPI to investigate school counselor leadership practices and concluded that practices such as alignment of the school counseling program mission statement with the school's mission and vision significantly contributed to vital programmatic service delivery. Janson (2009) also confirmed the importance of school counselor leadership through the examination of how school counselors perceive their leadership behaviors and found that the school context may impact how school counselors lead. Most important in the school counseling profession, the ASCA National Model (American School Counselor Association [ASCA], 2005, 2012) acknowledges the strength of leadership to design comprehensive school counseling programs and integrate with the lateral themes of advocacy, collaboration, and systemic change. Consequently, the need for visible and intentional school counselor leadership is not disputable (Chen-Hayes, Ockerman, & Mason, 2013; Education Trust, 1996; Hanson & Stone, 2002; Hines & Lemon, 2011; House & Hayes, 2002; National Office for School Counselor Advocacy, 2011; Sink, 2009; Young & Miller-Kneale, 2013).

Two models of leadership appear most pertinent to the current study. One of the earliest models of school counselor leadership is from Dollarhide (2003). Using Bolman and Deal's Four Framework Approach (1997, 2008), Dollarhide identified four contexts in which successful school counselor leadership occurs: *structural leadership* (creating successful school counseling programs), *human resource leadership* (empowering and inspiring others to want to follow), *political leadership* (using the formal and informal power structures in the school to accomplish the goals of the school counseling program), and *symbolic leadership* (framing the goals of the school counseling program in symbolic terms that the followers can identify). In a longitudinal qualitative study following the leadership efforts of five new school counselors, Dollarhide, Gibson, and Saginak (2008) found that the leadership challenges faced by new school counselors included balancing all four leadership frames and implementing human resource leadership. The respondents reported feeling alone and isolated in their leadership efforts, prompting the implication that new school counselors need leadership mentors to help them navigate the political leadership and human resource leadership frames of the model.

Second, in a quantitative study, Young and Bryan (2015) identified five dimensions of school counselor leadership practices that provide preliminary factors based on an instrument developed from the only survey normed with school counselors. The first dimension, *Resourceful Problem Solving*, suggests that school counselor leadership practices involve innovation, promote student achievement, and require problem-solving strategies to accomplish and exceed goals. The second dimension,

Systemic Collaboration, highlights skills required to coordinate and work with others to initiate new programs resulting in systemic outcomes for all K-12 students. The third dimension, *Interpersonal Influence*, addresses persuasiveness skills needed to promote the instructional vision and gain buy-in to share innovative ideas. The fourth dimension, *Social Justice Advocacy*, addresses aspects of social justice and advocacy skills that challenge status quo barriers to equitable opportunities. Last, the fifth factor, *Professional Efficacy*, focuses on the ability to believe in oneself. The results suggest that school counselors from all levels (elementary, middle, high, and supervisory) engage in practices that align with skills previously suggested as effective by educational leaders (Marzano, 2010) and recommended by authors of studies related to school counseling leadership (Janson, Stone, & Clark 2009; Mason & McMahon, 2009; Shillingford & Lambie, 2010).

Together, these two models provide macro and micro views of leadership for school counselors. Dollarhide (2003) provided some insight into the process of leadership from a macro perspective, offering how leadership might be engaged from a systemic view of establishing a program, recruiting colleagues, accessing power structures, and inspiring others. Young and Bryan (2015) provided a micro view of school counselor leadership; they captured the dimensions of leadership practices from professional school counselors in the field and outlined leadership behaviors from a quantitative perspective in terms of resourceful problem solving, systemic collaboration, interpersonal influence, social justice advocacy, and professional efficacy. What is still unknown about school counselor leadership is how practicing school counselors describe characteristics of school counselor leaders. This becomes important when considering the following example: efforts generated by a leader who is not trusted by his or her followers may likely fail because the individual does not possess or exhibit leadership characteristics of trustworthiness. Therefore, this survey-based study was undertaken to examine how school counselors describe leadership characteristics.

METHOD

The current study is part of a national study designed to articulate and validate a framework for school counseling leadership. An exploratory factor analysis was conducted after analyzing Likert items and open-ended comments developed from focus groups and used in pilot studies with school counselors, school counseling supervisors, and graduate school counseling students. A confirmatory factor analysis concluded that the Likert items were reliable and an effective measure for school counselors and school counseling supervisors' leadership practices. The findings from the exploratory and confirmatory analyses were used for separate quantitative research articles. This current survey-based study (Wiersma & Jurs, 2009) focused on what practicing school counselors identified as important characteristics of school counselor leaders. The study was designed to capture and analyze the open-ended responses of practicing school counselors and supervisors.

PARTICIPANTS

The stratified sample consisted of school counselors and school counselor supervisor members from the American School Counselor Association (ASCA) database and was believed to provide a wide national representation for this study. Therefore, an e-mail link survey request was sent to approximately 18,000 school counselor members, of whom 1577 from a variety of backgrounds and experiences responded and were deemed appropriate for a Web-based study (Wiersma & Jurs, 2009). Of those, 1,316 participants responded to the one open-ended question. However, due to the number of blank responses throughout the survey, the following demographics do not represent all 1,316 participants' responses for the open-ended statement. Percentages are presented in terms of the total responses for each question. In terms of school setting, respondents included 371 (28%) elementary counselors, 205 (16%) middle school counselors, 437 (33%) high school counselors, and 303 (23%) counselors across multiple levels. The sample also represented 257 (20%) school counseling supervisors. The respondents were dispersed in terms of school counseling experience; 475 (40%) reported fewer than 7 years of experience, 415 (35%) reported between 7 and 15 years of experience, and 300 (25%) reported more than 15 years of experience (total n for this question = 1,190). For gender, 174 (14%) of the respondents indicated male and 1066 (86%) indicated female (total n = 1240). In terms of school context, 323 (26%) were from urban schools, 375 (30%) were from rural schools, and 532 (43%) were from suburban schools (total n = 1,230). Last, in terms of leadership experience in the past 2 years in a professional association, 365 (30%) indicated yes and 868 (70%) indicated no (total n = 1,233).

PROCEDURE

The authors obtained Institutional Review Board (IRB) approval prior to distributing the survey to a stratified sample of school counselors and school counselor supervisors who were members of ASCA. Participants were emailed a link with instructions to complete the School Counselor Leadership Survey (SCLS), with weekly reminders e-mailed for 30 days.

As previously mentioned, questions posed to the respondents included demographics about school counseling setting; status as a school counseling supervisor; years of school counseling experience; gender; urban, rural, or suburban school setting; and leadership in a professional association in the past two years. Participants were also invited to respond to Likert scale items that were not used for this study and to the open-ended statement used for this study. The open ended statement asked respondents to "List two characteristics that you believe are essential for school counselor leaders." The statement was asked at the end of the SCLS and used to capture participants' ideas about leadership characteristics (Marshall & Rossman, 2006; Young & Bryan, 2015).

RESEARCH TEAM

The analysis of the open-ended responses involved content exploration; therefore, the researcher-as-instrument (Creswell, 2013) was an important part of the research process. In this study, the two first authors were both school counselor educators who have written and researched extensively in school counseling leadership (from quantitative and qualitative perspectives, respectively), and the third author was a doctoral student with research experience. All three authors were women with experience in the field and in academia. The first author collected the data as outlined above and the second and third authors analyzed and coded the data. To minimize research biases and increase confirmability, the first author acted as auditor (Hunt, 2011). Assumptions of the three researchers included a belief that understanding school counseling leadership was imperative and that school counselor leadership could be learned and should be taught to all school counselors. Although the first and second authors have written about school counseling leadership using different conceptual leadership models, those models were set aside during data analysis so that the data would be analyzed free from preexisting structures (Jackson & Trochim, 2002).

DATA ANALYSIS

An overall description of the data analysis in this study was concept mapping using phenomenological, not statistical, clustering strategies (Jackson & Trochin, 2002; Moustakas, 1994). Due to the high number of responses (usable responses = 1,316) and the multiple responses from each respondent, the dataset was very large. The initial examination of the data found that some responses were long sentences describing one idea; in other cases, respondents had strung together multiple descriptors, creating wide variety in the number of actual descriptors from each respondent. For example, one respondent stated "Proactive, innovative, and accountable" for one response, then "advocate, empathic, and compassionate" for the second response. In this example, each word in the string represents a unique "meaning unit" and was coded separately to allow full understanding of the response, consistent with concept mapping (Jackson & Trichim, 2002). The authors selected QSR NVivo 10 (http://qsrinternational.com) as the most appropriate tool to organize, analyze, categorize, and code open-ended survey responses (Wiersma & Jurs, 2009, p. 199) from these 1,316 respondents.

Data analysis involved six steps (Jackson & Trichim, 2002). In the first step of analysis, the second and third authors established the meaning units as words by having the system do a word count. In this list of words, they could then select and read the responses in which that word appeared. To account for all the responses, the authors followed this procedure for all words that appeared twice or more, not including "the", "and", prepositions, and qualifiers that did not alter the meaning of the response (Jackson & Trochim, 2002). For example, "a good communicator" and "should have great communication skills" were both coded as "communication" in the nodes that developed from the data. This level of analysis revealed misspellings and other issues that the authors were able to capture for analysis, and they were able to ensure that all responses were represented in the results.

The second step, sorting, involved the initial coding of meaning units, called "child nodes" (QSR NVivo 10). During this step of the analysis, the authors monitored the meaning of each response before coding to a node to ensure fidelity to the respondent's intent, and monitored the size and scope of each node to be sure that the meaning of the node was internally consistent (Jackson & Trochim, 2002). For example, the response "knowledge of school counseling" and "knowledge of students' issues" were both brought up in the initial code for "knowledge," but the responses clearly had different meaning. The first response was hand coded under "school counseling", and the second response was hand coded under "students." In this way, the authors ensured that all data was captured and ensured congruence with the respondents' meaning (Moustakas, 1994).

For the third step, the second and third authors examined the child nodes and grouped them under "parent nodes," or themes. In concept mapping, this is called clustering (Jackson & Trochim, 2002). In this iterative process, relationships between child nodes emerged and were grouped together. The process included multiple discussions and configurations, with time for reflection and individual analysis between meetings and continued thematic groupings (Moustakas, 1994). In the fourth step, the themes were examined for internal consistency, called final cluster solution (Jackson & Trochum, 2002), with movement of child nodes to create conceptually meaningful themes that were intuitive, consistent, and logical (Moustakas, 1994). The fifth step was labeling the clusters (Jackson & Trochim, 2002), a step designed to capture the textual and structural elements of the responses in a unified statement (Moustakas, 1994).

In the sixth and final step, the first author served as an outside reader to validate the findings (Hunt, 2011; Jackson & Trochim, 2002). In the Results section, below, thematic descriptors and discrete elements of each theme were maintained as parent and child nodes. The child nodes represent the discrete meaning units from the original data, and the parent nodes capture the thematic descriptor of all the related child nodes. The counts for the parent nodes were then defined as the aggregate of the child nodes within that thematic descriptor.

In qualitative research, four quality indices help the reader evaluate the integrity of the findings (Hunt, 2011; Marshall & Rossman, 2006): credibility, transferability, dependability, and confirmability. Because the examination of responses to this open-ended survey statement involved coding and thematic grouping, the authors applied these criteria of soundness. To achieve *credibility*, the data were carefully analyzed to preserve the meaning of the respondents, including extensive verification of the child nodes and presentation of all child/parent nodes for the reader to evaluate. To address *transferability*, the authors primarily applied triangulation: first, this study was grounded in (but not bounded or structured by) leadership literature in counselor education, school counseling, and educational administration; and second, the data analysis took place in multiple stages and from multiple perspectives within the research team, creating triangulation in the literature and triangulation from multiple researchers. In terms of *dependability*, the authors felt that the size and diversity of the respondent pool provided some confidence that the question of study was adequately covered. Last, in terms of *confirmability*, the authors provided transparent views of the data analysis process, the research team, and the child/parent nodes so that the reader could evaluate the veracity of the findings.

RESULTS

Respondents provided a total of 2,465 meaningful ideas for school counselor leadership qualities. As can be seen in Table 2.1, a total of five major themes emerged from the data: Leadership Attributes, Relationship Attributes, Communication and Collaboration, Exemplary Program Design, and Advocacy. Each of these major themes aggregated from six to 14 child nodes per theme, which are listed in Table 2.1; note that all descriptors within each individual node are listed, including misspelled words found in the raw data. As with any attempt to quantify and categorize complex interpersonal phenomenon, some level of overlap between themes is possible, but the rationale behind the division of individual responses into themes was as follows. Responses dealing with diversity, inclusion, justice, and outreach were grouped together under the theme of Advocacy; responses that directly related to the qualities required for the creation and development of a school counseling program were gathered under Exemplary Program Design; responses that directly related to how school counselor leaders utilized core communication skills were organized under Communication and Collaboration; responses identifying qualities that related directly to the ability of school counselor leaders to develop healthy and genuine relationships with their colleagues and stakeholders were grouped under Relationship Attributes; and, last, responses that identified qualities that were directly related to willingness and proficiency in the work of leadership, such as driving programs forward or having vision for the future of the program, were gathered under Leadership Attributes. Each of these major themes is presented individually, from the theme with highest number of responses to that with the lowest (see also Table 2.1).

The theme with the largest number of responses was Leadership Attributes (915 references), which included 37% of the total recorded responses. This theme was used to capture leader-specific behaviors and qualities based on existing literature. Example responses that were coded under this theme included “flexible, adaptable” ($n = 136$), “confident” ($n = 117$), “creative, innovative, problem solver” ($n = 79$), and “vision, visionary” ($n = 41$).

The theme with the second largest number of responses was Relationship Attributes, with 530 references and 22% of the total responses. This theme captured those relational attributes that are relationship, not leadership, qualities. This theme included descriptors such as “empathy, opening minded, approachable” ($n = 206$), “compassion, caring, kindness, love” ($n = 167$), “patience, calmness, poise, poised” ($n = 49$), and “ethical, honest, integrity” ($n = 49$). A full list of references under this theme can be found in Table 2.1.

The third most populated theme was Communication and Collaboration, with 503 references, and 20% of the total responses. This theme was characterized by communication and collaboration skills that were distinct from leadership and personality characteristics. This theme captured responses that included “communication, interactions” ($n = 214$), “collaborator, collaboration” ($n = 50$), “listening, listener, listen” ($n = 80$), and “stakeholders” ($n = 63$). Other responses in this category included “rapport, friendly, supportive” ($n = 37$).

The theme with fourth largest number of responses was Exemplary Program Design, with 343 references, or 14% of the total responses. This theme described program-related qualities and perspectives, including the instructional purpose of education, goal and data driven, holistic and systemic, expertise, comprehensive program, knowledge of resources and research, student focused, visionary, and hard working. This theme had a large number of responses with similar numbers; those with the highest number of references included “knowledge and expertise” ($n = 81$), “goal and data driven” ($n = 58$), “comprehensive program” ($n = 55$), and “student focused” ($n = 54$).

The fifth and final theme was Advocacy, with 175 references, or 7% of the response set. This theme was derived from descriptors of a specific activity that was unique from leadership, communication, or personality. In this theme are “advocate, advocacy” ($n = 97$), “change agent” ($n = 33$), “diversity, equity, and justice” ($n = 15$), and “willingness to advocate” ($n = 26$).

TABLE 2.1. RESULTS: "CHARACTERISTICS OF SCHOOL COUNSELOR LEADERS"

NAME	REFERENCES
LEADERSHIP ATTRIBUTES	915
commitment, dedication	15
humility, service	6
high expectations, belief, student achievement	56
vision, visionary	41
delegate	4
determination, tenacity	19
drive, motivation, motivated	21
follow through	7
leadership, lead, leader	40
multitask, multitasking, multi task, prioritize	9
objectivity	3
organization, time management, organizational, efficient (2)	72
persistent, persistance, perserverance, perseverance	19
professionalism, role model, professional	36
resourcefulness, resourceful	12
visibility	4
confidence, confident, strength, strengths	117
courage, guts, risk taker	28
decision, decisive	4
flexibility, flexability, adaptable, adaptability	136
intelligent, intelligence	5
passion, energy, enthusiasm, energetic, passionate	72
positive attitude, positivity, optimism	67
Proactive	12
resilient, thick skin, tough skin	8
solution focused	12
strategies, plans, analytical, analyze	6
thinking outside box, creative, innovative, innovator, creator, ideas, problem solver, problem solve, question status quo, initiative, independent	79
wisdom	5
RELATIONSHIP ATTRIBUTES	530
boundaries	3
compassion, caring, kindness, love	167
empathy, open minded, approachable, understanding,	206
mind, approachability, empathic, empathetic	10
help, helping	
ethical, honesty, integrity, honest	49
patience, calmness, poise, poised	49
respect, unconditional regard, non-judgmental	23
tolerance	5
trust, trustworthiness, genuine	18

NAME	REFERENCES
COMMUNICATION & COLLABORATION	502
articulate	4
assertive	8
collaborator, collaborative, collaboratively, collaboration	50
communication, communications, interactions, interaction, communicators, communicator	214
conflict resolution	4
cooperation	4
diplomacy, negotiate, negotiation, negotiator, compromise, policital, political	9
listening, listener, listen	80
networking	3
public speaking, public relations	3
rapport, interpersonal, engaging, friendly, supportive, connect, connections (2)	37
sense of humor	7
stakeholders, parents, teachers, administrators, faculty, staff, community, families, everyone, people	63
team	16
EXEMPLARY PROGRAM DESIGN	343
classroom, teaching, instructional	8
goal driven, data driven, data-driven, goal-driven, driven, accountable, accountability, impact	58
holistic, big picture, systems, systemic, building-wide, school-wide	35
knowledge, expertise, education, competent, competency, competancy, experience	81
program, essential, comprehensive, school counseling	55
resources, research, information, best current practices, lifelong learning	26
student focused, needs	54
work, working	26
ADVOCACY	175
advocate, advocacy, advocating	97
change agent	33
different, diverse, diversity, cultural	12
equity, justice	3
right, stand	4
willingness, willing	26

DISCUSSION

This study was designed to capture school counselors' and school counseling supervisors' perspectives of school counseling leadership characteristics. A total of 1,316 respondents yielded 2,465 descriptors in open-ended statement format. These responses were then analyzed using NVivo and hand coding in a six-step qualitative analysis using phenomenological concept mapping (Jackson & Trochim, 2002; Moustakas, 1994). The findings resulted in five themes: Leadership Attributes, Relationship Attributes, Communication and Collaboration, Exemplary Program Design, and Advocacy. Several frameworks can help contextualize these results.

The findings of this study not only confirm existing characteristics and behaviors of the school counselor literature, but the large data set also contributes to the uniqueness of the participants. For example, the larger context that these findings address is the ASCA National Model (ASCA, 2012). The four themes of the ASCA National Model are Leadership, Advocacy, Collaboration, and Systemic Change, which are represented in the findings of this study in the major themes of Advocacy, Communication and Collaboration, and Leadership Attributes. Further conceptualizing the remaining findings of this study is possible, namely, Relationship Attributes and Exemplary Program Design as the means by which the delivery system of the ASCA National Model (ASCA, 2012) would be provided in the school. Given that the respondents of this study were drawn from the membership of ASCA, it is possible that the foundation concepts of the professional association, as articulated in the ASCA National Model, may also be internalized by members as crucial leadership characteristics.

Another framework is applicable when examining the results of this study with the ASCA Leadership Components of the ASCA National Model (ASCA, 2012) based on Dollarhide's (2003) research. In this model, structural leadership, or the building of viable comprehensive school counseling programs, can be seen in the themes of Exemplary Program Design and Relationship Attributes. Human resource leadership, or the empowerment and inspiration of followers, is woven through Communication and Collaboration (see rapport and sense of humor) and Leadership Attributes (see leadership). Political leadership, or the use of interpersonal power and organizational power, appears in Communication and Collaboration in terms of diplomacy and networking, although it represents a very small number of responses. Last, symbolic leadership appears in Leadership Attributes in vision/visionary. Although not the only lens through which to view these results, the leadership structure articulated by Dollarhide (2003) does provide a context for much of these findings.

A third framework that can be applied to the results of this study are the five dimensions identified in the School Counselor Leadership Survey (SCLS) that categorizes leaders' practices for school counselors and school counselor supervisors (Young & Bryan, 2015). The Resourceful Problem Solving dimension mirrors Leadership Attributes as evident in the responses that refer to flexibility, adaptability, thinking outside the box, and resourcefulness. Consistent alignments also exist with exemplary program design and specific correlations with goal driven, data driven, program, essential, comprehensive, school counseling, and student-focused needs. The Social Justice Advocacy dimension is unanimously integrated with all characteristics identified in Advocacy and Relationship Attitudes. Systemic Collaboration appears solely in Communication and Collaboration and Relationship Attributes. Professional Efficacy is noted in comments related to confidence within Leadership Attributes and Communication and Collaboration. For example, responses such as confidence and positive attitude align with Leadership Attributes responses and although small, assertive relates to Communication and Collaboration. Interpersonal Influence is noted within characteristics such is as rapport, interpersonal, engaging and communication noted in Communication and Collaboration. Interpersonal Influence is also present within high expectations, belief, and student achievement in Leadership Attributes.

This study is unique in that it is the first leadership instrument exclusively normed and developed for school counselors. The magnitude of the response rate from participants in this study also contributes to the uniqueness. More important, the authentic voices of practicing school counselors and school counselor supervisors that emerged from the open-ended statement responses substantiate the importance of school counselors engaging in leadership behaviors (Janson, 2009). The authors did encounter surprises such as the presence of likability in relational qualities and the absence of a data and accountability theme. Research by Harland, Harrison, Jones, and Palmon (2005) supports the importance of likability as a leadership quality; however, the responses in this study provide a unique and interesting perspective with the categorical identification of relationship attributes that highlight the value of likability in school counselor leaders. Also notable are the low responses around the use of data and advocacy, yet this is congruent with the Likert scale responses (Young & Bryan, 2015). A possible reason is that school counselors view use of data as a strategy and not a characteristic.

LIMITATIONS

As with any study, this one had limitations that must also be acknowledged. First, the survey was administered to practicing school counselors and supervisors who are members of ASCA, so the authors cannot state what non-ASCA school counselors and supervisors might identify as school counselor leadership characteristics. Participants may not be representative of all ASCA school counselors. For example, fewer middle school counselors participated than other levels, 20% of the returned surveys were supervisors who may not have been school counselors themselves, most of the participants had limited (1–7 years) of school counseling experience, and most participants had never held a school counselor leadership position. Further, qualitative analysis of data is always subject to researcher bias and interpretation, and although qualitative quality measures were put in place, bias could always be possible. Other readers could have organized these findings into other themes, so the categories in which the results were located are researcher specific. Transparency in design and analysis can, however, provide some assurance that interpretations were made without a priori assumptions.

IMPLICATIONS

COUNSELOR EDUCATORS AND RESEARCHERS

The results of this study have potential implications for how counselor educators can promote the leadership growth of prospective school counselors. First, examining the leadership characteristics that K-12 school districts seek can help counselor education programs (a) refine their criteria for admission to identify students with the potential to become leaders as professionals, (b) develop curricula such as leadership courses to facilitate their professional growth and identity, and (c) aid the identification of school counselors who demonstrate the characteristics suggested in this study and other evidence of leadership as field supervisors for practicum and internship. Second, counselor educators can use this study's results to prepare professional development conferences and direct outreach to schools targeted to help school counselors identify these characteristics within themselves, and further the opportunities for school counselors to demonstrate leadership within the schools.

These results are also useful for future researchers in counselor education. Existing school counselor leadership models can be compared to these results; the level of congruence with previous models can provide additional support to those conceptualizations, or suggest areas where the existing model may not capture the practitioner-level experience of leadership. New areas of inquiry could include how school counselors develop their understanding of leadership, and how these identified characteristics intersect with existing models in practice with school counselor leaders currently in the field. Future research also could explore whether programs led by school counselors displaying these characteristics have more effective outcomes than programs led by school counselors without these qualities, and to what extent these characteristics and existing models such as Dollarhide's (2003) framework and the School Counselor Leadership Survey (Young & Bryan, 2015) account for the effectiveness of school counselor leaders in the field.

SCHOOL COUNSELORS

Because the ASCA National Model (ASCA, 2012) highlights leadership as one of the its four themes, professional school counselors will want to explore developing their own leadership potential using these results. For example, they might identify with leadership characteristics identified in this study and seek professional development trainings to increase their leadership capacity. There are also benefits from these results to school counselors in the field both emergent and experienced. Many of the characteristics identified by the participants as essential for school counselor leaders overlap with the characteristics of skilled school counselors in general, which may encourage practicing school counselors to feel competent and empowered to seek out professional development and leadership opportunities. These characteristics can also provide a starting point to help emergent school counselors identify peer mentors who can aid them in developing their own leadership characteristics (Dollarhide, Gibson & Saginak, 2008). They can help emergent school counselors reflect on what characteristics are important to them as leaders, and assist them in identifying other leaders among their peers who could help them grow to become stronger leaders, and collaborators, themselves. For district level personnel, these results can also be useful in developing assessments targeted at evaluating school counselor leadership characteristics and performance, evaluating current assessments for potential revision or refinement, and for developing hiring criteria for positions of school counselor leadership, such as directors of counseling.

CONCLUSION

This analysis of qualitative responses from a national study of school counselors offers a deeper understanding of what school counselors value about leadership. Respondents identified their preferred traits, strong personal and professional attributes, sound communication preferences, the ability to create and maintain a comprehensive program, and the willingness to advocate for students and the profession. With this information, counselor educators and researchers can refine programs to nurture these characteristics in students and help practitioners further develop these characteristics.

REFERENCES

American School Counselor Association. (2005). *The ASCA National Model: A framework for school counseling programs* (2nd ed.). Alexandria, VA: Author.

American School Counselor Association. (2012). *The ASCA National Model: A framework for school counseling programs* (3rd ed.). Alexandria, VA: Author.

Armstrong, S. A., McDonald, J. H., & Stillo, S. (2010). School counselors and principals: Different perceptions of relationship, leadership, and training. *Journal of School Counseling*, 8(15), 1–28.

Bolman, L. G., & Deal, T. E. (2008). *Reframing organizations: Artistry, choice and leadership* (4th ed.). San Francisco, CA: Jossey-Bass.

Chen-Hayes, S. F., Ockerman, M. S., & Mason, E. C. M. (2013). *101 Solutions for school counselors and leaders in challenging times.* Thousand Oaks, CA: Sage

Creswell, J. W. (2013). *Qualitative inquiry and research design: Choosing among five approaches* (3rd ed.). Los Angeles, CA: Sage.

Dollarhide, C. T. (2003). School counselors as program leaders: Applying leadership contexts to school counseling. *Professional School Counseling, 6*, 304–309.

Dollarhide, C. T., Gibson, D., & Saginak, K. (2008). New counselors' leadership efforts in school counseling: Themes from a year-long qualitative study. *Professional School Counseling, 11*(4), 262–271. doi:10.5330/psc.n.2010-11.262

Dufour, R., Dufour, R., Eaker, R., & Many, T. (2010). *Learning by Doing* (2nd ed.). Bloomington, IN: Solution Tree.

Education Trust. (1996). *The national guidance and counseling reform program.* Washington, DC: Author.

Finnigan, K. S., & Stewart, T. J. (2009). Leading change under pressure: An examination of principal leadership in low-performing schools. *Journal of School Leadership, 19*(5), 586–618.

Hanson, C., & Stone, C. B. (2002). Recruiting leaders to transform school counseling. *Theory into Practice, 4*(3), 163–168.doi:10.1207/s15430421tip4103_4

Harland, L., Harrison, W., Jones, J., & Palmon, R. (2005). Leadership, behaviors and subordinate resilience. *Journal of Leadership & Organizational Studies, 11*(2), 2–14. doi:10.1177/107179190501100202

Hines, P., & Lemon, R. (2011). *Poised to lead: How school counselors can drive college and career readiness*. Washington, DC: The Education Trust. Retrieved from https://edtrust.org/resource/poised-to-lead/

House, R. M., & Hayes, R. L. (2002). School counselors: Becoming key players in school reform. *Professional School Counseling, 5*, 249–261.

Hunt, B. (2011). Publishing qualitative research in counseling journals. *Journal of Counseling & Development, 89*, 296–307.doi:10.1002/j.1556-6678.2011.tb00092.x

Jackson, K. M., & Trochim, W. M. K. (2002). Concept mapping as an alternative approach for the analysis of open-ended survey responses. *Organizational Research Methods, 5*(4), 307–336. doi:10.1177/109442802237114

Janson, C. (2009). High school counselors' views of their leadership behaviors: A Q methodology study. *Professional School Counseling, 13*(2), 86–97. doi:10.5330/PSC.n.2010–13.86

Janson, C., Stone, C., & Clark, M. A. (2009). Stretching leadership: A distributed perspective for counselor leaders. *Professional School Counseling 13*(2), 98–105. doi:10.5330/psc.n.2010–13.98

Kouzes, J., & Posner, B. (2011). *The five practices of exemplary leadership* (2nd ed.). San Francisco, CA: The Leadership Challenge.

Leithwood, K., Day, C., Sammons, P., Harris, A., & Hopkins, D. (2006). *Successful school leadership: What it is and how it influences student learning* (Research Report 800). London, UK: Department for Education.

Marshall, C., & Rossman, G. B. (2006). *Designing qualitative research* (4th ed.). Thousand Oaks, CA: Sage.

Marzano, R. (2010). High expectations for all. *Educational Leadership, 68*, 82–85.

Marzano, R., Waters, T., & McNulty, B, (2005). *School leadership that works: From research to results*. Alexandria, VA: Association for Supervision and Curriculum Development.

Mason, E. C. M., & McMahon, H. G. (2009). Leadership practices of school counselors. *Professional School Counseling, 13*, 107–115. doi:10.5330/psc.n.2010-13.107

Moustakas, C. (1994). *Phenomenological research methods*. Thousand Oaks, CA: Sage.

National Office for School Counselor Advocacy. (2011). *The principal-counselor relationship*. Retrieved from http://nosca.collegeboard.org/research-policies/annual-survey

Shillingford, M. A., & Lambie, G. W. (2010). Contribution of professional school counselors' values and leadership practices to their programmatic service delivery. *Professional School Counseling, 13*, 208–217. doi:10.5330/psc.n.2010–13.208

Sink, C. (2009). School counselors as accountability leaders: Another call for action. *Professional School Counseling, 13*(2), 68–74. doi:10.5330/psc.n.2010–13.68

Stone, C., & Clark, M. A. (2001). School counselors and principals: Partners in support of academic achievement. *NASSP Bulletin, 85*, 46–53. doi:10.1177/019263650108562407

Wiersma, W., & Jurs, S. G. (2009). *Research methods in education: An introduction* (9th ed.). Boston, MA: Pearson.

Young, A., & Bryan, J. (2015). The school counselor leadership survey: Instrument development and exploratory factor analysis. *Professional School Counseling, 19*, 1–15.

Young, A., & Miller-Kneale, M. (2013). *School counselor leadership: The essential practice*. Alexandria, VA: American School Counselor Association.

CHAPTER 3

Improving the Effectiveness of School Counseling

Consensus, Collaboration, and Clinical Supervision

Karen Walker

ABSTRACT

In this literature review, factors influencing the effectiveness of the services and programs provided by school counsellors are examined. Specific influences reviewed were professional identity, collaborative working practices, and clinical supervision. Analysis revealed that the principles of egalitarianism, relationship, and connectedness permeate everything that school counsellors do, and that collaborative working practices, clinical supervision, and the concept of professional identity are inextricably linked. Implications for practice are discussed and recommendations for future research are provided. Researchers are challenged to address the dearth of literature on Canadian school counselling practices.

Canadian schools are dynamic, energetic, and diverse. At the heart of Canadian schools are school counsellors, who act in many roles: educational leaders, advocates, and change agents (British Columbia School Counsellors Association, n.d.; Manitoba School Counsellors' Association, 2002; New Brunswick Department of Education, 2002; Northwest Territories Education, Culture, and Employment, 2004; Nova Scotia Department of

Karen Walker, "Improving the Effectiveness of School Counselling: Consensus, Collaboration, and Clinical Supervision," *Canadian Journal of Counselling and Psychotherapy*, vol. 49, no. 3, pp. 275-295.

Education, 2010; Ontario School Counsellors' Association, n.d.; Prince Edward Island Department of Education, 2005).[1] Now, as their profession develops, school counsellors are taking on a broader range of duties and facing new challenges (Culbreth, Scarborough, Banks-Johnson, & Solomon, 2005). Therefore, it is becoming increasingly necessary to reexamine how school counsellors will continue to support the students in their care.

In this article, I analyze and synthesize the literature on school counselling to determine what factors contribute to, or detract from, the effectiveness of the services and programs that school counsellors offer. I then evaluate this information to determine how the literature can inform—and ultimately improve—the practice of school counsellors. I review variations in conceptualizations of the school counsellor's role across Canada, as well as how these views have changed over time. School settings are unique in that many people are involved in the lives of students. Therefore, I also examine the extent to which school counsellors collaborate with other stakeholders in order to support students, as well as any barriers to collaboration. Finally, I discuss the nature of supervision that school counsellors receive, as well as how this helps to support them in their various roles.

The existing literature has not examined the role of Canadian school counsellors and the effectiveness of the services and programs they offer. In this article, I aim to highlight some of these knowledge gaps and make recommendations for future research studies. I propose that consensus on the role of the school counsellor, collaborative working practices, and clinical supervision are key factors influencing the effectiveness of school counselling.

THE STORY SO FAR

My main focus in this article is to examine how school counsellors help to make a difference to the lives of their students. For the purposes of this article, I have defined an effective school counselling program (SCP) as one that helps students to make positive changes in one or more domains of their lives. The definition is in line with this guideline in the Prince Edward Island (PEI) Department of Education's (2005) handbook for counsellors: "the primary goal of school counselling services is to enhance and promote student learning" (p. 5), and to address the personal, social, emotional, and career needs of students. The term has been similarly defined by Alberta Education (2012), the BC Ministry of Education (2013), the Manitoba SCA (2002), and the NS Department of Education (2010).

School counsellors face a double challenge: they must show how the services they provide positively influence student outcomes, and they must also demonstrate their worth in order to ensure that their services continue to receive funding (Oberman, Studer, & Womack, 2006). Oberman et al. (2006) offered a model to help school counsellors implement action research projects that would determine the effectiveness of the services they offer and improve accountability. Cain's (2013) research affirmed that such a model might be useful to Canadian school counsellors, who are also aware of the links between credibility and educational funding. The 41 school counsellors who participated in Cain's survey said that to develop effective SCPs, they needed to establish a clear professional identity and demonstrate how they contribute to the well-being of students in their care. Cain recommended that Canadian school counsellors establish a national network to advocate for their profession.

Such an organization could help focus research on SCPs in Canada, which until now has been lacking. In the absence of such research, I have used available international literature to gain insight into factors that contribute to effective SCPs. In a case study aimed at turning around a failing American high school, Salina et al. (2013) recognized that, because of their heavy workload, school counsellors were often unable to meet the students' needs. The researchers, in conjunction with the school-based team, decided to use an evidence-based approach to identify at-risk students. The team gathered data in order to track students who were at risk of not graduating. The school counsellors then made this information available to students, staff, and parents. By working collaboratively, rather than in isolation, the school counsellors were able to engage parents and staff, increasing support to these students and helping them to fulfill their graduation requirements (Salina et al., 2013).

Salina et al. (2013) argued that the more staff knew about their students, the more likely they would be to feel connected to them. In turn, this would increase the likelihood that they would build relationships and offer support (Salina et al., 2013). Their study showed how data-driven programs and collaborative working relationships could have a positive effect on student outcomes. The findings of this study were supported by Gruman, Marston, and Koon (2013) and Poynton and Carey (2006); these authors also advocated the practice of gathering data and using it to inform and improve SCPs. I therefore propose that, when developing or evaluating SCPs, educational staff should consider how to infuse collaborative working practices and data gathering into their approach.

According to Gruman et al. (2013), effective school counsellors take on the roles of leaders and advocates. This stance is endorsed by the American School Counselor Association (2010), and has also been adopted in many of the provincial guidelines for Canadian school counsellors (BCSCA, n.d.; Manitoba SCA, 2002; NWT Education, Culture, and Employment, 2004; NS Department of Education, 2010; Ontario SCA, n.d.; PEI Department of Education, 2005), making Gruman et al.'s study relevant to Canadian school counsellors. In their case study on a rural American high school, Gruman et al. found that the two school counsellors who participated in the study faced many barriers in providing students with the support they needed. Consistent with other literature (Brown, Dahlbeck, & Sparkman-Barnes, 2006; Shallcross, 2013), Gruman et al. asserted that school counsellors were often stretched too thin to provide mental health support to students on top of fulfilling their other duties. Cain (2013) also found that Canadian counsellors experienced difficulties meeting the needs of their students due to a lack of resources. Gruman et al. discovered that when school counsellors led the way in evaluating their programs and developing and implementing a data-driven decision-making model, their students experienced positive changes, including increased graduation rates. The data gathered provided school counsellors with the impetus to advocate on behalf of their students and obtain permission from management to redistribute their resources. As a result, counsellors spent less time on administrative tasks, and more time providing support to students (Gruman et al., 2013). These studies demonstrate that when school counsellors challenge the status quo, and take on the roles of leaders and advocates, improvements can be made to how services are provided.

A survey of 415 secondary school students in the United Kingdom found that 84% of students rated their school counselling services positively. The respondents specifically cited the importance of having someone to talk to about problems such as bullying, home issues, and school issues. Following the survey component of the study, researchers conducted nine focus groups, with a range of three to seven students in each group. Responses from the focus groups indicated that many students valued the guarantee of confidentiality. However, some were more cautious about confidentiality, believing that others could find out what they had said in discussions with a school counsellor (Fox & Butler, 2007). Another common theme was that students shared a desire to get to know their school counsellor well, but noted concerns about the limited time the counsellor was available, as well as the lack of choice of whom they go to see (Fox & Butler, 2007).

These themes illustrate the importance of trusting relationships in effective SCPs. Fox and Butler's (2007) research indicated that students talk to school counsellors about a wide range of personal and sensitive issues that are difficult to discuss with other people. A precursor to students utilizing school counselling services is that they need to perceive the school counsellor as approachable and readily accessible (Fox & Butler, 2007). This finding suggests that school counsellors must maintain a visible presence in the school so that students can begin to build connections and foster relational trust. In addition, school counsellors must organize their workload so that that they are able to get to know the students they serve. I elaborate on these concepts in the next section on the importance of using a systemic approach to change.

USING A SYSTEMIC APPROACH TO CHANGE

A systemic approach toward improving SCPs is likely to be better than trying to implement change on a case-by-case, individual basis (Fitch & Marshall, 2004). A survey of 62 school counsellors in Kentucky found that participants in high-achieving schools allocated more time to program management, evaluation, and research, compared to participants in low-achieving schools. By gathering information and identifying themes across the school population, these school counsellors were able to place resources where they were needed most and implement systemic change that reached a large number of students (Fitch & Marshall, 2004). This American research is relevant to Canadian school counsellors because its focus on using data to drive change efforts would be easily replicable in Canadian schools. It is also important because it points to ways that school counsellors could make most efficient use of their time and resources; as mentioned, many Canadian school counsellors feel burdened by a workload that negatively impacts their ability to meet their students' needs (Cain, 2013). Salina et al. (2013) also concluded that a collaborative, systemic approach to school counselling improved outcomes for students and increased staff morale, and noted the importance of relationship to educational practices generally.

In the many provinces and territories across Canada, school counsellors possess a high level of training (BCSCA, n.d.; Manitoba SCA, 2002; NS Department of

Education, 2010; PEI Department of Education, 2005), which empowers them to offer a unique perspective on school protocols. It is important that school counsellors have the opportunity to use their knowledge and training to improve outcomes in their work with students. However, ambiguity about the role of the school counsellor can act as a barrier, so consensus on the role of the school counsellor is important (Salina et al., 2013).

CONSENSUS ON THE ROLE OF THE SCHOOL COUNSELLOR

Historically, the role of the school counsellor has lacked clear definition and has evolved to include a broad range of duties (Culbreth et al., 2005). Although school counsellors across Canada may have different responsibilities, some common themes do emerge from the literature. A review of publicly accessible provincial guidelines for Canadian school counsellors showed that most school counsellors are no longer responsible for simply implementing the classroom guidance curriculum; they are also providing counselling services, addressing mental health issues, intervening during crises, and providing support to students with regard to course choices and career goals. In addition, these guidelines also highlight the fact that school counsellors should consult and coordinate with teachers, parents, health professionals, and community agencies (Alberta Education, 2012; BCSCA, n.d.; Manitoba SCA, 2002; NB Department of Education, 2002; NWT Education, Culture, and Employment, 2004; NS Department of Education, 2010; Ontario SCA, n.d.; PEI Department of Education, 2005). The fact that school counsellors now take on such a broad range of duties has led the PEI Department of Education (2005) to ask "just what is a school counsellor?" (p. 5). Potential answers to this question are explored below.

The wide range of role demands (Gruman et al., 2013) faced by school counsellors include both counselling and noncounselling duties (Perera-Diltz & Mason, 2008). Perera-Diltz and Mason (2008) speculated that, when school counsellors perform noncounselling duties that do not match the typical job description of a school counsellor, they might be acting on direction given from their supervisors. In many schools, principals influence the design and purpose of SCPs (Amatea & Clark, 2005). Therefore, it would be important to understand how principals' views of the role of the school counsellor correlate with school counsellors' views of their own roles. A thorough review of the literature did not find any research on Canadian principals' views of the roles and responsibilities of a school counsellor. Therefore, I used American research to gain insight into the degree of agreement between the two stakeholders' opinions.

A survey of 53 school counsellors and administrators found that these important stakeholders often had different opinions on the role of the school counsellor (Brown et al., 2006). Brown et al. (2006) discovered that, although some administrators recognized the role that school counsellors played in supporting the mental health needs of students, 35% of administrators who responded did not consider that intervening with the mental health needs of students was a primary function of school counsellors. In contrast, only 18% of school counsellors held this view (Brown et al., 2006). Brown et al. speculated that principals might be concerned about whether school counsellors were competent to provide mental health support, and also that providing mental health interventions could take up a large amount of school counsellors' limited time.

Given that principals are often the direct line-managers of school counsellors, this difference of opinion might prevent some school counsellors from using their training to meet the mental health needs of students (Armstrong, MacDonald, & Stillo, 2010). This difference in opinion, coupled with an inability to perform the functions important for school counsellors, might lead to low job satisfaction (Armstrong et al., 2010). Lack of clarity in job responsibilities has been shown to lead to burnout in counsellors who work in the area of sexual abuse or substance abuse recovery, a factor that in turn inhibits counsellor competence (Wallace, Jayoung, & Sang Min, 2010). Further research might possibly reveal that these findings are generalizable to school counsellors.

Contrary to the above findings, a study of American school principals in the rural Midwest found that principals valued counsellors' abilities to offer individual counselling and to intervene during a crisis (Bardhoshi & Duncan, 2009). School principals in the state of Florida also found that supporting the mental health needs of students was an appropriate activity for counsellors (Zalaquett & Chatters, 2012). However, despite recognizing the importance of offering counselling, the Florida study raised concerns about the lack of time counsellors might have to dedicate to offering this type of support (Zalaquett & Chatters, 2012). Clearly, a divergence of opinions exists between counsellors and principals, and between principals and counsellors in different geographical areas. More research is needed on factors influencing principals' perceptions of the role of the school counsellor.

For Armstrong et al. (2010), trusting relationships between counsellors and their principals were vital to the success of SCPs. Survey findings indicated that, although both elementary and secondary counsellors felt supported by their principals, there were statistically significant differences between the perceptions of secondary counsellors and their principals regarding the roles and functions of school counsellors (Armstrong et al., 2010). For example, while 62% of school counsellors thought they had similar views as their principals on how to handle a crisis, 89% of principals thought they had similar views to their counsellors. Second, whereas 91% of principals believed they understood the role of the counsellor, only 67% of counsellors thought principals understood their role (Armstrong et al., 2010). Armstrong et al. asserted that a lack of consensus on the role of the school counsellor could be a contributing factor to poor relationships between counsellors and principals. Consensus (or lack of it) on the role of school counsellors is clearly an influencing factor in the effectiveness of SCPs.

Research by Meyers (2005) suggested that poor relationships between counsellors and principals could increase the stress levels of school counsellors. Previous research has identified links between high stress levels and compromised clinical practice (Barnett, Baker, Elman, & Schoener, 2007; Myers et al., 2012). Therefore, it is vital for school counsellors and principals to be consistent, to allow each member of the team to stay healthy and make positive contributions to student success and the overall school environment.

Perhaps the time has come for school counsellors to focus on establishing an identity that recognizes them as both educational leaders and mental health professionals (DeKruyf, Auger, & Trice-Black, 2013). However, there might be barriers to establishing such a "conjoint professional identity" (DeKruyf et al., 2013, p. 272). One barrier might be the perceptions of those who design and develop SCPs (Brown et al., 2006). That is, if principals (or others in charge of SCPs) prefer school counsellors to focus on academic and career counselling rather than on the mental health needs of students, it is unlikely that counsellors in such schools would be able to successfully establish the latter as part of their identity (Mason & Perera-Diltz, 2010). Another barrier might be variations in the training level of school counsellors across Canada. Cain (2013) noted that training levels vary by jurisdiction. For example, school counsellors in the NWT require a bachelor's degree with a speciality in guidance, whereas school counsellors in PEI require a master's degree in counselling or a related discipline (PEI Department of Education, 2005). More research needs to be done in Canada to determine the extent to which training levels vary between jurisdictions and between individual school counsellors, as well as the impact this difference has on the ability of school counsellors to establish a clear professional identity.

Many of the concerns cited in the above research regarding role demands and the credibility of school counsellors are also identified in Cain's (2013) study of the school counselling profession in Canada. Cain's recommendation that school counsellors should establish a national network in Canada also suggests that she found a desire among Canadian school counsellors to establish and stabilize a strong professional identity for themselves.

COLLABORATIVE WORKING PRACTICES

A key focus in this [chapter] is to examine how collaborative working practices can influence the effectiveness of SCPs. In this section, I examine the research to determine current collaboration practices that counsellors use with other stakeholders, the barriers to collaborative practice, and the links between collaborative working practices and the effectiveness of SCPs.

Collaboration, a bringing together of people to address a situation, is important to all organizations (Miller & Katz, 2014). For example, Miller and Katz (2014) proposed that collaboration between individuals in an organization allows people to share their knowledge and wisdom so that new solutions, which otherwise would have gone unrecognized, can be generated. However, Miller and Katz also noted that many barriers to collaboration exist, including the fact that people have learned to work in an isolated fashion, either within their department or even completely on their own. They speculated that working in isolation bred fear and mistrust, ultimately decreasing people's desire to collaborate with others. Cain's (2013) Canadian research supported these ideas. It showed that many Canadian school counsellors felt isolated in their work, which might act as a barrier to implementing collaborative working practices.

In a phenomenological study, Trice-Black, Riechel, and Shillingford (2013) found correlations between trust and the desire to collaborate. The more trust a school counsellor had in a colleague's ability to treat shared information with respect, the more likely the school counsellor was to work in partnership with that person (Trice-Black et al., 2013). Participants in this same study said that trusting relationships were reciprocal in nature—one counsellor described having increased opportunities to connect with students because staff trusted her enough to bring up their concerns (Trice-Black et al., 2013). Another counsellor said that, as he gained experience, his administrator showed faith in his ability to meet the needs of students and did not question his decisions about the limits to confidentiality (Trice-Black et al., 2013). These findings suggest that collaborative working practices can improve the quality of services that students receive. If so, it is important for educational leaders to create and maintain the conditions for good collaboration (Cisler & Bruce, 2013).

Armstrong et al. (2010) asserted that the role of the school counsellor and the role of the principal were interdependent and that a positive relationship between them based on respect was likely to lead to improved outcomes for students. Research carried out by Salina et al. (2013) supported this finding. Their transformative program, fittingly named All Hands on Deck (AHOD), stressed the importance of collaboration among principals, counsellors, teachers, parents, and students. Specific to the relationship between counsellors and principals, Salina et al.'s research emphasized the importance of shared power and recognition of the expertise that counsellors contribute to the school setting. In this study, when the principal neutralized the power imbalance between himself and the counsellors, and listened to what the counsellors had to contribute, he engaged them in the process of making systemic changes to educational practice in the school. In turn, this raised student achievement and improved graduation rates, demonstrating how collaborative practice can lead to improved outcomes for students (Salina et al., 2013).

Despite the importance of collaborative practice, barriers to it exist. Principals and counsellors work in a hierarchical system and sometimes lack knowledge on how to work together because of their distinct roles and skill sets (Williams & Wehrman, 2010). School counsellors and principals are trained independently of each other, with little opportunity to find out about each other's roles in the formal education setting. Williams and Wehrman (2010) hypothesized that this lack of knowledge on how to work together could contribute to difficulties in navigating challenging issues such as how to manage confidential information. It is important to examine how information is shared between educational stakeholders, and counsellors must seek a balance between confidentiality and collaboration that works in the school setting, because collaborative working relationships are important to the overall success of SCPs (Armstrong et al., 2010; Salina et al., 2013).

Managing the limits to confidentiality is one of the main challenges facing all counsellors (Bodenhorn, 2006). The literature suggests that confidentiality is a key component in successful therapy (Glosoff & Pate, 2002; Jenkins, 2010) and that students must be able to trust their counsellors if they are going to share sensitive information with them (Fox & Butler, 2007). A number of challenges to confidentiality are posed in the school setting (see Isaacs & Stone, 1999). The number of stakeholders involved in the lives of students is one such challenge. Principals and counsellors may have different perceptions of confidentiality, causing friction that can negatively affect school counselling services (Williams & Wehrman, 2010). Confidentiality is especially pertinent for those working with minors (Jenkins, 2010). While recognizing the importance of confidentiality in the counselling setting, Jenkins (2010) offered words of caution to counsellors in working with minors: "Their very age and vulnerability as a nonadult mean that their entitlement to unfettered respect for their right to autonomy, self-determination, and independence is unlikely to be fully implemented, without at least some degree of qualification" (p. 264). School counsellors must therefore find a balance between a student's desire for privacy and the vulnerabilities associated with his or her developmental age and stage.

For this reason, organizations have recognized the need for counsellors to be aware of ethical issues when working with young people, and have issued specific guidance to support helping professionals (Canadian Counselling and Psychotherapy Association [CCPA], 2011; College of Alberta Psychologists [CAP], 2010). It is important for school counsellors to be aware of the major variations between both provinces and employers. For example, the College of Alberta Psychologists (2010) advised their members that minors cannot legally consent to services until they are more than 18 years of age. In addition, CAP advised that minors should be made aware that their parents have a right to access all information disclosed during sessions. However, exceptions to the rule existed, and, in Alberta, school counselling was one of those exceptions. CAP highlighted a policy by Alberta Learning that defined guidance and counselling services as part of the school program. As such, students in Alberta do not need parental permission to see the school counsellor.

This example provides evidence of the challenge counsellors face when working in a school setting: they must balance the child's need for privacy with the rights of parents to be involved in their child's welfare (Isaacs & Stone, 1999). Counsellors should carefully consider what information is to be shared, and with whom. A legal precedent was set in 2000, when a parent in BC attempted to gain access to a school counsellor's notes pertaining to her children. The school counsellor refused access to the information, and this was supported by the local Board of Education (Office of the Information and Privacy Commissioner, 2000). The provincial Office of the

Information and Privacy Commissioner (2000) investigated and supported the school counsellor's decision to withhold access to the information shared in the counselling sessions. The investigator asserted that children have a right to expect that such information will be kept private and that parental rights do not supersede this (Office of the Information and Privacy Commissioner, 2000).

Despite this ruling, there is a need for school counsellors to collaborate with the child's family (Bodenhorn, 2005). Bodenhorn (2005) identified families as the "primary providers of support for child development" (p. 319) and highlighted how children can benefit from a healthy modelling of partnership and good communication between school counsellors and parents. Although collaboration with parents may cause an ethical dilemma for counsellors, training in systems counselling can help to overcome these barriers (Bodenhorn, 2005). Research by Bryan and Holcomb-McCoy (2004) indicated that school counsellors recognize the importance of collaboration between school, family, and community. However, despite their willingness to be involved in family and community partnerships, school counsellors' lack of time creates a challenging barrier to effectively fostering such collaborative relationships (Bryan & Holcomb-McCoy, 2004). Bryan and Holcomb-McCoy speculated that clearly defining the role of the school counsellor might reduce some of the barriers to collaboration. This finding suggests that consensus on collaborative working practices and on the role of the school counsellor could be reciprocal factors influencing the effectiveness of SCPs.

The information presented above suggests there are benefits arising from collaborative working relationships, including identifying students who may require additional support (Trice-Black et al., 2013), improved student outcomes (Salina et al., 2013), and modelling of healthy communication patterns (Bodenhorn, 2005). However, due to the inherent hierarchical nature of school systems, implementing collaborative working practices requires educational leaders and other stakeholders to recognize the value of a school culture founded on the belief that people are of equal value, regardless of their role in the school. A commitment to this philosophy creates space for people to form relationships and contribute to student success (Salina et al., 2013). Despite the benefits, embracing collaborative working practices can present school counsellors with some challenges, including ethical dilemmas related to the sharing of information (Bodenhorn, 2005). This research brings into focus the importance of adequate supervision for school counsellors, an issue that is examined in the next section.

CLINICAL SUPERVISION

Although clinical supervision is not explicitly referred to in any of the provincial handbooks for Canadian school counsellors (Alberta Education, 2012; BCSCA, n.d.; Manitoba SCA, 2002; NB Department of Education, 2002; NWT Education, Culture, and Employment, 2004; NS Department of Education, 2010; Ontario SCA, n.d.; PEI Department of Education, 2005), the BCSCA (n.d.), the NS Department of Education (2002), and the Ontario SCA (2009) do specify in their ethical codes that school counsellors should consult with other professionals in order to effectively help students. This guidance is in line with the ethical guidelines of other professional bodies that regulate the counselling and psychology professions in Canada (CCPA, 2007; Canadian Psychological Association, 2000). In addition, the PEI Department of Education (2005) acknowledged in their handbook that their school counsellors might also be affiliated with other regulatory bodies, such as the CCPA (2007). Because the CCPA requires certified counsellors to obtain supervision, it is likely that some of the school counsellors who work for the PEI Department of Education recognize the importance of clinical supervision in their practice. However, more research needs to be completed in this area to gauge the opinions of Canadian school counsellors with regard to clinical supervision and the extent to which they are accessing such services.

Dollarhide and Miller (2006) noted the distinct differences between clinical supervision and administrative supervision. These authors proposed that the latter focuses on broader organizational issues, while the former concentrates on counselling-related matters. Shepard and Martin (2012) supported this distinction, asserting that while administrative supervision focuses on "matters of organizational functioning" (p. 5), clinical supervision relates to the "development of the supervisee, as well as the safety and quality of the services delivered" (p. 5). For purposes of this article, I will use Shepard and Martin's definitions distinguishing the two types of supervision that school counsellors may encounter.

A review of the literature revealed that little has been written about clinical supervision and the Canadian school counsellor. In addition, gaps exist in the recent international literature on clinical supervision and school counsellors. In the absence of more recent literature, I have had to draw on foundational studies to gain insight into the clinical supervision of school counsellors. Research carried out in the United States in 2001 indicated that although the majority of school counsellors received administrative supervision from their principal, few had access to clinical supervision: only 13% of participants had access to individual clinical supervision, and only 10% had access to group clinical supervision (Page, Pietrzak, & Sutton, 2001). The results from Page et al.'s (2001) national study were similar to previous results from state-level studies done by Sutton and Page (1994) and Roberts and Borders (1994). Interestingly, Page et al. found that the majority of participants in their study expressed a desire for clinical supervision in order to improve their practice. This finding shows that, although many school counsellors are knowledgeable about the benefits of clinical supervision, they may experience difficulty accessing it in their workplace (Page et al., 2001). Therefore, it is important to examine not only the perceived benefits of clinical supervision, but also the barriers to obtaining it. Further research in this area would likely help to illuminate the connections between clinical supervision and the effectiveness of SCPs.

It is evident from the provincial counselling guidelines that individual and group counselling is a function that many school counsellors across Canada perform (Alberta Education, 2012; BCSCA, n.d.; Manitoba School Counsellors' Association, 2002; NB Department of Education, 2002; NWT Education, Culture, and Employment, 2004; NS Department of Education, 2010; Ontario SCA, n.d.; PEI Department of Education, 2005). For these counsellors, clinical supervision helps to enhance their clinical competence and improves their clinical skills (Ellis, 2010; Herlihy, Gray, & McCollum, 2002). In addition, "supervision is a rite of passage, the means by which skills are refined, [and] theory and practice integrated" (Dollarhide & Miller, 2006, p. 242). These findings are important, particularly because, in the American research, counsellors perceived that their training did not adequately prepare them to deal with the complex realities of working in the school system, especially in the area of resolving ethical dilemmas (Trice-Black et al., 2013). Nova Scotia research into ethical practice supported these concerns (Lehr, Lehr, & Sumarah, 2007). The authors of the Nova Scotia study found that school counsellors had concerns about how to manage the limits to confidentiality, which they believed could lead to inconsistencies in standards of practice between counsellors (Lehr et al., 2007). All the above concerns suggest that school counsellors could benefit from ongoing professional supervision; it would help them refine their skills, ensure they are adhering to ethical guidelines, and provide the best quality services for students in their care.

SELF-AWARENESS AND MULTICULTURAL COMPETENCY

Clinical supervision is an effective method for helping counsellors to increase their levels of self-awareness (Vallance, 2004), and self-awareness is essential if counsellors are to avoid potential harm to clients (Collins & Arthur, 2010). Page et al. (2001) highlighted the wide range of issues that American school counsellors face, including drug use, violence, and sexual health issues. Canadian school counsellors also face these kinds of issues (PEI Department of Education, 2005). Risk-taking behaviours such as these can present ethical dilemmas for counsellors, necessitating them to examine their own values (Stone, 2013).

Ellis (2010) recognized the importance of examining one's own worldview and advocated that the supervisory relationship is an appropriate forum in which to do so, particularly when working with a diverse population. Working with issues of diversity may present some unique challenges for counsellors (Collins & Arthur, 2010). Canada is a diverse nation; few countries have as many foreign-born residents (Statistics Canada, 2008). Figures drawn from the 2006 Census indicated that approximately 20% of people living in Canada were born elsewhere (Statistics Canada, 2009), and projections indicate this trend will continue (Statistics Canada, 2008). It seems, then, that as the population diversifies, so too will the Canadian student body. Ellis (2010) proposed that our value systems are not black and white; rather, they exist along a continuum. He asked, "[W]here are you on the continuum of racism or sexism, and what are you doing about it?" (Ellis, 2010, p. 96). Perhaps an analogous question for this forum would be "How are Canadian school counsellors being supported to ensure they examine their values and practice in a culturally competent manner?"

A culture-infused approach (Arthur & Collins, 2010b) to school counselling is particularly important because of the impact that discrimination can have on the mental health and academic progress of those from nondominant groups (Chang & Le, 2010). In addition, Canadian Certified Counsellors are required to practice in a manner that takes account of the cultural backgrounds of their clients and shows sensitivity to diversity (CCPA, 2007). One of the ways counsellors can do this is to take on the responsibility of examining their biases and learning to work with diverse clients in the counselling setting, rather than simply referring students to other counsellors (Stone, 2013). These are challenging situations, providing counsellors opportunities for growth so that they can create space for all students without marginalizing certain groups (Stone, 2013).

The variations in the levels of training between school counsellors across Canada (Cain, 2013) is likely to mean that although some school counsellors will feel well equipped to audit their ability to practice in a culturally sensitive manner, others might not possess the skills to do so. Moreover, because counsellors continue to evolve throughout their career, an ongoing commitment to the development of cultural competency is essential for all practitioners, regardless of their level of training (Arthur & Collins, 2010a). Canadian Certified Supervisors can offer support to counsellors in order to develop their competence in the area of cultural awareness and sensitivity to diversity (Shepard & Martin, 2012). Arthur and Collins (2010b) asserted that failure to develop cultural awareness in relation to self and others is likely to act as a barrier to effective counselling practice, making a strong case for the implementation of clinical supervision for school counsellors.

Despite these perceived benefits, a thorough review of the literature did not uncover any studies focusing on the issue of clinical supervision for Canadian school counsellors. American research indicated that few school counsellors there have access to this type of support as well (Page et al., 2001). Although little has been written about clinical supervision for Canadian school counsellors, the available literature can be used to hypothesize about the potential barriers to accessing this service.

One potential barrier is the lack of time (Herlihy et al., 2002) that some school counsellors experience; they feel overstretched and lack the resources that they need to fulfill their duties (Brown et al., 2006; Bryan & Holcomb-McCoy, 2004; Cain, 2013). Participating in formal clinical supervision would be just one more item on the already full plate of school counsellors (Herlihy et al., 2002).

A second potential barrier is some school counsellors' belief that do not they need clinical supervision (Page et al., 2001). In Page et al.'s (2001) study, 33% of respondents indicated that they did not need supervision. This finding is in line with foundational research carried out by Sutton and Page (1994), who found that 37% of school counsellors did not view clinical supervision as a priority. Herlihy et al. (2002) drew links between a perceived lack of need for clinical supervision and role ambiguity. These authors proposed that school counsellors might not be engaged in a great deal of clinical work, making clinical supervision unnecessary (Herlihy et al., 2002). In Canada, Cain's (2013) study highlighted the variations in training across jurisdictions, and more research needs to be done to determine whether differences in levels of training influence school counsellors' beliefs about the necessity of supervision. However, because Page et al.'s (2001) research indicated that a majority of school counsellors desired clinical supervision, it might be more likely that other barriers were getting in the way. These barriers could include financial obstacles, lack of knowledge on how to obtain supervision, or a lack of administrative support for such an endeavour (Herlihy et al., 2002).

Although these foundational studies provide some insight into the opinions of school counsellors on clinical supervision, there is a need to address the knowledge gaps in relation to clinical supervision and Canadian school counsellors.

IMPLICATIONS FOR SCHOOL COUNSELLORS

An interesting consideration that arises from this literature review is that relationships between educational stakeholders are a major contributing factor to the overall success of the services and programs that school counsellors offer (Armstrong et al., 2010; Salina et al., 2013). When school counsellors feel respected and valued by their leaders, they are motivated to strive to improve their practices, and this leads to improved outcomes for their students (Salina et al., 2013). Furthermore, when there is relational trust between school staff and parents, students benefit from witnessing the model healthy ways of communicating (Bodenhorn, 2005). A team approach helps to ensure that at-risk students are identified and offered appropriate support (Trice-Black et al., 2013). Therefore, it seems apparent that educational leaders must look for opportunities to create and nurture the conditions in which relationships can develop (Cisler & Bruce, 2013).

For school counsellors, working in isolation can increase their workload and decrease their ability to meet students' needs (Salina et al., 2013). Educational leaders, including principals and school counsellors, should therefore consider setting aside times throughout the school year to discuss policies and protocols, student progress, and any perceived hurdles to collaborative working practices. The American School Counselor Association's national model (2012) suggests that principals and school counsellors meet at the beginning of the school year to discuss roles and responsibilities. These preliminary meetings would be ideal forums for discussing complex issues such as student confidentiality (Trice-Black et al., 2013). Furthermore, I argue that such regular meetings might help staff to build relationships and overcome barriers to collaboration, as they find out more about each other's perceptions of their roles and responsibilities. Although lack of time might be a perceived barrier to organizing such meetings, research has shown how collaborative working practices can actually save time (Gruman et al., 2013; Salina et al., 2013), and educating school staff on this finding might help to overcome any resistance to changes in practice.

Mason and Perera-Diltz (2010) emphasized the importance of creating opportunities for school counsellors and principals to find out more about each other's work; they recognized that this did not always happen in the formal education setting. Educators in graduate counselling programs and educational leadership programs should consider designing innovative coursework that allows school counsellors and principals to learn about each other's roles (Amatea & Clark, 2005; Mason & Perera-Diltz, 2010).

Cisler and Bruce (2013) also recognized the need for school counsellors and principals to increase their knowledge about how to work together. These authors suggested that school counsellors and principals might benefit from participating in joint professional development workshops that focus on problem solving in the school setting (Cisler & Bruce, 2013). Such professional development workshops could focus on how to resolve complex ethical dilemmas or respond to crises. The ethical challenges offered by Froeschle and Crews (2010) and Hicks et al. (2014) might provide the substance for discussions during workshops, allowing for thought-provoking debates about how to respond to dilemmas in ways that would take local policies and protocols into account. Time could also be set aside to design and implement action research projects, using the model outlined by Oberman et al. (2006) to determine the overall success of various aspects of the SCP. Making improvements to the way school counsellors and principals are educated (Amatea & Clark, 2005; Mason & Perera-Diltz, 2010), as well as increasing opportunities for ongoing professional development (Cisler & Bruce, 2013) and action research (Oberman et al., 2006), might ameliorate the divergence of opinion between them (Brown et al., 2006) on the roles and functions of the school counsellor. Moreover, such measures could help to develop consensus on the role of the school counsellor, and in turn establish a strong professional identity for Canadian school counsellors and improve the effectiveness of the services they offer.

A second observation that arises from the findings presented above is that there is a direct link between consensus on the role of the school counsellor and access to clinical supervision. An analysis of the literature suggests that the role of the school counsellor needs to be better defined. For example, school counsellors provide individual and group counselling and are thus already addressing mental health needs of students (Alberta Education, 2012; BCSCA, n.d.; Manitoba School

Counsellors' Association, 2002; NWT Education, Culture, and Employment, 2004; NS Department of Education, 2010; Ontario SCA, n.d.; PEI Department of Education, 2005). Until such roles are formally recognized, it is unlikely that the need for clinical supervision will be acknowledged, to ensure that school counsellors are practicing in an ethical manner. Reinforcing the reciprocal relationship between professional identity and clinical supervision, Dollarhide and Miller (2006) pointed out that clinical supervision is necessary if novice school counsellors are to develop an understanding of the parameters of their profession. Without this support, it would be left to administrators to define the functions of the school counsellors, and previous research has shown that this may take the profession in a direction away from meeting the needs of those it serves (Mason & Perera-Diltz, 2010). These findings appear to suggest a need for school counsellors to join forces in order to strengthen advocacy efforts for their profession, and to ensure that they are receiving the support they need(i.e., appropriate training, professional development, and clinical supervision) to do their job well (Cain, 2013).

Cain (2013) identified many ways that school counsellors could build connections nationally, including participating in the CCPA's School Counsellors' Chapter and through organizing a Canadian School Counselling week (which took place for the first time in 2014; CCPA, 2014). However, I also suggest that it is important to build local networks within one's own school district. Peer consultation groups, where fellow counsellors provide critical and supportive feedback (Haag Granello, Kindsvatter, Granello, Underfer-Babalis, & Hartwig Moorhead, 2008), could be a beginning step in developing such connections. These groups have been shown to help participants develop new knowledge (Barlow & Phelan, 2007) and consider alternative viewpoints (Haag Granello et al., 2008), a necessary precursor to developing increased self-awareness. In addition, peer consultation groups have been linked to improved self-care practices among grief counsellors (Barlow & Phelan, 2007). This finding is important because Canadian Certified Counsellors have an ethical responsibility to ensure they participate in self-care activities (CCPA, 2007). However, as Cain (2013) noted, there are variations in training across jurisdictions, and it is likely that many school counsellors are not members of a professional association. Therefore, further research is required to determine the extent to which school counsellors believe they have an ethical requirement to participate in self-care activities, and whether Barlow and Phelan's (2007) findings are generalizable to school counsellors. I speculate that, in addition to the aforementioned benefits, establishing peer consultation groups might also help school counsellors to strengthen their voice within their school districts and increase advocacy efforts for systemic changes, such as implementing clinical supervision. However, this latter idea needs to be explored in more detail to determine if the projected outcome would be achieved. The recommendation to consider peer consultation groups should not be interpreted to mean that this type of support should take the place of individual or group supervision with a qualified supervisor, but merely that each journey begins with a small step. Peer consultation groups might be such a first step in increasing the connectedness between school counselling colleagues, thus strengthening professional solidarity and identity, as well as providing the motivation to advocate for changes.

RECOMMENDATIONS FOR FUTURE RESEARCH

A limitation of this review is its reliance on international data to gain insights into the experiences of Canadian school counsellors. Field research that explores the daily roles and functions of Canadian school counsellors, as well as the perceptions of other educational stakeholders on the roles and functions of school counsellors, could address some of the gaps in the literature. In addition, future research should seek to determine the extent to which educational stakeholders are working collaboratively and how this affects student outcomes in Canadian schools. It would also be useful to discover more about the perceived barriers to collaborative working practices and the steps that are being taken to overcome these barriers. Finally, there is a need to address the knowledge gaps in relation to clinical supervision and Canadian school counsellors. Field research that explores how many Canadian school counsellors have access to clinical supervision, the type of supervision they are engaging in (e.g., individual or group), and the perceived benefits of clinical supervision would be a useful starting point for this discussion. In addition, there is a need to examine current models of supervision to determine whether they are appropriate for the school setting (Luke & Bernard, 2006). Lastly, Swank and Tyson (2012) asserted that school counsellors benefit from receiving training prior to providing others with supervision. Therefore, it would be useful to investigate how many school counsellors have the training to provide clinical supervision, as well as the perceived benefits of participating in such training.

CONCLUSION

Many factors influence the effectiveness of SCPs, and the research presented in this article has shown that an evidence-based approach ensures that school counsellors remain accountable for the services they provide. Furthermore, clearly defined school counsellor roles and responsibilities, consistent with their education and training, provide the basis for collaborative working practices that lead to improved outcomes for students. Consensus on the role of the school counsellor and a commitment to collaborative working practices would create space for school counsellors to demonstrate their need for clinical supervision, a provision that would enhance clinical competency, thus improving the efficacy of the services provided to students. Although dealt with separately in this article, the concepts of consensus on the role of the school counsellor, collaborative working practices, and clinical supervision are inextricably linked, each one laying the foundation for and supporting the development of the other. Moreover, egalitarianism, relationships, and connectedness are the glue that unites these three realms. In addition to advocating for the needs of their students, school counsellors must now take seriously their responsibility for refining and advocating for their own professional identity. By joining together, school counsellors could create the conditions necessary for systemic change and ensure that their profession continues to develop in a way that meets the ever-changing needs of their students.

REFERENCES

Alberta Education. (2012). *Guide to education: ECS to Grade 12*. Edmonton, AB: Author. Retrieved from http://www.education.alberta.ca/media/6719891/guidetoed2012.pdf

Amatea, E. S., & Clark, M. (2005). Changing schools, changing counselors: A qualitative study of school administrators' conceptions of the school counselor role. *Professional School Counseling*, 9(1), 16–27. Retrieved from http://schoolcounselor.metapress.com/home/main.mpx

American School Counselor Association. (2010). *Ethical standards for school counselors*. Retrieved from http://www.schoolcounselor.org/asca/media/asca/Resource%20Center/Legal%20and%20Ethical%20Issues/Sample%20Documents/EthicalStandards2010.pdf

American School Counselor Association. (2012). *The ASCA national model: A framework for school counseling programs* (3rd ed.). Alexandria, VA: Author.

Armstrong, S. A., MacDonald, J. H., & Stillo, S. (2010). School counselors and principals: Differ-ent perceptions of relationship, leadership, and training. *Journal of School Counseling*, 8, 1–27. Retrieved from http://jsc.montana.edu/

Arthur, N., & Collins, S. (2010a). Future directions in culture-infused counselling. In N. Arthur & S. Collins (Eds.), *Culture-infused counselling* (2nd ed., pp. 449–466). Calgary, AB: Counselling Concepts.

Arthur, N., & Collins, S. (2010b). Introduction to culture-infused counselling. In N. Arthur & S.Collins (Eds.), *Culture-infused counselling* (2nd ed., pp. 3–25). Calgary, AB: Counselling Concepts.

Bardhoshi, G., & Duncan, K. (2009). Rural school principals' perception of the school counselor's role. *Rural Educator, 30*(3), 16–24. Retrieved from http://www.ruraleducator.net/

Barlow, C. A., & Phelan, A. M. (2007). Peer collaboration: A model to support counsellor self-care. *Canadian Journal of Counselling/Revue Canadienne de Counseling, 41*(1), 3–15. Retrieved from http://cjc-rcc.ucalgary.ca/cjc/index.php/rcc/index

Barnett, J. E., Baker, E. K., Elman, N. S., & Schoener, G. R. (2007). In pursuit of wellness: The self-care imperative. *Professional Psychology: Research and Practice, 38*(6), 603–612. doi:10.1037/0735-7028.38.6.603

Bodenhorn, N. (2005). American School Counsellor Association ethical code changes relevant to family work. *Family Journal: Counseling and Therapy for Couples and Families, 13*(3), 317–320. doi:10.1177/1066480705276292

Bodenhorn, N. (2006). Exploratory study of common and challenging ethical dilemmas experienced by professional school counselors. *Professional School Counseling, 10*(2), 195–202. Retrieved from http://schoolcounselor.metapress.com/home/main.mpx

British Columbia Ministry of Education. (2013). *Special education services. A manual of policies, procedures and guidelines*. Victoria, BC: Author. Retrieved from http://www.bced.gov.bc.ca/specialed/special_ed_policy_manual.pdf

British Columbia School Counsellors Association. (n.d.). *Legal and ethical guidelines*. Retrieved from http://www.bcschoolcounsellor.com/legal-ethical-guidelines

Brown, C., Dahlbeck, D. T., & Sparkman-Barnes, L. (2006). Collaborative relationships: School counselors and non-school mental health professionals working together to improve the mental health needs of students. *Professional School Counseling, 9*(4), 332–335. Retrieved from http://schoolcounselor.metapress.com/home/main.mpx

Bryan, J., & Holcomb-McCoy, C. (2004). School counselors' perceptions of their involvement in school-family-community partnerships. *Professional School Counseling, 7*(3), 162–171. Retrieved from http://schoolcounselor.metapress.com/home/main.mpx

Cain, M. (2013). *A national network for school counsellors: Supporting the school counselling profession in Canada*. Retrieved from http://www.ccpa-accp.ca/_documents/SC_Chapter/Research_Report_June_2013.pdf

Canadian Counselling and Psychotherapy Association. (2007). *Code of ethics*. Ottawa, ON: Author. Retrieved from http://www.ccacc.ca/_documents/CodeofEthics_en_new.pdf

Canadian Counselling and Psychotherapy Association. (2011). *Standards of practice*. Ottawa, ON: Author. Retrieved from http://www.ccpa-accp.ca/en/standardsofpractice/

Canadian Counselling and Psychotherapy Association. (2014). *School counsellors chapter*. Retrieved from http://www.ccpa-accp.ca/en/chapters/schoolcounsellors/

Canadian Psychological Association. (2000). *Canadian code of ethics for psychologists* (3rd ed.). Ottawa, ON: Author. Retrieved from http://www.cpa.ca/cpasite/userfiles/Documents/Canadian%20Code%20of%20Ethics%20for%20Psycho.pdf

Chang, J., & Le, T. N. (2010). Multiculturalism as a dimension of school climate: The impact on the academic achievement of Asian American and Hispanic youth. *Cultural Diversity and Ethnic Minority Psychology, 16*(4), 485–492. doi:10.1037/a0020654

Cisler, A., & Bruce, M. A. (2013). Principals: What are their roles and responsibilities? *Journal of School Counseling, 11*(10), 1–27. Retrieved from http://jsc.montana.edu/

College of Alberta Psychologists. (2010). *Limits to confidentiality and consent for services: Special issues in working with minors*. Retrieved from http://www.cap.ab.ca/pdfs/limitconf.pdf

Collins, S., & Arthur, N. (2010). Self-awareness and awareness of client cultural identities. In N. Arthur & S. Collins (Eds.), *Culture-infused counselling* (2nd ed., pp. 67–102). Calgary, AB: Counselling Concepts.

Culbreth, J. R., Scarborough, J. L., Banks-Johnson, A., & Solomon, S. (2005). Role stress among practicing school counselors. *Counselor Education and Supervision, 45*(1), 58–71. doi:10.1002/j.1556-6978.2005.tb00130.x

DeKruyf, L., Auger, R. W., & Trice-Black, S. (2013). The role of school counselors in meeting students' mental health needs: Examining issues of professional identity. *Professional School Counseling, 16*(5), 271–282. doi:10.5330/PSC.n.2013-16.271

Dollarhide, C. T., & Miller, G. M. (2006). Supervision for preparation and practice of school counsellors: Pathways to excellence. *Counselor Education & Supervision, 45*(4), 242–252. doi:10.1002/j.1556-6978.2006.tb00001.x

Ellis, M. V. (2010). Bridging the science and practice of clinical supervision: Some discoveries, some misconceptions. *Clinical Supervisor, 29*(1), 95–116. doi:10.1080/07325221003741910

Fitch, T. J., & Marshall, J. L. (2004). What counselors do in high-achieving schools: A study on the role of the school counselor. *Professional School Counseling, 7*(3), 172–177. Retrieved from http://schoolcounselor.metapress.com/home/main.mpx

Fox, C. L., & Butler, I. (2007). "If you don't want to tell anyone else you can tell her": Young people's views on school counselling. *British Journal of Guidance & Counselling, 35*(1), 97–114. doi:10.1080/03069880601106831

Froeschle, J. G., & Crews, C. (2010). An ethics challenge for school counselors. *Journal of School Counseling, 8*(14), 1–25. Retrieved from http://jsc.montana.edu/

Glosoff, H. L., & Pate, R. H., Jr. (2002). Privacy and confidentiality in school counseling. *Professional School Counseling, 6*(1), 20–27. Retrieved from http://schoolcounselor.metapress.com/home/main.mpx

Gruman, D. H., Marston, T., & Koon, H. (2013). Bringing mental health needs into focus through school counseling program transformation. *Professional School Counseling, 16*(5), 333–341. doi:10.5330/PSC.n.2013-16.333

Haag Granello, D., Kindsvatter, A., Granello, P. F., Underfer-Babalis, J., & Hartwig Moorhead, H. J. (2008). Multiple perspectives in supervision: Using a peer consultation model to enhance supervisor development. *Counselor Education & Supervision, 48*(1), 32–47. doi:10.1002/j.1556-6978.2008.tb00060.x

Herlihy, B., Gray, N., & McCollum, V. (2002). Legal and ethical issues in school counselor supervision. *Professional School Counseling, 6*(1), 55. Retrieved from http://schoolcounselor.metapress.com/home/main.mpx

Hicks, J. G. F., Noble, N., Berry, S., Talbert, S., Crews, C., Li, J., & Castillo, Y. (2014). An ethics challenge for school counselors: Part 2. *Journal of School Counseling, 12*(1), 1–23. Retrieved from http://jsc.montana.edu/

Isaacs, M. L., & Stone, C. (1999). School counselors and confidentiality: Factors affecting professional choices. *Professional School Counseling, 2*(4), 258–266. Retrieved from http://schoolcounselor.metapress.com/home/main.mpx

Jenkins, P. (2010). Having confidence in therapeutic work with young people: Constraints and challenges to confidentiality. *British Journal of Guidance & Counselling, 38*(3), 263–274. doi:10.1080/03069885.2010.483128

Lehr, R., Lehr, A., & Sumarah, J. (2007). Confidentiality and informed consent: School counsellors' perceptions of ethical practices. *Canadian Journal of Counselling/Revue Canadienne de Counseling, 41*(1), 16–30. Retrieved from http://cjc-rcc.ucalgary.ca/cjc/index.php/rcc/index

Luke, M., & Bernard, J. M. (2006). The school counseling supervision model: An extension of the discrimination model. *Counselor Education and Supervision, 45*(4), 282–295. doi:10.1002/j.1556-6978.2006.tb00004.x

Manitoba School Counsellors' Association. (2002). *Guidelines for comprehensive guidance and counselling in Manitoba*. Retrieved from http://www.msca.mb.ca/images/stories/downloads/msca_guidelines_2002.pdf

Mason, K. L., & Perera-Diltz, D. M. (2010). Factors that influence pre-service administrators' views of appropriate school counselor duties. *Journal of School Counseling, 8*(5), 1–28. Retrieved from http://www.jsc.montana.edu

Meyers, P. (2005). Relationships are everything. *ASCA School Counselor, 42*(5), 10–15.

Miller, F. A., & Katz, J. H. (2014). Four keys to accelerating collaboration. *OD Practitioner, 46*(1), 6–11. Retrieved from http://www.odnetwork.org/?page=Publications

Myers, S. B., Sweeney, A. C., Popick, V., Wesley, K., Bordfeld, A., & Fingerhut, R. (2012). Selfcare and perceived stress levels among psychology graduate students. *Training and Education in Professional Psychology. 6*(1), 55–66. doi:10.1037/a0026534

New Brunswick Department of Education. (2002). *Implementing a comprehensive and developmental SCP*. Retrieved from http://www.gnb.ca/0000/publications/ss/NBSchoolCounsellingREV.pdf

Northwest Territories Education, Culture, and Employment. (2004). *Honouring the spirit of our children: Handbook for SCPs in the Northwest Territories*. Retrieved from http://www.ece.gov.nt.ca/files/K-12/Student-Support/framework-school-counselling-programs-nwt/Handbook-for-School-Counselling-Programs.pdf

Nova Scotia Department of Education. (2010). *Comprehensive guidance and counselling program*. Retrieved from https://studentservices.ednet.ns.ca/sites/default/files/Comp%20Guidance%20and%20Couns%20Prog.pdf

Oberman, A. H., Studer, J. R., & Womack, R. H. (2006). Producing evidence to show counseling effectiveness in the schools. *Professional School Counseling, 9*(5), 392–400. Retrieved from http://schoolcounselor.metapress.com/home/main.mpx

Office of the Information and Privacy Commissioner. (2000, August 14). *Inquiry regarding Southeast Kootenay School Board records* (Order 00-40). Retrieved from http://www.oipc.bc.ca/rulings/orders.aspx

Ontario School Counsellors' Association. (2009). *Ethical guidelines for Ontario school counselors* (7th ed.). Bridgenorth, ON: Author.

Ontario School Counsellors' Association. (n.d.). *The role of the guidance teacher counsellor*. Retrieved from https://www.osca.ca/images/Role_of_Counsellor.pdf

Page, B. J., Pietrzak, D. R., & Sutton, J. M., Jr. (2001). National survey of school counselor supervision. *Counselor Education & Supervision, 41*(2), 142–150. doi:10.1002/j.1556-6978.2001.tb01278.x

Perera-Diltz, D. M., & Mason, K. L. (2008). Ideal to real: Duties performed by school counselors. *Journal of School Counseling, 6*(26), 1–36. Retrieved from http://jsc.montana.edu/

Poynton, T. A., & Carey, J. C. (2006). An integrative model of data-based decision making for school counseling. *Professional School Counseling, 10*(2), 121–130. Retrieved from http://schoolcounselor.metapress.com/home/main.mpx

Prince Edward Island Department of Education, Student Services Division. (2005). *School counselling services. Standards and guidelines. Handbook for school counsellors.* Retrieved from http://www.gov.pe.ca/photos/original/ed_couns_svcs.pdf

Roberts, E. B., & Borders, L. (1994). Supervision of school counselors: Administrative, program, and counseling. *School Counselor, 41*(3), 149–157.

Salina, C., Girtz, S., Eppinga, J., Martinez, D., Kilian, D., Lozano, E., & Shines, T. (2013). All hands on deck: A comprehensive, results-driven counseling model. *Professional School Counseling, 17*(1), 63–75. doi:10.5330/PSC.n.2014-17.63

Shallcross, L. (2013). Claiming their rightful place at the table. *Counseling Today, 56*(2), 34–43. Retrieved from http://ct.counseling.org/

Shepard, B., & Martin, L. (2012). *The supervision of counselling and psychotherapy handbook: A handbook for Canadian certified supervisors and applicants.* Ottawa, ON: Canadian Counselling and Psychotherapy Association.

Statistics Canada. (2008). *Canadian demographics at a glance.* Retrieved from http://www.statcan.gc.ca/pub/91-003-x/91-003-x2007001-eng.pdf

Statistics Canada. (2009). *Ethnic diversity and immigration.* Retrieved from http://www41.statcan.gc.ca/2008/30000/ceb30000_000-eng.htm

Stone, C. (2013). *School counseling principles: Ethics and law* (3rd ed.). Alexandria, VA: American School Counselor Association.

Sutton, J., Jr., & Page, B. J. (1994). Post-degree clinical supervision of school counselors. *School Counselor, 42*(1), 32–43.

Swank, J. M., & Tyson, L. (2012). School counseling site supervisor training: A web-based approach. *Professional School Counseling, 16*(1), 40–48. doi:10.5330/PSC.n.2012-16.40

Trice-Black, S., Riechel, M. E. K., & Shillingford, M. A. (2013). School counselors' constructions of student confidentiality. *Journal of School Counseling, 11*(12), 1–46. Retrieved from http://www.jsc.montana.edu

Vallance, K. (2004). Exploring counsellor perceptions of the impact of counselling supervision on clients. *British Journal of Guidance & Counselling, 32*(4), 559–574. doi:10.1080/03069880412331303330

Wallace, S., Jayoung, L., & Sang Min, L. (2010). Job stress, coping strategies, and burnout among abuse-specific counselors. *Journal of Employment Counseling, 47*(3), 111–122. doi:10.1002/j.2161-1920.2010.tb00096.x

Williams, R. L., & Wehrman, J. D. (2010). Collaboration and confidentiality: Not a paradox but an understanding between principals and counselors. *National Association of Secondary School Principals Bulletin, 94*(2), 107–119. doi:10.1177/0192636510374229

Zalaquett, C. P., & Chatters, S. J. (2012). Middle school principals' perceptions of middle school counselors' roles and functions. *American Secondary Education, 40*(2), 89–103. Retrieved from https://www.ashland.edu/coe/about-college/american-secondary-education-journal

NOTE

1. Hereafter these titles are referred to as BCSCA, n.d.; Manitoba SCA, 2002; NB Department of Education, 2002; NWT Education, Culture, and Employment, 2004;

NS Department of Education, 2010; Ontario SCA, 2009, or Ontario SCA, n.d.; and PEI Department of Education, 2005.

PART II

School Counselor Intervention

CHAPTER 4
Bringing Brilliance Out

A Counseling Intervention for Underachieving Students

Carolyn Berger

ABSTRACT

This study evaluated the impact of a small group counseling intervention designed for students who underachieve. The results of the study demonstrated significant improvement for ninth- and tenth-grade underachieving students in the areas of organizational skills, time management, and motivation. The author discusses implications and recommendations for school counselors working with underachieving students.

Two significant issues on which school counselors must focus are graduation rates and college and career readiness (Carr & Galassi, 2012; College Board Advocacy & Policy Center, 2010; Dockery, 2012; Public Agenda, 2010). Although high school graduation rates have improved over the years, there is still a need for progress in this area. Among public high school students in the class of 2009–2010, the average freshman 4-year graduation rate was 78% (Aud et al., 2013). The 4-year graduation rate among public high school students (class of 2004) in the 50 largest cities in the U.S. was only 52% (Editorial Projects in Education Research Center,

Carolyn Berger, "Bring Out the Brilliance: A Counseling Intervention for Underachieving Students," *Professional School Counseling*, vol. 17, no. 1, pp. 86-96.

2008). Each year, approximately 1.2 million students do not graduate and only 70% earn their high school diploma on time (Alliance for Excellent Education, 2009).

Although no study to date has directly examined the graduation rate of underachieving students, a possible hypothesis is that students who underachieve are contributing to lowering the graduation rate. School counselors recognize that working with students who underperform is a crucial issue to raising graduation rates. In a survey of 55 high school counselors who worked in urban areas, one of the top five reported needs included training regarding effective services for underachieving students who consistently earn low to failing grades (Owens, Pernice-Duca, & Thomas, 2009).

The need for school counselors to raise students' college and career readiness is also crucial. In 2010, Public Agenda, a group sponsored by the Bill and Melinda Gates Foundation, published a report that demonstrated concerns with U.S. high school students' college and career readiness (Public Agenda, 2010). This report outlined the challenges school counselors face, including their high student caseloads. However, one of the report's findings was that, overall, school counselors did not adequately prepare students for college. More than two thirds of those surveyed reported their school counselor did a "fair" or "poor" job of helping them decide which college they should attend. Similarly, 62% of respondents reported that their school counselor did a "fair" or "poor" job of helping them think about the types of careers they might want to pursue. In addition, the American College Testing (ACT) organization, in its recent college and career readiness report, found that only 23% of students were ready to enter college-level courses without remediation (ACT, 2011).

Students who do not perform up to their potential are at risk for one or both of these two major issues: dropping out of school and/or not succeeding in college and careers. Although many external factors affect graduation rates, one factor contributing to this problem is the large number of high school students who underachieve. One study (Hodis, Meyer, McClure, Weir, & Walkey, 2011) supported the theory that identifying underachieving students early in their education would prevent students from school failure and dropout. Studies have shown that students who underachieved in high school ended up receiving lower wages later in life (Dougherty, 2003; Murnane, Willett, & Levy, 1995). Peterson (2000) found that of the underachieving students who attended college, only 52% finished college in four years as compared to 83% of achieving students. McCall, Evahn, and Kratzer (1992) found that underachieving students are less likely to pursue a college degree and more likely to drop out of postsecondary education than students of comparable mental ability. Intervening with underachieving students is crucial for educators so that these students are more likely to graduate and be successful in college and in careers.

If school counselors can implement an approach to address underachievement and intervene with students who underachieve, student graduation rates and college/career readiness are likely to improve. This study focuses on a small group counseling intervention that was designed to help underachieving students improve their school performance and school success skills.

DEFINING UNDERACHIEVEMENT

Underachievement is a controversial and debated topic in the literature (Smith, 2005). The most common definition of underachievement is a discrepancy between a student's ability and his/her actual achievement (Reis & McCoach, 2000). The definition of underachievement used in this article is:

> Underachievers are students who exhibit a severe discrepancy between expected achievement (as measured by standardized achievement test scores or cognitive or intellectual ability assessments) and actual achievement (as measured by class grades and teacher evaluations) (Reis & McCoach, 2000, p. 157).

However, considering other factors, such as environmental influences, socioeconomic status, and family background, is important when identifying underachieving students to reduce the bias in this process (Smith, 2005; Thorndike, 1963).

Reis and McCoach's definition was the basis for the method of identifying underachieving students for this study. Therefore, one of the inclusion criteria for the participants was that their expected achievement (as measured by the Florida Comprehensive Assessment Test) was higher than their actual achievement (as measured by letter grades in school). The process for identifying students is addressed more thoroughly in the method section.

CONSIDERING THE NEEDS OF UNDERACHIEVING STUDENTS

After identifying an underachieving student, a school counselor must examine the student's characteristics, behaviors, and attitudes that might contribute to his or her low school performance. Over the past few decades, researchers have identified characteristics of underachieving students. These characteristics are at times disparate, indicating that underachieving students can think, act, and behave quite differently from one another (Mandel & Marcus, 1988, 1995; Rimm, 2008). Personality characteristics of underachieving students include: easy-going, sociable, dependent, anxious, perfectionist, depressed, and possessing low self-esteem (Bruns, 1992; Mandel & Marcus, 1995; Rimm, 2008; Van Boxtel & Monks, 1992). Underachieving students also behave in a variety of ways. For example, they have been shown to procrastinate, use defense mechanisms, question authority, externalize problems, blame failure on others, lack goal-directed behavior, and fail to use self-regulation strategies (Bruns, 1992; Mandel & Marcus, 1995; Rimm, 2008; Van Boxtel & Monks, 1992; Whitmore, 1980).

Since underachieving students have been shown to demonstrate different characteristics from each other, researchers have developed typologies (or categories) of underachieving students. For example, Mandel and Marcus (1995) proposed a typology consisting of six underachievement patterns linked to major personality types: (a) the Anxious Underachiever, (b) the Wheeler-Dealer, (c) the Coaster, (d) the Identity-Search Underachiever, (e) the Defiant Underachiever, and (f) the Sad or Depressed Underachiever. Researchers who examine underachieving students through a typology lens suggest that educators should consider the type of the underachieving student in the formulation of an intervention plan (Mandel & Marcus, 1995; Rimm, 2008).

In addition to the literature on underachievement typologies, another helpful line of research is the work regarding motivation as it relates to student achievement. The Achievement-Orientation Model (AOM) provides a framework that enables school counselors to help raise the motivation level of underachieving students (Rubenstein, Siegle, Reis, McCoach, & Burton, 2012). Since the AOM focuses on each student's unique perceptions, this model integrates well with the research regarding underachievement typologies. The AOM is based on the idea that students' perceptions in three areas regulate motivation and achievement. These three areas include self-efficacy, goal valuation (meaningfulness), and environmental perception. Students with high self-efficacy are more likely to work harder at tasks and persevere even if the task gets difficult (Bandura, 1986). The tasks must also be meaningful to students; therefore, students need to see a link between their school tasks and their future goals. Environmental perception refers to the students' perceptions of teachers' and parents' expectations and support. If students do not feel supported by caring adults, they will not be productive at school tasks (Rubenstein et al., 2012).

When students function highly in the areas of self-efficacy, meaningfulness, and perceptions of the environment, they set realistic goals and are able to regulate themselves in order to accomplish a task. Therefore, self-regulation is an additional component to the AOM (Rubenstein et al., 2012). Interventions that focus solely on self-regulation with underachieving students have not been found to be successful (Stoeger & Zigler, 2005). However, other research has addressed teaching students skills such as organization and time management (Brigman, Webb, & Campbell, 2007; Zimmerman, Bonner, & Kovach, 1996). Therefore, including self-regulation as a component of a group intervention for underachieving students is important.

The author took into consideration the research regarding the effectiveness of counseling format. Research has supported the premise that low-achieving and underachieving students benefit from the small group counseling format (Whiston & Quinby, 2009; Wilson, 1986). One study to date has examined the impact of an AOM small group counseling intervention with gifted students and, while the results were positive, more research needs to be done to examine the effectiveness of the AOM in small group counseling format (Rubenstein et al., 2012).

GROUP COUNSELING INTERVENTION DESIGN AND FORMAT

Prior to developing the Bring out the Brilliance group, the author developed a six-session group counseling curriculum based on recommendations from the literature on typologies of underachieving students (Mandel & Marcus, 1995; Rimm, 2008). However, the data from the original group did not show any significant results. The author consulted with school counseling professionals and examined the literature to determine ways to make the group more effective. As a result of examining the research and consulting with school counseling professionals, the author integrated the Achievement-Orientation Model into the original group counseling intervention. To include all the essential components, the group sessions were increased from six to eight. The Bring out the Brilliance group was the result of this collaboration. This eight-session group was primarily based on the AOM, but with consideration for the different typologies of underachieving student characteristics (Mandel & Marcus, 1995; Rimm, 2008). The objectives and activities for each session can be found in Figure 4.1.

METHOD

PURPOSE AND HYPOTHESES

The main purpose of this study was to determine whether or not Bring out the Brilliance, a small group counseling intervention based on the AOM, was effective at raising achievement data and achievement-related data of underachieving students. The hypothesis was that the Bring out the Brilliance intervention will lead to an increase in student achievement data, specifically grade point average. Achievement-related data were also hypothesized to improve, with decreases in both absences and disciplinary referrals. A further hypothesis was that the organizational skills and time management scores would increase, while the students' low motivation and test anxiety would decrease. The author used the School Motivation and Learning Strategies Inventory (SMALSI) to measure students' organizational skills, time management, low motivation, and test anxiety.

A secondary purpose of the study was to learn underachieving students' perceptions of what they need to be more successful academically. The final session of Bring out the Brilliance asked students to answer questions that assessed whether or not they felt the group intervention was helpful and what else the students needed to become more academically successful.

SETTING

Three high schools in South Florida were chosen for the Bring out the Brilliance groups. The schools were chosen using convenience sampling; the research team had a relationship with each school. The school counseling interns who ran the Bring out the Brilliance groups were placed in the school settings at the time of the study, and the author was the university supervisor for these interns. The enrollments of the three schools ranged from approximately 1300 to 2200. The smallest school's

FIGURE 4.1. BRING OUT THE BRILLIANCE SESSION OBJECTIVES AND ACTIVITIES

	SESSION OBJECTIVES* STUDENTS WILL:	SESSION ACTIVITIES
Session 1	1. Develop connection between group members and group leader (Greenberg, 2003) 2. Build self-efficacy (Peters, 2000; Rimm, 2008)	• Paper Bag Self (Amatea, 1975): Students use art supplies and magazines to decorate the outside of a small paper bag with how they think people view them. The students also cut out pictures and words from magazines to place inside of the paper bag that represent how the students view themselves. In processing the students' Paper Bag Selves, the group leader focuses on the students' strengths and the commonalities between group members.
Session 2	1. Build self-regulation skills through setting long-term and short-term goals 2. Understand the link between their school tasks and future goals (meaningfulness)	• Guided imagery: Students visualize they are receiving an academic degree or an award for an accomplishment • Goal setting: Students reflect on this visualization to help them write long and short-term goals • Processing activity: Discussion of role school success plays in relation to goals • Challenge activity: Students research how a role model became successful
Session 3	1. Continue working on self-regulation/goal valuation skills by developing strategies for overcoming obstacles that might get in the way of their goals	• Follow up on last session's "challenge activity" • Externalization activity (Winslade & Monk, 1999): Students draw their main obstacle to achievement by giving it a face and a name. The counselor helps students discuss how they can keep this obstacle from leading them to fail in school.
Session 4	1. Learn time management strategies for self-regulation 2. Discuss their support team who will help them reach their goals (environmental perception)	• Time management activity: several methods of time management are demonstrated and students practice them during group • Students choose one time management method to practice • Students discuss people who support them and make a concrete plan for using support people to help them stay on track with their time management

Session 5	1. Follow up on time management strategies 2. Discuss effective ways to manage procrastination (self-regulation) 3. Discuss support team (environmental perception)	• Report back on time management plan • Guided imagery for managing procrastination (Fiore, 1989) • Discuss how using their support team will help them avoid procrastination and feel less stressed/anxious/etc. • Compare "Procrastinator Talk" with "Producer Talk"
Session 6	1. Be able to identify feelings 2. Identify feelings that are related to their achievement (e.g., school grades, test scores, etc.) 3. Practice relaxation strategies for dealing with unpleasant feelings (Mandel & Marcus, 1995)	• Read poems and have students identify feelings in the poems using a feelings list • Students will write down feelings related to times when they did not achieve in school • Teach muscle relaxation and breathing exercises to overcome unpleasant feelings
Session 7	1. Review goals and the link between school achievement and future goals 2. Make a plan for practicing the skills they learned in group after group ends	• Students will go over goals they set in session two and revise as needed • Students will write a concrete plan for how they will reach goals, and how they will reward themselves if they reach their short-term goals
Session 8	1. Celebrate their accomplishments 2. Build self-efficacy	• Bring treats to celebrate end of group • Highlight students' accomplishments • Give a card or small poster board for each student. All group members and the group leader will write positive feedback in each person's card.

*All objectives are based on the Achievement-Orientation Model (Rubenstein et al., 2012) unless otherwise noted.

student demographics were: 59% White, 19% Hispanic, 12% Black, 4% Asian, 5% Bicultural, and < 1% Native American. The demographics of the mid-sized school's students were: 20% White, 55% Hispanic, 20% Black, 3% Asian, 2% Bicultural, and < 1% Native American. At the largest school, the student demographics were: 57% White, 27% Hispanic, 12% Black, 2% Asian, 2% Bicultural, and < 1% Native American. The graduation rate for the school district was approximately 74%, and the truancy rate was approximately 6.5% (21 days or more of school missed per school year).

PARTICIPANTS AND PROCEDURES

The Bring out the Brilliance group participants were 13 students from the three high schools. Three separate groups were conducted, one at each of the three high schools. Four ninth-grade students were in the group at the smallest school, three students (one in tenth grade and two in ninth grade) were in the group at the mid-sized school, and six tenth-grade students comprised the group at the largest school. The demographics of the participating students were: Black/ African American (5 students = 38%), White/Caucasian (6 students = 46%), Hispanic (1 student = 7.5%), and Native American (1 student = 7.5%). In order for a student's data to be considered in the study, he or she had to attend at least six of the eight group sessions with their peers. The participants were in attendance 84.7% of the time. When a student missed a session, he or she met with the group leader individually for approximately 15–20 minutes to cover the material that was missed.

The group leader was a counselor educator who previously served as a school counselor in middle and high school settings. The group leader trained two school counseling interns to assist with leading the groups. The interns helped lead the sessions in each of the three schools, in collaboration with the group leader. The school counselors assigned to each of the three schools were crucial for helping to set up the group, recruit students, and assist with monitoring student progress. The school counselors gave the group leader and interns insight on the students' academic progress to provide information that would assist with facilitating the group.

Each student in the group was identified as underachieving by at least one teacher and by the school counselor, in accordance with Reis and McCoach's (2000) definition of underachievement. Teachers were asked to refer students whose actual academic performance was less than their expected performance (i.e., students who were not performing up to their potential). A total of 33 students were referred by teachers to participate in the group. The school counselors then looked at the referred students' academic profiles for evidence of a discrepancy between actual performance (i.e., grades) and expected performance (i.e., standardized test scores). The student had to achieve a level 3, 4, or 5 on the Florida Comprehensive Assessment Test (FCAT) in both math and reading, which is at or above proficiency. The students' report cards had to reflect grades with a C average or below in reading and/or math. For example, if the student currently had an F in a math class, but scored at or above grade level on the math standardized test, he or she could be identified as underachieving. However, if the student had below average test scores and below average grades, then the student would not qualify for the group but would need to receive other counseling services instead to assist with low achievement (e.g., tutoring and other academic resources). Students selected for the group could not have a diagnosed learning disability, nor could they be in the English Language Learners program, as these factors would complicate their identification as an underachieving student.

Once the school counselors screened for the inclusion criteria, 30 students remained as potential group participants. The school counselors contacted the parents/guardians of these 30 students to obtain written consent for participation. The students were also contacted to obtain assent to participate in the study. All risks and benefits were clearly explained. Parents and/or students could opt out of participating in the group. Out of the 30 students who met the inclusion criteria for the group, 12 students did not return the consent and assent forms for participation, leaving a total of 17 students to participate in the groups. Of these 17 students, two students transferred schools during the timeframe the groups were meeting. Two other students stopped attending the group after 1–2 sessions. These four students' data were excluded from the study, resulting in 13 student participants. These 13 participants averaged a 1.38 GPA, well below the 2.0 minimum GPA required for graduation.

The groups met eight times for 45-minute sessions over a 9- to 11-week period. Each group typically met once per week, although holidays and/or testing dates required the group to reschedule on occasion. The method of pulling students from class varied from school to school. One school had a 45-minute lunch period and utilized this time to hold the group. One school had common elective periods and used elective class periods for group meeting times. The third school used a rotating schedule so students would not miss the same class period on a regular basis. The group schedule was determined by consulting with the administration.

Each group session included a check-in and a summary of the previous group meeting's topic (refer to Figure 4.1). If students were given a task in the last group (e.g., to practice relaxation exercises), the students were asked to share how this task went for them this past week. Honesty in self-reflection was encouraged as it was important for each student to find what worked for him or her.

One important consideration that the group leader and student interns kept in mind for each group was the importance of keeping the group on task. Since the groups were composed of students identified as underachieving, straying from the main topic of the activity or discussion was common for them. Therefore, it was crucial that the person running the group redirected the students as needed to help them remain on task. The activities in each group kept the students busy, and this reduced the likelihood that students would stray off the topic.

INSTRUMENTS

The School Motivation and Learning Strategies Inventory (SMALSI), a scale that has been tested for reliability and validity, was used to measure change in student motivation before and after the Bring out the Brilliance group (Stroud & Reynolds, 2006). The SMALSI has a teen form (ages 13-18) and a child form (ages 8–12). Since all group participants were 13 years of age or older, the group leaders gave students the Teen Form version of the SMALSI. The scale includes ten subscales; however, for the purposes of this study, only four of the subscales were used. These subscales included: Organizational Techniques (ORG), Time Management (TIME), Low Academic Motivation (LOMOT), and Test Anxiety (TANX). The alpha coefficients for these scales are strong and range from .79 to .91, thereby supporting the reliability of these subscales (Stroud & Reynolds, 2006). The remaining subscales on the SMALSI were not directly relevant to the goals of this small group counseling intervention, and since time was a factor, reducing the number of items helped students complete the survey more quickly.

Two of the SMALSI subscales, Time Management and Organization, assessed student strengths. Therefore, improvement in these areas would be supported if the students' scores increased on these two subscales. The remaining two subscales, Low Academic Motivation and Test Anxiety, assessed student liabilities. Improvement in these areas would be supported if the students' scores decreased on these two subscales.

In addition to collecting quantitative data from the SMALSI, the group leaders collected qualitative data at the end of the study. This qualitative data was in the form of a seven-item, short-answer questionnaire, the End of Group Survey. Students were asked questions such as, "Do you think this intervention plan helped you? Why or why not?" and "What skills (if any) did you learn through this group that help you with your schoolwork?" The purpose of this qualitative survey was to give the group leaders insight into how to make the group more effective to meet students' needs in the future, and to assess students' perspectives regarding the overall effectiveness of the group. The qualitative data was analyzed using thematic analysis (Braun & Clarke, 2006).

DATA COLLECTION AND ANALYSIS

In addition to collecting students' perception data using the SMALSI and End of Group Survey, the group leaders collected school achievement and achievement-related data. This data included grade point average (GPA), attendance, and discipline. The researchers compared GPAs from progress report grades immediately prior to the beginning of the group to GPAs from progress reports approximately 2 to 4 weeks after the group ended.

Comparing attendance and discipline referrals pre- and postgroup was complex because each of the three separate groups met at different points during the fall semester of school. One of the groups started in mid-September and the other two groups began in late September/early October. To make the comparisons as equivalent as possible, the researcher gathered attendance and discipline referral data on the 30 school days immediately prior to the group. This pregroup attendance and discipline referral data were compared to the attendance and discipline referrals of the 30 school days towards the end of the group sessions (starting at week 5 of the group).

RESULTS

The researcher used paired-sample *t* tests to analyze the mean differences between students' pregroup and postgroup scores on the SMALSI (see Table 4.1 for a summary of all pretest and posttest data). Posttest scores for the Organizational Skills and Time Management subscales were significantly higher than pretest scores. Posttest scores for the Low Motivation subscale were significantly lower than pretest scores. Posttest scores for the Test Anxiety subscale were higher than pretest scores; however, these results were not significant.

The researcher also used a paired-sample *t* test to analyze the mean differences between students' pregroup and postgroup school achievement and achievement-related data. Although none of the mean differences in achievement and achievement-related data were found to be significant, these types of data did show

TABLE 4.1. PAIRED SAMPLES T-TEST DATA

	PRETEST		POSTTEST			
MEASURE	*M*	*SD*	*M*	*SD*	*t*	*df*
SMALSI-ORG	19.63	4.99	24.67	4.91	-3.372*	11
SMALSI-TIME	12.50	4.07	17.92	6.53	-3.308*	11
SMALSI-LOMOT	21.63	8.37	17.08	8.46	3.716*	11
SMALSI-TANX	13.38	6.04	14.83	9.00	-.674	11
Progress GPA	1.39	1.13	1.57	.77	-.947	12
Discipline Referrals	1.22	2.11	1.11	1.38	.222	12
Unexcused Absences	5.41	7.49	2.19	.70	1.463	10
Excused Absences	1.07	1.28	1.57	.68	-1.372	10

$^{*}p < .01$.

movement in the desired direction. Grade point averages increased .18 points between grading periods, while discipline referrals went down an average of .11 for all three groups. Unexcused absences decreased on average 3.22 per student. Excused absences increased by .5.

The students took a survey at the end of the group so the researcher could determine the students' perception of the effectiveness of the group. Eleven students reported they felt that the group helped them in some way. The remaining two students did not return the end of group survey. These survey results were analyzed using thematic analysis (Braun & Clarke, 2006). The two main themes were coded as "Realization" and "Skills." Students reported that the group helped "open [their] eyes," "realize I need to reach my goal," and "introspect on [their] future." These types of responses were coded as "realization" because students reported that they learned something new about themselves, whether it was in relation to their future goals, their academic behaviors, or their motivation. The second main theme was termed "skills" because students reported a wide variety of skills that they gained from participating in the group. Students reported the group taught them skills such as: ways to reduce procrastination, goal setting, time management, organizational skills, and how to de-stress.

Secondary themes that emerged included "Connections" and "Improved Academics." Students reported that the group helped them make connections with their peers and with the individual leading the group. They reported that it helped them to share their school problems with each other and to come up with solutions together. In terms of "improved academics," students reported feeling pleased that their grades improved, or at least that they were now making an effort to improve their grades.

The final question of the survey asked students to share ways educators can more effectively encourage achievement. The most common feedback was that educators need to make school more interesting for all students. For example, one student wrote that educators should "focus on the students' learning type to get better results." The second most common feedback was that teachers and counselors need to get to know students on a more personal level to individualize instruction and education plans. One student wrote, "[teachers and school counselors need to] make a bigger effort to make a personal connection with students."

Several students demonstrated significant changes in grade point average. Below are two students' success stories that demonstrate the effectiveness of this group counseling intervention.

1. "Sam" is a ninth-grade student who should be in the 10th grade due to retention in middle school. He came into the group with a .40 grade point average on his progress report. Sam's standardized test scores demonstrated that he is proficient in math and reading, yet his math and English grades at the beginning of the group were both Fs. Sam loved to be a disc jockey (DJ) at school events and parties, and he wrote music on his keyboard in his spare time. When asked about his goals, he said he wanted to pursue a career in music but didn't know where to begin. In the group, we discussed possible careers in music and the training he would need to pursue these careers. The group leader encouraged him to pursue extracurricular activities in music; although Sam expressed interest, he did not sign up for these activities by the end of the group. Sam shared that he never really talks about his goals with anyone, and he frequently skips school because he'd rather just hang out at home and doesn't see the point in going to school. By the end of the group, Sam started to make connections between his schoolwork and his goals to study music. His attendance improved from 13 missed absences before group to 7 absences at the end of the group. His progress report GPA increased from .40 to 2.00. Sam reported that the group helped him really think about why school is important and motivated him to get out of bed in the morning and come to school.
2. "Eva" was a 10th-grade student who frequently missed school and therefore had a 2.25 GPA on her pregroup progress report. Her test scores met the requirement to qualify her for honors level courses; however, she was almost held back in the ninth grade because she failed a few courses the previous school year. Eva had a tumultuous

home life and was currently living with a friend (with her mother's permission). Eva knew she could get into college if she tried but was surrounded by chaos in her home life that made it difficult to get work done. She was often overwhelmed emotionally by her life situation, and adding school stress into the mix was too much for her to bear. By the end of the group, Eva improved her GPA from 2.25 to 2.75. Her absences went from 10 to 4.25. Eva reported that the group helped her process her anxieties and stress regarding school, helped her set goals for herself, and helped her realize that these goals are within her reach and her control.

DISCUSSION

The students in the Bring out the Brilliance groups had GPAs that averaged below the state's requirement to graduate from high school. However, these students' teachers reported that they had potential to succeed, and the students all demonstrated proficient or above proficient standardized test scores. These students had different characteristics from each other and underachieved for various reasons. The Bring out the Brilliance group focused on the dimensions of the Achievement-Orientation Model (AOM), including self-efficacy, goal valuation (meaningfulness), self-regulation, and environmental perception (Rubenstein et al., 2012). The group also incorporated the need for underachieving students to process their emotional struggles that lead to underachievement (Mandel & Marcus, 1995; Rimm, 2008).

The focus on the elements of self-efficacy, self-regulation, meaningfulness, and environmental perception led the students to show significant improvements in organizational skills, time management, and motivation as demonstrated in the SMALSI results. Although the remaining data were not shown to be significant, these findings demonstrate that the group had the overall desired effect on the students by raising achievement and improving achievement-related data. The lack of significant findings may be due to the fact that the group's impact may come with more time and may not yet be reflected in the current grades, discipline referrals, and attendance rates.

The group leader and the school counseling interns shared the results of the Bring out the Brilliance group with the school counselors and administrators. All three administrators were supportive of the counseling intervention. One administrator in particular was excited about the results at his school, and he requested his school counselors to continue using the Bring out the Brilliance group session curriculum in the future. All of the school counselors planned to follow up with the students in the group to keep them on the right track.

One limitation of Bring out the Brilliance is that some students may need additional supports that are not met by the eight sessions of this group. For example, if a student is from a family with low income and needs help gaining access to basic resources, the school counselor may need to work this student in additional ways. School counselors always need to take into consideration the individual needs of each student.

A second limitation of this study is that the students' school counselors were not the individuals leading the group. School counselors have particular insight into students' needs and personal motivations that could help make the group more successful. Students may connect more with their school counselors than with an individual coming from outside of the school. The students' school counselors also understand the school climate, specific student-teacher relationships, and other dynamics within the school that an outside person does not understand.

A potential limitation to implementing this program could be the length and frequency of group meetings. Each of the eight group sessions lasted approximately 45 minutes, and finding that amount of time in the school setting may be challenging for school counselors. Some students may not want to be in a group counseling environment, and therefore Bring out the Brilliance would not be a good fit for those individuals. If the school has resources for incentives, bringing food or drinks to the group may help to encourage students to attend. A school counselor who is interested in implementing Bring out the Brilliance may want to consider delivering the content over a longer period of time to increase the impact of the group. For example, rather than doing eight sessions in 8 weeks, a counselor could spread out the material into 12 sessions and deliver the lessons throughout an entire semester.

IMPLICATIONS AND RECOMMENDATIONS

The Bring out the Brilliance group provides an example of how school counselors and researchers can effectively work with underachieving students on a variety of key elements that impact achievement. The students' improvement in motivation, organizational skills, and time management could lead to continued improvement in their grades. This study supports an intervention that considers multiple dimensions of needs such as those outlined in the Achievement-Orientation Model, as well as the considerations outlined by researchers studying typologies of underachievement (Mandel & Marcus, 1995; Rimm, 2008; Rubenstein et al., 2012). Teaching underachieving students basic school success strategies (e.g., study skills, organizational skills, time management) is not enough (Rubenstein et al., 2012). Therefore, researchers and school counselors need to pay attention to counseling services that consider the wide array of underachieving students' needs.

The primary recommendation for increasing the effectiveness of the Bring out the Brilliance intervention is for the students' school counselor to lead the group. The author recommends this for several reasons. The school counselor would have insight on students' histories, backgrounds, and family information. The school counselor usually has some rapport built with the students already and this connection is very important to implementing an effective intervention. The school counselor's insight on the students' needs would help him or her tailor the counseling lessons accordingly.

Another reason to have the school counselor lead the group is to help students feel more connected to adults in the school setting. In the postgroup feedback, the students communicated that they want to feel like teachers and counselors connect with them. The students liked that they could share their feelings and thoughts with peers in the group, and also that they had an educator with whom they could connect to discuss their situation in school. The school counselor is an ideal person to connect with the students and to foster connections between the students and teachers. During the counseling sessions, students shared feedback regarding their academic needs. The school counselor can advocate for these students' needs with both teachers and administration. If students see that caring adults at the school are willing to help meet their needs, they are more likely to succeed.

School counselors are also in an ideal position to incorporate three additional elements into the group counseling unit: weekly grade checks, weekly parent communication, and booster sessions. Most school counselors today can use technology to easily pull up students' current grade status. School counselors have access to teachers to gain feedback on students' academic or behavioral progress in class. School counselors can also e-mail or call parents to gain more feedback on students' progress at home. Booster sessions would have increased the likelihood that students continue to stay on the right path. Many of the students in the group expressed a wish that the group could last throughout the year to help them stay motivated. While a year-long group is not realistic in a school setting, having the group convene on a monthly or bi-monthly basis would be possible to follow up with the students regarding their goals and specific objectives for overcoming barriers.

In the feedback given at the end of the group, students shared a need for more positive connections with teachers and adults at school. School counselors can help foster these connections by communicating with teachers, coaches, and other key adults within the school to set up an advisement or mentorship program. Having an adult mentor or advisor within the school will help underachieving students feel more connected, which can increase achievement as outlined in the AOM model (i.e., environmental perception).

Students also shared feedback at the end of the group regarding the need for relevancy and connection between their goals/dreams and their schoolwork. School counselors and researchers should consider more systemic services that focus on developing this relevancy and connection school-wide. School counselors can hold professional development trainings to remind teachers of the importance of making these connections with students.

CONCLUSION

The Bring out the Brilliance study demonstrated support for a group intervention that looks at a variety of factors that affect performance. Future school counseling research could examine interventions for underachieving students that incorporate elements such as self-regulation, goal valuation, self-efficacy, and others described in this study. However, underachieving students may need other systemic interventions as well. Parents, teachers, administration, and community members can come together to best serve the needs of underachieving students through a variety of school-based academic supports. Underachieving students have a wide variety of needs and therefore intervention plans for these students need to be complex. A group like Bring out the Brilliance will help school counselors recognize other systemic needs of underachieving students within their schools.

REFERENCES

American College Testing. (2011). *The condition of college and career readiness.* Retrieved from http://act.org/ research/policymakers/cccr11/index. html

Alliance for Excellent Education. (2009). *There's a crisis in America's high schools.* Retrieved from http://www. all4ed.org/about_the_crisis

Amatea, E. (1975). *The yellow brick road: A sourcebook of career guidance strategies for the elementary teacher and counselor.* Tallahassee, FL: Career Education Center, Florida Department of Education.

Aud, S., Wilkinson-Flicker, S., Kristapovich, P., Rathbun, A., Wang, X., Zhang, J., ... Dziuba, A. (2013). *The condition of education 2013.* (NCES 2013–037). Washington, D.C.: National Center for Education Statistics. Retrieved from http://nces.ed.gov/pubsearch/pubsinfo.asp?pubid=2013037

Bandura, A. (1986). *Social foundations of thought and action: A social cognition theory.* Englewood Cliffs, NJ: Prentice-Hall.

Braun, V., & Clarke, V. (2006). Using thematic analysis in psychology. *Qualitative Research in Psychology, 3,* 77–101. doi:10.1191/1478088706qp063oa

Brigman, G. A., Webb, L. D., & Campbell, C. (2007). Building skills for school success: Improving the academic and social competence of students. *Professional School Counseling, 10,* 279–288.

Bruns, J. H. (1992). *They can but they don't : Helping students overcome work inhibition.* New York, NY: Viking.

Carr, C. V., & Galassi, J. P. (2012). The role school counselors believe they should adopt in dropout prevention. *Journal of School Counseling,* 10(1). Retrieved from http://www.jsc.montana.edu/ articles/v10n1.pdf

College Board Advocacy & Policy Center. (2010). *Eight components of college and career readiness counseling.* Retrieved from http://nosca.collegeboard.org/ tools-resources?affiliateId=-noscahero& bannerId=resources

Dockery, D. J. (2012). School dropout indicators, trends, and interventions for school counselors. *Journal of School Counseling,* 10(12). Retrieved from http://www.jsc.montana.edu/articles/ v10n12.pdf

Dougherty, C. (2003). Numeracy, literacy and earnings: Evidence from the National Longitudinal Survey of Youth. *Economics of Education Review, 22,* 511–521. doi:10.1016/s02727757(03)00040-2

Editorial Projects in Education Research Center. (2008). *Cities in crisis: A special analytic report on high school graduation.* Retrieved from http://www.edweek.org/ media/citiesincrisis040108.pdf

Fiore, N. (1989). *Overcoming procrastination.* New York, NY: MJF Books.

Greenberg, K. R. (2003). *Group counseling in K-12 schools: A handbook for school counselors.* Boston, MA: Allyn and Bacon.

Hodis, F. A., Meyer, L. H., McClure, J., Weir, K. F., & Walkey, F. H. (2011). A longitudinal investigation of motivation and secondary school achievement using growth mixture modeling. *Journal of Educational Psychology, 103*(2), 312–323. doi:10.1037/a0022547

Mandel, H. P., & Marcus, S. I. (1988). *The psychology of underachievement.* New York, NY: John Wiley & Sons.

Mandel, H. P., & Marcus, S. I. (1995). *Could do better.* New York, NY: John Wiley & Sons.

McCall, R. B., Evahn, C., & Kratzer, L. (1992). *High school underachievers: What do they achieve as adults?* Newbury Park, CA: SAGE Publications.

Murnane, R. J., Willett, J. B., & Levy, F. (1995). The growing importance of cognitive skills in wage determination. *The Review of Economics and Statistics,* 77(2), 251–266.

Owens, D., Pernice-Duca, F., & Thomas, D. (2009). Post-training needs of urban high school counselors: Implications for counselor training programs. *Journal of School Counseling, 7*(17). Retrieved from http://www.jsc.montana.edu/ articles/v7n17.pdf

Peters, R. (2000). *Overcoming underachieving*. New York, NY: Broadway Books.

Peterson, J. S. (2000). A follow-up study of one group of achievers and under-achievers four years after high school graduation. *Roeper Review, 22*(4), 217–224. doi:10.1080/02783190009554041

Public Agenda. (2010). *Can I get a little advice here? How an overstretched high school guidance system is undermining students' college aspirations*. Retrieved from http://www.publicagenda.org/ theirwholelivesaheadofthem?qt_ active=1

Reis, S. M., & McCoach, D. B. (2000). The underachievement of gifted students: What do we know and where do we go? *Gifted Child Quarterly, 44*(3), 152-170. doi:10.1177/001698620004400302

Rimm, S. (2008). *Why bright kids get poor grades*. Scottsdale, AZ: Great Potential Press, Inc.

Rubenstein, L. D., Siegle, D., Reis, S. M., McCoach, D. B., & Burton, M. G. (2012). A Complex quest: The development and research of underachievement interventions for gifted students. *Psychology in the Schools, 49*, 678–694. doi:10.1002/pits.21620

Smith, E. (2005). *Analysing underachievement in schools*. New York, NY: Continuum International Publishing Group.

Stoeger, H., & Zigler, A. (2005). Evaluation of an elementary classroom self-regulated learning program for gifted mathematics underachievers. *International Education Journal, 6*(2), 261–271.

Stroud, K. C., & Reynolds, C. R. (2006). *SMALSI: School Motivation and Learning Strategies Inventory*. Los Angeles, CA: Western Psychological Services.

Thorndike, R. L. (1963). *The concepts of over and underachievement*. New York, NY: Teachers College Press.

Van Boxtel, B. W., & Monks, F. J. (1992). General, social and academic self-concepts of gifted adolescents. *Journal of Youth and Adolescence, 21*(2), 169–187.

Whiston, S. C., & Quinby, R. F. (2009). Review of school counseling outcome research. *Psychology in the Schools, 46*, 267–272. doi:10.1002/pits.20372

Whitmore, J. R. (1980). *Giftedness, conflict, and underachievement*. Boston, MA: Allyn & Bacon.

Wilson, N. S. (1986). Counselor interventions with low-achieving and underachieving elementary, middle, and high school students: A review of the literature. *Journal of Counseling and Development, 64*, 628–634.

Winslade, J., & Monk, G. (1999). *Narrative counseling in schools*. Thousand Oaks, CA: Corwin Press, Inc.

Wittmer, J., & Thompson, D. W. (2006). *Large group guidance activities: A K-12 sourcebook* (2nd ed.). Warminster, PA: Educational Media Corp.

Zimmerman, B. J., Bonner, S., & Kovach, R. (1996). *Developing self-regulated learners: Beyond achievement to self-efficacy*. Washington, D.C.: American Psychological Association.

CHAPTER 5

Academically Resilient Low-Income Students' Perceptions of How School Counselors Can Meet Their Academic Needs

Joseph Williams, Sam Steen, Tracy Albert, Betty Dely, Brian Jacobs, Chelsea Nagel and Anese Irick

ABSTRACT

This phenomenological, qualitative study examined a national sample of academically resilient, low-income middle school students' (N = 24) perspectives of what school counselors can do to promote their academic achievement. Three main themes and nine subthemes were identified: build meaningful relationships, build on the cultural wealth of students, and provide mental health services in schools. This article discusses implications for school counselor practice and future research.

For the first time in recent history, a majority (51%) of the nation's public school children come from families living below, at, or not far above the poverty line (Suitts, 2015). More troubling than the high number of low-income students are the long-term trends and impact of poverty on

Joseph Williams, Sam Steen, and Tracy Albert, "Academically Resilient Low Income Students' Perceptions of How School Counselors Can Meet Their Academic Needs," *Professional School Counseling*, vol. 19, no. 1, pp. 155-165.

the academic achievement of students at all levels, pre-K through college (Lacour & Tissington, 2011). For example, Reardon (2011) found that the gap in standardized test scores between affluent and low income students grew by 40% since the 1960s. Reading scores data from the National Association of Educational Progress (NAEP, 2011) continues to show that fourth graders who were eligible for free or reduced lunch scored 29 points lower than those not eligible, and a similar pattern exists for eighth graders (NCES, 2011). Furthermore, according to the U.S. Department of Education (USDOE, 2014b), from 1990 to 2012, the status dropout rates (i.e., the percentage of 16- through 24-year-olds who are not enrolled in school and have not earned a high school credential) for those in higher income families remained consistently and significantly lower than the rates for those from families with lower incomes. Similarly, between 1990 and 2012, significant gaps in college-going rates persisted across income levels (USDOE, 2014a). For instance, in 2012, the immediate college enrollment rate for high school completers from high-income families (81%) was 29 percentage points higher than the rate for those from low-income families (52%) and 16 percentage points higher than the rate for those from middle-income families (65%; USDOE, 2014a).

Yet, despite these grim statistics, many K-12 students from low-income households go on to succeed academically (Wyner, Bridgeland, & DiIulio, 2007). These students are often referred to as academically resilient, and research on resilient students has the potential to provide school counselors and other stakeholders with insights into the drivers of achievement among students from low-income backgrounds (Williams & Bryan, 2013). The ASCA National Model (American School Counselor Association [ASCA], 2012) calls for school counselors to implement comprehensive school counseling programs that support the academic achievement of all students, especially marginalized student populations (e.g., low-income students). But without insights into which areas of support might be most fruitful to address, well-intended programs and counseling services to improve outcomes for students from low-income families will likely be ineffective (Williams & Bryan, 2013).

Several studies demonstrate that, when asked, marginalized students have much to say about the challenges they face and how school personnel can help them succeed academically despite those challenges (e.g., Cook-Sather, 2002; Downey, 2002; Mitra, 2009, Williams & Bryan, 2013; Williams & Portman, 2014). However, student perspectives in the school counseling literature have been relatively absent (Alfaro, Umaña-Taylor, & Bámaca, 2006; Stinson, 2008; Williams & Portman, 2014). The authors surmise that the ability to identify appropriate services and solutions will be limited if student voices remain silent in conversations related to how school counselors can best address the needs of students from lower income backgrounds. Therefore, the main purpose of this phenomenological study was to understand academically resilient, low-income middle school students' perspectives on what school counselors can do to promote students' academic achievement.

ACADEMIC RESILIENT STUDENTS

Resilient students are described by Alva (1991) as those who maintain high levels of achievement motivation and performance despite the presence of stressful events and conditions that place them at risk of poor performance. The capacity for academic resilience varies from one student to the next and can grow or decline over time based on individual and environmental protective factors that reduce or eliminate the impact of risk factors associated with poor academic outcomes (Borman & Rachuba, 2001). Research on resilient students is very recent and limited. The findings have typically revealed that several factors differ significantly between resilient and non-resilient students, including social competence; problem-solving skills; internal locus of control; a sense of purpose; motivation and goal orientation; academic self-efficacy; learning environment; relationships that provide care and support; nonparental sources of support or counsel from peers, siblings, and teachers; and availability of community organizations and services (e.g., Wong, 2008; Gizir & Aydin, 2009; Martin & Marsh, 2006; Morales, 2010; Vanderbilt-Adriance & Shaw, 2008). Although these studies identified a number of predictors of academic resilience, the vast majority used comparative or correlational analysis of large samples. Few studies approached the topic of academic resilience from the perspective of resilient students. Even fewer studies have focused on resilient students' perceptions of what they need to succeed academically despite exposure to adversity.

METHOD

The researchers used a qualitative, phenomenological study to gain an in-depth understanding of students' perspectives and the meanings they attached to them (Creswell, 2007). Phenomenological methods have been shown to be effective at gathering the experiences and perceptions of individuals from their own perspectives in prior counseling research (Hays & Singh, 2012). The authors chose to focus on middle school students because most academic problems either begin or accelerate in middle school for many poor and minority students (e.g., Goldstein, Boxer, & Rudolph, 2015; Midgley, Arunkumar, & Urdan, 1996; Steele & Aronson, 1995). Middle school students from low-income families contend with environmental and social pressures that put them at greater risk of negative outcomes than their peers who only have to cope with pubertal and school change during this developmental period (Goldstein et al., 2015). The decision to select academically resilient, low-income students offered a more defined perspective given their success in school despite the presence of adverse conditions associated with living in poverty. The research question established as the basis for this study was: What are academically resilient, low-income middle school students' perspectives on how school counselors can help poor students get good grades?

RESEARCH TEAM

The research team consisted of a faculty member (first author), a doctoral student (third author), and four masters-level students (fourth through seventh authors) in a counselor education program at a large Mid-Atlantic public university. Four members of the research team identified as African American, and the other two as European American, with a mean age of 26 years (*SD* = 2.9). Two members of the research team were males and the other four team members were females. The first author developed the methodology and provided qualitative research training to the team. The third author conducted and transcribed four interviews; the fourth through seventh authors each conducted and transcribed five interviews. To include independent and consensus coding, the first and third author shared in the responsibility of data analysis to include independent and consensus coding. The team was a diverse group in terms of race and ethnicity, age, gender, and background.

PARTICIPANTS

Stratified purposeful sampling was used to identify 24 out of 115 potential participants drawn from a national sample of applicants pursuing a foundation-funded scholarship program (Jack Kent Cooke Young Scholars Program) for academically successful low-income students. This number fell within the recommended size for phenomenological studies (Creswell, 2007). The strata were formed based on income, sex, race, and geographical locale. Participants represented diverse racial groups, including Caucasian/European American ($n = 5$), African American or Black ($n = 5$), Hispanic or Latino ($n = 5$), Asian, Asian American, or Pacific Islander ($n = 4$), Multiracial ($n = 4$), and Middle Eastern ($n = 1$). Half of the participants were males ($n = 12$) and the other half females ($n = 12$). Participants lived and attended school in diverse geographic locales, including urban areas ($n = 8$), suburban areas ($n = 8$), and rural areas ($n = 8$). Students were representatives from the District of Columbia and 19 states across the four major United States regions (West, Midwest, South, and Northeast). The participants were age 13 ($n = 13$) or age 12 ($n = 11$) at the time of the study. The average gross family income was below $18,000 per year for the sample population, as indicated by IRS-reported adjusted gross income.

The participating students met the following criteria for inclusion: (a) seventh graders enrolled in middle school; (b)evidence of academic success as indicated by grades earned (mostly A's with no C's in core academic subjects [English/language arts, math, science, social studies/history, foreign language] since sixth grade) and high standardized test scores (i.e., at or above the proficient level in reading, mathematics, and science in the state in which they resided); (c) eligible for free or reduced-price lunch; (d) living in low-income households (i.e., students with IRS-reported adjusted gross income of less than $24,000 per year were classified as low income for the purposes of this report); and (e) applicants to the 2012 cohort of the Jack Kent Cooke Young Scholars program.

PROCEDURES AND DATA COLLECTION

The researchers obtained Institutional Review Board (IRB) approval before the study commenced. Participants were selected from a national sample of applicants pursuing a foundation-funded scholarship program (Young Scholars program) that provides high-achieving, low-income students with scholarships and educational support to maintain their academic success. The researchers selected applicants because they represented a diverse and representative group of students from low-income backgrounds that have excelled academically. Access to the applicant pool was granted to the first author for approved use and was governed by the director of research for the foundation. The Young Scholars program is selective and only 65 students out of over 1,000 applicants are selected each year. The Young Scholars selection criteria include academic measures and income indicators. Thirty participants were invited to participate in this study and 24 of the invited potential participants agreed to participate. This study examined 24 applicants who made it to the penultimate round of selection for the Young Scholars program 2012 cohort. This study draws upon two data sources: the Young Scholars application and semi-structured qualitative interviews.

Applications. When applying to the Young Scholars program, students provided grades, test scores, student essays, letters of recommendation, and demographics (including age, family status, race/ethnicity, gender, residency information, and income). These data provided the researchers with student profiles and ensured that students met the study criteria.

Interviews. Once a list of potential candidates for the present study was generated, the researchers mailed the candidates a description of the research study and parental consent and student assent forms. The potential candidates were also informed that they would receive $10 as an incentive for participating following the interview. Once the consent and assent documents were returned, students received a phone call from a member of the research team to coordinate a time for the phone interview. The interview protocol included the following open-ended question: "What can school counselors do to help students from low-income backgrounds succeed in school?" After this initial question was posed and the conversation progressed, the interviewers asked probing questions to encourage participants to concentrate on specific points and to check for more detail or clarification (Patton, 2015). The use of probing questions varied according to the interviewee's response. For instance, an example of a probing question was, "What do you mean by support?" Each phone interview was conducted by one research team member and lasted 32 to 45 minutes ($M = 40$). According to Miller (2003), 30 to 40 minute interviews are appropriate for phenomenological research, given the age and developmental level of the participants. Each research team member interviewed four student participants. After the interviews, each participant received a thank-you statement with $10 via U.S. mail.

To insure the accuracy of data collection, researchers used a digital audio recorder during each interview to record responses (Hays & Singh, 2012). As recommended by Patton (2015), after the completion of each individual session, the established digital files were transcribed verbatim by the research team member. Once transcribed, the transcript was checked again against the taped interview, to make sure that nothing was missed. Next, in order to do an initial member check, each transcription was sent in an e-mail attachment or via U.S. mail to the appropriate interviewee for review, comment, and correction to ensure adequate representation of their ideas and comments (Patton, 2015). All participants reported that the transcripts accurately depicted their ideas and comments. Every participant's responses were assigned a code number and participants' names were deleted from the data to maintain confidentiality. The interviewers conducted follow-up interviews with each of the 24 student participants to clarify and expand upon their responses during the analysis process. This was done via telephone 4 weeks after the conclusion of the semistructured interview, and the follow-up interviews lasted on average 25 to 30 minutes. An example of the questions posed during the follow-up interviews was, "Can you think of anything else that counselors can do or maybe they are doing that works well?"

TRUSTWORTHINESS PROCEDURES

The researchers used several techniques to ensure the trustworthiness of the present study. For example, before engaging in the research process, they met as a team to discuss the assumptions related to school counselors' effectiveness in working with low-income students, and team members recognized their unanimous negative assumptions that school counselors were not meeting the academic and psychosocial needs of low-income students. The researchers found that they had developed assumptions based on personal experiences and their knowledge of the literature related to the negative bias and low expectations prevalent among educators and counselors regarding these students and their families. Acknowledging their biases and bracketing their assumptions allowed for epoché, a foundational element of phenomenology, which implies that our assumptions and beliefs will not affect the perspectives of the participants reported in the results (Patton, 2015).

Strategies for trustworthiness also included peer debriefing and member checking. Peer debriefing involved enlisting the support of two colleagues with experience conducting qualitative research to discuss evolving suppositions and findings from the study (Patton, 2015). Next, the present study used member checking by asking participants to (a) review the interview questions to check for clarity, (b) review their personal interview transcripts to ensure adequate representation of their ideas and comments, and (c) comment on the themes and expressions of emerging patterns that contributed to the results. The participants believed the findings accurately depicted their ideas and comments and it was apparent that saturation occurred naturally during the progress of the study once incremental learning became minimal.

DATA ANALYSIS

The authors used Braun and Clarke's (2006) approach to thematic analysis for analyzing the phenomenological data acquired in this study. Thematic analysis is a method for identifying, analyzing, and reporting patterns (themes) within data. Thematic analysis is not wed to any pre-existing theoretical framework, so it can be used within different theoretical frameworks. Braun and Clarke (2006) offered the following six steps for conducting a thematic analysis: (a) familiarizing yourself with your data, (b) generating initial codes, (c) searching for themes, (d) reviewing and refining themes, (e) defining and naming themes, and (f) writing up the results.

For the first step, two research team members (the first and third authors) read all transcribed interviews before they began coding. While reading the transcripts, both took notes and marked ideas for coding that were later revisited in subsequent phases. Next, the two research team members reread the transcripts to detect recurring words, phrases, or thoughts that might form the basis of repeated patterns (themes) across the data set; these were then categorized using codes. They also took note of contradictions or discrepancies in students' responses. In the third step, they sorted the codes into potential themes, then collated all the relevant coded data extracts within the identified themes. In this step, the researchers considered the relationship between codes, between themes, and between different levels of the themes. Step four consisted of the entire team of researchers conducting a separate examination to identify overlapping themes or uncoded text and subsequently refining and revising each category. During the fifth step, the research team compared themes and found a high degree of consensus (95%) between codes. Coding decisions that differed were discussed and modified slightly, and the theme names were jointly agreed upon until the team reached 100% consensus on content and wording. The sixth and final step consisted of writing up the findings.

FINDINGS

The participants' perspectives of what school counselors can do to promote the academic achievement of students from low-income backgrounds is presented below. These participants (identified by pseudonyms) reflected three main themes: (a) build meaningful relationships, (b) build on the cultural wealth of students, and (c) provide mental health services in schools. Each theme had corresponding subthemes and is described below.

BUILD MEANINGFUL RELATIONSHIPS

Students in the current study perceived meaningful counselor–student relationships as a protective factor for students from low-income backgrounds. According to these students, such relationships are essential for school counselors to learn about the challenges students from low-income backgrounds face, help students navigate those challenges, and show students how much counselors care. Students also identified specific ways school counselors can build positive relationships with their students from low-income backgrounds, such as (a) show students you care, (b) challenge personal biases about poor students, and (c) be visible and accessible.

Show students you care. Most participants (n = 20) reported that, to nurture academic resilience, students from low-income backgrounds need a school counselor who provides care and support, who believes in them, and encourages and challenges them to do their best. As Carlos remarked, "students need a school counselor who cares about them, someone to encourage them and challenge them, when needed." Similarly, Jessica noted, "school counselors and teachers need to find ways to let students know that they care about them; without a caring relationship, nothing they say or do is going to matter." Jacob shared that "school counselor[s] can show that they care by listening to and taking a personal interest in students and providing extra help to students when necessary." Lauren also described ways that teachers can show that they care, such as "being respectful towards students and being warm and approachable."

Challenge personal biases about poor students. Some of the participants (n = 14) indicated that school counselors should challenge their understandings of and attitude about people in poverty. As Andreal stated, "I'm poor, not stupid.

Sometimes I have to remind my friends and teachers about that." Another student, Jasmine, mentioned that school personnel need to

> do a better job of recognizing poor students who have potential for honors class, even if the student hasn't quite met the requirements. I feel like I get passed up a lot because I live on the wrong side of the tracks, per se.

According to Malique, "I feel like I have to work extra hard to prove that I can compete with my friends whose families have more money than I do."

Be visible and accessible. Most of the participants ($n = 20$) indicated that school counselors need to be more visible and accessible in the school. According to these students, increased visibility would make students more aware of the supports available to them and how to work with their school counselor. For instance, Jessica stated, "If [school counselors] were advertised and around more in the school, students would know more about what they're about, see them as helpful, and actually use them." Stephanie noted that "school counselors need to be more visible and let people know what they do, apart from academic scheduling." Another student, Lauren, suggested that "school counselors can find creative ways to be more readily accessible to students and families."

BUILD ON THE CULTURAL WEALTH OF STUDENTS

Student participants emphasized the importance of finding ways to discover and mobilize low-income students' strengths and resources related to their goals. The participants offered two examples of personal strengths and resources that school counselors can utilize to promote their academic achievement: (a) nurturing *aspirational capital* (i.e., the ability to maintain high hopes and dreams in the face of real obstacles and barriers) and (b) leveraging *social capital* (i.e., networks of people, contacts, and community resources that enable the achievement of goals).

Nurture students' aspirational capital. Participants ($n = 17$) expressed the belief that school counselors should help nurture students' hopes and dreams for themselves, even in the face of struggle. According to students, hopes and dreams shape the choices they make and the success they achieve. For example, Benjamin said,

> School counselors should not only motivate and encourage you to reach your dreams, but also kind of help you understand why am I taking this class and why am I learning this, and how does it help me reach my goals. Some [students] don't have the actual drive or want to succeed, so I think helping them answer these questions will help them do better in school.

Diana shared that "school counselors should get students thinking early about what's important to them and why and how education can help—this might help them make better choices." Similarly, Josh commented that school counselors should "help [students] believe in who [they] are and what [they] can accomplish despite obstacles in your path like a lack of money."

Leverage students' social capital. Over half of the participants ($n = 14$) indicated that school counselors should tap into the informal sources of support (i.e., friends, family, neighbors, church members, or other contacts) that low-income students use to achieve academic success. These participants believe that informal and/or personal networks of support are essential to facilitating academic resilience among students from low-income backgrounds. For instance, Sarah shared,

> I feel like they need to recognize and acknowledge that students don't really talk to their school counselor. At least I don't. Instead we go to our friends and family for help, so maybe they can link up with them to figure out what's going on and how they can help.

Similarly, Thomas stated, "I know not every child has a lot of resources, but most of us know someone who can help us when we face challenges; school counselors might want to figure out who that someone is." Another student, Stacy, said, "School counselors can identify the resources that students have and use it to help or add to it." Jamie stated, "Counselors can use our strengths and the supports available in our families and communities to help us overcome our problems."

PROVIDE MENTAL HEALTH SERVICES IN SCHOOLS

Many participants ($n = 19$) indicated that students from low-income backgrounds would benefit from personal counseling services offered in schools. According to many of these students, such services would help them to resolve personal concerns that may hinder their academic success. For example, David stated,

> The reason poor students perform badly is because there's something that's not going good in their lives and I think the counselors can try to talk it out with them and work on what's going on at home, in the community, or like with the student personally and try to fix that problem to help them focus on learning.

Candace remarked:

> School counselors shouldn't limit their focus to school stuff only, because some students may not want to talk about their low academic performance, but about what's going on in their life, so school counselors can focus on those things first, then move to academic performance.

Refer students and their families to needed resources. Participants (n = 17) reported that school counselors should assess students' needs and match their needs with appropriate external resources. Students participating in this study realized that school counselors alone cannot meet all their needs. As Ashley shared, "[school counselors] can try to find programs, services and different activities in the community that can prevent student from heading down the wrong direction." Carlos noted that "counselors should help kids find money for field trips, afterschool events, or school supplies if they can't afford them so they won't be singled out and embarrassed." He later mentioned that "being poor distracts you from focusing on school." Andreal said, "Counselors need to know outside resources to refer families in need; where else are they going to get that type of information."

Teach life skills. More than half of the participants (n = 15) believed that school counselors can help low-income students develop life skills (e.g., stress management, help-seeking, cognitive skills, and emotional coping skills) that they can use both in school and outside of school, immediately and in the future. For instance, Aran stated that "school counselors can teach kids how to deal with daily stress like having to take care of your siblings after school, living in bad neighborhoods, or having stressed-out parents." Hung explained, "Some kids have trouble with paying attention and concentrating in school because of what happens once they leave school." Rachael mentioned that school counselors "can help students find trustworthy adults who they can go to and ask for help when they need it." Miguel suggested that school counselors help students "look for the good in themselves and not dwell on the fact that they are poor ... because sometimes being poor can be hard to live with."

DISCUSSION

These findings support the notion that marginalized students have important insight into how school counselors can best help them succeed in school (e.g., Williams & Portman, 2014). For example, building meaningful relationships was recommended by nearly all the participants as a way to help students who live in poverty succeed in school. This recommendation is supported by research showing that low-income students who report having a close, positive, and supportive relationship with at least one adult in the school do better academically than those without this support (Lapan, Wells, Petersen, & McCann, 2014). Several studies have noted that students feel more connected to their school when they believe that the adults and other students at school not only care about how well they are learning, but also care about them as individuals (e.g., Lapan et al., 2014; Niehaus, Rudasill, & Rakes, 2012).

The participants suggested three ways school counselors can build meaningful relationships with students from low-income backgrounds. First, students suggested that school counselors show students they care for them. Research indicates that school personnel with caring and supportive relationships with low-income students are better able to build rapport with, relate to, and uncover the strengths, capabilities, and motivations of students than those without such relationships (Niehaus et al., 2012). Second, students suggested that school counselors recognize and address any bias or preconceived notions they may have against students from lower socioeconomic backgrounds. This suggestion is consistent with existing evidence indicating that such biases make it difficult for counselors, educators, and school administrators to accept, understand, and effectively work with their students (Boysen, 2010). Furthermore, these biases shape students' perceptions of counselor competency (Constantine & Sue, 2007). Third, students recommended that school counselors be more visible and accessible to them. According to the participants, increased visibility would make students more aware of the supports available to them and how to work with their school counselors. This recommendation connects to previous research indicating that school counselors serving predominately low-income students are unable to provide adequate support to students due to disproportionate student-to-school-counselor ratios and noncounseling tasks and fair-share responsibilities that are assigned to them (e.g., Corwin, Venegas, Oliverez, & Colyar, 2004).

Next, students emphasized the importance of assessing and utilizing existing resources and assets with which students respond to the poverty-related barriers to academic achievement. Specifically, students recommended fostering the aspirational capital of students and leveraging students' social capital. Yosso (2005) defines aspirational capital as the ability to maintain hopes and dreams for the future, even in the face of real and perceived barriers. Research connects middle school students' academic achievement to their educational and career aspirations (e.g., Creed, Conlon, & Zimmer-Gembeck, 2007; Garg, Kauppi, Lewko, & Urajnik, 2002; Mau, 2003). According to Yosso (2005), social capital refers to networks of people, contacts, and community resources that enable the achievement of goals that otherwise would not have been possible individually. This view is supported by research suggesting that students from economically disadvantaged backgrounds function more effectively when they have networks that support students' efforts to succeed in school and provide guidance to students about school or personal matters (Hayes, Blake, Darensbourg, & Castillo, 2015; Baker, Grant, & Morlock, 2008; Williams & Bryan, 2013).

Last, students recommended that mental health services be provided in schools. According to ASCA (2012), students' unmet mental health needs can be a significant barrier to a student's academic, personal-social and career development, and even compromise school safety. The provision of mental health services within their schools for students from economically disadvantaged backgrounds can improve the academic performance, attendance rates, social competence, test scores, and personal/social success of students (Hoagwood et al., 2007; Walker, Kerns, Lyon, Bruns, & Cosgrove, 2010; Whiston, Tai, Rahardja, & Eder, 2011). This study's participants suggested three types of mental health services: mental health counseling, referral services, and psychoeducation.

Students suggested that school counselors offer direct counseling services to help students resolve personal concerns. ASCA (2012) recommends that school counselors recognize and respond to student mental health crises and needs by offering education, prevention, crisis, and short-term individual and/or group counseling services until the student is connected with available community resources. Second, students suggested that school counselors refer students and their families to needed resources. This is consistent with Kaffenberger and O'Rorke-Trigiani (2013), who suggest that school counselors network with other school counselors in nearby school districts to learn what resources exist in the surrounding community that can provide information, support, and sources for referral. Third, students discussed life skills training as a mental health treatment. According to Hodge, Danish, and Martin (2013), psychoeducational life skills training offers students tools for effectively managing their lives (mentally, emotionally, interpersonally, and behaviorally) in the midst of the nonacademic and social issues confronting low-income students on a daily basis.

IMPLICATIONS FOR SCHOOL COUNSELORS

These findings have clear and direct implications for how elementary and middle school counselors can best serve their students from low-income backgrounds. First, school counselors can work on school improvement teams (represented by school staff, economically disadvantaged students, and their families) to help schools create focused, school-wide strategies to enhance conditions of care. Such strategies might include consulting with school personnel to create counseling, academic, discipline, instructional, and classroom strategies and interventions that create caring teacher–student relationships, or implementing culturally relevant behavioral and communicative strategies that relay caring and support, high expectations, and affirmations for students from low-income backgrounds (Britzman, 2005; Cunningham & Sandhu, 2000; Musheno & Talbert, 2002; Williams & Bryan, 2013).

Second, school counselors might be wise to explore their own biases and prejudices (implicit and explicit), especially regarding social class, that could get in the way of communicating care toward students (Miller, Miller, & Stull, 2007). Attending professional development workshops centered on raising awareness of implicit bias among counselors (and how it might affect their work with students) and skills training to control or reduce implicit bias is essential for building caring relationships with students from low-income families (see Boysen & Vogel, 2008). Hill (2003) suggested several methods counselors can use to promote and maintain school-wide intentions to reduce implicit bias, such as: (a) setting goals related to implicit bias at the school level, (b) developing committees to address implicit bias within the school community, (c) setting aside specific funds and time for professional development related to implicit bias, and (d) providing opportunities to assess personal implicit biases and process the results.

Third, school counselors might consider sharing data with their administrators about non-school-counseling activities that affect their ability to build relationships with and meet the unique needs of students from economically disadvantaged backgrounds (ASCA, 2012). Presenting data to demonstrate the impact of specific interventions on individual students and to inform administrators how counselors are contributing to closing gaps and the mission of the school could help reduce the noncounseling tasks and fair-share responsibilities assigned to school counselors (ASCA, 2012). School counselors should also create a plan to challenge the noncounseling tasks assigned and develop the support needed to build relationships with students from low-income families (Scarborough & Culbreth, 2008).

Fourth, developing and implementing a comprehensive guidance curriculum that includes identity development, explores poverty-related barriers to learning and achievement, and fosters hope about the future would help to grow and maintain low-income students' aspirations and expectations (Creed et al., 2007). Using small groups or classroom lessons to raise aspirations will not only disseminate information but also may affect the school and classroom culture. Specifically, school counselors might consider using academically resilient students and/or alumni to lead workshops, serve on panels, and visit elementary and middle schools, thereby reinforcing presenting students' own aspirations and plans. School counselors also can use professional development, common planning time, or school counselor-created incentives (e.g., coffee talks) to educate teachers and school staff about the importance of setting high expectation for and nurturing the career and academic aspiration of students from low-income families and the barriers some students may face.

Fifth, school counselors must meet the needs of students in a way that builds on the assets of students and their communities. Community asset maps can be used to identify the resources (individual and community) that are already available to students (Griffin & Farris, 2010). Griffin and Farris (2010) provide a detailed description of a four-step approach to organizing and developing a community asset map, including (a) developing a multidisciplinary team, (b) examining and assessing current and potential resources, (c) contacting individual and community resources, and (d) developing and maintaining a community resource guide. Community asset mapping can enable school counselors to locate resources that meet the needs of students from low-income families.

Along the same lines, school counselors should build alliances within the school community with other student support professionals to better serve the mental health needs of students in the school (DeKruyf, Auger, & Trice-Black, 2013; Kaffenberger & O'Rorke-Trigiani, 2013). School counselors might also benefit from seeking additional training and clinical supervision to improve the direct services offered and learn evidence-based skills and strategies that can be used and modified in school settings (Kaffenberger & O'Rorke-Trigiani, 2013).

Last, small groups and classroom guidance lessons can be used to teach everyday life skills that students from low-income families need in order to effectively cope with the daily challenges related to poverty. Many skills development groups incorporate elements of psychoeducational and support; however, the primary goal is on building or strengthening behavioral or cognitive resources to cope better in their environment (Thompson, 2013).

LIMITATIONS

The present study had several limitations. First, the sampling may have been biased due to self-selection. More specifically, the participants, all of whom were applicants to a competitive, foundation-funded scholarship program, were not necessarily representative of the larger low-income student population. These students might have more parental involvement and school recognition than average low-income students. Second, the developmental level of participants may have affected both their self-report and their member checking. Next, although the researchers engaged in epoché, it is possible that their preconceived biases still affected the analysis. Last, in phenomenological research, finding meaning and understanding the subjective experiences of study participants is difficult to ascertain. These limitations are provided to caution the reader and to serve as a starting point for future research by providing factors that others should consider when conducting similar research.

CONCLUSION

It seems apparent that some students know what they need in order to succeed in school despite the presence of adverse conditions associated with living in poverty.

This qualitative inquiry revealed three powerful themes and nine subthemes that came directly from the students themselves and indicate ways in which school counselors could more effectively assist these students. The voices of these students offer unique understanding of student achievement for high-achieving poor students. Moreover, these comments can serve as points of reflection for school counselors in evaluating their own professional dispositions, school counselor roles, school counseling programs, and efforts to promote academic success among students from economically disadvantaged backgrounds.

REFERENCES

Alva, S. A. (1991). Academic invulnerability among Mexican American students: The importance of protective resources and appraisals. *Hispanic Journal of Behavioral Sciences*, 13, 18–34.

Alfaro, E. C., Umaña-Taylor, A. J., & Bámaca, M. Y. (2006). The influence of academic support on Latino adolescents' academic motivation. *Family Relations*, 55, 279–291. doi:10.1111/j.1741-3729.2006.00402.x

American School Counselor Association. (2012). ASCA National Model: A framework for school counseling programs (3rd ed.). Alexandria, VA: Author.

Baker, J. A., Grant, S., & Morlock, L. (2008). The teacher-student relationship as a developmental context for children with internalizing or externalizing behavior problems. *School Psychology Quarterly*, 23(1), 3. doi:10.1037/1045–3830.23.1.3

Borman, G. D., & Rachuba, L. (2001). *Academic success among poor and minority students: Analysis of competing models of school effects. Report No.* 52. Baltimore, MD: Center for Research on the Education of Students Placed at Risk, Johns Hopkins University.

Boysen, G. A. (2010). Integrating implicit bias into counselor education. *Counselor Education and Supervision*, 49, 210–227.

Boysen, G. A., & Vogel, D. L. (2008). The relationship between level of training, implicit bias, and multicultural competency among counselor trainees. *Training and Education in Professional Psychology*, 2(2), 103–110. doi:10.1037/1931–3918.2.2.103

Braun, V., & Clarke, V. (2006). Using thematic analysis in psychology. *Qualitative research in psychology*, 3(2), 77–101. doi:10.1191/1478088706qp063oa

Britzman, M. (2005). Improving our moral landscape via character education: An opportunity for school counselor leadership. *Professional School Counseling*, 8, 293–296.

Constantine, M. G., & Sue, D. W. (2007). Perceptions of racial microaggressions among black supervisees in cross-racial dyads. *Journal of Counseling Psychology*, 54, 142–153. doi:10.1037/0022-0167.54.2.142

Cook-Sather, A. (2002) Authorizing students' perspectives: Toward trust, dialogue, and change in education. Educational Researcher, 4, 3–14. doi:10.3102/0013189X031004003

Corwin, Z. B., Venegas, K. M., Oliverez, P. M., & Colyar, J. E. (2004). School counsel: How appropriate guidance affects educational equity. *Urban Education*, 39, 442–457.

Creed, P. A., Conlon, E. G., & Zimmer-Gembeck, M. J. (2007). Career barriers and reading ability as correlates of career aspirations and expectations of parents and their children. *Journal of Vocational Behavior*, 70(2), 242–258. doi:10.1016/j.jvb.2006.11.001

Creswell, J. W. (2007). *Qualitative inquiry and research design: Choosing among five traditions*. Thousand Oaks, CA: Sage.

Cunningham, N. J., & Sandhu, D. S. (2000). A comprehensive approach to school–community violence prevention. *Professional School Counseling, 4*, 126–133.

DeKruyf, L., Auger, R. W., & Trice-Black, S. (2013). The role of school counselors in meeting students' mental health needs: Examining issues of professional identity. *Professional School Counseling, 16*, 271–282. doi:10.5330/PSC.n.2013-16.271

Downey, J. (2002). Exploring children's beliefs about educational risk and resilience. *Academic Exchange Quarterly, 6*, 126–131.

Garg, R., Kauppi, C., Lewko, J., & Urajnik, D.(2002). A structural model of educational aspirations. *Journal of Career Development, 29*(2), 87–108.doi:10.1023/a:1019964119690

Gizir, C., & Aydin, G. (2009). Protective factors contributing to the academic resilience of students living in poverty in Turkey. *Professional School Counseling, 13*, 38–49.

Goldstein, S. E., Boxer, P., & Rudolph, E. (2015). Middle school transition stress: Links with academic performance, motivation, and school experiences. *Contemporary School Psychology, 19*(1), 21. doi:10.1007/s40688-014-0044-4

Griffin, D., & Farris, A. (2010). School counselors and school-family-community collaboration: Finding resources through community asset mapping. *Professional School Counseling, 13*, 248–256. doi:10.5330/psc.n.2010-13.248

Hayes, D., Blake, J. J., Darensbourg, A., & Castillo, L. G. (2015). Examining the academic achievement of Latino adolescents: The role of parent and peer beliefs and behaviors. *The Journal of Early Adolescence, 35*(2), 141–161. doi:10.1177/0272431614530806

Hays, D. G., & Singh, A. A. (2012). *Qualitative inquiry in clinical educational settings*. New York, NY: The Guilford Press.

Hill, N. R. (2003). Promoting and celebrating multicultural competence in counselor trainees. *Counselor Education and Supervision, 43*, 39–51.

Hoagwood, K. E., Olin, S. S., Kerker, B. D., Kratochwill, T. R., Crowe, M., & Saka, N. (2007). Empirically based school interventions targeted at academic and mental health functioning. *Journal of Emotional and Behavioral Disorders, 15*, 66–92. doi:10.1177/10634266070150020301

Hodge, K., Danish, S., & Martin, J. (2013). Developing a conceptual framework for life skills interventions. *The Counseling Psychologist, 41*, 1125–1152.

Kaffenberger, C. J., & O'Rorke-Trigiani, J. (2013). Addressing student mental health needs by providing direct and indirect services and building alliances in the community. *Professional School Counseling, 16*, 323–332. doi:10.5330/PSC.n.2013-16.323

Lacour, M., & Tissington, L. D. (2011). The effects of poverty on academic achievement. *Educational Research and Reviews Journal, 6*, 522–527. Retrieved from http://www.academicjournals.org/article/article1379765941_Lacour%20and%20Tissington.pdf

Lapan, R., Wells, R., Peterson, J. & McCann, L. A. (2014). Stand tall to protect students: School counselors strengthening school connectedness. *Journal of Counseling & Development, 92*, 304–315. doi:10.1002/j.1556-6676.2014.00158.x

Lester, S. (1999). *An introduction to phenomenological research*. Retrieved from http://devmts.org.uk/resmethy.pdf

Martin, A. J., & Marsh, H. W. (2009). Academic resilience and academic buoyancy: Multidimensional and hierarchical conceptual framing of causes, correlates and cognate constructs. *Oxford Review of Education, 35*(3), 353–370. doi:10.1080/03054980902934639

Mau, W. C. (2003). Factors that influence persistence in science and engineering career aspirations. *The Career Development Quarterly, 51*(3), 234–243. doi:10.1002/j.2161-0045.2003.tb00604.x

Midgley, C., Arunkumar, R., & Urdan, T. C. (1996). "If I don't do well tomorrow, there's a reason": Predictors of adolescents' use of academic self-handicapping strategies. *Journal of Educational Psychology,* 88(3), 423. doi:org/10.1037//0022-0663.88.3.423

Miller, S. (2003). Analysis of phenomenological data generated with children as research participants. *Nurse Research,* 10, 68–82.

Miller, K. L., Miller, S. M., & Stull, J. C. (2007). Predictors of counselor educators' cultural discriminatory behaviors. *Journal of Counseling & Development,* 85(3), 325. doi:10.1002/j.1556-6678.2007.tb00481.x

Mitra, D. L. (2009). Student voice and student roles in education policy and policy reform. In D. N. Plank, G. Sykes, & B. Schneider (Eds.), *AERA handbook on education policy research* (pp. 819–830). London, UK: Routledge.

Morales, E. E. (2010). Linking strengths: Identifying and exploring protective factor clusters in academically resilient low-socioeconomic urban students of color. *Roeper Review: A Journal on Gifted Education,* 32(3), 164–175. doi:10.1080/02783193.2010.485302

Musheno, S., & Talbert, M. (2002). The transformed school counselor in action. *Theory Into Practice, 41,* 186–191. doi:10.1207/s15430421tip4103_7

National Center for Education Statistics. (2011). *The nation's report card: Reading 2011* (NCES 2012-457). Washington, DC: Author. Retrieved from http://nces.ed.gov/nationsreport card/pubs/main2011/2012457.asp

Niehaus, K., Rudasill, K. M., & Rakes, C. R. (2012). A longitudinal study of school connectedness and academic outcomes across sixth grade. *Journal of School Psychology,* 50, 443–460.

Patton, M. Q. (2015). *Qualitative research and evaluation methods* (4th ed.). Los Angeles, CA: Sage Publications.

Reardon, S. F. (2011). The widening academic achievement gap between the rich and the poor: New evidence and possible explanations. In R. Murnane & G. Duncan (Eds.), *Whither opportunity? Rising inequality and the uncertain life chances of low-income children* (pp. 91–116). New York, NY: Russell Sage Foundation Press.

Scarborough, J. L., & Culbreth, J. R. (2008). Examining discrepancies between actual and preferred practice of school counselors. *Journal of Counseling & Development, 86*(4), 446–459. doi:10.1002/j.1556-6678.2008.tb00533.x

Stinson, D. W. (2008). Negotiating sociocultural discourses: The counter-storytelling of academically (and mathematically) successful African American male students. *American Educational Research Journal,* 45, 975–1010. doi:10.3102/0002831208319723

Steele, C. M., & Aronson, J. (1995). Stereotype threat and the intellectual test performance of African Americans. *Journal of Personality and Social Psychology, 69*(5), 97. doi:10.1037//0022-3514.69.5.797

Suitts, S. (2015). A new majority: Low income students now a majority in the nation's public schools. SEF Research Report Update. *Southern Education Foundation.* Retrieved from http://www.southerneducation.org/Our-Strategies/Research-and-Publications/New-Majority-Diverse-Majority-Report-Series/A-New-Majority-2015-Update-Low-Income-Students-Now

Thompson, R. A. (2013). *School counseling: Best practices for working in the schools.* New York, NY: Routledge.

U.S. Department of Education, National Center for Education Statistics. (2014a). *The condition of education 2014 (NCES 2014-083): Immediate transition to college.* Retrieved from http://nces.ed.gov/programs/digest/d13/tables/dt13_302.30.asp

U.S. Department of Education, National Center for Education Statistics. (2014b). *The condition of education 2014 (NCES 2014-083): Status dropout rates.* Retrieved from http://nces.ed.gov/programs/digest/d13/tables/dt13_219.76.asp

Vanderbilt-Adriance, E., & Shaw, D. S. (2008). Protective factors and the development of resilience in the context of neighborhood disadvantage. *Journal of Abnormal Child Psychology, 36,* 887–901. doi:10.1007/s10802-008-9220-1

Walker, S. C., Kerns, S. E. U., Lyon, A. R., Bruns, E. J., & Cosgrove, T. J. (2010). Impact of school-based health center use on academic outcomes. *Journal of Adolescent Health, 46,* 251–257. doi:10.1016/j.jadohealth.2009.07.002

Whiston, S. C., Tai, W. L., Rahardja, D., & Eder, K. (2011). School counseling outcome: A meta-analytic examination of interventions. *Journal of Counseling & Development, 89,* 37–55. doi:10.1002/j.1556-6678.2011.tb00059.x

Williams, J. M., & Bryan, J. (2013). Overcoming adversity: High-achieving African American youth's perspectives on educational resilience. *Journal of Counseling & Development, 91,* 291-300. doi:10.1002/j.1556-6676.2013.00097.x

Williams, J. M., & Portman, T. A. A. (2014). "No one ever asked me": Urban African American students' perceptions of educational resilience. *Journal of Multicultural Counseling and Development, 42,* 13–30. doi:10.1002/j.2161-1912.2014.00041.x

Wong, M. M. (2008). Perceptions of parental involvement and autonomy support: Their relations with self-regulation, academic performance, substance use and resilience among adolescents. *North American Journal of Psychology, 10,* 497–518.

Wyner, J. S., Bridgeland, J. M., & DiIulio, J.J., Jr. (2007). Achievement Trap: HowAmerica is failing millions of high-achieving students from lower-income families. *Civic Enterprises.* Retrieved from http://www.jkcf.org/assets/1/7/Achievement_Trap.pdf

Yosso, T. J. (2005). Whose culture has capital? A critical race theory discussion of community cultural wealth. *Race ethnicity and education,* 8(1), 69–91. doi:10.1080/136 1332 052000341006

CHAPTER 6

Beyond Stereotypes

Understanding, Working With Twice Exceptional Children

Lois Baldwin, Stuart N. Omdal, and Daphne Pereles

The term twice exceptional was coined to describe students who have a disability and who also have characteristics and traits associated with giftedness. These students may appear to be capable and bright but do not demonstrate that ability when asked to produce work in the classroom. Recognizing these students may be challenging, as the disability may overshadow the gift, the gift may mask the effect of the disability, or both remedial and advanced learning needs may go completely unnoticed. Strategies for serving twice-exceptional students include addressing the student's strengths and interests; providing appropriate social and emotional support; offering adaptations for academic strengths and accommodations for learning needs; and creating a supportive, safe, problem-solving culture that values the success of every student. What do twice-exceptional learners "look like? The students profiled in this article provide a glimpse into the variety of ways twice exceptionality can present in the classroom environment.

Lois Baldwin, Stuart N. Omdal, and Daphne Pereles, "Beyond Stereotypes: Understanding, Working with Twice Exceptional Children," *Teaching Exceptional Children*, vol. 47, no. 4, pp. 216-225.

STUDENT PROFILES

LANCE

Lance is a second-grade student with autism spectrum disorder. He spends half of his day in the special education classroom, where he receives reading and math instruction as well as social skills training. The other half of his day is spent in a second-grade general education classroom with support from a paraprofessional for social studies and science. He is progressing at an average pace in reading decoding but is still struggling with complex comprehension questions that require character analysis and evaluation. Lance likes school and the teachers say that he works hard, but he finds it to be confusing and unpredictable, particularly when instruction or directions are presented orally with few or no visuals. When he is stressed or confused, he will twirl his hair, flap his hands, or begin to cry. His classmates usually don't pay attention to these behaviors. Although he sits with other students at lunch, he does not have any friends. He spends most of his recess time wandering the periphery of the playground, talking to himself.

Lance says that he likes science class and demonstrates advanced knowledge and vocabulary in the area of botany and some aspects of biology. After having students read about places where plants and animals live, his teacher asked the students what that was called. Several students answered that it was their "environment." Lance, however, answered that it was a "habitat" because, as he explained, the word *environment* means a larger area. He said it was like the difference between *house* and *neighborhood*. He was insistent that everyone use the right word. At home, Lance has developed his own "scientific lab" in his bedroom with different types of plants growing on his windowsill and bedside stand. He is keeping a journal in which he draws diagrams and pictures of the growth and parts of each plant. His mother is surprised by the sophistication and accuracy of the drawings and his vocabulary. Not only does he know the scientific name for many of the plants; he insists on using them both in his journal and when he's speaking about his favorite topic. Lance likes to read nonfiction books and to watch science programs on television about botany.

HADLEY

Hadley, an active, verbally precocious, and social fifth grader, was identified for the gifted program when she was in second grade. In both her general education class and the gifted pull-out program, Hadley demonstrates creativity, curiosity, and advanced humor. She also has an excellent memory as demonstrated by her ability to remember facts and details that she learns in lessons, particularly social studies. She has a strong sense of social justice and will come to the aid of students who are being teased on the playground or at lunch. She also becomes emotional when the television news describes children who are being abused or hurt by war or other similar circumstances. She was so upset about the fact that girls in Afghanistan were not being allowed to go to school that she persuaded her gifted resource teacher to support a fund-raising activity for those students. Hadley developed a plan, organized the student activities, and demonstrated leadership abilities. She is popular with all of the students in both her classroom and the gifted resource room and is well liked by the teachers.

Given that she is in the gifted program, her classroom teacher was surprised to see that her fall universal screening scores in reading placed her in the 40th percentile. Although this scoring does not put her in the "at-risk" category, she is not demonstrating reading achievement commensurate with her intellectual ability. Her math universal screening scores are in the 95th percentile, and her progress in class would indicate that the assessment is accurate. The teacher is concerned because she has noticed that although Hadley uses advanced and descriptive vocabulary when she is speaking, her writing does not demonstrate any of this verbal richness. Her writing is limited to short sentences, few descriptions, and basic vocabulary. Hadley's mother has complained to the teacher that Hadley is overwhelmed by the amount of homework, particularly in social studies, even though it is a subject she loves. Her mother often finds Hadley playing games on her laptop rather than reading the textbook or doing the worksheet or homework questions. She frequently says she finished her homework in school or makes up excuses. An assignment that should take her a half hour may take her at least twice that amount of time. Her teacher has also noticed that her pace is slow and labored.

PEDRO

Pedro is a ninth grader at a large urban high school. He likes his physical education and music classes, but he really enjoys his pre-engineering computer-aided design (CAD) class and shows great aptitude. He participates on the school's football and track teams. Although he consistently earns average grades in all content areas, his teachers are frustrated because he often appears to be daydreaming or doodling, not following instructions on how to do particular assignments, and always looking for but rarely finding his homework papers. His notebook is a "disaster," with scattered papers and no discernable system of organization. This has caused him to get in trouble numerous times due to missed deadlines on papers and projects. His English and history teachers have noted that he will contribute interesting insights or make connections between literature and historical events that other students miss or do not understand. But they also indicate that they are concerned because he disrupts the flow of the lesson by calling out the information or the answers. He is late for his first-period math class two or three times a week because he has stayed up late and has overslept.

At home he likes to take apart old computers and small appliances and combine parts from them to make new devices. He often works past midnight if he is working on a new project. One of his creations was the basis for his science fair project last year, winning him a first-place award. His content-area teachers and other students were very impressed, as they had not seen evidence of that kind of performance from him before. Several teachers questioned if he really had done the work because it was so well done and more sophisticated than what he produces on a regular basis in his content classes. Although his father sees Pedro's greater potential, as a single father who works two jobs, he has little time to meet with school personnel to discuss his son's mediocre performance and tardiness.

DEFINITION OF *TWICE EXCEPTIONALITY*

Are these students' profiles familiar? Do their profiles demonstrate the confusion that occurs when a student who appears to be capable and bright does not demonstrate that ability when asked to produce work in the classroom, particularly on written assignments? Is the lack of work often accompanied by inappropriate behaviors, such as calling out, disorganization, disinterest, or acting out? Teachers find such students to be confusing enigmas. Students who demonstrate gifts and talents but also have a disability are known as *twice exceptional* and do not fit the stereotypical characteristics of students with a disability or giftedness (Baum & Owen, 2004).

Through a better understanding about the nature of disabilities and a broadened conception of giftedness, the term *twice exceptional* has entered the mainstream literature. Much of the literature on twice exceptionality addresses students who are gifted and have learning disabilities, though the term can be applied to other disabilities, such as behavioral and emotional disabilities, sensory and physical disabilities, attention deficit hyperactivity disorder (ADHD), and autism spectrum disorder. Professional organizations, like the Council for Exceptional Children, have developed definitions of twice exceptionality. Recently a group of professional organizations, including the Council for Exceptional Children, collaborated through a Community of Practice approach to create an agreed upon definition that could be used nationally (see box).

Passed by Congress in 1989 and continuing for over 20 years, the Jacob K. Javits Gifted and Talented Students Education Act was the impetus for multiple projects and research activities to further educators' understanding of the complex needs of twice-exceptional students. In 2004, with the reauthorization of the Individuals with Disabilities Education Act (IDEA), for the first time there was federal acknowledgement that students with disabilities could also be gifted. At the current time, there is an increased interest in this special population as indicated by the number of research studies and projects (e.g., Iowa's Belin-Blank Center for Gifted Education, Colorado Department of Education Twice-Exceptional Project), publications (e.g., the *Twice-Exceptional Newsletter*), and symposia (e.g. NAGC Twice-Exceptional Symposium). A common thrust of these projects focuses on the recognition and potential strategies for meeting the needs of twice-exceptional students.

RECOGNIZING CHARACTERISTICS OF TWICE-EXCEPTIONAL STUDENTS

In the case of twice-exceptional students, their educational needs—whether advanced or remedial—may not be observed for a variety of reasons. Baum and Owen (2004) identified three types of conditions that make it difficult for educators to recognize these special students. In the first condition, the disability is recognized but not the strengths. The second condition is the reverse: giftedness is recognized but not the disability. For the last condition, neither strengths nor disabilities are recognized.

DEFINITION OF TWICE EXCEPTIONALITY, NATIONAL TWICE-EXCEPTIONAL COMMUNITY OF PRACTICE

The following definition was created by the National Twice-Exceptional Community of Practice in 2014:

> Twice exceptional (2e) individuals evidence exceptional ability and disability, which results in a unique set of circumstances. Their exceptional ability may dominate, hiding their disability; their disability may dominate, hiding their exceptional ability; each may mask the other so that neither is recognized or addressed.
>
> 2e students, who may perform below, at, or above grade level, require the following:
>
> - Specialized methods of identification that consider the possible interaction of the exceptionalities
> - Enriched/advanced educational opportunities that develop the child's interests, gifts and talents while also meeting the child's learning needs
> - Simultaneous supports that ensure the child's academic success and social-emotional well-being, such as accommodations, therapeutic interventions, and specialized instruction.

Working successfully with this unique population requires specialized academic training and ongoing professional development. (personal correspondence, May 1. 2014)

Lance, Hadley, and Pedro each represent one of these three conditions. Lance's disability is recognized early and special education services are begun. Because the focus is on remediation, however, educators are unaware of or are not looking for his gifts or talents. This is a common situation for some twice-exceptional students. For example, for students with a reading disability, the focus may be on the decoding or fluency issue even though they may be capable of understanding and analyzing complex literature and participating in analytical discussions. The disability focus creates a barrier to advanced educational opportunities. In Lance's case, the school team acknowledges his disability and supports him academically and socially in those areas of need. However, the team has not recognized nor addressed his exceptional ability and advanced needs in science.

Hadley's experience exemplifies when giftedness is noted at a young age and nurtured. Twice-exceptional students like Hadley may be identified for gifted education programming or may demonstrate their abilities of advanced thinking and conceptualization in classroom activities. However, it is not unusual for these students to "hit a wall" beginning in middle school or later when they are no longer able to compensate with their ability to memorize material or to verbalize responses (McEachern & Bornot, 2001). In Hadley's case, she memorized words and passages until she could no longer "fake" her ability to read and write on grade level. It is not unusual to hear adults mistakenly say that a student is "lazy" or "not trying hard enough" when an apparent mismatch between skills and performance occurs.

Pedro's remedial and advanced needs of twice exceptionality are completely unrecognized. Researchers refer to this phenomenon as students whose talents are "masked" by the disability or the disability is "masked" by the advanced ability, making the students appear average (Baum & Owen, 2004). These students often struggle or fail in school. The students are frequently confused and frustrated by their ability to conceptualize and think at a faster rate than most of their peers but at the same time are unable to keep up with the course requirements because of their disability. Educators may see glimmers of the gift or talent, like Pedro's CAD teacher or the science fair coordinator, but for the most part, the educational experience is rarely at a level commensurate with the student's intellectual or talent ability. Likewise, educators may see behavioral issues, such as Pedro's tardiness or calling out, but those issues likely would not, in themselves, demonstrate a need for further investigation.

It is not easy to recognize twice-exceptional students. As Reis, Baum, and Burke (2014) noted, "successful identification and programming depend on both the depth of educators' understanding about giftedness and disabilities and their intersection or comorbidity" (p. 218). Therefore, educators must become familiar with characteristics of giftedness and disabilities that may point to a potential twice-exceptional condition. Because educators, including special education teachers, interact with these students on a daily basis, it is important for teachers to recognize and understand the characteristics of twice-exceptional learners. Table 6.1 is a compilation of characteristics and behaviors that are associated with giftedness. In addition, it includes a column about how a disability may influence that behavior. Please note that not all behaviors apply to all gifted students, nor do all of the behaviors of twice-exceptional students in the second column apply to all twice-exceptional students. These are merely indicators to determine further investigation of student need.

TABLE 6.1. COMPARISONS OF CHARACTERISTICS OF GIFTED STUDENTS AND TWICE-EXCEPTIONAL STUDENTS

INDICATOR	RECURRENT BEHAVIORS AND CHARACTERISTICS OF GIFTED STUDENTS	POSSIBLE BEHAVIORS AND CHARACTERISTICS OF TWICE EXCEPTIONAL STUDENTS
Learning	Possesses ability to learn basic skills quickly and easily and retain information with less repetition	Often struggles to learn basic skills; may demonstrate need for strategies in order to acquire basic skills and information
Verbal skills	Exhibits high verbal ability	May demonstrate high verbal ability but may also show extreme difficulty in written language area; may use language in inappropriate ways and at inappropriate times
Reading skills	Acquires reading skills early	Reading problems can be evident early; may demonstrate need for strategies in phonics, phonemic awareness, and fluency; may mask reading deficits through compensation until shifting from "learning to read" to "reading to learn"
Organizational skills	Organizational skills can vary; some gifted students can be very organized whereas others struggle	Usually struggles with organization of things, ideas, and time
Observational skills	Has keen powers of observation	Has strong observation skills but may demonstrate deficits in memory
Critical thinking/ problem-solving skills	Adept at critical thinking, problem solving, and decision-making skills	May excel in solving "real-world" problems; can demonstrate outstanding critical thinking and decision-making skills; often independently develops compensatory skills
Attention	Has long attention span; may demonstrate persistent, intense concentration	Attention is frequently affected; may be able to concentrate for long periods of time in areas of interest
Curiosity	Demonstrates questioning attitude	May demonstrate a strong questioning attitude, may appear disrespectful when questioning information and facts presented by the teacher

(*continued*)

INDICATOR	RECURRENT BEHAVIORS AND CHARACTERISTICS OF GIFTED STUDENTS	POSSIBLE BEHAVIORS AND CHARACTERISTICS OF TWICE EXCEPTIONAL STUDENTS
Creativity	Generates creative thoughts, ideas, actions; may be innovative	Imagination may be unusual; may frequently generate original and at times rather "bizarre" ideas; is extremely divergent in thought; may appear to daydream when generating ideas
Risk taking	Takes risks	Is often unwilling to take risks with regard to academics or areas of deficit; takes risks in nonschool areas without consideration of consequences
Sense of humor	Possesses unusual, often highly developed sense of humor	Humor may be used to divert attention from school failure; may use humor to make fun of peers or to avoid trouble
Maturity	May mature at different rates than age peers	Sometimes appears immature by using anger, crying, and withdrawal to express feelings and to deal with difficulties
Independence	Has a strong sense of independence and self-efficacy	Requires frequent teacher support and feedback in deficit areas; is highly independent in other areas; often appears to be extremely stubborn and Inflexible
Social skills	May not be accepted by other children and may feel isolated	May be perceived as a loner; sometimes has difficulty being accepted by peers due to poor social skills
Leadership	Exhibits leadership ability	May be a leader among the more nontraditional students; can demonstrate strong "streetwise" behavior; the disability may interfere with ability to exercise leadership skills
Broad interests	Is interested in a wide range of topics	Is interested in many topics, but often, learning problems impede pursuit of them
Focused interests	Shows very focused interest, that is, a passion about a certain topic to the exclusion of others	Often demonstrates a very focused interest, that is, a passion about a certain topic to the exclusion of others—often not school-related subjects

Note: Adapted from ***Comparisons of Characteristics of Gifted Students With*** or ***Without Disabilities,*** by E. Nielsen, D. Higgins, L. Baldwin, D. Pereles, 2000, unpublished manuscript. Adapted with permission.

STRATEGIES FOR SERVING TWICE-EXCEPTIONAL STUDENTS

The purpose of recognizing the strengths and needs of twice-exceptional students is to employ appropriate strategies and accommodations to meet the dual individual educational needs. A problem-solving process is effective for bringing multiple sources of information in order to make decisions that will have the best outcomes for these students. The problem-solving process involves (a) defining area of need, (b) collecting and analyzing data, (c) implementing a plan and (d) evaluating the progress. Effective problem-solving teams include family members; teachers from general, special, and gifted education; administrators; and other school personnel involved with the student and who can contribute to the process. As the team reviews data from multiple sources that address the different facets of the student, it will become evident that a variety of strategies will be necessary to support the unique needs of the twice-exceptional student.

Research indicates that twice-exceptional students require a dual-emphasis approach—one that focuses on strengths and talents while supporting and addressing the disability (Assouline & Whiteman, 2011; Baum, Cooper, & Neu, 2001; Berninger & Abbott, 2013; Mccoach, Kehle, Bray, & Siegle 2001; Nicpon, Allmon, Sieck, & Stinson, 2011; Willard-Holt & Morrison, 2013). Whereas it is possible to think of strategies that work for students with high ability or potential and other strategies that have been successful for addressing the needs of specific disabilities, the fact that the twice-exceptional student requires both types of support necessitates an integrated, whole-child approach (Pereles, Omdal, & Baldwin, 2009). Addressing only the area of remediation or only the area of strengths and interests is inadequate.

In reviewing the literature on twice exceptionality, one will encounter many lists under the heading of "Strategies for Twice-Exceptional Students" (Baum et al., 2001; Baum & Owens, 2004; Coleman, 2005). It is tempting for teachers to look at the lists and come to the conclusion that the strategies listed are of a universal nature and any one of them would work equally well with any twice-exceptional student. It must be noted that though some common characteristics may exist, each twice-exceptional student should be regarded as having a unique profile requiring a tailored set of evidence-based strategies reflecting his or her personal strengths and challenges.

STRENGTHS AND INTERESTS

When planning for instruction of twice-exceptional students, the first critical consideration is identification of the student's academic and intellectual strengths, talents, and interests in and outside of school and other personal factors, such as creativity, intrinsic motivation, and sustained attention. Focusing on the student's strengths before addressing the challenges is well supported in the literature (King, 2005; Olenchak, 2009; Reis et al., 2014). There are a number of important questions that the problem-solving team can ask in order to begin the process of determining how to address the student's strengths and interests. Figure 6.1 provides some questions teams can use to identify strengths and areas of need.

FIGURE 6.1. QUESTIONS TO HELP DETERMINE NEED IN THE AREA OF STRENGTHS AND INTERESTS

- In what subjects does the student excel?
- Does the student show evidence of higher level thinking in this subject?
- What is the student's favored mode of learning information and skills?
- What is the student's favored mode of expressing him/herself?
- Does the student qualitatively extend assignments and projects beyond the requirements? (Not just writing more pages for a report, but adding insights reflecting a deeper and more complex understanding.)
- In what topics does the student have interest and knowledge that is far above the level of a typical student of the same age? Does the student have an intense focus on a single topic that may be considered unusual?
- In what school-based or out-of-school activities does the student participate, and/or perform at a higher level than his/ her age-mates and/or has received recognition?
- To what degree does the challenge/disability impact the ability of the student to pursue this area of interest?
- How has the student utilized his/her strengths to compensate or mediate the areas of challenge?

Questions targeting the student's learning strengths and interests guide the problem-solving team's development of a comprehensive plan for the student. Determining a student's strengths and interests can be ascertained through a variety of assessments, such as student, parent, and teacher interviews and checklists. Observation and anecdotal information, often collected via student interest forms, is also helpful in developing a profile of the student's strengths and interests. For example, *Scales for Rating the Behavioral Characteristics of Superior Students* by Renzulli et al. (2010) addresses areas of learning, creativity, motivation, and leadership as well as the option to gather information on content areas, the arts, communication, and planning. A student interest form (see Yssel, Adams, Clarke, & Jones, 2014) for parents to fill out requests information regarding the student's favorite books, after-school activities, a passionate interest, vocabulary, and so on. The *Interest-A-Lyzer Family of Instruments* (Renzulli, 1997) is a survey for students that requests information about areas of interest in which the student has already been involved in order to create opportunities for further investigation or creative productivity. This type of instrument is easy for parents to complete and garners helpful information from a very important source: the student. Sitting down with the student one-on-one is also extremely important, especially for younger students who might not be able to fill out a form on their own. This kind of information can help fill in the gaps not addressed by more formalized assessments.

Once the problem-solving team has this important information as part of a comprehensive data set, they can begin to determine a plan for the student to develop identified strengths and interests. Plans will be tailored to the student's particular strengths, learning needs, and personality. A sample of some of the strategies that have frequently been suggested are acceleration; content extension to include greater depth, complexity, and novelty; and higher-level thinking activities, such as analysis, evaluation, and synthesis (Baum et al., 2001; Baum & Owens, 2004; Bianco, Carothers, & Smiley, 2009; Coleman, 2005; McEachern & Bornot, 2001). Examples for addressing strengths and interests are given in the section "Twice-Exceptional Student Plans."

LEARNING NEEDS

The second critical consideration involves the student's learning needs. Like the strengths-and-interests area, there are questions for the problem-solving team to ask to help them determine a plan. In Figure 6.2, questions that can inform the process of developing plans to address the particular learning needs of a twice-exceptional student are presented.

FIGURE 6.2. QUESTIONS TO HELP DETERMINE NEED IN THE AREA OF CHALLENGE OR DISABILITY

- In what subject(s) does the student have difficulty?
- What is the nature of the learning difficulty?
- What is the student's favored mode of learning information and skills?
- What tasks or learning activities does the student avoid?
- Does the student demonstrate negative or unexpected behaviors during certain learning tasks or activities?
- What is the student's favored mode of expressing him/herself? Does the student prefer oral versus written responses?
- What learning/academic incongruities are present (e.g. advanced comprehension of material presented visually and/or aurally, but low comprehension if read)?
- To what degree does the challenge/disability impact the ability of the student to pursue strengths and interests?

Some of the same information from the strengths-and-interests area will be useful here as well. It is beneficial to review the student's cumulative records to determine if changes in student performance or observations from teachers has recently occurred (Assouline, Nicpon, & Huber, 2006). As noted earlier, a perceptive teacher may notice that a student's scores on the universal screener are discrepant. If a student's score is very high on a math assessment, for example, but in the low-average range in reading, that can be a trigger for further investigation. The teacher could review classwide reading assessments, writing samples, and reports from the student's previous teacher. Informal observations of the ways the student approaches or struggles during specific academic tasks can also be very helpful. If the data support the teacher's initial impressions that the student needs academic or behavioral help, then a plan for classroom intervention should be implemented. If progress monitoring indicates that the student is not making adequate progress, a problem-solving team meeting should be convened. The problem-solving team might recommend that the support be increased in duration or intensity. In some cases, the problem-solving team may request a further assessment because of the severity of the student's needs.

Pedro, for example, might require further evaluation. His overall average grades and test scores may not raise any "red flags" about his potential ADHD. However, signs, such as his extreme disorganization and inattention, as well as the need for the teacher to redirect his off-task behavior, indicate that there might be a disability.

The problem-solving team could make the recommendation for a more thorough assessment and evaluation. The section "Twice-Exceptional Student Plans" provides examples of how a problem-solving team might address students' specific needs due to disability.

SOCIAL AND EMOTIONAL NEEDS

The third area concerns the social-emotional dimension. In the effort to address the needs of the whole child, the student's social and emotional needs must be addressed. It is common for the academic self-concept of twice-exceptional students to be very low as they often see themselves as imposters or as inadequate. Researchers have noted that twice-exceptional students experience high levels of anxiety, poor self-concept, and anger because of the discrepancies between what they can and cannot do (Baldwin, 1995; Baum & Owen, 2004; Reis et al., 2014; Schiff, Kaufman, & Kaufman, 1981). Because these students often experience feelings more intensely, it is crucial that they feel supported. Figure 6.3 provides questions members of the problem-solving team might ask in regard to the social and emotional needs of twice-exceptional students.

FIGURE 6.3. QUESTIONS TO HELP DETERMINE THE NEED IN THE AREA OF SOCIAL-EMOTIONAL CONCERNS

- What triggers, if any, set the student off?
- What behaviors does the student exhibit that interfere with learning?
- To what degree does the student exhibit heightened empathy and sensitivity?
- Does the student make derogatory comments such as 'I'm dumb" about him/herself?
- What, if any, uneven development exists physically, emotionally and/or socially?
- What evidence exists that would indicate extreme perfectionistic tendencies that would prevent the student from taking risks?
- How does the student hide their strengths and/or their disabilities to fit in with peers?
- Does the student avoid peers or do they avoid the student?
- Describe the circumstances of when the student appears anxious or agitated.
- Describe when the student becomes angry and/or refuses to participate or follow class rules?

As the questions indicate, the social-emotional dimension related to students with twice-exceptionality is varied and complex. Students may be confused because of high abilities in some academic subjects and the dichotomy of learning difficulties in other subjects or within the same subject. Teachers and other school personnel can help these students by ensuring that the school environment is designed to be accepting and safe. A variety of people can support twice-exceptional students' social and emotional needs. Teachers, psychologists, family members, administrators, coaches, mentors, community members, and peers who share the same strengths, talents, or passions can be called upon for support. In addition, Neumeister, Yssel, and Burney (2013) stressed that family members are instrumental in nurturing and supporting their child's social and emotional needs. Because the concept of twice exceptionality is still new for many educators, acceptance, willingness, and an interest in meeting the needs of twice-exceptional students needs to be present and part of the culture of the school. A nurturing, safe environment is crucial for a twice-exceptional student to be willing to take risks necessary to address the challenges.

TWICE-EXCEPTIONAL STUDENT PLANS

The three critical considerations discussed-strengths, academic needs, and social and emotional needs—demonstrate how each can be addressed to support the success of twice-exceptional students. Lance's, Hadley's, and Pedro's plans show how their schools' problem-solving teams developed integrated plans. The plans address the students' strengths and interests as well as learning needs with research-based strategies and accommodations in both areas (National Association for Gifted Children, n.d.). In addition, the plans describe the social-emotional dimension and how that area will be addressed. The intent is that the progress of the students will be monitored and plans will be reviewed regularly in a flexible, continuous improvement cycle. In school systems where the environment and culture are conducive for recognizing and meeting the varied and individual needs of twice-exceptional learners, educators and families can develop integrated individualized plans that address the needs of the whole child.

LANCE

Strengths and Interests, Accommodations

- Gifted education teacher will work with the classroom teacher to facilitate curriculum compacting for possible subject acceleration or enrichment.
- The classroom teacher had pretested Lance to determine which content standards were met and which he still needed to learn. He tested out of four of the nine science units for the year. It was determined that it would be more appropriate to develop enrichment activities for him during weeks when the teacher is teaching those four science units.
- Gifted education teacher will facilitate the development of an independent investigation based on a specific science topic of his choice and create a contract that breaks down tasks that includes the following: (a) problem finding, (b) research tools, (c) a rubric, (d) specific time lines for completion, (e) key concepts to be addressed, (f) check-in dates, and (g) method of presentation.

Learning Needs, Accommodations and Modifications

- Teachers will collaborate to locate video and audio resources and teach him how to acquire information from these resources. The special education teacher will teach him how to use data charts and graphic organizers to record and summarize his information. She will also assist him with the writing associated with the final product. His other teachers will reinforce the strategies.
- The family will read and discuss some of the more difficult resource reference books with him.
- The gifted teacher will help Lance determine the type of product (e.g., PowerPoint, oral presentation, cartoon strip, and different types of charts) that will best represent and communicate his knowledge.

Social-Emotional Needs, Support

- The school psychologist will meet with Lance once a week as part of a social group of second-grade peers during lunch.
- The family will take him to the Nature Center after school once a week to be part of their organized plant and animal classes with the hope of finding other children who share the same intense interests.
- The science coordinator will invite Lance to join the Junior Scientist Club.

HADLEY

Strengths and Interests, Accommodations

- Hadley will continue in the gifted program. The gifted education teacher will integrate learning accommodations into her activities to make them accessible to Hadley, such as audio books, videos, and graphic organizers.
- The gifted education teacher will meet with Hadley to determine an independent project based on her social justice interests, such as poverty or Afghanistan.

Learning Needs, Accommodations and Modifications

- As per the problem-solving team, the reading teacher gave Hadley reading and writing assessments and determined that she was a candidate for more intense reading support from a reading specialist. Hadley will receive a specific and systematic reading and writing approach three times a week for 30 minutes plus specific, coordinated instruction in the general education class during reading instruction.
- The teachers, including the new reading interventionist, will collaborate to create a reading plan that can be applied across all of her educational settings. She will have access to the highest-level reading and discussion groups.
- The family will have her practice keyboarding 20 minutes a day using any of the high-interest keyboarding programs available for home use.
- The gifted teacher will teach her to utilize voice-activated recognition software to capture her creative ideas and advanced thinking.

Social-Emotional Needs, Support

- The gifted teacher will recommend audio books, articles, and videos to Hadley on the lives of adults (e.g., Henry Winkler, Whoopi Goldberg, and Jewel, the singer) who have had similar learning issues but who learned how to compensate for them.
- The principal will invite Hadley to join the School Superintendent's Youth Task Force on Mediation and Bullying Prevention.

PEDRO

Strengths and Interests, Accommodations and Modifications

- The pre-engineering CAD teacher knows that Pedro demonstrates more skill and knowledge than other students in his classes. He will provide Pedro subject acceleration or a supervised project of his choice.

- The pre-engineering CAD teacher will add Pedro to the high school Engineering Olympiad Team. The team is building a robot for sorting recycled materials.

Learning Needs, Accommodations and Modifications

- The English teacher volunteered to teach Pedro how to color-code his notebooks and to access his homework online.
- Pedro will check in with the English teacher once a week after school to organize his materials and review homework and project timelines.
- The family agreed to provide a dedicated study space for him and an area in the basement where he can organize his supplies for his academics and his projects.

Social-Emotional Needs, Support

- Pedro's participation on the high school Engineering Olympiad Team will provide him with the opportunity to positively interact with other students who have a shared interest and skill level.
- The pre-engineering CAD teacher also teaches at the nearby middle school. The teacher has several students whom he asked Pedro to tutor in 3-D printing application.

As demonstrated in the case examples of Lance, Hadley, and Pedro, comprehensive, individualized, flexible plans that address the whole child work best for twice-exceptional students. The composite profiles of these three twice-exceptional students provide insight into the multidimensional nature of this phenomenon, including characteristics and challenges associated with recognition of either gifts and talents or disability in order to facilitate the delivery of appropriate services, and specific strategies to support students' needs across the spectrum. For the twice-exceptional student to be successful, educators need to set aside preconceived notions of disability and giftedness. The focus should be on the unique needs of twice-exceptional students to create an integrated, individualized approach rather than trying to fit them into an existing system.

REFERENCES

Assouline, S. G., Nicpon, M. F., & Huber, D. H. (2006). The impact of vulnerabilities and strengths on the academic experiences of twice-exceptional students: A message to school counselors. *Professional School Counseling.* 10, 14–24.

Assouline, S. G., & Whiteman, C. S. (2011). Twice-exceptionality: Implications for school psychologists in the post-IDEA 2004 era. *Journal of Applied School Psychology.* 27, 380–402.

Baldwin, L. (1995). *Portraits of gifted learning disabled students: A longitudinal study* (Unpublished doctoral dissertation). Teachers College, Columbia University, New York, NY.

Baum, S., Cooper, C., & Neu, T. (2001). Dual differentiation: An approach for meeting the curricular needs of gifted students with learning disabilities. *Psychology in the Schools, 38,* 477–490.

Baum, S., & Owen, S. (2004). *To be gifted and learning disabled: Strategies for helping bright students with LD, ADHD, and more.* Mansfield, CT: Creative Learning Press.

Berninger. V. W., & Abbott, R. D. (2013). Differences between children with dyslexia who are and are not gifted in verbal reasoning. *Gifted Child Quarterly. 57,* 223–233.

Bianco, M., Carothers, D. E., & Smiley, L. R. (2009). Gifted students with Asperger syndrome: Strategies for strength-based programming. *Intervention in School and Clinic, 44,* 206–215.

Coleman, M. R. (2005). Academic strategies that work for gifted students with learning disabilities. *TEACHING Exceptional Children, 38*(1). 28–32.

King, E.W. (2005). Addressing the social and emotional needs of twice-exceptional students. *TEACHING Exceptional Children, 38*(1), 16–20.

McCoach, D. B., Kehle, T. J., Bray, M.A., & Siegle, D. (2001). Best practices in the identification of gifted students with learning disabilities. *Psychology in the Schools, 38,* 403–411.

McEachern, A.G., & Bernot, J. (2001). Gifted students with learning disabilities: Implications and strategies for school counselors. *Professional School Counseling, 5,* 34–41.

National Association for Gifted Children. (n.d.) *Research support for the 2013 Teacher Preparation Standards in Gifted Education.* Retrieved from http://ektron. nagc.org/uploadedFiles/lnformation_ and_Resources/NCATE_standards/ research% 20support % 20for%20 2013%20 stands.pdf

Neumeister, K. S., Yssel, N., & Burney, V. H. (2013). The influence of primary caregivers in fostering success in twice-exceptional children. *Gifted Child Quarterly, 57,* 263–274.

Nicpon, M. F., Allmon, A., Sieck, B., & Stinson, R. D. (2011). Empirical investigation of twice-exceptionality: Where have we been and where are we going? *Gifted Child Quarterly, 55,* 3–17.

Nielsen, M. E., Higgins, D., Baldwin. L., & Pereles, D. (2000). *Comparisons of characteristics of gifted students with or without disabilities.* Unpublished manuscript.

Olenchak, F. R. (2009). Effects of talents unlimited counseling on gifted/learning disabled students. *Gifted Education International, 25,* 144–164.

Pereles, D. A., Omdal, S. N., & Baldwin, L. (2009). Response to intervention and twice-exceptional learners: A promising fit. *Gifted Child Today, 32*(3). 40–51.

Reis, S. M., Baum, S. M., & Burke, E. (2014). An operational definition of twice-exceptional learners: Implications and applications. *Gifted Child Quarterly, 58,* 217–230.

Renzulli, J. S. (1997). *Interest-A-Lyzer Family of Instruments: A manual for teachers.* Waco, TX: Prufrock Press.

Renzulli, J. S., Smith, L. H., White, A. J., Callahan, C. M., Hartman, R. K., Westberg, K. L., ... Sytsma. R. E. (2010). *Scales for rating the behavioral characteristics of superior students: Technical and administration manual* (3rd ed.). Waco, TX: Prufrock Press.

Schiff, M. M., Kaufman, A. S., & Kaufman, N. L. (1981). Scatter analysis of WISC-R profiles for learning disabled children with superior intelligence. *Journal of Learning Disabilities. 14,* 400–404.

Willard-Holt. C., & Morrison, K. (2013, Fall). Uncovering buried treasure: Effective learning strategies for twice-exceptional students. *Teaching for High Potential,* pp. 14–16.

Yssel, N., Adams, C .. Clarke, L., & Jones, R. (2014). Applying an RTI model for students with learning disabilities who are gifted. *TEACHING Exceptional Children, 46*(3), 42–52.

CHAPTER 7
Demonstrating School Counselor Effectiveness in Counseling Using Play Therapy Techniques

Jolie Ziomek-Daigle and Kelly Cowart

The purpose of this chapter is to highlight the efficacy of play therapy used by school counselors. In this chapter we first discuss the evolution of the school counseling specialty over the last century. Next, a discourse on the transforming school counseling initiative (TSCI) (Education Trust, 1997) will follow and information will be provided as to how this movement took shape on the cusp of the era of accountability. Accountability and assessment measures of the No Child Left Behind Act (NCLB, 2002) will be presented as well as the American School Counselor Association's (ASCA) response with the introduction to the ASCA *National Model* (2012). In the next section we examine advocacy and social justice strategies used to increase student achievement. The practice of using play therapy in the schools to improve student achievement, behavior, and connectedness will be the following section. Finally, a case study is included so that the reader can integrate all of the content presented in this chapter.

A BRIEF HISTORY OF THE SCHOOL COUNSELING PROFESSION

At the turn of the 20th century, the roots of school counseling began through the work of Frank Parsons and the founding of the vocational guidance movement. Impending social issues at that time included child labor, immigration, and urbanization thus the vocational guidance movement was created to assist in transitions from school or home to the workforce (Herr & Erford, 2011). The next 2 decades brought related allied professionals to the vocational movement along with their respective knowledge gained from curriculum offerings and practices. Professionals in student personnel, psychology, social work, and psychiatry all began to contribute to the vocational guidance movement. Individuals working in the area of vocational guidance were now bringing discipline-specific strategies in administration, testing, behavior management, advocacy, systemic work, and diagnosis and treatment. Toward the middle of the 21st century, counseling theories began to emerge. Once such theory was the person-centered approach in which the client and counselor work more collaboratively to achieve goals rather than counselor directed interventions. Herr and Erford (2011) suggest that the arrival of collaborative counseling theories (i.e., developmental and systems), which were proactive and adaptive in nature, provided fertile soil for school counseling models to grow.

The next few decades brought further definition of the school counseling specialty as well as special recognition and support from the federal government. This change occurred post World War II. The launching of Sputnik in 1957 helped the government conclude that the country was behind in math and science advances. The concern resulted in the passing of the National Defense Education Act of 1958 so that high achieving students could be identified and attend college. Federal funds were now being spent on the preparation and employment of school counselors who, in turn, would identify talented students for college majors in engineering, mathematics, and science. Herr and Erford (2011) concluded that this was the era when legislation and professionalization defined the field of school counseling. This professionalization of the school counseling specialty included the birth of several national organizations such as the ASCA and state standards for school counselor certification.

Several acts passed during the following decades that increased responsibilities for school counselors. The Carl D. Perkins Act of 1984 and the Elementary School Counseling Demonstration Act of 1995, along with local and state mandates for school counselors to become involved in issues of child abuse, drug abuse, and career education, all took place during this time. Due to school counselors assuming more responsibilities across developmental domains, comprehensive program models began to emerge to ensure accountability and cohesion of program components (Gysbers & Henderson, 1994). Also, toward the end of this era, we saw the birth of the TSCI (Education Trust, 1997) and the passage of NCLB (2002). The following section will describe how the school counseling profession increased accountability measures in training and practice.

TRANSFORMING SCHOOL COUNSELING AND ACCOUNTABILITY

The mid-90s brought standards-based reform, accountability measures, and advanced technologies (House & Martin, 1998). Leaders in the field wanted school counselors engaged in critical conversations regarding student achievement and prepared to show evidence-based results; particularly in student outcomes. Discussions as to whether school counselors should address issues of equity and access, as well as assume roles as advocates and leaders, were occurring (Paisley & Hayes, 2003). This transformative shift in school counseling would leave behind a more clinical, mental health model focused on the individual needs of students and create a greater focus on comprehensive program development in the areas of academic, career, and college aspirations of all students. As a result of this discourse and a response to the educational climate, many training programs made a commitment to value all the contributions school counselors can offer and meet both the academic and mental health needs of youth. Presently, students are being trained under a model that develops counselors to become skilled practitioners and educational leaders in the schools (Paisley & McMahon, 2001; Ziomek-Daigle, McMahon, & Paisley, 2008).

Educational reform efforts during this time also stimulated organizations such as the ASCA to develop national standards for programs. Additionally, ASCA's standards development concentrated on student competence in three broad domains: personal/social, academic, and career. Later, ASCA published the *ASCA National Model: A Framework for School Counseling Programs* (ASCA, 2012) to assist counselors in developing standards-based programs in four primary areas: foundation, management system, delivery system, and accountability.

Given that this is the age of accountability and educational reform, school counselors should not be complacent by only developing programs based on comprehensive models but should also present results that show positive student outcomes. So, the question is reframed from *"What do counselors do?"* to *"How are students different because of what school counselors do?"* (ASCA, 2012, p. 17). As Brown and Trusty (2005) suggest, "If school counselors expect to be credited with raising student achievement, they must provide clear-cut evidence that this occurs because of their interventions" (p. 13). Demonstrating outcomes like increasing graduation rates, improving standardized test scores, and decreasing behavior referrals is important to mark yearly progress and is often included in school wide improvement goals. However, data must clearly establish that the results are linked to school counseling interventions. Mixed methods of data collection and analysis such as observations, document analysis, focus groups, and multiple assessments may offer school counselors additional support in terms of substantiating effectiveness. An example of a school counselor using multiple assessments and data points will be discussed in the case study section of this chapter.

ADVOCACY AND SOCIAL JUSTICE WORK IN SCHOOLS

Recent accountability measures and transformative practices have allowed school counselors to identify educational and attainment gaps of all students but particularly those who might be poor and underrepresented. The school counseling profession has progressed from appreciating diversity and promoting multiculturalism to using advocacy and social justice strategies in schools. The United States is more diverse than ever and it is estimated that minority groups will outnumber majority groups by 2020 (Wasow, 2005). Interestingly, ASCA's skills of collaboration, advocacy, and use of data support school counselors in discovering gaps and developing appropriate interventions for traditionally marginalized students. Guided by Brofenbrenner's (1979) theory of ecological systems, school counselors can work within contextual influences and collaborate multisystsemically at the microlevel (with teachers, principals, allied professionals, and parents), at the mesolevel (with community leaders, agency administrators, and school district supervisors), and at the macrolevel (within state or national entities that deal with counseling and student achievement matters). Students from marginalized groups could benefit from school counselors advocacy efforts that affect student outcomes. Examples include the efforts of a school counselor to sponsor a student-led organization for lesbian, gay, bisexual, transgender (LGBT) youth and families (micro), advocate to increase gifted and advanced placement testing for minority students (meso), and present research to lawmakers when potential bills may cut funding (macro).

ASSESSING THE EFFECTIVENESS OF PLAY THERAPY IN SCHOOLS

The evolution of the school counselor whose focus was on the individual adjustment of students to the current transformative practitioner has occurred. As aforementioned, training programs are graduating students who have skills to work with K-12 youth as mental health specialists and educational leaders. By responding to student needs in the personal/social domain, school counselor practices may have the potential to impact other aspects of student growth and development, for example academics. Counseling strategies that have been used in schools for decades, such as play therapy, can be linked to increasing student achievement (Blanco & Ray, 2011; Baggerly & Bratton, 2010).

School counselors are professional educators with expertise in mental health who deliver "comprehensive developmental school counseling programs that promote healthy development, and provide prevention and intervention services as needed" (ASCA, 2012, p. 3). Prevention services anticipate potential problem areas and proactively offer learning opportunities (Gysbers & Henderson, 1994). Further, school counselors have the skill set to recognize and intervene when students experience emotional distress, academic difficulties, social complications, behavior problems, or other prevailing concerns that may impact academic achievement (Ziomek-Daigle, McMahon, & Paisley, 2008). The school counselor is trained in issues of mental health and may be the first, if not only person to whom a student is referred (Paisley & Hubbard, 1994).

Identifying early interventions that are effective for children and can be delivered in a highly accessible setting such as schools is a critical need for the 21st century (Landreth, Ray, & Bratton, 2009). According to Kochhar-Bryant (2010) an increasing proportion of the general school population is at-risk of academic failure, school dropout, and suicide. In particular, one in five children between the ages of nine and 17 have diagnosable mental health or behavioral disorders (Kochhar-Bryant, 2010). Over 20% of school age children experience mental health concerns and nearly 80% of these students will not receive any mental health services (Blanco

& Ray, 2011). Students of low socioeconomic status may lack social capital (i.e., social relations that have productive benefits) and are likely to only receive these services from a school counselor as they may not have access to resources in their own communities. Even when resources do exist in the community, families may encounter other barriers such as no transportation or parents who work during nonschool hours on nights and weekends and therefore can't take their child for counseling services.

Blanco and Ray (2011) state that younger children are susceptible to a lack of mental health attention and the subsequent effects on student outcomes. Academic achievement is a significant predictor of whether or not young people will have either stable or marginalized economic lives in our increasingly complex world (Lapan, 2004). As child development specialists in the schools, counselors are uniquely qualified to create educational environments that promote the optimal cognitive, emotional, social, and behavioral development of children (White & Flynt, 1999). Academic self-efficacy is enhanced when school counselors provide developmentally appropriate interventions aimed at improving attitudes toward learning and academic skills. Academic competence allows students to maximize the instruction offered by teachers (Landreth, 2002). Experts contend that play therapy with youth in grades prekindergarten through high school and with diverse populations is a research-based and developmentally appropriate method of facilitating student growth (Baggerly & Bratton, 2010; Ray, Bratton, Rhine, & Jones, 2001). Therefore, play therapy offers students the opportunities to develop in the academic as well as personal/social and career domains during 30-minute sessions, a typical intervention time in the schools (Blanco & Ray, 2011).

PLAY AS A COMPONENT OF A SCHOOL COUNSELING PROGRAM

Play has the power to facilitate normal child development as well as alleviate potentially delayed or disrupted behaviors (Reynolds & Stanley, 2001). Piaget (1962) identified play as being vital to the cognitive, social, and emotional development of children. It is the native language of children (Landreth, 2002) and the therapeutic modality of choice when working with children (Dougherty & Ray, 2007). School counselors can embrace play therapy as a viable method of addressing a variety of social, emotional, behavioral, and developmental issues and view that counseling through play is not an adjunct to the school counseling program but is ideally infused into large group guidance, small group interventions, and individual counseling (Landreth, Strother, & Barlow, 1985). School counselors who value play therapy are likely to also incorporate it into their work with teachers and parents (e.g., kinder training, filial therapy).

Comprehensively integrating play therapy into the school-wide counseling program requires conceptualizing the modality in a much broader form than playroom-based delivery (Ray, Muro, & Schumann, 2004); for example, play can be integrated in the classroom, the small group setting, and in one-on-one work with students School counselors deliver services to students through classroom guidance, small group counseling, and individual counseling. Careful planning is essential when a school counselor intends to infuse play therapy into the counseling program. When designing the guidance curriculum, several questions are helpful to consider: (a) What does this specific population of students need? (b) How will students be different as a result of the guidance curriculum? (c) Are play therapy lesson plans empirical? and (d) How will learning be assessed? (Dimmitt, 2009).

PLAY IN CLASSROOM GUIDANCE

Classroom guidance is where prevention and developmental education primarily take place. It is an instructional program that is comprehensive in scope, preventative and proactive, and developmental in design (ASCA, 2012). Through well-crafted, engaging lessons counselors are able to provide every student with the knowledge, attitudes, and skills that prepare them for a successful academic career, healthy relationships, and a promising future.

The ASCA *National Model* (2012) recommends that elementary level counselors spend 45% of their time engaged in classroom guidance, while middle school and high school counselors dedicate 35 and 25% of their time respectively. With nearly half of their time committed to classroom guidance, this seems the most logical place for elementary counselors to begin implementing play and play therapy techniques. Class sizes can vary from fifteen to thirty or more students. Therefore, directive play therapy interventions such as games, art, music, drama, and bibliotherapy are best suited for this form of delivery. Many practitioners have authored articles and books filled with play therapy and play-based interventions that can be adapted or modified for classroom guidance (Ashby, Kottman, & Degraaf, 2008; Goodyear-Brown, 2002;

Hall, Kaduson, & Schaefer, 2002; Kaduson & Schaefer, 2010; Lowenstein, 1999; Swank, 2008).

The standards and competencies of the ASCA *National Model* (2012) have been established to ensure that every student receives instruction in the domains of academic development, personal/social development, and career development. For example, a competency in the academic domain may read, "Students will articulate feelings of competence and confidence as learners" (ASCA, 2012, p. 114). The developmental crosswalking tool assists counselors in deciding if this competency will be taught K–2, 3–5, 6–8, and/or 9–12. In an elementary setting, for example, this particular competency might be delivered through classroom guidance in kindergarten through second grade, remediated through small group counseling in third and fourth grade, and be identified as a strength during individual academic planning in fifth grade. As stated earlier, knowledge regarding the needs of specific populations drives the design of curricula at individual schools (Dimmitt, 2009). This knowledge is gained through needs assessment, review of critical data elements, and garnering the perspectives of multiple stakeholders (i.e., conversations with advisory council, interview with administrators). Once the competencies of each grade level have been identified, the curriculum crosswalking tool provides a written format for planning the scope, and sequence, of yearlong guidance curriculum plans. This is the time for counselors to plan for the systematic incorporation of play into the classroom through guidance lessons.

PLAY IN SMALL GROUPS

Many children require additional supports in order to reach their full academic, social, and emotional potential. Small groups provide counselors a forum for offering individualized prevention and remediation instruction in a time-efficient manner. The types of groups that counselors implement are as varied as the student populations they serve. Traditional groups may be remedial in nature, crisis oriented, or preventative in design. Play therapy groups allow counselors to focus on individual and group issues concurrently (White & Flynt, 1999). Interactions in small groups often reflect how children interact with others in the classroom. Small group counseling is the most authentic medium for children to learn about others, the ways in which they interact with others, and their impact on others (Ziomek-Daigle, McMahon, Paisley, 2008).

Children can, but do not have to be grouped by similar concerns (White & Flynt, 1999). Scheduling is less of a challenge when groups are comprised of children with varying counseling needs. For example, a kindergarten play group may be comprised of three students from the same classroom. The group might consist of one student experiencing transition to school difficulties, another student exploring issues regarding retention in kindergarten, and a third student adjusting to a new sibling at home. Groups may also be structured around a similar issue with students of varying ages and relationships. Baggerly (2004) demonstrated that elementary-aged siblings whose family had recently become homeless benefitted from sibling group play therapy to process the dramatic change in life circumstances. Research indicates that group play counseling has been effective with children receiving speech therapy services at school (Danger & Landreth, 2005), raising the self-esteem of fourth, fifth, and sixth grade students (Post, 1999), increasing the moral reasoning of ninth grade students (Paone, Packman, Maddux, & Rothman, 2008), and reducing anxiety in children who have witnessed domestic violence (Tyndall-Lind, Landreth, & Giordano, 2001).

PLAY IN INDIVIDUAL COUNSELING

Students who are experiencing crisis or intense levels of disruption in their lives may necessitate the use of individual play therapy. Some children are not candidates for group therapy due to aggressive behaviors, sexual acting out, or severe emotional issues and need one-on-one assistance (White & Flynt, 1999). While school counselors are not trained nor can they spend their day providing in-depth therapy, as previously mentioned, many children do not have access to healthcare or a mental health provider.

Students who are struggling in the classroom may benefit academically from individual play therapy. Blanco and Ray (2010) found that individual child-centered play therapy significantly improved the academic achievement for at-risk first grade students. Further, an increase in students' self-efficacy was seen after just six individual play therapy sessions (Fall, 1999). In a study conducted by Ray, Henson, Schottelkorb, Brown, and Muro (2008) individual play therapy occurring at least twice weekly was shown to reduce teacher's perceptions of relationship stress with children demonstrating behavioral and social issues. The play therapy literature is rich in efficacious interventions with individual children. A review and analysis of such studies may be beneficial to school counselors hoping to reproduce such effective outcomes through play.

COUNSELOR AS CONSULTANT IN TRAINING OTHER SCHOOL-BASED PROFESSIONALS

Current research indicates that the relationship between student and teacher impacts achievement, connectedness to school, and interactions with peers (Edwards, Varjas, White, & Stokes, 2009). Positive teacher-student relationships are characterized by support, understanding, and invigorating learning experiences (White, Flynt, & Draper, 1997). A quality relationship enhances students' social bonding, resilience, and brain development resulting in effective learning and functional peer relationships (Chaloner, 2001; Edwards et al., 2009). Children who dislike school or their teacher are at risk of developing such hostility that they withdraw from the educational process altogether (Kuykendall, 2004). These feelings manifest in multiple behaviors such as: refusal to enter the classroom, wandering around the classroom, noncompliance with directions, incomplete work, disengagement from group activities, continual arguing with and aggression toward peers, crying, refusal to be consoled, frequent visits to the school nurse, absenteeism, and poor academic growth exacerbate negative teacher-student relationships (Chaloner, 2001; Draper, White, O'Shaunghessy, Flynt, & Jones, 2001). School counselors may have the opportunity to develop positive relationships among teachers and students by using consultation or staff development to present the basic facilitative skills of play therapy.

An example of an intervention, known as kinder therapy, engages teachers as part of the therapeutic process and teaches the use of basic play therapy skills for the classroom (White, Flynt, & Draper, 1997). Kinder Therapy is an adaptation of filial therapy. The kinder training manual developed by White, Draper, Flynt, and Jones (2000) outlines teacher learning, facilitator supervision, and classroom coaching procedures. Additionally, it allows school counselors to maintain an emphasis on developmental and preventative interventions for greater numbers of students. Teachers who participated in kinder training reported improved classroom management skills and student behavior as well as enhanced teacher child relationships (Edwards et al., 2009).

ASSESSMENT OF PLAY THERAPY IN A SCHOOL COUNSELING PROGRAM

"Accountability and evaluation of the school counseling program are absolute necessities" (ASCA, 2012, p. 7). As Young and Kaffenberger (2009) emphasize:

> For school counseling programs to be considered a pivotal and valued resource to the learning environment requires school counselors to commit to formulating and executing services that link school counselors' work to the instructional mission and concretely demonstrate accountability for student academic success. (p. 59)

Fortunately, the ASCA *National Model* (2012) establishes clear steps for accomplishing this important task beginning with garnering support from administrators and stakeholders. Assessment of play therapy based interventions must be conducted and shared in order for school administrators and other stakeholders to clearly acknowledge the alignment of a play therapy infused curriculum with the academic mission of the school. By using play interventions that have shown positive outcomes, counselors are more likely to be able to communicate to administrators, teachers, parents how students are different because of a developmental, comprehensive counseling program (Reynolds & Stanley, 2001).

The ASCA *National Model* (2012) encourages the collection of process, perception, and results data to measure the evaluation of the effectiveness of interventions implemented as part of the counseling program. Dimmitt (2009) defines the three types of data in the following way: (a) *process data* is evidence that the intervention took place. It is data that answers the questions of who received the services, when the client received the intervention, and duration of intervention; (b) *perception data* identifies what children learned as evidenced by a change in feelings or beliefs, mastery of new skills, or an increase in knowledge, and (c) *results data* is the application of process and perception data to prove that an intervention either has or has not positively impacted achievement or achievement-related behavior such as attendance, discipline, or work completion.

Perception data can be acquired through assessment. There are many ways to evaluate student learning such as multiple choice tests, rating scales or rubrics, role plays, skill demonstration, portfolios, journals, informal or formal observation of student behavior, or student self- assessment (Holcomb-McCoy, 2007). Surveys and scaled questions that use a Likert-type scale can be used to identify changes in beliefs, attitudes, or opinions. Packaged curricula typically include pre- and posttests to aid in identifying and measuring impact (Dimmitt, 2009; Holcomb-McCoy, 2007).

To demonstrate the effectiveness of a first grade classroom guidance lesson regarding the process of making mistakes in order to learn, a school counselor begins with a survey for the teacher (see Appendix A). The teacher is asked to list students whose grades are being impacted due to difficulty completing work because of a fear of making mistakes (i.e., perfectionism). Students are given a pre-test examining their beliefs about mistakes based on five scaled questions (see Appendix B). The pretest provides information to the counselor regarding students whom the teacher has expressed concerns about, perceptions of students regarding the teacher's expectations of perfection, and reveals students who may have perfectionistic tendencies or anxieties that have gone unnoticed by the teacher.

A play-based lesson is then taught using bibliotherapy and drawing. The counselor reads *Ish* by Peter Reynolds. The counselor and children then discuss how beginning efforts when learning something new are close-*ish* but not perfect. A Mr. Potato Head is set up where every child can see it. Each child is given paper and crayons and then asked to draw a picture that looks Mr. Potato Head-*ish*. Students then discuss with partners the parts of their drawings they are proud of and the parts that are -*ish* and may improve with practice. The counselor leads a discussion of how it felt to know that the drawing was intended to be Mr. Potato Head-*ish* and not perfect. Students identify tasks at school that they are willing to be-*ish* and not perfect. The pictures, with names omitted to protect the confidentiality of the students, are then hung in the hallway in an "*Ish* Gallery." The counselor follows up two weeks when returning for the next guidance lesson. The students complete the scaled questions and the teacher reports on the grades and work attempts of the students previously identified on the survey (see Appendix C). The perception data is analyzed for any changes in student beliefs. The results data is determined by analyzing student grades and teacher reports regarding number of work attempts before and after the lesson. The amount of positive change indicates the degree of effectiveness of the lesson.

Any results data indicating an efficacious impact on change in student attitudes, behaviors, and grades can be shared with stakeholders, such as administrators and the advisory council, to illustrate exactly how counselor-led, play-based interventions positively influence student achievement. Expanding the discussion to include ways in which successful large group lessons are translated into small group and individual interventions enhances stakeholders' understanding of the varied ways school counselors use play to meet the academic, social, and career needs of students.

CASE STUDY

Macey is a White, energetic, bright, healthy 6-year-old. Macey lives with her mother who is employed part-time, and two older sisters. The children qualify for the free lunch program at school. One sister is in fourth grade and the other is in sixth grade. Macey is of average size for first grade, is athletically built, and enjoys playing with the boys in her class. Academically, she is mastering the knowledge and skills of first grade. Macey is referred to the school counselor after being sent to an administrator for continual verbal arguments and name calling with her peers.

Working from a holistic perspective, the school counselor consulted with the teacher and parent in order to fully understand the child's world. Operating from the belief that children and adults can use play-based media to express themselves, the school counselor placed a basket of fidget toys, a bowl of moon sand, and Silly Putty on the table used for consultations. The use of the toys by Mrs. Jenkins, the teacher, allowed her to engage in anxiety reducing behaviors while encouraging the discussion of her feelings regarding Macey. Mrs. Jenkins reported that Macey exhibits difficulty staying on task, completing work, and frequently disrupts instruction by bickering with other students. In the teacher's words, Macey is "bullying" other students on the playground. Mrs. Jenkins expressed that she has a difficult time liking Macey. She feels this may be due, in part, to the fact that she is exasperated with the number of times a day different students report to her that Macey is bothering them or calling them "fat," "annoying," or "rambunctious." Mrs. Jenkins is frustrated that Macey's mother has not responded to invitations for a parent conference and that Macey regularly does not have any completed homework. Feelings of resentment, anger, and hopelessness were expressed by the teacher.

The counselor reflected the teacher's feelings and frequently offered encouragement regarding the positive strategies implemented by Mrs. Jenkins. The counselor offered to contact the mother for a conference and agreed to start seeing Macey individually in the play room. The school counselor asked the teacher to begin keeping data. Mrs. Jenkins would record daily the two significant behaviors creating concern: student reports regarding Macey's social interactions and the number of redirections Macey needed to complete her work. Weekly classroom assessments would be used as well for achievement data purposes.

The school counselor called Macey's mom, explained her role at the school, and stated that she had some ideas about how to improve things for Macey. The counselor appealed to mom as the expert on her child and explained that the school needed her expertise. Macey's mom agreed to come in 2 days later. Both the assistant principal and Mrs. Jenkins were in attendance for the meeting. During the course of the conference, Macey's mom articulated her own feelings of disconnectedness from her child. She reported that as a petite woman with two other petite daughters she often found herself commenting to Macey about her weight and allowing the other daughters to call Macey "fat." The two older sisters enjoy quiet activities and are soft spoken while Macey is "rambunctious" and frequently "annoying." Macey's mother reported that she frequently feels overwhelmed by Macey and can understand how other children might feel 'bullied' by Macey. The school counselor helped the mom reframe her vision of Macey using words such as "athletic," "exuberant," "lively," "assertive," and "outgoing."

Mrs. Jenkins left the conference with a new understanding of her student. Knowledge of her student's home life created a sense of urgency within the teacher to affirm and encourage Macey. Mrs. Jenkins and the counselor collaborated to create a plan allowing Macey to have 10 minutes of one-on-one play time with Mrs. Jenkins every day. The counselor discussed with the teacher how to improve her relationship with Macey by adopting the therapeutic attitude of Axline's (1969) eight basic principles for therapists who work with children:

1. The therapist is genuinely interested in the child and develops a warm, caring relationship;
2. The therapist experiences unqualified acceptance of the child and does not wish that the child were different in some way;
3. The therapist creates a feeling of safety and permissiveness in the relationship, so the child feels free to explore and express herself completely;
4. The therapist is always sensitive to the child's feelings and gently reflects those feelings in such a manner that the child develops self-understanding;
5. The therapist believes deeply in the child's capacity to act responsibly, unwaveringly respects the child's ability to solve personal problems, and allows the child to do so;
6. The therapist trusts the child's inner direction, allows the child to lead in all areas of the relationship, and resists any urge to direct the child's play or conversation;

7. The therapist appreciated the gradual nature of the therapeutic process and does not attempt to hurry the process;
8. The therapist establishes only those therapeutic limits necessary to anchor the session to reality and which help the child accept personal and appropriate relationship responsibility.

The counselor also provided instruction on the language of encouragement (Dinkmeyer, McKay, & Dinkmeyer, 1980; Kottman, 1993) and the basic tracking skills of play therapy (Landreth, 2002) to be used during the ten minutes of play time. Mrs. Jenkins also read *Responsibility in the Classroom* (Lew & Bettner, 1995) at the counselor's suggestion. Macey's mother was agreeable to learning strategies to enhance her relationship with Macey. Using a modified version of child-centered filial play therapy (Landreth & Bratton, 2006), Macey and her mother were able to share connections through play. Macey's mother began affirming strengths that she observed in Macey while enjoying time with her daughter. Macey also participated in small group play therapy with the school counselor. After 2 weeks of play therapy with the counselor, Mrs. Jenkins, and her mother, Macey's mother and teacher began noticing differences in Macey at home and at school. Macey became more cooperative with her sisters, more compliant with her mother's requests, and initiated friendly conversations with her peers. After 4 weeks of play therapy with her teacher and counselor, as well as filial play with her mother, Macey began reporting to her mother, teacher, and the assistant principal how much she enjoys school.

The achievement data from grades, achievement-related data from the time-on-task record (see Appendix D), parent perception survey, and the results from the peer interaction data (see Appendix E) at the end of eight weeks indicated that Macey was consistently finishing her work without redirection, few students were reporting incidents regarding Macey to Mrs. Jenkins, her math and reading grades had improved by one letter grade, and both Macey and her mother reported increased happiness at home. The school counselor created a data report for the administrators indicating the interventions used and pre- and postintervention achievement data. The principal later requested that the school counselor offer a staff development session to the faculty regarding the outcomes and the skills the teacher learned. The integration of play therapy into every facet of the intervention and the use of data to document its effectiveness confirms that the school counselor's work contributed substantially to the success of this student.

CONCLUSION

Integrating play therapy into a comprehensive program is a promising option for school counselors. It is helpful to remember that play therapy is not just about techniques, rather it is "a way of being with children based on a deep commitment to certain beliefs about children and their innate capacity for growth" (Landreth, Ray, & Bratton, 2009). A commitment to developmentally appropriate practice with students must be built on an evidence-based foundation. In this age of accountability, it is crucial for school counselors to show intent and impact in their work with students. The collection and analysis of process, perception, and results data are central practices of today's school counselors. As leaders in the school building, counselors must to advocate for children's rights to participate in programming conducted in their first language of play. Effectively assessing student learning and outcomes enables school counselors to articulate to all stakeholders that play and play-based interventions work in tandem with academic instruction to achieve the mission of schools in valuable, concrete ways.

APPENDIX A

Perfectionistic or Risk Anxiety Referral Form

Teacher Name ________________

Please answer the following questions before the "Ish" guidance lesson. Thank you!

Name of Student	Academic Context of Behaviors	Types of Behaviors Displayed	Tally the # of Times Child Exhibits Behaviors During the Academic Context Identified for 1 Week	Number of Assignments Completed in Academic Context Over 1 Week
Example: *Ryder*	*Writer's Workshop (or any writing)*	*Starts and then erases over and over again, asks to go to the bathroom, can become irritable, doesn't complete work and hides it.*		

APPENDIX B

Pre- and Postassessment for *Ish* Lesson

What do you think about mistakes?

☺ = YES ☹︎ = I don't know ☹ = NO

All of my work has to be completed perfectly.

☺ 😐 ☹

It is okay to try even if I might make a mistake.

☺ 😐 ☹

I am afraid to make a mistake on my work.

☺ 😐 ☹

My work can be close-ish.

☺ 😐 ☹

My teacher says it is okay to make mistakes.

☺ 😐 ☹

APPENDIX C

Perfectionistic or Risk Anxiety Follow-Up Form

Teacher Name ____________________

Please record the following information

Name of Student	Academic Context of Behaviors	Types of Attempted Behaviors Observed	Tally the # of Times Student Attempts Work in the Identified Context for 1 Week	Number of Assignments Completed in Context Over 1 Week
Example: *Ryder*	*Writer's Workshop (or any writing)*	*Starts and then erases and then starts again. Shows his work to another student to ask if it is "ish." Starts and seeks reassurance from teacher.*		

APPENDIX D

Time On-Task Record

Teacher Name ________________ Student Name ________________________

Please place a tally mark in the box each time you redirect the student to get back on-task.

	Monday	**Tuesday**	**Wednesday**	**Thursday**	**Friday**
Week of: Total:					
Week of: Total:					
Week of: Total:					
Week of: Total:					

APPENDIX E

Peer Interaction Record

Teacher ______________________ Student __________________________

Please tally the number of times **other students** *report ______________ engaging in any of the following behaviors:*

*name calling,
*instigating conflict,
*inappropriately touching others.

	Monday	Tuesday	Wednesday	Thursday	Friday	Total
Week of:						
Week of:						
Week of:						
Week of:						

REFERENCES

American School Counselor Association. (2012). *The ASCA National Model: A Framework for School Counseling Programs, Third Edition*. Alexandria, VA: Author.

Ashby, J., Kottman, T., & Degraaf, D. (2008). *Active Interventions for Kids and Teens: Adding Adventure and Fun to Counseling*. Alexandria, VA: American Counseling Association.

Axline, V. (1969). *Play therapy*. New York, NY: Ballantine Books.

Baggerly, J. (2004). Applying the ASCA national model to elementary school students who are homeless: A case study. *Professional School Counseling, 8*(2), 116–123.

Baggerly, J., & Bratton, S. C. (2010). Building a firm foundation in play therapy research: Response to Phillips (2010). *International Journal of Play Therapy, 19*(1), 26–38.

Blanco, P. J., & Ray, D. C. (2011). Play therapy in elementary schools: A best practice for improving academic achievement. *Journal of Counseling & Development, 89*, 235–243.

Brofenbrenner, U. (1979). *Ecology of human development*. Cambridge, MA: Harvard Univeristy Press.

Brown, D., & Trusty, J. (2005). The ASCA National Model, accountability, and establishing causal links between school counselors' activities and student outcomes: A reply to Sink. *Professional School Counseling, 9*(1), 13–15.

Chaloner, W. B. (2001). Counselors coaching teachers to use play therapy in classrooms: The Play and Language to Succeed (PALS) early, school-based intervention for behaviorally at risk children. In A. Drewes, L. Carey, Y. C. Schaefer (Eds.), *School-based play therapy* (pp. 368–390). New York, NY: John Wiley.

Danger, S., & Landreth, G. (2005). Child-centered group play therapy with children with speech difficulties. *International Journal of Play Therapy, 14*(1), 81–102.

Dimmitt, C. (2009). Why evaluation matters: Determining effective school counseling practices. *Professional School Counseling, 12*(6), 395–399.

Dinkmeyer, D., McKay, G., & Dinkmeyer, D. (1980). *Systematic training for effective teaching*. Circle Pines, MN: American Guidance Services.

Dougherty, J., & Ray, D. (2007). Differential impact of play therapy on developmental levels of children. *International Journal of Play Therapy, 16*(1), 2–19. doi:10.1037/1555-6824.16.1.2

Draper, K., White, J., O'Shuaunghessy, T., Flynt, M., & Jones, N. (2001). Kinder training: Play based consultation to improve the school adjustment of discouraged kindergarten and first grade students. *International Journal of Play Therapy. 10*(1), 1–29.

Education Trust. (1997). *Transforming school counseling*. Retrieved from http:// www.edtrust.org/main/school_counseling.asp

Edwards, N. A., Varjas, K. M., White, J. F., & Stokes, S. A. (2009). Teachers' perceptions of kinder training: Acceptability, integrity, and effectiveness. *International Journal of Play Therapy, 18*(3), 129–146. doi:10.1037/a0015170

Fall, M. (1999). A play therapy intervention and its relationship to self-efficacy and learning behaviors. *Professional School Counseling, 2*(3), 194–204.

Goodyear-Brown, P. (2002). *Digging for buried treasure: 52 Prop-based play therapy interventions for treating the problems of childhood*. Nashville, TN: Sundog.

Gysbers, N. C., & Henderson, P. (1994). *Developing and managing your school guidance program* (2nd ed.). Alexandria, VA: American Association for Counseling and Development.

Hall, T. M., Kaduson, H. G., & Schaefer, C. E. (2002). Fifteen effective play therapy techniques. *Professional Psychology: Research and Practice, 33*(6), 515–522. doi:10.1037//0735-7028.33.6.515

Herr, E. L., & Erford, B. T. (2011). Historical roots and future issues. In B. T. Erford (Ed.), *Transforming the school counseling profession* (3rd ed., pp. 19–43). Columbus, OH: Pearson Merrill Prentice Hall.

Holcolmb-McCoy, C. (2007). *School counseling to close the achievement gap*. Thousand Oaks, CA: Corwin Press.

House. R. M., & Martin, P. J. (1998). Advocating for better futures for all students: A new vision for school counselors. *Education*, 779, 284–291.

Kaduson, H. & Schaefer, C. (2010). *101 Favorite Play Therapy Techniques*. Lanham, MD: Jason Aronson.

Kochhar-Bryant, C. A. (2010). *Effective collaboration for educating the whole child*. Thousand Oaks, CA: Corwin.

Kottman, T. (1993). Adlerian play therapy: A tool for school counselors. *Elementary School Guidance & Counseling*, 28(1), 42–53.

Kuykendall, C. (2004). *From rage to hope: Strategies for reclaiming black and hispanic students*. Bloomington, IN: Solution Tree.

Landreth, G. (2002). *Play therapy: The art of the relationship* (2nd ed.) New York, NY: Brunner-Routledge.

Landreth, G., & Bratton, S. (2006). *Child parent relationship therapy* (CPRT): *A 10-session filial therapy model*. New York, NY: Brunner-Routledge.

Landreth, G., Ray, D. C., & Bratton, S. C., (2009). Play therapy in elementary schools. *Psychology in the Schools, 46*(3). doi:10.1002/pits.20374

Landreth, G., Strother, J., & Barlow, K., (1985). Child-centered play therapy: Nancy from baldness to curls. *School Counselor, 32*(5), 347–356.

Lapan, R. (2004). *Career development across the K-16 years: Building the present to satisfying and successful futures*. Alexandria, VA: American Counseling Association.

Lew, A., & Bettner, B. A. (1995). *Responsibility in the classroom: A teacher's guide to understanding and motivating students*. Newton, MA: Connexions Press.

Lowenstein, L. (1999). *Creative Interventions for Troubled Children & Youth*. Toronto, Canada: Champion Press.

No Child Left Behind (NCLB) Act of 2001, Pub. L. No. 107-110, § 115, Stat. 1425 (2002).

Paisley, P. O., & Hayes, R. L. (2003). School counseling in the academic domain: Transformations in preparation and practice. *Professional School Counseling, 6*, 198–205.

Paisley, P. O., & Hubbard, G. T. (1994). *Developmental school counseling programs: From theory to practice*. Alexandria, VA: American Counseling Association.

Paisley, P. O., & McMahon, H. G. (2001). School counseling for the 21st century: Challenges and opportunities. *Professional School Counseling, 5*, 106–115.

Paone, T. R., Packman, J. Maddux, C., & Rothman, T. (2008). A school-based group activity therapy intervention with at-risk high school students as it relates to their moral reasoning. *International Journal of Play Therapy, 17*(2), 122–137. doi:10.1037/a0012582

Piaget, J. (1962). *Play, dreams, and imitation in childhood*. New York, NY: Routledge.

Post, P. (1999). Impact of child-centered play therapy on the self-esteem, locus of control, and anxiety of at-risk 4th, 5th, and 6th grade students. *International Journal of Play Therapy, 8*(2), 1–18.

Ray, D. C., Bratton, S. C., Rhine, T., & Jones, L. (2001). The effectiveness of play therapy: Responding to the critics. *International Journal of Play Therapy, 10*, 85–108.

Ray, D. C., Henson, R. K., Schottelkorb, A. A., Brown, A. G., & Muro, J. (2008). Effect of short- and long-term play therapy services on teacher-child relationship stress. *Psychology in the Schools, 45*(10), 994–1009. doi:10.1002/pits.20347

Ray, D. C., Muro, J., & Schumann, B. (2004). Implementing play therapy in the schools: Lessons learned. *International Journal of Play Therapy, 13*(1), 79–100.

Reynolds, C., & Stanley, C. (2001). Innovative applications of play therapy in school settings. In A. A. Drewes, L. J. Carey, & C. E. Schafer (Eds.), *School-based play therapy*. New York, NY: John Wiley.

Swank, J. M. (2008). The use of games: A therapeutic tool with children and families. *International Journal of Play Therapy, 17*(2), 154–167. doi:10.1037/15556824.17.2.154

Tyndall-Lind, A., Landreth, G. L., & Giordano, M. A. (2001). Intensive group play therapy with child witnesses of domestic violence. *International Journal of Play Therapy, 10*(1), 53–83.

Young, A., & Kaffenberger, C. (2009). *Making data work*. Alexandria, VA: American School Counselor Association.

Wasow, B. (2005). *Majority minority*. Retrieved from http://www.tcf.org/ list.asp?type=NC&pubid=1072

White, J., Draper, K., Flynt, M., & Jones, N. P. (2000). *Kinder training: Play-based teacher consultation to promote the adjustment and achievement of discouraged students*. Norcross, GA: Kid Choice.

White, J., & Flynt, M. (1999). Play groups in elementary school. In D. S. Sweeney & L. E. Homeyer (Eds.), *Group play therapy: How to do it, how it works, whom it's best for*. San Francisco, CA: Jossey Bass.

White, J., Flynt, M., & Draper, K. (1997) Kinder therapy: Teachers as therapeutic agents. *International Journal of Play Therapy, 6*(2), 33–49.

White, J., Flynt, M., & Draper, K. (1997). Kinder therapy: Teachers as therapeutic agents. *International Journal of Play Therapy, 2*(6), 33–49.

Ziomek-Daigle, J., McMahon, H. G., & Paisley, P. O. (2008) Adlerian-based interventions for professional school counselors serving as both counselors and educational leaders. *Journal of Individual Psychology, 64*(4), 450–467.

CHAPTER 8

Chalk Talk—Attention Deficit Hyperactivity Disorder

Excuse or Epidemic

Rachel Ainsworth

INTRODUCTION

Attention Deficit Hyperactivity Disorder (ADHD) is one of the most commonly diagnosed neurological disorders in children.[1] Over the past decade, ADHD diagnoses have increased approximately five percent per year.[2] In a 2012 Centers for Disease Control and Prevention (CDC) study, more than five million children ages three to seventeen were diagnosed with ADHD in the United States.[3]

The CDC determined that boys are nearly three times more likely than girls to be diagnosed with ADHD; Hispanic children are less likely to be diagnosed with ADHD than non-Hispanic children; and children raised by a single-mother are more likely to have ADHD than children raised by

1 *Facts About ADHD*, Attention—Deficit/Hyperactivity Disorder (ADHD). Centers for Disease Control and Prevention (Sep. 29, 2014), http://www.cdc.gov/ncbddd/adhd/facts.html.

2 *Data & Statistics*, Attention—Deficit/Hyperactivity Disorder (ADHD). Centers for Disease Control and Prevention (Sep. 29, 2014), http://www.cdc.gov/ncbddd/adhd/data.html.

3 Barbara Bloom et al., *Summary Health Statistics for U.S. Children: National Health Interview Survey, 2012*, Vital and Health Statistics Report (Dec. 2013) http//www.cdc.gov/nchs/data/series/sr_10/sr10_258.pdf.

two parents.[4] Additionally, southern states lead the nation in children's ADHD diagnoses.[5] At almost nineteen percent, Kentucky has the highest percentage of ADHD diagnoses in children.[6]

The recent influx of ADHD diagnoses in the United States has created dangerous dependencies on ADHD medication and has manifested a culture where many parents and teachers are more inclined to seek an ADHD diagnosis and administer ADHD medication than to eliminate unwanted behaviors through exercise and behavioral treatments.[7] For example, in Kentucky from 2009 to 2010, seventy-eight percent of children diagnosed with ADHD had taken corrective medication within a week of the survey, as compared to forty-five percent of ADHD diagnosed children that had received behavioral treatment within the last year. [8]

Inconsistent and subjective ADHD diagnoses and the prescription of stimulant medications for students' misbehavior or inattention are detrimental to all students, including those not diagnosed with ADHD. Those who are diagnosed with ADHD and rely on stimulant medication and/or disability accommodations may be kept from fully learning valuable lessons of self-control, accountability, and coping mechanisms that could provide for a more prepared, stable, and healthy lifestyle. Additionally, college students diagnosed with ADHD may be provided with excessive classroom and exam disability accommodations, arguably placing other students in a disadvantage in classroom settings.

Section II of this article will discuss the science behind ADHD and the cause of increasing diagnoses. Section III will examine how ADHD causes detrimental effects in classroom settings, particularly in university settings. Section IV will discuss how courts have ruled on ADHD issues in the classroom, and Section V will conclude with suggestions on how to maintain fair classroom settings apart from unnecessary accommodations for those students with unfounded diagnoses of ADHD.

---

4 *Id.*

5 *Data & Statistics, supra note* 2.

6 Laura Ungar, *Kentucky Tops U.S. for ADHD*, The Courier Journal (May 4, 2014), http://www.courier-journal.com/story/life/wellness/health/2014/05/02/kentucky-tops-us-adhd/8564911/.

7 John Breeding, *Does ADHD Even Exist?: The Ritalin Sham,* THE NATURAL CHILD PROJECT (July 2000), http://www.naturalchild.org/guest/john_breeding.html.

8 *Data & Statistics, supra note* 2.

THE SCIENCE BEHIND ADHD

ADHD is a common neurological disorder, usually diagnosed during childhood, that can continue through adolescence and adulthood.[9] The most prevalent symptoms of ADHD are exemplified by a student's classroom behavior and include difficulty staying focused, paying attention and controlling behavior, as well as hyperactivity.[10] Physical manifestations of ADHD include fidgeting, excessive talking, blurting inappropriate comments, and interrupting the activities of others.[11] Students who suffer from ADHD are more likely to struggle in school due to inattention, missing or misunderstanding information and instruction, not listening, and becoming disinterested.[12]

However, patients presenting with symptoms of ADHD tendencies may interact differently in individualized settings; therefore, doctors are not often fully able to evaluate reported behaviors of the patient in the clinical setting.[13] Doctors will instead ask questions to determine if the behaviors are excessive, if the behaviors affect all aspects of the patient's life, if the behaviors are more prevalent in that patient compared with the patient's peers, or how long the behaviors have been occurring[14] As a result, doctors' diagnoses typically are based on subjective evidence, including comments from parents, teachers, school counselors, and coaches regarding the patient's behaviors.[15]

Inconsistent and subjective ADHD diagnostic procedures are major factors in the increase of ADHD diagnoses.[16] A Ruhr-Universitaet-Bochum 2012 study concluded that ADHD is over-diagnosed due to heuristic-based diagnoses and that "in order to avoid a misdiagnosis of ADHD and premature treatment, it is crucial for therapists not to rely on the intuition [and] instead to strictly adhere to defined, established

---

9 *Attention Deficit Hyperactivity Disorder*, U.S. Dep't of Health and Human Servs., Nat'l Inst. of Mental Health, http://www.nimh.nih.gov/health/publications/attentiondeficit-hyperactivity-disorder/index.shtml (last visited Nov. 1, 2014).

10 *Id.*

11 *Id.*

12 *Id.*

13 *Id.*

14 *Id.*

15 *Id.*

16 Breeding, *supra* note 7.

diagnostic criteria."[17] Moreover, the Pope Center for Higher Education Policy reported that since there is no single test to determine whether a patint suffers from ADHD, "there can be—and there is—great variance in the diagnoses from specialist to specialist and from demographic group to demographic group."[18]

Because there is no cure for ADHD, stimulants such as methylphenidate and amphetamines are prescribed to neutralize ADHD symptoms to "activate brain circuits that support attention and focused behavior, thus reducing hyperactivity."[19] These medications have serious side effects, including decreased appetite, irritability, insomnia, and an increased potential for narcotic substance addiction and abuse.[20] The long-term effects of stimulant use are under-researched and unknown.[21] Nonetheless, over two-thirds of children and teens diagnosed with ADHD are on medication to suppress their symptoms.[22]

ADHD IN THE CLASSROOM

Under the Americans with Disabilities Act of 1990 (ADA), the Individuals with Disabilities Education Improvement Act of 1997 (IDEA), and the Rehabilitation Act of 1973, disabled students "must be provided with services, monitoring, assessment, and other aspects of treatment in publicly funded education."[23] Therefore, a multitude of schools and universities will provide disability accommodations for students with ADHD, whether as required by federal law or as determined by a school administrator.[24] However, because of the lack of uniformity in diagnosing

---

17 *ADHD is Over-diagnosed, Experts Say,* SCIENCE DAILY (Mar. 30, 2012), http://www.sciencedaily.com/releases/2012/03/120330081735.htm

18 Melana Z. Vickers, *Accommodating College Student with Leaming Disabilities: ADD, ADHD, and Dyslexia,* THE JOHN WILLIAM POPE CTR. FOR HIGHER EDUC. POLICY, 4, (March 2010), *available at* http://www.popecenter.org/acrobat/vickers-mar2010.pdf.

19 *Attention Deficit Hyperactivity Disorder, supra* note 9.

20 *Id.a*

21 William Pelham, *Public Health Issues in the Treatment of ADHD,* CTRS. FOR DISEASE CONTROL AND PREVENTION (June 1999), http://www.cdc.gov/ncbddd/adhd/workshops/treatment.html.

22 Amy Novotney, *Is It Really ADHD?,* AM. PSYCH. ASS'N (Apr. 2014), http://www.apa.org/monitor/2014/04/adhd.aspx.

23 Vickers, *supra* note 18, at 5.

24 *Id.*

ADHD and the growing number of students diagnosed with ADHD each year, school administrators must be certain that classroom disability accommodations for ADHD are fair reflections of each student's impairment.

At the university level, the increase of misdiagnosed ADHD students has infiltrated universities' disability centers, as many students who received ADHD disability accommodations in the K-12 setting apply for similar accommodations in college.[25] At the University of North Carolina at Chapel Hill, the number of students with learning disabilities (including ADHD) who applied for disability accommodations grew by 766% from 1990 to 2010.[26]

Moreover, in the United States in 2003, fifty-one percent of learning disabled students, including students with ADHD, received college disability services.[27] In comparison with only nineteen percent of mobility-impaired students and twenty-two percent of visually or hearing-impaired students receiving college disability services, it is possible that students claiming ADHD disabilities are being overly diagnosed, and ultimately, overly accommodated.[28] Overly accommodating students diagnosed with ADHD may be limiting that student's preparation for professional environments, as such environments likely will not offer **ADHD** accommodations and "will require them to process information and to exercise professional judgment in a setting filled with distractions."[29]

At the University of Louisville Brandeis School of Law, students who have been diagnosed with ADHD are able to obtain disability accommodations.[30] Such accommodations are determined on a case-by-case basis by the University of Louisville Disability Resource Center.[31] Although the ADHD accommodation list is not exhaustive or limiting, common ADHD accommodations include supplemented class notes, the option of taking exams in a separately designated room, and additional time for exams, which is typically time-and-a-half.[32]

---

25 *Id.*

26 *Id.* at 7.

27 Id. at 6.

28 *Id.*

29 *Id.*

30 *Services for Students with Attention Deficit Hyperactivity Disorder*, UNIV. OF LOUISVILLE DISABILITY RES. CTR. (last visited Sep. 29, 2014), https://louisville.edu/disability/students/services-for-students-with-attention-deficit-hyperactivity-disorder.

31 *Id.*

32 *Id.*

Additionally, over two-thirds of those diagnosed with ADHD take ADHD medication.[33] Thus, ADHD students receiving classroom disability accommodations may likely be taking ADHD medication designed to enhance the ability to focus and perform, which arguably mitigates the need for accommodations. [34]

Therefore, ADHD disability accommodations may affect the fairness among students during college exams. As the number of ADHD diagnoses excessively increases, providing accommodations to possibly misdiagnosed ADHD students likely receiving the beneficial effects of ADHD medication can disadvantage non-disability accommodated students required to take their own notes in class and observe the prescribed time limits for exams. Moreover, anonymity in exam grading creates potential unfairness because while a professor is grading exams on a curve, he or she does not know which three-hour exam was completed with additional time.

ADHD IN THE COURTROOM

In determining whether ADHD constituted a disability in a classroom setting, the Sixth Circuit held in *Knapp* v. *City of Columbus* that firefighters claiming an ADHD disability under the Americans with Disabilities Act (ADA) did not qualify as disabled persons under the act.[35] In *Knapp*, firefighter plaintiffs requested various accommodations from the Columbus Civil Service Commission, including an accommodation for testing.[36] The court determined that the firefighters did not present sufficient evidence to prove that their ADHD diagnoses affected their daily lives enough for disability protection under the ADA.[37]

Additionally, the United States District Court for the Eastern District of Pennsylvania held in *Centennial Sch. Dist.* v. *Phil L. ex rel. Matthew L.* that there was "sufficient evidence to conclude that [plaintiff's] medication controlled his ADHD and enabled him to think and function as an average person. Thus, the medication

33 Novotney, *supra* note 22.

34 *See id.*

35 192 F. App'x 323 (6th Cir. 2006).

36 *Id.*

37 *Id.* at 330.

mitigated [his] disability."[38] This illustrates a court's interpretation to support the consideration of ADHD medications as mitigating factors in determining whether a student's disability limits a major life activity in order to meet the requirements for special education.[39]

Similarly, the United States District Court for the Southern District of West Virginia determined whether an ADHD diagnosis qualified for additional time in medical school testing.[40] In *Price v. National Board of Medical Examiners*, three Marshall University Medical School students sought an injunction compelling the National Board of Medical Examiners to allot them more time and a separate room to take their board exam due to their alleged ADHD disabilities.[41] Although the court acknowledged that ADHD is an impairment potentially protected by the ADA, it held that "[those] students [did] not suffer from an impairment which substantially [limited] the life activity of learning in comparison with most people." Additionally, the court held that the plaintiffs had an average or greater than average learning ability and no evidence suggested that accommodations for the board exam were necessary.[42]

These courts were unwilling to require disability accommodations for plaintiffs with ADHD. In light of cases that held ADHD was not a disability that substantially limited life activities and recognized the mitigating effects of ADHD medications, school administrations must reevaluate ADHD accommodation policies to ensure that students receiving ADHD disability accommodations are not instead gaining advantages over other students.

ALTERNATIVES AND SUGGESTIONS

While the numbers of students diagnosed with other impairments remains steady, students diagnosed with ADHD continues to rise.[43] From 1981 to 2006, the percentage of students enrolled in K-12 public education diagnosed with a hearing, visual,

38 CIV.A. 08-982, 2010 WL 1174206 (E.D. Pa. Mar. 26, 2010).

39 *Id.*

40 Price v. Nat'l Bd. of Med. Exam'rs, 966 F. Supp. 419 (S.D.W. Va. 1997).

41 *Id.* at 427.

42 *Id.* at 424

43 Vickers, *supra* note 18, at 4.

orthopedic, or other impairment has varied only by 0.1 percent.[44] Students enrolled in K-12 public schools diagnosed with a speech or language impairment rose by only 0.1 percent.[45] In contrast, the percentage of students enrolled in K-12 public schools diagnosed with a learning disability, including ADHD, rose 3.6 percent.[46] Specifically, from 2003 to 2011, ADHD diagnoses alone have increased approximately five percent per year.[47]

To prevent over-diagnoses of ADHD, other alternatives must warrant additional research and consideration. These alternatives include methods to help young students expend their energies in constructive ways to promote attention and concentration before an ADHD diagnosis is necessary. For example, the American Academy of Pediatrics recognizes the importance of the exertion of energy in children, and therefore states that recess should not be withheld for punitive or academic reasons.[48]

Parents must also embrace alternatives to the immediate prescription of ADHD stimulant medication. David Stein, the author of *Unraveling the ADD/ADHD Fiasco: Successful Parenting without Drugs*, offers a parent-training program that helps children permanently learn appropriate behavioral and cognitive skills without prescription drug therapy.[49] Stein suggests that we must stop labeling poorly behaved children as "sick" or "diseased" since many of the symptoms of ADHD are still within the normal limits of child conduct.[50] Other strategies, such as coaching, reminding, warning, helping, assisting, and coaxing, may abolish the need and desire for medical interventions.[51]

Additionally, research has shown that students exhibiting ADHD tendencies benefitted by a variety of classroom changes, such as a teacher posting, re-posting, and reviewing classroom rules, frequently praising good behavior, reducing the length of assignments, providing students with assignment options, and

---

44 *Id.*

45 *Id.*

46 *Id.*

47 *Data & Statistics, supra* note 2.

48 Robert Murray & Catherine Ramstatter, *The Crucial Role of Recess in School*, American Academy of Pediatrics (2012), *available at* http://pediatrics.aappublications.org/content/131/1/183.full. pdf.

49 David B. Stein, Unraveling the ADD/ADHD Fiasco: Successful Parenting without Drugs 122 (2001).

50 *Id.* at 50.

51 *Id.* at 93.

reinforcing good behavior with the students' preferred activities.[52] Self-regulation, which encouraged the students to evaluate and monitor their own behaviors, improved their organizational skills.[53] Furthermore, a collaborative approach between school administrators, parents, and teachers to monitor and intervene the students' unwanted behaviors was beneficial to behavior improvement.[54] Therefore, as ADHD diagnoses continue to rampantly increase, it is possible that addressing unwanted behaviors during children's earlier development may avoid improper ADHD diagnoses, unnecessary stimulant prescriptions, and allow for more consistency in disability accommodations for properly diagnosed ADHD students.

Students claiming an ADHD disability should be held to stricter standards for receiving classroom disability accommodations. Doctors, parents, and school administrators must become more informed of the realities of ADHD over-diagnoses in order to ensure that disability accommodations are allotted fairly. To better guarantee that a student presenting with ADHD symptoms is substantially limited by ADHD to justify the allowance of disability accommodations, the mitigating effects of ADHD medication must also be considered.

Additionally, the Pope Center for Higher Education Policy suggested that "schools should have strict standards for determining eligibility and produce data on the numbers of accommodations granted, refused, and appealed per year," arguing that such reports would maintain student privacy but would also assist in exposing ADHD accommodation inconsistencies.[55]

CONCLUSION

The purpose of this note is not to completely discredit ADHD as a medical condition. However, there is currently a high propensity for the over-diagnosis of ADHD. Today's overly broad and inconsistent ADHD diagnostic procedures allow for

---

52 George J. DuPaul et al., *ADHD In the Classroom: Effective Intervention Strategies*, 50 Theory Into Practice 35, 35–42 (Jan. 2011), *available at* http://www.tandfonline.com/doi/pdf/ 10.1080/00405841.201 1.534935.

53 *Id.* at 37–38.

54 *Id.* at 39–40.

55 Vickers, *supra* note 18, at 14.

unnecessary diagnoses and stimulant prescriptions and ultimately result in unfair classroom settings through excessive disability accommodations.

Students' educations are at stake in these decisions, and there must be more research on the appropriateness of current ADHD diagnostic procedures and availability of classroom disability accommodations for ADHD. Before turning more students into victims of the ADHD epidemic, we must consider the consequences and possible alternatives to overly broad ADHD diagnoses and classroom accommodations.

CHAPTER 9

Preventing Relational Aggression in Schools Everyday Program

A Preliminary Evaluation of Acceptability and Impact

Stephen S. Leff, Tracy Evian Waasdorp, Brooke Paskewich, Rebecca Lakin Gullan, Abbas F. Jawad, Julie Paquette MacEvoy, Betsy E. Feinberg and Thomas J. Power

ABSTRACT

Despite recent research suggesting that relationally aggressive behaviors occur frequently and may lead to physically aggressive actions within urban school settings, there has been little prior research to develop and evaluate relational aggression prevention efforts within the urban schools. The current article describes the development and preliminary evaluation of the Preventing Relational Aggression in Schools Everyday (PRAISE) Program. PRAISE is a 20-session classroom-based universal prevention program, designed to be appropriate and responsive to the needs of youth within the urban school context. Results suggest strong acceptability for the program and feasibility of implementation. Further, the program was especially beneficial for girls. For instance, girls in classrooms randomly assigned to the PRAISE Program

Stephen S. Leff, et al., "The Preventing Relational Aggression in Schools Everyday Program: A Preliminary Evaluation of Acceptability and Impact," *School Psychology Review*, vol. 39, no. 4, pp. 569-586.

demonstrated higher levels of knowledge for social information processing and anger management techniques and lower levels of relational aggression following treatment as compared to similar girls randomly assigned to a no-treatment control condition. Further, relationally aggressive girls exhibited similar benefits from the program (greater knowledge and lower levels of relational aggression) plus lower levels of overt aggression following treatment as compared to relationally aggressive girls within the control classrooms. In contrast, the program was not associated with improvements for boys across most measures. The significance and implications of the findings for research and practice are discussed.

Although physical aggression, such as hitting, pushing, and threatening others, has long been recognized as a problem among school-age youth (see Leff, Power, Manz, Costigan, & Nabors, 2001; Nansel et al., 2001), and especially among young males (Crick & Grotpeter, 1995), there has been a more recent focus on the nonphysical forms of aggression (Card, Stucky, Sawalani, & Little, 2008; Crick & Grotpeter, 1995), such as manipulating others' social reputation through rumor spreading, threats of friendship withdrawal, and social exclusion (e.g., Björkqvist, Osterman, & Kaukiainen, 1992; Crick, 1995; French, Jansen, & Pidada, 2002; Galen & Underwood, 1997; Giles & Heyman, 2005). Crick and Grotpeter (1995) termed these behaviors *relational aggression* to emphasize that the function of these behaviors is to damage others' relationships.[1]

A number of studies have found that relational aggression occurs often among youth and is viewed as distressing and harmful, especially among girls (Crick, 1995; Galen & Underwood, 1997; Leff, Kupersmidt, & Power, 2003; Murray-Close, Ostrov, & Crick, 2007). Over the past 15 years there have been numerous studies demonstrating that relational aggression is associated with peer difficulties, social problem-solving deficits, internalizing problems, and psychosocial adjustment difficulties (see Card et al., 2008 for a meta-analysis). Relational aggression perpetration in school-age youth is relatively stable over time (Crick, 1996; Kuppens,

1 Although researchers have often used the terms *aggression* and *bullying* interchangeably, peer aggression is a broader construct that is defined as any negative action directed toward another peer or group of peers when angry or upset. Bullying represents a subset of aggressive behaviors in which the negative action occurs repeatedly over time and when there is a power differential between the bully and victim, either physically or socially (see Merrell, Gueldner, Ross, & Isava, 2008). Thus, all bullying behaviors are by definition aggression, although not all aggression is bullying.

Grietens, Onghena, Michiels, & Subramanian, 2008; Ostrov & Crick, 2007) and may be associated with a range of mental health disorders as the youth reach adolescence and early adulthood (Geiger & Crick, 2001; Werner & Crick, 1999). The extant research supports that girls are more likely than boys to express their anger through relationally, as opposed to physically, aggressive behaviors and that girls are more distressed by these behaviors (Crick, 1995; Galen & Underwood, 1997; Leff et al., 2003, Murray-Close et al., 2007; Waasdorp, Bagdi, & Bradshaw, 2010). Consequently, much of the literature on relational aggression has focused on girls. However, recent studies indicate that relational aggression impacts boys' relationships quite frequently as well (Juliano, Werner, & Cassidy, 2006; Swearer, 2008; Waasdorp et al., 2010), suggesting that boys would also benefit from programming for relational aggression.

In addition to the impact that relational aggression can have on individuals, recent studies suggest that it also has an impact on the broader school climate. For example, research has shown that in schools with higher levels of relational aggression, students feel less safe (Goldstein, Young, & Boyd, 2008). Further, students are more likely to use relationally aggressive strategies to solve problems in classrooms with higher overall levels of relationally aggressive behaviors (Kuppens et al., 2008). This is particularly troubling for students in schools located in urban, low-income communities. Students in these schools are already at an increased risk for school and community violence (Guerra, Huesmann, & Spindler, 2003; Morales & Guerra, 2006). In addition, relational aggression occurs frequently and often leads to physical aggression within the urban school context (Leff et al., 2009; Talbott, Celinska, Simpson, & Coe, 2002; Waasdorp et al., 2010). Although there are universal violence prevention programs implemented in inner-city schools, few incorporate relational forms of aggression (Leff et al., 2001). As such, additional programming for inner-city, minority youth is needed.

Aggression prevention programs designed for physically aggressive youth often include a social information processing component. Social information processing (SIP) is one of the strongest factors in the development and maintenance of aggression (see Orbio de Castro, Veerman, Koops, Bosch, & Monshouwer, 2002), and considerable research has documented that physical aggressors are deficient at all SIP steps (see Vasey, Dangleish, & Silverman, 2003). The reformulated SIP model posits that all youth process social situations in six sequential steps that interact with their biological predispositions, social schemas, and memories for past events to influence their behavior (Crick & Dodge, 1994). The six sequential steps that influence the response to each social situation are as follows: encoding of social cues, interpretation of cues, clarification of social goals, response access, response decision, and finally, behavioral enactment (see Crick & Dodge, 1994 for a detailed discussion of each step). Researchers have begun to examine whether relational aggressors exhibit social processing deficits similar to physically aggressive youth. For example, studies show that relationally aggressive youth, as compared with nonrelationally aggressive youth, experience a deficit at the second SIP step, and appear more likely to exhibit a hostile attributional bias (e.g., Crick, 1995; Crick, Grotpeter, & Bigbee, 2002; Delveaux & Daniels, 2000; Leff et al., 2003). Further, at SIP Step 4, they appraise aggressive solutions as positive (Crick & Werner, 1998), which may make them prone to respond more negatively towards others.

Taken together, the aforementioned findings regarding relational aggression, the broader school context, and SIP can help inform effective school-based programming. First, in order for school-based prevention programs to be most effective, they should take into account the important systemic and contextual factors related to aggression, such as the school classroom and race/ethnicity, in conjunction with the inclusion of all forms of aggression (Card et al., 2008; Murray-Close et al., 2007; Swearer, Espelage, Vaillancourt, & Hymel, 2010). Second, research suggests that designing interventions for all forms of aggressive behavior is critical. Despite this, however, programming that focuses on the reduction of relational forms of aggression is scarce. In fact, the majority of school-based aggression prevention and intervention efforts have been designed for overt (i.e., direct physical and verbal) aggression and have generally not been effective in preventing problems among girls (see Leff et al., 2001). Finally, programming for the reduction of all forms of aggression would likely benefit from incorporating social cognitive retraining into the curriculum.

In addition to acknowledging the aforementioned issues in creating a universal aggression prevention program, it is also important to adapt the interventions for use across different cultures and contexts. A participatory action research (PAR) approach can be beneficial in these efforts. This approach combines empirically based intervention techniques and strategies with input from key school and community stakeholders (see Leff, Costigan, Power, 2004; Nastasi et al., 2000). Using a PAR approach often empowers minority participants such that they can become involved in the research intervention and help to ensure that the resultant product is acceptable, meaningful, and respectful to the local community (Hughes, 2002; Leff et al., 2006). Given that urban minority populations have often felt disenfranchised and potentially disrespected by many prior research projects (e.g., Fantuzzo, Coolahan, & Weiss, 1997; Leff et al., 2006), a PAR approach holds particular promise for designing programs and for ensuring that they are culturally sensitive for particular ethnic minority groups.

The Friend to Friend Program (F2F), which focuses on aggression reduction and social skills promotion, was designed by using the PAR approach. As such, best practice, empirically supported techniques were adapted by meeting with stakeholder groups of youth, teachers, and parents in order to meet the specific needs of urban African American third-through fifth-grade relationally aggressive girls (Leff, Angelucci et al., 2007). In addition to enabling F2F to be one of the first interventions to address both relational and physical aggression among urban African American girls, the use of PAR also resulted in the design of culturally specific cartoons, videos, and role-plays (see Leff et al., 2006). F2F has been found to be highly acceptable to participants and was associated with decreases in participant's levels of relational and overt aggression, hostile attributions, and feelings of loneliness (Leff, Angelucci et al., 2007; Leff et al., 2009).

Teachers who participated in the F2F evaluation study expressed their desire for the program to be modified for implementation with all students in the classroom setting instead of with only high-risk girls in a pull-out group format. Considering this feedback and the recent literature illustrating the importance of the school classroom and the impact of relational aggression on boys, a universal adaptation of F2F was designed. The resulting program, called the Preventing Relational Aggression in Schools Everyday (PRAISE) Program, was based upon F2F and similarly combines a social cognitive retraining emphasis (e.g., Crick & Dodge, 1994), and an ecological/systems model of development (e.g., Bronfenbrenner, 1986).

OVERVIEW OF THE CURRENT STUDY

There were several goals in the current study. A primary goal of the study was to evaluate the acceptability and feasibility of the new program according to participating youth and teachers. Another primary goal was to conduct a preliminary evaluation of the effectiveness of PRAISE for girls, and especially relationally aggressive girls. We wished to see whether the program had similar positive effects for relationally aggressive girls as we had demonstrated in a previous study using the F2F-indicated group intervention. Specifically, we expected to find that relationally aggressive girls randomized to receive PRAISE within their classroom would have improved problem-solving skills (greater knowledge of social information processing steps and less of a hostile attributional bias) and lower levels of relational and overt aggression following treatment as compared to similar high-risk girls randomized to a no-treatment control classroom condition. In addition, we expected that PRAISE would be effective at improving problem solving and reducing or suppressing aggression over the school year for all girls. Finally, we wanted to explore whether this universal prevention program would demonstrate a similar pattern of findings for high-risk boys and all boys.

METHOD

RATIONALE FOR THE DEVELOPMENT OF THE PRAISE PROGRAM

The PRAISE Program was developed within the context of the F2F intervention (Leff, Angelucci et al., 2007; Leff et al., 2009). The research team first adapted the culturally specific cartoons used in F2F. That is, depictions of urban African American girls engaging in problem-solving strategies were created for boys as well. Next, researchers focused on adapting the F2F curriculum into a more comprehensive classroom-based intervention designed for boys and girls (PRAISE). Challenges in the transition from F2F to PRAISE included the following: (1) ensuring that materials and content were appropriate for presentation at the classroom level (as opposed to within a small group) and for nonaggressive girls and all boys (as opposed to only aggressive girls); (2) including sessions related to empathy awareness, perspective taking, and responding as the bystander of aggression, based on current research and well-known aggression and bullying prevention programming (e.g., Coping Power Program, Lochman & Wells, 2003, and Lochman & Wells, 2004; Bullying Prevention Program, Olweus, 1991; Second Step, Frey, Nolen, Van Schoiack-Edstrom, & Hirschstein, 2005, and Van Schoiack-Edstrom, Frey, & Beland, 2002); and (3) collapsing the social-cognitive retraining components of F2F into fewer sessions to leave time and space for sessions on the three new aforementioned topics.

In sum, PRAISE and F2F share similar core components, yet differ in several important ways. For example, F2F and PRAISE both address relational and physical subtypes of aggression and introduce the locations where these problems commonly occur. Following a social-cognitive retraining model, both programs help students explore and practice the identification of feelings, signs of physiological arousal, calming strategies, interpreting intentions of others, and generating and evaluating alternative behaviors to enact. So that PRAISE can also focus on the three new topics aforementioned, it dedicates 6 sessions to social-cognitive retraining, as compared to 10 sessions in F2F. PRAISE and F2F also focus on applying social-cognitive strategies to rumors and peer entry situations (4 vs. 3 sessions, respectively). In addition, PRAISE offers curriculum not included in F2F, such as empathy building, perspective taking, being a bystander in conflict situations, and developing a class plan to prevent or reduce the harm of aggression (9 sessions total). Finally, another difference between F2F and PRAISE is that F2F has a more explicit focus on leadership promotion, as girls participating in the small-group intervention assist group leaders in conducting 8 classroom-based sessions. See Table 9.1 for a more detailed comparison of the characteristics of the F2F and PRAISE programs, and Table 9.2 for more specific information about the PRAISE curriculum.

MODIFICATION OF F2F CURRICULUM IN ORDER TO DESIGN PRAISE

Three steps were taken to appropriately modify F2F for the classroom-wide PRAISE Program: (1) conduct an open pilot trial of the PRAISE Program, (2) conduct focus groups with ongoing participants from the initial open pilot trial, and (3) integrate feedback from a diverse group of key stakeholders.

Open pilot study. An initial open pilot study was conducted with four classrooms (one 3rd-grade, one 4th-grade, and two 5th-grade classrooms) across two schools. Results suggested that PRAISE would be highly acceptable to students and teachers and feasible to implement within the classroom context (Leff, Paskewich, & Gullan, 2008). An initial evaluation of program impact across all students within the four participating classrooms suggested that PRAISE may be associated with significant decreases in relational aggression and significant improvements in prosocial behavior and likability as rated by the teacher (Leff et al., 2008). Effect sizes for these findings were generally in the low to moderate range.

Focus groups. A series of focus groups with ongoing participants in the open pilot study were conducted on alternating weeks. Six boys and six girls provided feedback on specific aspects of program content and process (Leff et al., 2008). Children were chosen to participate in focus groups if they had high rates of school

TABLE 9.1. PROGRAM CHARACTERISTICS OF THE F2F AND PRAISE PROGRAMS

PROGRAM CHARACTERISTICS	F2F	PRAISE
Type	Indicated Preventative intervention	Universal Preventative intervention
Mode of operation	School based Pull-out small group	School based Classroom based
Format	20 small group sessions conducted over lunch-recess period 8 classroom sessions Conducted twice per week 40-min sessions	20 classroom sessions Conducted twice per week 40-min sessions
Program facilitators	1 master's-level research therapist 1 teacher partner	3 master's-level research therapists 1 teacher partner
Participants	Low socioeconomic status Inner city Predominantly African American 3rd–5th grade Relationally aggressive girls plus several nonaggressive positive role models	Low socioeconomic status Inner city Predominantly African American 3rd–4th grade All girls and boys
Program targets	Social-cognitive retraining	Social-cognitive retraining Empathy building Perspective-taking skills Responding as bystander of aggression
Leadership component	Targeted aggressors serve as youth leaders and cofacilitate 8 classroom sessions with research therapist and teacher	Not a primary focus

Note. F2F = Friend to Friend; PRAISE = Preventing Relational Aggression in Schools Everyday Program.

attendance, their teachers thought they would openly share their opinions, and they did not have a best friend in the focus group. Focus groups, conducted by an experienced facilitator who had limited knowledge of PRAISE, were audiotaped and transcribed by a research assistant. Then, following procedures outlined by Nastasi and Berg (1999), process notes were generated, the content was coded, cross-cutting themes were identified, and distribution tables were generated to indicate the frequency of comments pertaining to each theme.

Although a detailed description of the focus group results goes beyond the goals of the current article, several primary themes emerged across groups and gender. Participants indicated that they greatly enjoyed the program, thought it was respectful and fun, valued the teaching strategies and activities, greatly enjoyed learning through the modalities of videos, role-plays, and cartoons, and would recommend that others be involved in the program in the future. In addition, both boys and girls felt the program was relevant and they indicated that their parents, grandparents, and same-age peers would find the program acceptable and relevant as well. In contrast, they indicated that middle schoolers (sixth grade and above) may think that the acronyms used for the strategies taught may be too juvenile and suggested making more cartoon and video illustrations of boys.

Key stakeholder feedback. An advisory board consisting of five teachers from three different schools and two community members was formed to discuss perceptions of the new program, how it could be most impactful, and what further modifications were needed. Advisory board members were chosen if they had some familiarity with the PRAISE Program and a strong understanding of the classroom, school, and/or home context of the urban elementary schools in which the projects were being implemented. Care was taken to include a diverse group of adults on the advisory board in terms of years of experience, ethnicity, and prior exposure to the program. Members of the advisory board affirmed the importance and cultural sensitivity of the primary content, modalities, and outcome evaluations. Specific suggestions for improvement included the following: (a) increasing the intensity of retraining participants on intentionality attributions; (b) developing video testimonials from prior participants discussing how they had benefited from the program; (c) changing some terminology to ensure relevance for both boys and girls (e.g., using the term *rumors* as opposed to *gossip*); (d) adding a session related to peer group entry that was part of F2F but not originally included in PRAISE (i.e., how to recognize which groups to approach and how best to attempt to enter them); (e) fine-tuning the presentation of sessions on perspective taking; and (f) helping teachers develop a classroom plan to prevent aggression in order to maximize its relevance to the urban school context.

Finalizing the curriculum. Based on advisory board feedback, several modifications were made to the curriculum. First, in order for youth to have more opportunities to try out new strategies, three sessions were added: (1) a second

TABLE 9.2. MAIN COMPONENTS AND SESSION OUTLINE FOR PRAISE PROGRAM

COMPONENT	DESCRIPTION
Introduction	
Session 1: Discussing purpose, structure, and expectations for the program	
Session 2: Considering different types of FMPs and settings in which FMPs occur	
Social-cognitive retraining	
Session 3: Understanding and identifying a range of feelings	
Session 4: Identifying body's warning signs when one is becoming angry	
Session 5: Developing strategies for coping with anger	
Session 6: Interpreting intentions of others	
Session 7: Practicing interpreting intentions of others	
Session 8: Generating and evaluating alternatives and choosing a response to enact	
Applying social-cognitive strategies to rumors and peer entry situations	
Session 9: Determining what a rumor is and the effects of rumors	
Session 10: Applying strategies for dealing with rumors	
Session 11: Understanding peer group entry and applying strategies to peer entry situations	
Empathy building and perspective taking	
Session 12: Review what feelings are and signs of physiological arousal	
Session 13: Exploring identification of feelings of others and introduce understanding other people's perspective	
Session 14: Exploring and practicing the difficulties and benefits of perspective taking	
Session 15: Practicing perspective taking using personal or common situations	
Helping recognize that everyone plays a role in aggression reduction and friendship promotion	
Session 16: Introducing the role of the bystander in conflict situations	
Session 17: Exploring feelings of bystanders and challenges in intervening as a bystander	
Session 18: Developing a class plan to prevent or reduce the harm of FMPs	
Session 19: Reviewing and fine-tuning the class plan	
Session 20: Reviewing all strategies and class plan; wrap-up and goodbyes	

Note. PRAISE = Preventing Relational Aggression in Schools Program; FMPs = friendship making problems.

session related to retraining participants on attributions of intent, (2) a session related to peer group entry, and (3) a second session related to perspective taking. One of the two review sessions was also removed, resulting in a 20-session PRAISE curriculum. Second, the cartoons depicting boys were expanded and revised in line with suggestions. Unfortunately, the research team was unable to make additional video illustrations of boys or video testimonials of former participants, which were useful ideas for future applications. Third, in order to apply content to both boys and girls, several terms and strategies were renamed (e.g., cartoons depicting girls jumping rope changed to boys playing basketball) and/or broader examples were used.

PARTICIPANTS IN PRELIMINARY STUDY OF PRAISE

An initial trial of PRAISE across ten 3rd- and 4th-grade classrooms within one large urban elementary school was conducted with the finalized PRAISE curriculum over the following year. All 3rd- and 4th-grade teachers agreed for their classrooms to be randomized to the intervention or control (regular education curriculum) condition, blocked by the number of relational and overt aggressors within the classroom (as determined through a peer nomination procedure explained in the next section). All students in those classrooms ($n = 290$) were given the opportunity to participate in pre- and postassessment of the program.[2] All youth who provided child assent and parent permission ($n = 227$; 78%) participated in this evaluation of PRAISE.[3] The participating sample was comprised of 48.5% girls ($n = 110$) and 51.5% boys ($n = 117$). Of the 227, 115 children were in the intervention (drawn from three 3rd-grade and two 4th-grade classrooms) and 112 were in the control group (drawn from two 3rd-grade and three 4th-grade classrooms). On average, children were aged 113.2 months ($SD = 10.5$). Seventy-four percent of the sample were African American, 9% were biracial including African American, 5% were European American, and 12% included other ethnic minorities (e.g., Asian, Native American, Hispanic/Latino/Latina). With regard to the number of aggressors, 66.7% ($n = 78$) of males and 80.9% ($n = 89$) of females were designated as *not* being aggressive by the peer nomination procedures. No girls displayed only overt aggression, 11.8% of girls ($n = 13$) displayed only relational aggression, and 7.3% of girls ($n = 8$) displayed both relational and overt aggression.[4] Of the 21 relationally aggressive girls, 13 were in the intervention

---

2 As per the Children's Hospital of Philadelphia institutional review board, all students in intervention classes received the PRAISE Program as part of their regular school day but only those who provided parental permission in either intervention or control classrooms completed pre- and postevaluations.

3 At postintervention, 17 of the 227 children were unavailable to complete measures (i.e., had changed schools, were absent on the days of post-testing).

4 For subsequent analyses, *relationally aggressive girls* referred to the 21 girls with elevated levels of relational aggression, some of whom also had elevated levels of overt aggression.

classrooms and 8 were in control classrooms. Among boys, 7.7% ($n = 9$) exhibited only overt aggression, 4.3% displayed only relational aggression ($n = 5$), and 21.4% ($n = 25$) displayed both relational and overt aggression. Of the 39 aggressive boys, 21 were in the intervention classrooms and 18 were in control classrooms.

METHODS AND PROCEDURES

Peer nominations. A peer nomination procedure developed by Crick and Grotpeter (1995) was used to assess each child's level of relational aggression (5 items), overt aggression (3 items), and prosocial behavior (2 items) during the baseline period (Crick & Grotpeter, 1995; Leff et al., 2009). The concurrent and predictive validity, test–retest reliability, and the stability of the subscales across time have been well established across many different samples (e.g., Crick & Grotpeter, 1995; Olweus, 1991; Kupersmidt & Coie, 1990). In addition, several investigations have demonstrated strong correlations between peer nomination methods and teacher report indices of behavior for African American youth (Coie & Dodge, 1988; Hudley, 1993). An unlimited peer nomination procedure was used, whereby students could nominate as many youth within their grade that they felt met the behavioral description. This decision was based on research demonstrating that this approach demonstrates slightly stronger psychometric properties than the traditional limited nomination procedure (e.g., Terry, 2000).

Raw score nominations on the five items corresponding to relational aggression were standardized within each grade (the nominating group), resulting in a final relational aggression z score for each child. A parallel process was used to determine each child's z score related to overt aggression and prosocial behavior. Given that youth with moderate elevations on peer nominations of relational aggression ($z > 0.50$) exhibit high levels of teacher-reported relational aggression (see Leff et al., 2009), we chose to use a z-score cutoff point of .50 to designate students as being *relationally* and/or *overtly aggressive* for the purposes of the current study. As described previously, the number of relationally and overtly aggressive boys and girls within each classroom was also used as a blocking variable as part of the random assignment procedure.

Teacher reports of aggression. Students' levels of relational and overt aggression were determined by the teachers' completion of the Children's Social Behavior Questionnaire (Crick, 1996) at both pre- and postintervention periods. The primary subscales of the CSB have demonstrated strong reliability and validity for an ethnically diverse sample of youth (e.g., Crick, 1996), and the measure has been used in a number of studies with low-income youth (e.g., Crick, Murray-Close, & Woods, 2005; Leff et al., 2009; Murray-Close, Crick, & Galotti, 2006). In the current study, subscales demonstrated adequate internal consistency: 7-item Relational Aggression subscale ($\alpha = .95$) and 4-item Overt Aggression subscale ($\alpha = .94$).[5]

Cartoon-based hostile attributional bias measure. A widely used written vignette-based hostile attributional bias measure (Crick, 1995, Crick et al., 2002) was recently adapted to cartoons for use with urban African American boys and girls. The cartoon-based version is presented simultaneously with the written vignettes and is used to determine a hostile attribution bias in both relationally and instrumentally/overtly provocative social situations. This adapted measure has demonstrated strong psychometric properties and higher levels of acceptability among urban predominately African American girls (Leff et al., 2006) and African American boys (Leff, Simeral, Khera, & Grossman, 2007) than the traditional written vignette measure. This measure was used at both pre- and postintervention periods.

Knowledge of Anger Problem Solving (Leff, Cassano, MacEvoy, & Costigan, 2010). This 15-item multiple-choice test was designed to assess students' general knowledge of the steps underlying the social information processing model of aggression and of anger management techniques (Crick & Dodge, 1996). As compared to more traditional vignette measures, which determine one's interpretation of and reaction to a social situation (e.g., Crick, 1995; Crick et al., 2002), the Knowledge of Anger Problem Solving assesses a youth's general understanding of social problem-solving steps. The Knowledge of Anger Problem Solving has demonstrated strong ecological and convergent validity and adequate test–retest reliability among urban African American girls and boys (Leff et al., in press). In the current study, the Knowledge of Anger Problem Solving was used at pre- and postintervention time periods.

Intervention integrity. An integrity monitoring system was designed based upon previous systems developed through PAR (see Gullan, Feinberg, Freedman, Jawad, & Leff, 2009). It included several procedural integrity items from each session (i.e., the three or four key content areas to cover) and process items (i.e., student enthusiasm

---

5 Teacher reports of relational aggression were significantly correlated with peer nominations of relational aggression ($r = .36, p < .001$). Teacher reports of overt aggression were also significantly correlated with peer nominations of overt aggression ($r = .58, p < .001$).

in session, facilitator responsiveness to students and teachers, facilitators working well together, students' behavior, and so on). All items were rated through live observations on a 3-point scale that included 0 = *Not Implemented*, 1 = *Partially Implemented*, and 2 = *Fully Implemented*. Two coders were trained to criterion on the integrity monitoring system and then a random selection procedure was used to choose sessions to observe both individually and as a pair to determine inter-rater reliability. Approximately 50% of randomly selected sessions were coded, almost all of which were coded by the pair for inter-rater reliability.

Intervention acceptability and feasibility. A student acceptability questionnaire was developed for PRAISE based on previous acceptability measures used with urban intervention participants (Leff et al., 2009). Participants were asked to rate 16 items according to a 4-point scale including 1 = *Strongly Agree* (Denoting Strong Acceptability), 2 = *Agree* (Denoting Acceptability), 3 = *Disagree* (Denoting Unacceptability), and 4 = *Strongly Disagree* (Denoting Strong Unacceptability). Good internal consistency was found ($\alpha = .93$).

A teacher acceptability and feasibility questionnaire was also developed for PRAISE based on previous research (Leff et al., 2009). The three subscales, consisting of a total of 29 items, demonstrated adequate internal consistency in the current study: (1) teacher perception of student acceptability (13 items, $\alpha = .92$); (2) teacher acceptability (9 items; $\alpha = .71$); and (3) feasibility of program implementation (7 items, $\alpha = .89$).

RESULTS

OVERVIEW OF ANALYSES

First, we present descriptive analyses at the baseline period for boys and girls. Next, we present acceptability, feasibility, and integrity of the intervention. For our first aim, we explored the effects of the intervention using analyses of covariance (with pretreatment performance as covariate) to examine postintervention scores between treated and untreated relationally aggressive girls across all constructs of interest (i.e., knowledge, relational aggression, overt aggression, hostile attribution bias). Next, we examined the effects of the program comparing all girls in the treatment classrooms versus those who were not. For our final aim, we explored the effects of the program for all boys and high-risk boys. To control for Type 1 error rate, we used $p < .01$ as a cutoff when conducting analyses to account for the multiple comparisons.

DESCRIPTIVE ANALYSES AT BASELINE

Differences between boys and girls. At baseline, teacher CSB ratings indicated boys displayed higher levels of overt aggression ($M = 2.01$, $SD = 1.09$) than did girls ($M = 1.53$, $SD = 0.81$), $t(222) = -3.75$, $p < .001$. Likewise, according to peer nominations, boys were nominated as displaying more overt aggression ($M = 0.33$, $SD = 1.14$) than do girls ($M = -0.39$, $SD = 0.60$), $t(225) = -5.88$, $p < .001$. There were no significant differences between teachers ratings of boys' and girls' levels of relational aggression on the CSB ($M_{boys} = 1.80$, $SD = 0.87$; $M_{girls} = 1.70$, $SD = 0.93$). Similarly, there were also no significant gender differences in peer nominations of relational aggression ($M_{boys} = 0.07$, $SD = 1.06$; $M_{girls} = 0.06$, $SD = 0.92$). Boys displayed similar levels of a hostile attributional bias in relationally provocative social situations ($M = 4.41$, $SD = 2.50$) to the girls ($M = 4.93$, $SD = 2.80$) and in instrumentally provocative social situations ($M = 3.79$, $SD = 2.94$) as compared to the girls ($M = 3.57$, $SD = 3.05$). Finally, girls' knowledge for social information processing steps ($M = 6.64$, $SD = 2.67$) did not significantly differ from boys ($M = 6.13$, $SD = 2.26$).

Within-gender differences. On the CSB, girls displayed higher levels of relational than overt aggression, $t(109) = 2.70$, $p < .01$, and boys displayed higher levels of overt than relational aggression, $t(113) = -3.61$, $p < .001$. Similarly, peer nominations suggested that girls displayed more relational than overt aggression, $t(109) = -6.27$, $p < .001$, whereas boys were nominated as displaying more overt than relational aggression, $t(116) = 5.31$, $p < .001$. Girls displayed higher levels of hostile attributional biases in relationally provocative situations than instrumentally provocative situations, $t(105) = 5.95$, $p < .001$.

ACCEPTABILITY AND FEASIBILITY

The program was viewed as acceptable by participating girls ($M = 1.72$, $SD = 0.59$) and boys ($M = 1.65$, $SD = 0.56$) on a 4-point scale ranging from 1 = *Strongly Agree/Highly Acceptable* to 4 = *Strongly Disagree/Highly Unacceptable.* Boys and girls did not seem to differ remarkably in their responses to individual items, as girls' acceptability scores ranged from 1.52 to 1.92 and boys' acceptability scores ranged from 1.41 to 1.89 across the 16 items on a 4-point scale. Aggressive girls (M = 1.85, SD = 0.46) and aggressive boys (M = 1.82, SD = 0.66) also demonstrated relatively high levels of acceptability, with no noticeable differences across individual items.

Teachers found the program acceptable (M = 1.69, SD = 0.27) and indicated that students would also find the program acceptable (M = 1.40, SD = 0.35). In addition, they rated the program as relatively feasible to implement (M = 1.97, SD = 0.66) on a 4-point scale ranging from 1 = *Highly Feasible* to 4 = *Highly Unfeasible*. Item-level analyses revealed some variability in responses to specific items on the feasibility subscale. For instance, teachers gave higher ratings to the item indicating that it was easy to communicate with PRAISE team members (M = 1.20, SD = 0.45) and to the item that it was easy for children to transition back and forth between PRAISE sessions and regular classroom instruction (M = 1.80, SD = 0.45). In contrast, ratings were generally lower and more variable on an item indicating that the duration of the program (20 weeks) was not too long (M = 2.40, SD = 1.14) and on an item indicating that the program did not disrupt daily classroom routines (M = 2.20, SD = 0.84).

INTEGRITY MONITORING

Integrity analyses across sessions suggested that cofacilitators (therapists and teachers) fully implemented the majority of core content components (94%) and process dimensions (74%). Inter-rater reliability between coders, defined as the percentage of exact agreements on the 3-point Likert rating system, was adequate across content (99%) and process (89%) items.

PRELIMINARY FINDINGS OF PRAISE

Effects for aggressive girls. As shown in Table 9.3, relationally aggressive girls within intervention classrooms had significantly higher post-treatment knowledge scores as compared to relationally aggressive girls within control classrooms after controlling for baseline levels. For the relationally aggressive girls in the intervention classrooms, knowledge significantly increased from pre- to postintervention, whereas relationally aggressive girls in the control classrooms demonstrated smaller gains in knowledge (see Table 9.3). With regard to levels of aggressive behavior, relationally

TABLE 9.3. MEANS AND STANDARD DEVIATIONS OF PRIMARY VARIABLES FOR ALL GIRLS AND FOR AGGRESSIVE GIRLS

	Pre-Intervention		Post-Intervention			
Outcome Variable	*M*	*SD*	*M*	*SD*	*F*(1, 19)	*d*
			Aggressive Girls			
Knowledge						
Intervention	7.69	2.59	10.46	2.37	8.0*	0.63
Control	5.14	1.77	6.29	2.06		
Relational aggression						
Intervention	1.93	0.81	2.11	1.22	11.3*	1.38
Control	1.93	1.07	3.42	1.42		
Overt aggression						
Intervention	1.60	0.75	1.48	0.60	51.8**	3.13
Control	2.13	1.13	3.43	1.24		
HAB_relational						
Intervention	4.62	2.81	5.85	2.97	0.65	0.05
Control	6.50	1.87	7.83	0.75		
HAB_overt						
Intervention	2.85	3.24	4.92	3.68	2.07	0.90[a]
Control	4.57	2.70	4.00	3.11		
			All Girls		*F*(1, 100)	*d*
Knowledge						
Intervention	6.41	2.62	9.53	2.77	40.0**	1.24
Control	6.98	2.75	7.02	2.74		
Relational aggression						
Intervention	1.83	0.98	1.88	1.20	7.4*	0.60
Control	1.42	0.67	2.06	1.23		
Overt aggression						
Intervention	1.56	0.80	1.75	0.91	1.48	0.29
Control	1.40	0.69	1.86	1.17		
HAB_relational						
Intervention	5.06	2.99	5.31	2.89	0.38	0.09
Control	4.85	2.55	4.90	2.85		
HAB_overt						
Intervention	3.82	3.15	4.56	3.48	2.13	0.22
Control	3.36	3.08	3.48	3.21		

Note. Higher scores indicate greater knowledge of social information processing steps, and higher levels of relational aggression, overt aggression, and hostile attributional biases. HAB refers to hostile attribution bias.

[a] Although there was a relatively large effect size indicating that relationally aggressive girls in the intervention may have increased their hostile attributions in overtly aggressive situations as compared to girls in the control group, the nonsignificant finding ($p = .17$) raises questions about the validity of this result. Further, inspection of the data indicated that there was a disproportionate number of cases in the intervention condition (as compared to the control condition) who experienced a floor effect in their level of preintervention hostile attributions in overt situations, which may have contributed to this inconsistent pattern of results. When the youth who exhibited the floor effect were omitted from both groups, the effect size was $d = 0.43$.

* $p \leq .01$.

** $p < .001$.

aggressive girls in intervention classrooms had significantly lower levels of relational and overt aggression following treatment as compared to relationally aggressive girls in control classrooms after controlling for baseline levels (see Table 9.3). For relationally aggressive girls who received the intervention, levels of relational aggression increased minimally from baseline to postintervention, whereas levels of relational aggression increased markedly from baseline to postintervention for the control group. Further, relationally aggressive girls who received the intervention demonstrated a slight decrease in levels of overt aggression from pre- to postintervention, whereas levels of overt aggression increased substantially for the control group. There were no significant differences posttreatment for aggressive girls in intervention versus control classrooms on hostile attributional biases after controlling for pretreatment levels.

Effects for all girls. All girls within intervention classrooms had significantly higher scores in knowledge for social information processing and anger management following treatment as compared to all girls in the control classrooms after controlling for pretreatment scores (see Table 9.3). Girls within intervention classrooms demonstrated increased knowledge scores pre- to post-treatment, whereas knowledge for girls within control classrooms stayed the same. Girls within intervention classrooms also had significantly lower relational aggression scores posttreatment then girls within control classrooms after accounting for baseline levels. Girls within intervention classrooms demonstrated the same level of relational aggression from baseline to post-treatment, whereas girls in the control group showed increases in relational aggression during the same time period (see Table 9.3). Girls in intervention classrooms, as compared to girls in control classrooms, exhibited similar levels of overt aggression and hostile attributional biases at post-treatment after taking into account pretreatment scores.

Effects for all boys and aggressive boys. For aggressive boys, there were no significant differences in knowledge, levels of overt and relational aggression, or hostile attributions between intervention and control classrooms at posttreatment after controlling for baseline levels. All boys within intervention classrooms had significantly higher knowledge scores posttreatment as compared to boys within control classrooms after controlling for baseline knowledge scores, $F(1,108) = 15.5$, $p < .001$; $d = .58$). For boys in the intervention classrooms, knowledge increased from a mean of 6.41 ($SD = 2.31$) at baseline to a mean of 8.18 ($SD = 2.82$) post intervention. In contrast, for boys in the control classrooms, knowledge did not change considerably from a mean of 5.84 ($SD = 2.19$) at baseline to 6.11 ($SD = 2.42$) at posttreatment. There were no significant differences at posttreatment for intervention versus control boys with regard to relational and overt aggression, or hostile attributional biases.

DISCUSSION

The current study provides preliminary evidence of a culturally sensitive relational aggression prevention program for urban youth, specifically for girls. Further, the program was viewed as quite acceptable by participating youth and teachers, and was judged as relatively feasible to conduct within the busy urban classroom setting. Although the social cognitive retraining emphasis in PRAISE is not very different from a number of other classroom-based prevention programs (except for the emphasis on relational aggression), it is the modalities and engagement methods developed through PAR that allow for the content to be understood and appreciated by urban youth. For instance, the use of cartoons depicting urban African American girls and boys and role-plays created by youth of the same age illustrate how a PAR approach can be used to ensure that programs are culturally sensitive. This research is consistent with a number of prior studies suggesting that the use of a PAR approach leads to interventions that are well accepted and responsive to the needs of the partnering community (e.g., Israel, Schulz, Parker, & Becker, 1998; Leff et al., 2004; Nastasi et al., 2000). This type of approach may hold particular promise for under-resourced urban schools in which empirically supported prevention programs designed originally for suburban middle-class youth are often recommended without considering their applicability within the urban school setting.

Results of descriptive analyses comparing levels of relational and overt aggression between girls and boys are consistent with prior research suggesting that girls are more likely to display relationally as opposed to overtly aggressive behaviors, whereas boys are more apt to display their anger in overt and physical ways as compared to relational or social ways (see Card et al., 2008, and Crick & Grotpeter, 1995). We also found that boys are more overtly aggressive than girls, and that boys and girls have similar levels of relational aggression across teacher and peer report methods, which is consistent with a number of recent studies (Card et al., 2008; Kuppens et al., 2008; Smith & Gross, 2006). This is instructive for several reasons. First, most prior research studies comparing boys' and girls' rates of relational aggression have been conducted in nonurban and/or nonminority samples. Thus, our research within an under-resourced urban community suggests that relational aggression is a frequent occurrence for both boys and girls. Given recent research suggesting that relationally aggressive actions are viewed as extremely problematic (Leff et al., 2009; Talbott et al., 2002; Waasdorp et al., 2010), and often lead to more physical actions within urban minority samples (Talbott et al., 2002), the development of prevention programs addressing both forms of aggression for both genders is an important avenue of research.

The findings suggested that PRAISE may be beneficial to girls, and especially to high-risk relationally aggressive girls who are most in need of intervention. As hypothesized, findings from PRAISE are similar to the promising findings from F2F among high-risk girls. For instance, relationally aggressive girls whose classes were randomized to PRAISE experienced a relatively large aggression suppression effect (for both relational and overt aggression) as compared to relationally aggressive girls whose classes were randomized to the no-treatment control condition. Specifically, relationally aggressive girls in PRAISE exhibited no increase in problematic behaviors over the course of the intervention, whereas similar high-risk girls in control classrooms experienced a rather large worsening of relational and overt aggressive behavior. Similarly, all girls who received PRAISE experienced an aggression suppression effect related to relational aggression as compared to girls in the control condition. Prior studies examining the impact of promising aggression prevention programs have also found aggression suppression effects. For instance, two separate investigations of Second Step found aggression suppression effects (Cooke, Ford, Levine, Bourke, Newell, & Lapidus, 2007; Grossman et al., 1997). Further, researchers have found an increase in antisocial and aggressive behavior over the course of the school year for untreated elementary school students (Reid & Eddy, 1997; Taub, 2002). Given this, and the findings that students are more likely to use relationally aggressive strategies in classrooms with higher overall levels of relationally aggressive behaviors (Kuppens et al., 2008), the suppression of relational aggression across all girls suggests that this universal adaptation may impact the broader school climate over time.

The PRAISE Program was not associated with changes in levels of hostile attributional biases. This is somewhat surprising given research suggesting that deficits in SIP are a robust predictor of physically aggressive behavior and improvement in SIP has resulted in the reduction of physical aggression (Orbio de Castro et al., 2002; Vasey et al., 2003). Further, because aggressive girls participating in PRAISE demonstrated a strong aggression suppression effect for relational and overt aggression, we expected to see a corresponding change in hostile attributions. One possible reason such changes did not occur is that the focus on attribution retraining in PRAISE is less intensive than in indicated intervention programs. For instance, in the F2F Program (Leff, Angelucci et al., 2007; Leff et al., 2009), at-risk girls received 10 sessions involving attribution retraining and substantial individual attention, whereas at-risk girls in PRAISE received only 6 retraining sessions, which were classroom based. Future research could examine why hostile attributions are not being impacted by PRAISE and whether effects could be strengthened by providing additional support to high-risk youth. In general, it appears important to focus on the mechanisms by which aggression may be reduced in urban school-based prevention programs.

It is noteworthy, however, that despite no significant change in hostile attributions, substantial increases in knowledge of social information processing and anger management techniques were demonstrated by relationally aggressive girls and all girls who received PRAISE as compared to all girls in control classrooms. Given these strong findings, it would be beneficial to explore whether these changes in knowledge serve as a mediator to changes in aggressive behavior. Unfortunately, the small sample size in the current study made it impossible to explore a mediational model. Nevertheless, having an intervention presented within a classroom format may have some advantages to a pull-out group format with only high-risk girls. For instance, the teacher and all students in classrooms receiving PRAISE gained experience with the program and exposure to the principles and strategies related to aggression prevention and better problem solving. Although this may not immediately translate into a better outcomes, teachers become privy to program materials and strategies and are able to reinforce and practice them with their students. Programs delivered in a format such as PRAISE may therefore have a better chance of generalization and sustainability and it may be beneficial to examine effects over time.

The PRAISE Program was not particularly effective for boys. Although boys receiving the intervention demonstrated increased knowledge of social information processing steps and anger management techniques as compared to boys within the control condition, this did not translate into any type of aggression reduction or suppression effect. PRAISE may be less successful for boys because it was developed by expanding the F2F Program that was designed through an extensive partnership process specifically to address relational forms of aggression among girls (Leff, Angelucci et al., 2007; Leff et al., 2009). Even though the focus groups conducted during the adaptation phase of PRAISE indicated that boys found the materials and concepts to be enjoyable and important, the video illustrations were not able to be remade with male actors or to include mixed-gender groups. Perhaps this made the program less meaningful for boys. Another possibility is that although PRAISE addresses both forms of aggression, additional generalization strategies and supports for high-risk boys may be needed for them to benefit from the program. For example, research on physically aggressive urban boys has found that anger management within the context of competitive sports or activities is an important arena in which to intervene (see Stevenson, 2003). Thus, for programs such as PRAISE to be more meaningful or effective for boys, it may be important to put specific emphasis on helping them apply the problem-solving strategies within the context of competitive activities. It is also possible that conflicts among urban boys are qualitatively different than conflicts that occur among girls (Maccoby, 2004; Rose & Rudolph, 2006). Research suggests that boys more frequently aggress against peers outside of their friendship networks (i.e., acquaintances or strangers), whereas girls are more likely to use aggression within the context of their friendships (Crick & Nelson, 2002; Murray-Close et al., 2007; Turkel, 2007). Therefore, the intent and goals of using relational aggression may differ by gender (Maccoby, 2004; Rose & Rudolph, 2006). Finally, given that boys demonstrated no behavioral impact despite their strong acceptability ratings for PRAISE and suggestions of a knowledge effect, it would be helpful to talk with boys about what makes it difficult for them to put the strategies to use. Overall, better understanding these issues may help suggest ways of making the program more effective for boys and/or promoting the generalization of skills. Finally, future adaptations of PRAISE could incorporate more of an emphasis on building participants' leadership skills, similar to this focus within the F2F Program.

The current study had several limitations. First, although the development of PRAISE was based on research conducted across multiple schools within a large urban school district, only one school was included in this study. Despite this school's similarity to other schools within the district from which it was drawn, PRAISE should be replicated across more schools and classrooms. Second, the relatively small sample size of aggressive girls precluded an examination of potential mediating models or the effect of the nesting of students within classrooms. These are important areas for future research. Third, baseline means across some variables were different for the intervention versus control groups, although this was at least partially accounted for within the covariate analyses conducted. Finally, future research could compare PRAISE to an alternative treatment program to control for any nonspecific treatment factors.

Overall, the PRAISE program holds promise for increasing knowledge of problem-solving steps and for slowing the increase of relationally and overtly aggressive behavior that may occur for girls from low-income, urban settings over the course of the school year. In light of the recent reviews indicating a need for bullying and aggression programming sensitive to contextual and systemic factors (Swearer et al., 2010), PRAISE shows promise in reducing aggression among urban African American low-income female youth, a sample who previously showed minimal positive effects from school-based interventions (Leff et al., 2001). With regard to implications for school psychologists, this study suggests that classroom-based programming for relational aggression can be effective at stemming relational and overt aggression for girls living in high-risk environments. The results also suggest that additional modifications and/or evaluations of PRAISE are warranted before widespread implementation, specifically focusing on examining whether prevention and intervention programs should be adapted to be effective for each gender. In addition, more research is needed to determine whether programs such as PRAISE are cost-effective when conducted at the classroom level with all children. Finally, the study provides an illustration of a PAR process for adapting intervention and prevention programs so that they are developmentally and culturally appropriate for students. By partnering with teachers, students, and community members, school practitioners can ensure that interventions are responsive to the goals and preferences of key stakeholders while still adhering to key components of empirically supported practice.

REFERENCES

Björkqvist, K., Österman, K., & Kaukiainen, A. (1992). The development of direct and indirect aggressive strategies in males and females. In K. Björkqvist & P. Niemelä (Eds.), *Of mice and women: Aspects of female aggression* (pp. 51–64). San Diego, CA: Academic Press.

Bronfenbrenner, U. (1986). Ecology of the family as a context for human development: Research perspectives. *Developmental Psychology, 22*, 723–742.

Card, N. A., Stucky, B. D., Sawalani, G. M., & Little, T. D. (2008). Direct and indirect aggression during childhood and adolescence: A meta-analytic review of gender differences, intercorrelations, and relations to maladjustment. *Child Development, 79*, 1185–1229.

Coie, J. D., & Dodge, K. A. (1988). Multiple sources of data on social behavior and social status in the school: A cross-age comparison. *Child Development, 59*, 815–829.

Cooke, M. B., Ford, J., Levine, J., Bourke, C., Newell, L., & Lapidus, G. (2007). The effects of city-wide implementation of 'Second Step' on elementary school students' prosocial and aggressive behaviors. *The Journal of Primary Prevention, 28*, 93–115.

Crick, N. R. (1995). Relational aggression: The role of intent attributions, feelings of distress, and provocation type. *Development and Psychopathology, 7*, 313–322.

Crick, N. R. (1996). The role of overt aggression, relational aggression, and prosocial behavior in the prediction of children's future social adjustment. *Child Development, 67*, 2317–2327.

Crick, N. R., & Dodge, K. A. (1994). A review and reformulation of social information-processing mechanisms in children's social adjustment. *Psych. Bulletin, 115*, 74–101.

Crick, N. R., & Grotpeter, J. K. (1995). Relational aggression, gender, and social psychological adjustment. *Child Development, 66*, 710–722.

Crick, N. R., Grotpeter, J. K., & Bigbee, M. (2002). Relationally and physically aggressive children's intent attributions and feelings of distress for relational and instrumental peer provocations. *Child Development, 73*, 1134–1142.

Crick, N. R., Murray-Close, D., & Woods, K. (2005). Borderline personality features in childhood: A short-term longitudinal sample. *Development and Psychopathology, 17*, 1051–1070.

Crick, N. R., & Nelson, D. A. (2002). Relational and physical victimization within friendships: Nobody told me there'd be friends like these. *Journal of Abnormal Child Psychology, 30*, 599–607.

Crick, N. R., & Werner, N. E. (1998). Response decision processes in relational and overt aggression. *Child Development, 69*, 1630–1639.

Delveaux, K. D., & Daniels, T. (2000). Children's social cognitions: Physically and relationally aggressive strategies and children's goals in peer conflict situations. *Merrill-Palmer Quarterly, 46*, 672–692.

Fantuzzo, J. W., Coolahan, K., & Weiss, A. (1997). Resiliency partnership-directed research: Enhancing the social competencies of preschool victims of physical abuse by developing peer resources and community strengths. In D. Cicchetti & S. Toth (Eds.), *Developmental perspective on trauma: Theory, research and intervention* (pp. 463–490). Rochester: University of Rochester Press.

French, D. C., Jansen, E. A., & Pidada, S. (2002). United States and Indonesian children's and adolescents' reports of relational aggression by disliked peers. *Child Development, 73*, 1143–1150.

Frey, K. S., Nolen, S. B., Van Schoiack-Edstrom, L., & Hirschstein, M. K. (2005). Evaluating a school-based social competence program: Linking behavior, goals, and beliefs. *Journal of Applied Developmental Psychology, 26*, 171–200.

Galen, B. R., & Underwood, M. K. (1997). A developmental investigation of social aggression among children. *Developmental Psychology, 33*, 589–600.

Geiger, T. C., & Crick, N. R. (2001). A developmental psychopathology perspective on vulnerability to personality disorders. In R. E. Ingram & J. M. Price (Eds.), *Vulnerability to psychopathology: Risk across the lifespan* (pp. 57–102). New York: Guilford Press.

Giles, J. W., & Heyman, G. D. (2005). Young children's beliefs about the relationship between gender and aggressive behavior. *Child Development, 76*, 107–121.

Goldstein, S. E., Young, A., & Boyd, C. (2008). Relational aggression at school: Associations with school safety and social climate. *Journal of Youth Adolescence, 37*, 641–654.

Grossman, D. C., Neckerman, H. J., Koepsell, T. D., Liu, P. Y., Asher, K. N., Beland, K., et al. (1997). Effectiveness of a violence prevention curriculum among children in elementary school. *Journal of the American Medical Association, 277*, 1605–1611.

Guerra, N. G., Huesmann, L. R., & Spindler, A. (2003). Community violence exposure, social cognition, and aggression among urban elementary school children. *Child Development, 74,* 1561–1576.

Gullan, R. L., Feinberg, B. E., Freedman, M. A., Jawad, A., & Leff, S. S. (2009). Using participatory action research to design an intervention integrity system in the urban schools. *School Mental Health, 1,* 118–30.

Hudley, C. A. (1993). Comparing teacher and peer perceptions of aggression: An ecological approach. *Journal of Educational Psychology, 85,* 377–384.

Hughes, J. N. (2002). Commentary: Participatory action research leads to sustainable school and community improvement. *School Psychology Review, 32,* 38–43.

Israel, B. A., Schulz, A. J., Parker, E. A., & Becker, A. B. (1998). Review of community-based research: assessing partnership approaches to improve public health. *Annual Review of Public Health, 19,* 173–202.

Juliano, M., Werner, R. S., & Cassidy, K. W. (2006). Early correlates of preschool aggressive behavior according to type of aggression and measurement. *Journal of Applied Developmental Psychology, 27,* 395–410.

Kupersmidt, J. B., & Coie, J. D. (1990). Preadolescent peer status, aggression, and school adjustment as predictors of externalizing problems in adolescence. *Child Development, 61,* 1350–1362.

Kuppens, S., Grietens, H., Onghena, P., Michiels, D., & Subramanian, S. V. (2008). Individual and classroom variables associated with relational aggression in elementary-school aged children: A multilevel analysis. *Journal of School Psychology, 46,* 639–660.

Leff, S. S., Angelucci, J., Goldstein, A. B., Cardaciotto, L., Paskewich, B., & Grossman, M. (2007). Using a participatory action research model to create a school-based intervention program for relationally aggressive girls: The Friend to Friend Program. In J. Zins, M. Elias, & C. Maher (Eds.), *Bullying, victimization, and peer harassment: Handbook of prevention and intervention* (pp. 199–218). New York: Haworth Press.

Leff, S. S., Cassano, M., MacEvoy, J. P., & Costigan, T. E. (2010). Initial validation of a knowledge-based measure of social information processing and anger management. *Journal of Abnormal Child Psychology, 38,* 1007–1020.

Leff, S. S., Costigan, T. E., & Power, T. J. (2004). Using participatory-action research to develop a playground-based prevention program. *Journal of School Psychology, 42,* 3–21.

Leff, S. S., Crick, N. R., Power, T. J., Angelucci, J., Haye, K., Jawad, A., et al. (2006). Understanding social-cognitive development in context: Partnering with urban African American girls to create a hostile attributional bias measure. *Child Development, 77,* 1351–1358.

Leff, S. S., Gullan, R. L., Paskewich, B. S., Abdul-Kabir, S., Jawad, A. F., Grossman, M., et al. (2009). An initial evaluation of a culturally-adapted social problem solving and relational aggression prevention program for urban African American relationally aggressive girls. *Journal of Prevention and Intervention in the Community, 37,* 260–274.

Leff, S. S., Kupersmidt, J. B., & Power, T. J. (2003). An initial examination of girls' cognitions of their relationally aggressive peers as a function of their own social standing. *Merrill-Palmer Quarterly, 49,* 28–54.

Leff, S. S., Paskewich, B., & Gullan, R. L. (2008, February). The Preventing Relational Aggression in Schools Everyday (PRAISE) Program: Implications for school psychologists and counselors. In S. Leff (Chair), *Bullying prevention programming: Implications for school-based professionals.* Symposium conducted at the National Association of School Psychologists Annual Convention, New Orleans, LA.

Leff, S. S., Power, T. J., Manz, P. H., Costigan, T. E., & Nabors, L. A. (2001). School-based aggression prevention programs for young children: Current status and implications for violence prevention. *School Psychology Review, 30*, 343–360.

Leff, S. S., Simeral, C., Khera, G. S., & Grossman, M. B. (2007, March). Developing a hostile attributional bias measure for urban African American boys. In N. Werner (Chair), *Relational aggression and social information processing in middle childhood: Recent developments and future directions.* Symposium presented at the biennial meeting of the Society for Research in Child Development, Boston, MA.

Lochman, J. E., & Wells, K. C. (2003). Effectiveness of the Coping Power Program and of classroom intervention with aggressive children: Outcomes at a 1-year follow-up. *Behavior Therapy, 34*, 493–515.

Lochman, J. E., & Wells, K. C. (2004). The Coping Power Program for preadolescent aggressive boys and their parents: Outcome effects at the 1-year follow-up. *Journal of Consulting and Clinical Psychology, 72*, 571–578.

Maccoby, E. E. (2004). Aggression in the context of gender development. In M. Putallaz & K. L. Bierman (Eds.), *Aggression, antisocial behavior, and violence among girls* (pp. 3–22). New York: Guilford Press.

Merrell, K. W., Gueldner, B. A., Ross, S. W., & Isava, D. M. (2008). How effective are school bullying intervention programs? A meta-analysis of intervention research. *School Psychology Quarterly, 23*, 26–42.

Morales, J. R., & Guerra, N. G. (2006). Effects of multiple context and cumulative stress on urban children's adjustment in elementary school. *Child Development, 77*(4), 907–923.

Murray-Close, D., Crick, N. R., & Galotti, K. M. (2006). Children's moral reasoning regarding physical and relational aggression. *Social Development, 15*, 345–372.

Murray-Close, D., Ostrov, J. M., & Crick, N. R. (2007). A short-term longitudinal study of growth of relational aggression during middle childhood: Associations with gender, friendship intimacy, and internalizing problems. *Development and Psychopathology, 19*, 187–203.

Nansel, T. R., Overpeck, M., Pilla, R. S., Ruan, W. J., Simons-Morton, B., & Scheidt, P. (2001). Bullying behaviors among US youth. *Journal of the American Medical Association, 285*, 2094.

Nastasi, B. K., & Berg, M. (1999). Using ethnography to strengthen and evaluate intervention programs. In J. J. Schensul & M. D. LeCompte (Eds.), *The ethnographer's toolkit—Book 7, Using ethnographic data: Interventions, public programming, and public policy* (pp. 1–56). Walnut Creek, CA: AltaMira Press.

Nastasi, B. K., Varjas, K., Schensul, S. L., Silva, K. T., Schensul, J. J., & Ratnayake, P. (2000). The participatory intervention model: A framework for conceptualizing and promoting intervention acceptability. *School Psychology Quarterly, 15*, 207–232.

Orbio de Castro, B., Veerman, J. W., Koops, W., Bosch, J. D., & Monshouwer, H. J. (2002). Hostile attribution of intent and aggressive behavior: A meta-analysis. *Child Development, 73*, 916–934.

Olweus, D. (1991). Bully/victim problems among school-children: Basic facts and effects of a school based intervention program. In K. H. Rubin & D. Pepler (Eds.), *Development and treatment of childhood aggression* (pp. 411–448). Hillsdale, NJ: Erlbaum.

Ostrov, J. M., & Crick, N. R. (2007). Forms and functions of aggression during early childhood: A short-term longitudinal study. *School Psychology Review, 36*, 22–43.

Reid, J. B., & Eddy, J.M. (1997). The prevention of antisocial behavior: Some considerations in the search for effective interventions. In D. M. Stoff, J. Breiling, & J. D. Maser (Eds.), *The handbook of antisocial behavior* (pp. 343–356). New York: John Wiley & Sons.

Rose, A. J., & Rudolph, K. D. (2006). A review of sex differences in peer relationship processes: Potential trade-offs for the emotional and behavioral development of girls and boys. *Psychological Bulletin, 132*, 98–131.

Smith, R. G., & Gross, A. M. (2006). Bullying: Prevalence and the effect of age and gender. *Child & Family Behavior Therapy, 28*, 13–37.

Stevenson, H. C. (2003). *Playing with anger: Teaching coping skills to African American boys through athletics and culture.* Westport, CT: Greenwood Publishing, Praeger.

Swearer, S. M. (2008). Relational aggression: Not just a female issue. *Journal of School Psychology, 46*, 611–616.

Swearer, S. M., Espelage, D. L., Vaillancourt, T., & Hymel, S. (2010). What can be done about school bullying: Linking research to educational practice. *Educational Researcher, 39*, 38–47.

Talbott, E., Celinska, D., Simpson, J., & Coe, M. G. (2002). "Somebody else making somebody else fight": Aggression and the social context among urban adolescent girls. *Exceptionality, 10*, 203–220.

Taub, J. (2002). Evaluation of the Second Step Violence Prevention Program at a rural elementary school. *School Psychology Review, 31*, 186–201.

Terry, R. (2000). Recent advances in measurement theory and the use of sociometric techniques. In A. Cillessen & W. Bukowski (Eds.), *Recent advances in the measurement of acceptance and rejection in the peer system: New directions in child and adolescent development* (pp. 27–53). San Francisco, CA: Jossey-Bass.

Turkel, A. R. (2007). Sugar and spice and puppy dog's tails: The psychodynamics of bullying. *Journal of the American Academy of Psychoanalysts and Dynamic Psychiatry, 35*, 243–258.

Van Schoiack-Edstrom, L., Frey, K. S., & Beland, K. (2002). Changing adolescents' attitudes about relational and physical aggression: An early evaluation of a school-based intervention. *School Psychology Review, 31*, 201–216.

Vasey, M., Dangleish, T., & Silverman, W. (2003). Research on information-processing factors in child and adolescent psychopathology: A critical commentary. *Journal of Clinical Child and Adolescent Psychology, 32*, 81–93.

Waasdorp, T. E., Bagdi, A., & Bradshaw, C. P. (2010). Peer victimization among urban predominantly African American youth: Coping with relational aggression between friends. *Journal of School Violence, 9*, 98–116.

Werner, N. E., & Crick, N. R. (1999). Relational aggression and social-psychological adjustment in a college sample. *Journal of Abnormal Psychology, 108*, 615–623.

CHAPTER 10
Children With Mental Health Disorders

Implications for School Counselors

Dana Matthews, Maryann Meniru and Yue Dang

According to the Centers for Disease Control (CDC) (2017) children between the ages of 2 and 8 have been diagnosed with a mental, behavioral, or developmental disorder (MBDD). Boys were diagnosed with MBDD more often. The CDC further wrote that children between 3 and 17 years old have diagnoses of attention deficit/hyperactive disorder (ADHD), behavioral/conduct disorders, anxiety, depression, autism spectrum disorder, and Tourette's syndrome. Adolescents between the ages of 12 and 17 with mental disorders may also experience alcohol and drug abuse as well as cigarette dependence (CDC, 2017). The silent epidemic of mental illness among school-age children is a growing concern for school counselors (Anderson & Cardoza, 2016). There is a substantial number of children and adolescents who have been diagnosed with a mental disorder and some of these youth are not being treated (Auger, 2013b). Left untreated, mental disorders can be debilitating, thus causing some children an inability to thrive academically and socially in school settings. Students suffering from mental illness may at some point drop out of school, have chronic absenteeism, low academic achievement, and disruptive behaviors (Anderson & Cardoza, 2016). School counselors are aware that they may be the only mental health professional available. However, with having to perform unrelated counseling duties, they are not always able to provide services to students with mental health concerns. Kaffenberger and O'Rorke-Trigiani (2013) suggested that school counselors provide direct counseling services to students; however, barriers such as administrative tasks and large caseloads may prohibit them from performing counseling services to students. Students continue to attend school with undiagnosed and untreated mental illness while expected to do well behaviorally, academically, and socially.

School counselors are responsible for developing curriculum and programs geared toward students' academic, career, and personal/social needs. Within this paradigm, children are coming to school with mental health disorders that impede their academic success. For these students to become proficient in school where they are successful academically, school counselors will need to perform more school counseling related activities versus administrative tasks otherwise, children with mental disorders may continue to go unnoticed. Researchers have discussed the issues pertaining to mental health and school counselors (Anderson & Cardoza, 2016; Auger, 2013b; Carlson & Kees, 2013). However, additional discussions are warranted to give voice to this silent epidemic.

THE PROFESSIONAL SCHOOL COUNSELOR

School counselors are academically trained to address the growing concerns of mental health problems affecting children and adolescents. They are in essence trained mental health professionals who can identify mental disorders. Collaborating with school administrators is paramount to developing an effective school counseling program where counselors can incorporate behavioral prevention, early intervention, and crisis services (Schmidt, 2014). School counselors continue to have vague job descriptions that have an impact on school counselor's roles within the school. School counselors can make appropriate referrals to outside mental health agencies. However, parents may either choose not to follow through or may not have adequate resources to take their child to counseling outside of the school setting (Auger, 2013). The lack of access to mental health services outside of the school makes the school counselor's role paramount in addressing student mental health needs (Carlson & Kees, 2013).

As key stakeholders working extensively with school-age children, it is important for school administrators to be more aware of the role school counselors play at their schools. Often school counselors are given administrative tasks and clerical duties versus direct services that entail providing individual and group counseling services (Zalaquett & Chatters, 2012). The position statement of the American School Counselor Association (ASCA) on student mental health is clear regarding the role of school counselors in addressing mental illness. However, school counselors are finding it difficult to provide direct counseling services to students (Kaffenberger & O'Rorke-Trigiani, 2013). In addition, school counselors are developing prevention programs aimed at identifying symptoms that could potentially be signs of a mental disorder. They are also providing education in the community and bringing about mental health and children and offering outside resources within the community.

IMPACT OF MENTAL HEALTH ISSUES ON SCHOOL-AGE CHILDREN

School-age children face various challenges ranging from general issues (e.g., academic) to specific issues (e.g., psychological) in school settings. Although general issues are more common, researchers have suggested a high prevalence rate of mental health issues among school-age children (Auger, 2013; Erickson & Abel, 2013; Hill, Ohmstede, & Mims, 2012). These children usually experience a wide range of mental health related issues including but are not limited to: anxiety (Thompson, Robertson, Curtis, & Frick, 2013), depression (Dugger & Jones, 2016), autism spectrum disorders (Auger, 2013a), and bullying (Black, Banks, Patience, & Lund, 2014). Of the mental health issues presented by school-age children, many issues are not appropriately addressed and therefore inadequately treated (Auger, 2013). When left untreated, the mental health issues that school-age children present are likely to impact other areas of their daily functioning (Auger, 2013b; Hill et al., 2012). For example, a student who presents excessive anxiety may experience difficulties concentrating in class (academic) and interacting with peers and teachers (social).

As a key stakeholder working extensively with school-age children, school counselors play a significant role in preventing and intervening on behalf of children with mental health issues (Auger, 2013b; Carlson & Kees, 2013). It is imperative that school counselors attend to mental health issues among students and provide appropriate help to meet the students' mental health needs. School counselors are equipped with the knowledge and skills to address and promote mental health awareness across a diverse student body in school settings. The increased mental health awareness may promote increased student functioning in other areas (e.g., academic, social) (Hill et al., 2012). For example, school counselors may promote students' awareness and knowledge about bullying by implementing bully prevention programs. Such effort may help ensure a safe school environment and reduce students' anxiety level concerning bullying in school settings. The enhanced school environment and the decreased stress level among students may contribute to positive student learning outcomes. Based on an empirical study from the perspectives of school administrators, school counselors, and school psychologists, Hill and colleagues (2012) shed light on the ongoing need to provide mental health services for school-age children (e.g., bully prevention, individual counseling, crisis intervention).

CHALLENGES FACING SCHOOL COUNSELORS

Despite the need to respond to students' mental health issues, school counselors often encounter numerous challenges as they attempt to prevent and intervene in mental health issues among students. First, the high prevalence rate of mental health issues with inadequate interventions present challenges for school counselors as they navigate their roles in responding to these issues (Auger, 2013). For instance, when working with students with undiagnosed developmental issues, school counselors may need to refer the students for a psychological assessment prior to being able to provide help and support to meet the presenting concern. Second, school counselors often act in multiple roles with various responsibilities in school settings (e.g., counseling, academic, administrative), which may potentially limit their ability to fully exercise their primary role as school counselors (Gruman, Marston, & Koon, 2013; Walley & Grothaus, 2013). Third, school counselors often carry big caseloads on a regular basis, which can hinder their ability to attend to the mental health needs across diverse student populations at the individual level (Gruman et al., 2013; Kaffenberger, 2011; Kaffenberger & O'Rorke-Trigiani, 2013; Walley & Grothaus, 2013). In other words, the constant demands to attend to the general mental health needs presented by a large group may overshadow school counselors' effort to address specific mental health issues presented by individual students. Fourth, the availability of mental health services in school settings is often limited when compared with community mental health services (Hill et al.,

2012). Yet, school counselors are constantly challenged to respond to a wide range of mental health issues presented by students. As a result, it is possible that some students' mental health needs are not adequately addressed. Fifth, school counselors may need additional training to effectively respond to specific mental health issues among school-age children (Kaffenberger, 2011; Kaffenberger & O'Rorke-Trigiani, 2013). Based on a qualitative study that explored school counselors' training in addressing students' mental health concerns, Walley and Grothaus (2013) wrote that counselor education programs must provide additional training specifically designed to help school counselors respond to mental health issues among school-age children. In a recent study that sampled ASCA members, it was revealed that school counselors tended to be relatively comfortable at addressing general student issues (e.g., academic concerns, relationship concerns, stress management) than they did with specific mental health issues (e.g., sleep disorders, eating disorders) (Carlson & Kees, 2013). The results point to a need to examine school counselors' preparedness and readiness to respond to mental health issues in school settings. Graduate counselor training is an essential avenue through which school counselors obtain school counseling related knowledge and skills needed to effectively work in the field. Carlson and Kees (2013) suggested that relevant counseling coursework (e.g., diagnosis, addition) may enhance school counselors' comfort level in address mental health issues among school-age children.

The above discussion points to the urgent need to address mental health issues in school aged students. It is a given that the mental well-being of a child has a large impact on his or her academic progress, behavioral and psychological well-being. The impact has been studied extensively and can be seen in increased diagnoses of depression and anxiety related conditions. These diagnoses will affect behavior, academic, social, and overall outlook for any child diagnosed. One way to articulate implications of mental health counseling for school-age children is to look at ASCA's mission. The mission stipulates reduction of barriers including mental disorders that may prevent young school-age children from achieving their academic goals and becoming responsible citizens in the future.

IMPLICATIONS FOR SCHOOL COUNSELORS

School counselors advocate as well as refer to other mental health professional. The need for school counselors to address the mental health concerns in students can not be underestimated. This type of approach if encouraged would help in identifying and treating early signs of mental health needs among school-age children (Brown et al., 2006). In addition, collaborating with students families is as important as collaborating with outside agencies (Schmidt, 2014). Unaddressed mental health concerns can manifest as behavioral concerns. It is important that students dealing with mental health issues are supported and treated early.

Without addressing underlying mental health needs some school-age children may struggle to achieve academic goals. Also when students mental health needs are not identified and adequately attended to they are likely to be disengaged, dismissed, or drop out of school. Mental health problems such as ADHD that tend to present as behavioral concerns may not be diagnosed early enough to benefit the student.

CONCLUSION

The degree or variability with which mental health services are provided will depend on availability of resources such as the ratio of counselor to students. A support system that takes cognizance of mental health needs of its pupils, actual staff, and collegial support and policies to support school counselors is critical. More importantly as discussed above is the conflicting role definitions that school counselors face. Their role albeit complicated by administrative responsibilities. School counselors are trained mental health professionals and are in a unique positive to effectively develop preventative mental health programs.

REFERENCES

Anderson, M., & Cardoza, K. (2016). Mental health in schools: A hidden crisis affecting millions of students. Retrieved from https://www.npr.org/sections/ed/2016/08/31/464727159/mental-health-in-schools-a-hidden-crisis-affecting-millions-of-students

Auger, R. W. (2013b). School counselors and children's mental health: Introduction to the special issue. *Professional School Counseling, 16*(4), 208–210.

Auger, R. W. (2013a). Autism spectrum disorders: A research review for school counselors. *Professional School Counseling, 16*(4), 256–268.

Black, J. J., Banks, C. S., Patience, B. A., & Lund, E. M. (2014). School-based mental health professionals' bullying assessment practices: A call for evidence-based bullying assessment guidelines. *Professional School Counseling, 18*(1), 136–147.

Centers for Disease Control. (2017). *Children's mental health.* Retrieved from https://www.cdc.gov/childrensmentalhealth/data.html

Carlson, L. A., & Kees, N. L. (2013). Mental health services in public schools: A preliminary study of school counselor perceptions. *Professional School Counseling, 16*(4), 211–221.

Dugger, S. M., & Jones, K. R. (2016). Depressive disorders in children and adolescents: What every school counselor needs to know. *Journal of Professional Counseling: Practice, Theory & Research, 43*(1), 32–50.

Erickson, A., & Abel, N. R. (2013). A high school counselors' leadership in providing school-wide screenings for depression and enhancing suicide awareness. *Professional School Counseling, 16*(5), 283–289.

Gruman, D. H., Marston, T., & Koon, H. (2013). Bringing mental health needs into focus through school counseling program transformation. *Professional School Counseling, 16*(5), 333–341.

Hill, J., Ohmstede, T., & Mims, M. (2012). A look in to mental health in the schools. *International Journal of Psychology: A Biopsychosocial Approach/Tarptautinis psichologijos zurnalas: Biopsichosocialinis poziuris, 11,* 119–131. doi:10.7220/1941-7233.11.6

Kaffenberger, C. (2011). Helping students with mental and emotional disorders. In B. T. Erford (Ed.), *Transforming the school counseling profession* (3rd ed., pp. 342–370). Upper Saddle River, NJ: Merrill Prentice-Hall.

Kaffenberger, C. J., & O'Rorke-Trigiani, J. (2013). Addressing student mental health needs by providing direct and indirect services and building alliances in the community. *Professional School Counseling, 16*(5), 323–332.

Mason, M. J., Sabo, R., & Zaharakis, N. M. (2017). Peer network counseling as brief treatment for urban adolescent heavy cannabis users. *Journal of Studies on Alcohol & Drugs, 78*(1), 152–157.

Schmidt, J. J. (2014). *Counseling in schools: Essential services and comprehensive programs* (4th ed.). Needham Heights, MA: Allyn & Bacon.

Thompson, E. H., Robertson, P., Curtis, R., & Frick, M. H. (2013). Students with anxiety: Implications for professional school counselors. *Professional School Counseling, 16*(4), 222–234.

Thornton, S. (2015). We urgently need to address the rising mental health crisis. *British Journal of School Nursing, 10*(1), 36–38.

Walley, C. T., & Grothaus, T. (2013). A qualitative examination of school counselors' training to recognize and respond to adolescent mental health issues. *Journal of School Counseling, 11*(11), 1–32.

Zalaquett, C. P., & Chatters, S. J. (2012). Middle School Principals' Perceptions of Middle School Counselors' Roles and Functions. *American Secondary Education, 40*(2), 89–103.

CHAPTER 11
Students With Anxiety
Implications for Professional School Counselors

E. Heather Thompson, Phyllis Robertson and Russ Curtis

Anxiety is one of the most pervasive mental health concerns affecting students, yet a significant number of students with anxiety disorders remain underserved. If left untreated, anxiety can hinder students' personal/social, academic, and career development. The purpose of this article is to provide professional school counselors with helpful information about the etiology of anxiety disorders and brief, evidence-based prevention and intervention options. The authors discuss specific recommendations for the identification, assessment, and treatment of anxiety that fit within the unique school environment.

Anxiety is the most commonly diagnosed mental health issue for children and adolescents (Costello, Mustillo, Erkanli, Keeler, & Angold, 2003; Essau, Conradt, & Petermann, 2002; Muris, Merckelbach, Mayer, & Prins, 2000). The hallmark symptoms of an anxiety disorder are persistent and debilitating fear or worry that impairs a child's functioning (American Psychiatric Association [APA], 2000) and exceeds what is considered developmentally normal (Keeley & Storch, 2009). Experiencing anxiety that is short-lived and representative of developmentally age-appropriate fears is common for children. According to the American Academy of Child and Adolescent Psychiatry (AACAP, 2007), infants have a developmental tendency to be fearful of loud noises and strangers. In early childhood, children may experience considerable distress when separated from a primary caregiver. Toddlers often have fears of the dark, monsters, or animals. Young school-aged children may be fearful of natural disasters or concerned about injury or death. Adolescents may worry about how they are perceived by others, their level of competency in school or other activities, and health concerns (AACAP, 2007).

Excessive fear and worry that meets the clinical criteria for an anxiety disorder is experienced by 10-20% of the general population of children (Dadds, Spence, Holland, Barrett, & Laurens 1997; Muris et al., 2000). Frequently occurring anxiety disorders in youth include phobias, generalized anxiety disorder, and separation anxiety disorder, whereas agoraphobia, posttraumatic stress disorder, panic disorder, and obsessive-compulsive disorder are less frequently diagnosed in children and adolescents (Costello et al., 2003).

Anxiety disorders can significantly impair children's social skills, academic success, (Langley, Bergman, McCracken, & Piacentini, 2004; Neil & Christensen, 2009; Wood, 2006) and emotional wellbeing (Ost & Treffers, 2000; Rapee, Schniering, & Hudson, 2009). For example, a child's ability to concentrate on important academic tasks and recall previously learned material may be impaired by physiological arousal, inordinate attention to a perceived threat, and excessive worry (Ma, 1999). An anxious child's ability to do well in school may also be compromised by somatic discomfort such as stomachaches, headaches, and nausea (Dorn et al., 2003; Hughes, Lourea-Waddell, & Kendall, 2008; Van Ameringen, Mancini, & Farvolden, 2003). Somatization can lead to poor school attendance and diminished school performance (Bernstein et al., 1997), which may adversely influence social skill development (Barrett & Heubeck, 2000; La Greca & Harrison, 2005; Langley et al., 2004). Research also indicates that children who report being bullied experience higher levels of anxiety and, conversely, children who experience higher levels of anxiety are more likely to report being bullied (D'Esposito, Blake, & Riccio, 2011; La Greca & Harrison, 2005; Storch & Masia-Warner, 2004). If left untreated, anxiety disorders increase the risk of depression, addictions, and suicidality for children and adolescents (Ost & Treffers, 2000). Sareen et al. (2005), for instance, found that anxiety is the most significant risk factor for suicidal ideation and attempts.

To help address the prevalence of anxiety and its deleterious effect on the academic, personal/social, and career development of students, this article first provides an overview of the etiology of anxiety disorders, including intrapersonal and environmental factors that may impact and/or reinforce symptomology. Second, a table lists brief assessment instruments that school counselors may use to detect student anxiety and monitor treatment outcomes. Third, the authors discuss responsive services that can be realistically utilized within schools. These include prevention programs, individual and group counseling, play therapy, and computerized Cognitive Behavior Therapy (CBT) intervention programs. The article concludes with specific prevention and early intervention recommendations for professional school counselors.

RISK FACTORS FOR THE DEVELOPMENT OF CHILDHOOD ANXIETY

No single risk factor can universally account for the development of anxiety in children (Wood, McLeod, Sigman, Hwang, & Chu, 2003); however, empirical evidence indicates that several salient intrapersonal and environmental risk factors are associated with the development of clinical anxiety disorders in children and adolescents. Intrapersonal risk factors include behavioral inhibition (Hirshfeld-Becker et al., 2008), heightened physiological responding (Weems, Zakem, Costa, Cannon, & Watts, 2005), negative emotionality (Carthy, Horesh, Apter & Gross, 2009), emotional dysregulation (Carthy et al., 2009; Farach & Mennin 2007; Suveg & Zeman 2004), limited attention control (Muris, Meesters, & Rompelberg, 2006), and emotional self-efficacy (Suveg & Zeman, 2004). Environmental risk factors associated with anxiety disorders in young people include anxious and overprotective parenting (van Brakel, Muris, Bogels, & Thomassen, 2006), mothers with depression (Field, Hernandez-Reif, & Diego, 2006; Pelaez, Field, Pickens, & Hart, 2008), and exposure to domestic violence (Briggs-Gowan et al., 2010; Litrownik, Newton, Hunter, English, & Everson, 2003).

INTRAPERSONAL RISK FACTORS

Many studies indicated varying degrees of overlap in genetic and environmental contributions to anxiety (Eley & Stevenson, 2000; Legrand, McGue & Iacono, 1999; Thapar & McGuffin, 1995; Warren, Schmitz, & Emde, 1999). Twin studies indicated that 30-50% of the variance in anxiety is due to genetic influences (Clifford, Murray, & Fulker, 1984; Eley & Gregory 2004; Stevenson, Batten, & Cherner 1992; Thapar & McGuffin, 1995). According to Eysenck and Eysenck (1985), neuroticism, the biological temperamental contribution to anxiety, is evidenced in young children as behavioral inhibition, which is defined as a child's consistent tendency to display fear, restraint, or withdrawal from novel stimuli such as unfamiliar people, places, objects, or situations (Mian, Wainwright, Briggs-Gowan & Carter, 2011). Studies during the past 20 years have revealed that behavioral inhibition is a significant risk factor for the development of anxiety (Hirshfeld-Becker et al., 2008).

Anxiety disorders are often characterized by hyperarrousal in response to mildly threatening stimuli (Weems et al., 2005). Research has demonstrated that elevated amygdala responses (Thomas et al., 2001), sympathetic arousal (Beidel, 1991), and cortisol levels (Carrion et al., 2002) are associated with anxiety disorders in children. The amygdala plays a key role in physiological reactions such as elevated heart rate and the release of stress hormones. In a functional neuroimaging study, Thomas et al. (2001) found that in comparison to children without anxiety, anxious children experienced an exaggerated amygdala response when shown pictures of fearful faces. Findings also indicated a robust correlation between responsiveness of the amygdala and the degree of anxiety symptoms. Weems et al. (2005) found that elevated heart rate in response to threatening visual stimuli was associated with children's self-reports of anxiety. Carrion et al. (2002) found that children with posttraumatic stress disorder (PTSD) experienced elevated cortisol levels, which are associated with behavioral inhibition (Kagan, Reznick, & Snidman, 1988).

Much like behavioral inhibition, negative emotionality is a risk factor for the development of anxiety disorders (Shaw, Keenan, Vondra, Delliquadri, & Giovannelli, 1997). Negative emotionality, often associated with depression and other childhood psychopathology, is characterized by irritability, difficulty being soothed, and elevated negative emotional reactivity (Sanson, Hemphill, & Smart, 2004). Research indicates that anxious children demonstrate elevated negative emotional reactivity to stress-producing stimuli and have more difficulty using reappraisal methods to deescalate their emotional response when compared to children who do not have anxiety (Carthy et al., 2009).

Although research is in the early phases, emotional dysregulation, or a combination of heightened emotional responding and difficulty regulating emotional reactions, appears to play a pivotal role in the development and maintenance of anxiety disorders in children (Carthy et al., 2009; Suveg & Zeman 2004). Carthy et al. (2009) found that children with anxiety exhibited more intense and frequent emotional responses to mildly threatening stimuli and used less emotional regulation strategies than children who did not have anxiety disorders. Children with anxiety also tended to use anxiety suppressing techniques (Carthy et al., 2009), which diminished outward symptoms of anxiety but did not reduce the internal physiological experience associated with anxious feelings (Gross, 2002). For example, outwardly suppressing feelings of anxiety while taking a test does not actually diminish the experience of the anxious feelings and may increase the sympathetic activation of the cardiovascular system (Gross, 2002). Conversely, cognitive reappraisal that happens earlier in the emotional response process is more likely to transform anxious feelings and reduce physiological responding. Examples of ways for students to manage physiological reactions through Ellis' ABC model of reappraisal techniques are provided in the implications section of this [chapter].

Self-regulation of attention, or attention control, is the ability to concentrate on a particular task, thoughtfully process an experience, solve a problem, or purposefully shift attention from one stimulus to another. The gradual enhancement of attention regulation abilities throughout childhood and adolescence enables children to better self-regulate their emotions (Rueda, Posner, & Rothbart, 2004). Research reveals that children who struggle with anxiety are less capable of controlling or shifting their attention (Muris et al., 2006). Furthermore, anxious children demonstrate attention bias in that they are hyperattentive to threatening stimuli and have a tendency to show a negatively biased interpretation of seemingly neutral stimulus (Chorpita, Yim, Moffitt, Umemoto, & Francis, 2000; Vasey & MacLeod, 2001).

Another factor that is likely to influence emotional regulation is the degree to which a child feels capable of attenuating symptoms of anxiety (Suveg & Zeman, 2004). In a study comparing 26 children ages 8 to 12 years old with anxiety disorders to children without anxiety, Suveg and Zeman (2004) found that anxious children reported lower self-efficacy in regulating their anxiety and sadness. Children with diminished emotion-regulation self-efficacy may be less inclined to actively engage in adaptively managing emotions during anxiety-provoking situations. In fact, evidence suggests that individuals with anxiety have a tendency to suppress emotionally expressive behavior, which is likely to increase sympathetic activation of cardiovascular systems (Gross, 2002). In other words, the suppression of anxious feelings and behaviors does not lessen the internalized physiological experience of those feelings and may lead to diminished self-efficacy in managing emotionally arousing situations.

ENVIRONMENTAL RISK FACTORS

Parenting. Although genetic and personality contributions to anxiety are moderate, environmental factors such as parenting practices also play a significant role in children's manifestations of anxiety (Muris & Broeren, 2009). Children with anxious parents are up to seven times more likely to develop anxiety than children of non-anxious parents (Turner, Beidel, & Costello, 1987). Research indicates that anxious parents are more likely to model interpretation bias (Muris, Steerneman, Merckelbach, & Meesters, 1996) and predict that their children will perceive stimuli to be threatening (Barrett, Rapee, Dadds, & Ryan, 1996). In studies utilizing direct observation and questionnaires, anxious parents have been shown to be more controlling (van Brakel et al., 2006), more critical (Hudson & Rapee, 2000), and selectively focused on negative outcomes than parents who are not anxious (Barrett, Rapee, Dadds, & Ryan, 1996). Parenting styles of depressed mothers are also considered potential contributors to the development and maintenance of childhood anxiety. Observational studies of depressed mothers' interactions with their children have shown depressed mothers to be withdrawn (Field et al., 2006; Pelaez et al., 2008), less nurturing (Pelaez et al., 2008), and more inconsistent (Gelfand & Teti, 1990) than non-depressed mothers. Rapee (2001) posited that a relationship exists between parents and anxious children that creates a maladaptive pattern in which parents of anxious children attempt to remediate their children's vulnerability by becoming overly involved. Their attempt to reduce their child's anxiety serves to diminish the child's autonomy, sense of self-efficacy, and perceived control over threats while reinforcing avoidance behaviors. Ultimately, the parents' response to their child's high level of arousal reinforces the child's perception that the world is a dangerous place from which the child needs protection (Rapee, 2001). In a recent review of publications over the past decade on parenting practices related to childhood anxiety, controlling parenting behaviors were most consistently linked to childhood anxiety (Wood et al., 2003). School counselors should be aware of this potential dynamic and be mindful not to recreate an interactional pattern that reinforces an anxious child's sense that the world is a scary place and he or she is limited in his or her ability to manage anxious feelings.

Intimate Partner Violence. Exposure to violence in childhood is associated with a wide range of developmental concerns that include but are not limited to anxiety disorders. Edleson (1999) reviewed 31 empirical studies that explored the relationship between exposure to intimate partner violence (IPV) and adjustment concerns for child-witnesses. This review revealed that, across studies exploring problems associated with exposure to IPV, findings consistently showed that child-witnesses exhibited anxiety and symptoms of posttraumatic stress disorder. In an attempt to examine the relationship between anxious, depressed, and aggressive problem behaviors and exposure to IPV, 682 children (ages 4 to 6 years old) and their mothers completed a battery of assessments that revealed that exposure to violence between intimate partners in the home was associated with symptoms of anxiety and depression and aggressive behavior problems (Litrownik et al., 2003). In a more recent study of 213 children 2 to 4 years old, Briggs-Gowan et al. (2010) found that exposure to violence was associated with an increased risk of separation anxiety and posttraumatic stress disorder.

ASSESSING FOR ANXIETY IN SCHOOLS

Anxiety disorders can often go unnoticed and the concomitant problems associated with student anxiety can easily get misinterpreted as a host of unrelated learning issues (e.g., hostility, poor performance, hyperactivity). As such, the authors recommend that professional school counselors utilize brief screening tests that can quickly identify students who are at risk of experiencing anxiety-related symptoms. Also, as is best practice in school counseling, interventions should include an assessment component to determine the potential effectiveness of the interventions used. Information about commonly used measures for the assessment of anxiety symptoms is provided in Table 11.1.

SCHOOL-BASED PREVENTION AND INTERVENTIONS FOR STUDENTS WITH ANXIETY

PREVENTION PROGRAMS

The American School Counseling Association (ASCA) states that a vital element of a comprehensive school counseling program is the delivery of school-wide prevention programs that are comprehensive, developmentally appropriate, aimed at enhancing student achievement, and grounded in data that indicates a need for services (ASCA, 2005). Fortunately, research indicates that school-wide anxiety prevention programs are effective in reducing anxiety symptoms among students. The FRIENDS program is an evidenced-based, cognitive behavior therapy (CBT) prevention program offered through classroom guidance curriculums aimed at the prevention of anxiety symptoms (Barrett, Webster, Turner, & May, 2003). This manualized CBT prevention program, which is widely endorsed by the World Health Organization (2004), is an adaptation of the Coping Cat Curriculum created by Kendall (1994). Comparisons of pre- and post-test scores on anxiety revealed that children who participated in the FRIENDS program exhibited significantly fewer anxiety symptoms than children in the control group at completion of the intervention (Barret & Turner, 2001; Lowry-Webster, Barrett, & Dadds, 2001) and at 12-month follow-up (Essau, Conradt, Sasagawa, & Ollendick, 2011). Results from these studies indicate that the FRIENDS school-wide prevention program is an effective approach to reducing anxiety symptoms experienced by children.

INDIVIDUAL COUNSELING

Cognitive behavioral therapy (CBT) for children and adolescents experiencing anxiety typically addresses the relationship between thoughts, feelings, behaviors, and physiological symptoms of anxiety; learning ways of reacting that lead to more desirable outcomes; instruction and practice of progressive muscle relaxation, guided imagery, and deep breathing; changing negative self-talk; cognitive restructuring; exposure; assertiveness training; and problem-solving techniques. CBT strategies may include helping children with anxiety learn to identify and understand emotions, recognize potential triggers that may initiate negative emotions, and identify the type of regulation style they typically utilize to cope with those emotional reactions so antecedent responses can be developed, rehearsed, and improved (Carthy et al., 2009). Research shows that anxious individuals have a tendency to experience emotions more quickly and intensely in the emotion-generation and regulation process (Mennin, Turk, Heimberg, & Carmin, 2004); therefore, an effective approach may be to help anxious children learn to develop a tolerance for emotional discomfort and to reframe emotional reactions from being undesirable and in need of being controlled to being a source of information that can help them interpret and make decisions (Decker, Turk, Hess, & Murray, 2008).

Research on the effectiveness of CBT with children with anxiety was initially sparked by Kendall's (1994) examination of the effectiveness of the Coping Cat

TABLE 11.1. BRIEF ANXIETY ASSESSMENTS THAT CAN BE USED BY SCHOOL COUNSELORS

ANXIETY ASSESSMENT	AGE IN YEARS	TAKEN BY	COMPLETED IN MINUTES	AVAILABLE
Beck Anxiety Inventory for Youth (BYI)	7–18	Student Parent Counselor	5–10	http://www.pearsonclinical.co.uk/Psychology/ ChildMentalHealth/ChildMentalHealth/BeckYouthInventories-SecondEditionForChildrenand Adolescents(BYI-II)/BeckYouth-Inventories-Second Edition-ForChildrenandAdolescents (BYI-II) .aspx
Multidimensional Anxiety Scale for Children (MASC)	8–19	Parent Student	15	http://www.mhs.com/product.aspx?gr=edu&prod= masc2&id=overview
Revised Children's Manifest Anxiety Scale (RCMAS-2)	6–9	Student	10	http://www.proedinc.com/customer/ProductView. aspx?ID=1759
Self-Report for Childhood Anxiety Related Emotional Disorders (SCARED)	8–18	Parent Student	5	http://psychiatry.pitt.edu/sites/default/files/Documents/ assessments/SCARED%20Child.pdf **FREE**
Social Anxiety Scale-Child Adolescent version (LSAS-CA)	8–14	Parent Student Counselor	20–30	Available by request from Carrie Masia-Warner, NYU Child Study Center, 215 Lexington Avenue, 13th Floor, New York, NY 10016 USA, carrie.masia@med.nyu.edu
Social Phobia and Anxiety Inventory for Children (SPAI-C)	8–14	Student	20–30	http://www.mhs.com/product.aspx?gr=edu&prod=spaic&id=overview
The Spence Children's Anxiety Scale	8–14	Parent Student	10	http://www.scaswebsite.com/index.php?p=1_6 **FREE**
Behavioral Assessment System for Children, Second Addition (BASC 2)	6–21	Parent Teacher Student	10–20	http://www.pearsonassessments.com/HAIWEB/Cultures/ en-us/Productdetail.htm?Pid=PAa30000
The Child Behavior Checklist (CBCL)	6–18	Parent Teacher Student	15	http://www.aseba.org/

Curriculum with 47 children (ages 9 to 13 years old) with an anxiety diagnosis who participated in either a 16-session CBT Coping Cat intervention or a waitlist control condition. Findings from pre- and post-treatment diagnostic evaluations revealed that 64% children who participated in the Coping Cat intervention no longer met diagnostic criteria for anxiety after a 1-year follow-up. In a follow-up study of 94 children (ages 9 to 13 years old) with an anxiety diagnosis, Kendall et al. (1997) found that 50% of the children who participated in the CBT Coping Cat program no longer met the diagnostic criteria for anxiety at the time of post-treatment evaluation and at a 1-year follow-up. A review of evidence-based treatments shows that at least 25 randomized control intervention studies have demonstrated that CBT is an efficacious intervention for decreasing a variety of anxiety disorders in children and adolescents (see Silverman, Pina, & Viswesvaran, 2008).

Although limited in nature, research also indicates that the academic performance and social development of anxious youth can be enhanced through CBT interventions. For example, Wood (2006) explored the effects of a CBT intervention on academic performance and social functioning for 40 children aged 6 to 13 years old. Findings revealed that children who experienced a decrease in anxiety also demonstrated improvement in their school performance and social development (2006).

Related to improved academic performance, Ramirez and Beilock (2011) found that having ninth-grade students write about their test anxiety for 10 minutes immediately before taking final exams significantly improved test scores compared to control groups. Furthermore, habitually test-anxious students (high-test-anxious) in the expressive writing group significantly outperformed the high-test-anxious control group. The high-test-anxious expressive writing group also performed at or above the low-test-anxious students, suggesting that high-test-anxious students benefit most from the expressive writing intervention (Ramirez & Beilock).

GROUP COUNSELING

In the school setting, group cognitive behavioral therapy (GCBT) is likely to be the treatment of choice for ameliorating childhood anxiety because it is evidence based and is a more efficient treatment modality than individual counseling. Furthermore, group counseling that is based on clearly evidenced school and community needs is deemed an essential element of comprehensive school counseling programs (ASCA,

2008). Pre- and post-test comparison studies consistently have shown GCBT to be effective in reducing the anxiety symptoms of children in treatment interventions in comparison to those in control or waitlist conditions (Barrett, 1998; Cobham, Dadds, & Spence, 1998). GCBT interventions that include some aspect of family involvement also have been shown to be helpful in reducing anxiety symptoms (Barrett et al., 1996). Many GCBT interventions can easily be adapted to include family members and primary caregivers of children with anxiety.

GROUP PLAY THERAPY INTERVENTIONS

Emotional regulation and CBT strategies may be difficult to teach to young children. Instead, utilizing play therapy interventions may be more appropriate to help children who are preoperational in their cognitive development. Research with preschool-age and school-age children has shown a positive relationship between play, emotion regulation, and emotional competence (Lindsey & Colwell, 2003; Russ & Schafer, 2006).

Intervention studies have shown that play can reduce anxiety in young children (Baggerly & Jenkins, 2009; Shen, 2002; Wettig, Coleman, & Geider, 2011). For example, Shen (2002) investigated the potential effectiveness of play therapy group on reducing levels of anxiety and depression for elementary-age children in Taiwan who experienced an earthquake in 1999. Upon completion of the intervention, the experimental group scored significantly lower than the control group on self-reported anxiety. Baggerly and Jenkins (2009) explored the effects of a play therapy group for young children who were homeless. Statistical analysis revealed that the play therapy group had a moderate effect in reducing anxiety.

COMPUTERIZED COGNITIVE BEHAVIORAL INTERVENTIONS

Computerized CBT (CCBT) interventions for anxiety may enhance the efficiency and accessibility of mental health services to students with anxiety. Such interventions may help school counselors reach youth who have been identified with anxiety but choose not to participate in group counseling, are not appropriate for group counseling, or need support in addition to group counseling or school-wide guidance curriculums aimed at preventing or reducing anxiety symptoms. The following CCBT interventions may be helpful to school counselors: Cool Teens, Camp Cope-a-Lot, and the Brave Program.

A recent study of 43 adolescents with an anxiety diagnosis who were assigned to either the Cool Teens intervention or a waitlist revealed that those teens who participated in the intervention experienced a greater reduction in their anxiety symptoms in comparison to teens on the waitlist (Wuthrich et al., 2006). Khanna and Kendall (2010) studied the effectiveness of the Camp Cope-a-Lot intervention for 49 children (ages 7 to 13 years old) who were randomly assigned to Camp Cope-A-Lot, individual CBT, or computer-assisted education and support. Their findings revealed that at post-intervention and a 3-month follow-up, children who participated in Camp Cope-A-Lot demonstrated greater improvements and reductions in anxiety diagnoses than children in the computer-assisted education group and similar improvements and reductions in diagnoses to children who received individual CBT counseling sessions. March, Spence, and Donovan (2009) examined the potential effectiveness of the Brave Program with a sample of 73 children with anxiety diagnoses (ages 7 to 12 years old) who were randomly assigned to the Brave Program condition or no treatment condition. Post-treatment assessments revealed that children in the treatment condition experienced a greater reduction in the severity of their anxiety symptoms in comparison to children in the no treatment condition. However, there were no significant differences between the groups in terms of a reduction in the number of anxiety diagnoses at post-treatment.

CCBT programs are cost-effective, convenient, interactive, and accessible to youth who may not be willing or able to engage in face-to-face counseling. Although CCBT interventions have shown to be effective in treating adults with anxiety, research on CCBT programs for anxious youth is still burgeoning. Fortunately, this new research indicates that CCBT has promise as an anxiety-reducing intervention for children. Specific information about school-based interventions that can be used to address childhood anxiety is provided in Table 11.2.

COUNSELING IMPLICATIONS

Based on the literature review, the authors make the following recommendations to enhance the responsive services provided for students who have anxiety disorders.

TABLE 11.2. SCHOOL-BASED INTERVENTIONS FOR CHILDHOOD ANXIETY

INTERVENTION	DESCRIPTION	AGE IN YEARS	INFORMATION AVAILABLE
FRIENDS	10-week CBT intervention 2 booster sessions offered at 1 and 3 month follow-up 4 supplemental sessions offered for parents Facilitator manual and workbook for children	7 to 16	An order form for the FRIENDS curriculum is available on the final page of the Introduction to Friends handbook (Barrett, Webster, Turner, & May, 2003) which can be found at http://www.friendsinfo.net/downloads/friendsintro.pdf
Coping Cat	16-session CBT intervention Facilitator manual and workbook for children	6 to 13	A helpful review of the content, sequence, implementation considerations, and videos of the Coping Cat program and the FEAR plan is provided by Podell et al. (2010).
Cool Teens	12-session computer-delivered interactive intervention	adolescents	Cool Teens can be purchased at the Center for Emotional Health, http://www.centreforemotionalhealth.com.au/ pages/resources-products.aspx
Camp Cope-a-Lot	12-session computer-assisted intervention	7 to 13	Camp Cope-a-Lot can be purchased at http://cope-a-lot.com/instruction.htm.
Brave Program	10 on-line sessions	7 to 18	More information about registering for the Brave Program can be found at http://brave.psy.uq.edu.au/index.html? site=public&page=about.

1. School-wide anxiety reduction programs should be initiated at the beginning of each academic year to increase all students' ability to recognize symptoms of anxiety and learn coping mechanisms.

2. Students who exhibit frequent somatic complaints, poor attendance, poor academic performance (uncharacteristic of ability), hostility and irritability, hyperactivity, tearfulness, sensitivity, and persistent isolation from other students should be screened with one of the aforementioned brief instruments to determine if significant anxiety symptoms are present.

3. Students who meet criteria for having anxiety-related issues should be carefully screened to determine if they could learn from a group setting. Students who exhibit symptoms of social anxiety, for instance, may not be the best candidates for group

until they can develop confidence in their coping skills (Curtis, Kimball, & Stroup, 2004). Students who are deemed too socially anxious for groups could be encouraged to use computerized anxiety reduction programs to enhance their coping skills.

4. Regardless of age and grade, students should be educated about how sugar and caffeine can exacerbate anxiety.

5. In concert with guardian collaboration, students should be encouraged to possibly reduce or eliminate fear-provoking or violent TV programs, movies, or video games. This could also include limiting exposure to traumatic news events (Curtis, Garrett, Forst, & Looney, 2006).

6. Specifically for high-test-anxious students, writing about their fears and concerns for ten minutes immediately prior to taking exams could reduce excessive worry, which hinders academic performance (Ramirez & Beilock, 2011). As such, identifying high-testanxious students early in the academic year would be helpful and allow educators to arrange accommodations for the expressive writing intervention.

7. Whether in group or individual counseling, CBT is an effective evidence-based treatment option for anxious students. Although myriad versions of CBT are used to treat anxiety, most programs contain the following three components: (a) education about the nature of stress and anxiety and how it affects emotions, thoughts, behavior, and physiology; (b) coping skills that are taught and practiced; and (c) encouragement and reinforcement of students practicing facing fearful situations (e.g., asking questions in class, giving a speech) while using coping skills.

Coping skills can include a cadre of cognitive and behavioral strategies. Christophersen and Mortweet (2001) had students move or dance as robots (stiff, tight, constrained) and then as ragdolls (loose, relaxed) to demonstrate the contrast between feeling tense and relaxed. They also used a feeling-face chart to help students identify the range of emotions they experience and to normalize the existence of such emotions (Christophersen & Mortweet, 2001). Once students are able to identify feeling words and when/how they experience them, school counselors may introduce how the students' thoughts increase the intensity of emotions. School counselors may introduce Ellis's ABC model (Ellis & Harper, 1975) and explain how having thoughts (B) about what happens (A) and about themselves, results in increased anxiety (C). For example, thinking about how classmates will laugh at them (B) when they give a class presentation (A) results in increased feelings of anxiety (C). Students are then instructed to develop alternative ways to think about giving a class presentation that will not increase anxiety. Similarly, younger students may be taught the concept of "stinking thinking" and the connection between negative thoughts and emotions (Altiero, 2006). Counselors may use visual aids such as a volcano or thermometer to demonstrate how negative thoughts increase the "temperature" of their emotions, such as in anxiety or anger, and the importance of recognizing the negative thoughts early in order to reduce anxiety, anger, or sadness.

Once students become comfortable recognizing and replacing unproductive thoughts and behaviors, school counselors may use the game "Red Light, Green Light" to help students monitor when they need to stop and think (red light) about their thoughts and choices before proceeding (green light) with actions that are unhelpful. Actions may include replacing negative coping statements with positive affirmations, such as "I think I can" from *The Little Engine that Could* (Piper, 1930), or calming words. School counselors also may consider using bibliotherapy to demonstrate how characters in stories work through anxiety and increase confidence. An example of this is Henkes's (2000) book, *Wemberly Worried*, and other resources from stressfreekids. com. When working with adolescents, counselors may have them choose their favorite music to create personal theme songs that inspire relaxation, motivation, and hope. Students who express themselves in writing or art may benefit from journal activities to monitor the events, thoughts, and resulting emotions they are experiencing, or by drawing, coloring, or painting with colors and images that depict what they are feeling.

When using counselor directives, or homework assignments, school counselors should consider students' age and maturity, and assess their level of understanding the directives. School counselors may use worksheets for students to practice skills on their own and incorporate into their daily lives with the help of their family and friends, when possible. For younger students, assigning one skill task per week is more useful for reinforcing learning techniques, rather than addressing multiple skills.

Somatic management techniques, or relaxation techniques, are another tool to manage physiological arousal and counter anxious responding related to distressing thoughts and feelings. Specific techniques include practicing deep breathing, guided imagery, and progressive muscle relaxation. One example of practicing deep breathing is having students place a teddy bear on their abdomens and have them practice taking deep breaths and watch the teddy bear move outward from their bodies. This will help students practice taking deeper breaths than the more common shallow breaths found in the upper chest. One elementary counselor noticed positive results when teaching breathing exercises that had students inhale as if smelling flowers or fresh baked cookies and exhale as if blowing out a candle (Van Horne, 2012). School counselors may teach guided imagery by first having students look at peaceful images (e.g., outdoor scenery) and then have students imagine what they would enjoy doing in those scenes. Or, school counselors may have students create their own images of a relaxing or safe space where they can retreat or have a "mental vacation." Integrated with deep breathing, students may practice imagining their relaxing scene as soon as symptoms of anxiety emerge. School counselors also may teach students progressive muscle relaxation and have students audiotape themselves reading a script that instructs them to breathe, tense, and relax different muscle groups. Primary caregivers or parents should also be included in learning somatic management techniques to model the relaxation skills and help their children practice at home (Simpson, Suarez, & Connolly, 2012).

CONCLUSION

Students have identified multiple stressors that can contribute to heightened anxiety in their interactions at school. These include but are not limited to fear of failure, school phobia, difficulty in peer and adult interactions, fear of violence and/or bullying, separation anxiety, and uncertainty about future aspirations. Despite a wealth of research on evidence-based interventions and prevention programs, a significant number of youth who struggle with anxiety do not receive mental health services (Essau, 2005) because of cost, time constraints, and limited access to available services (Barrett & Pahl, 2006). If left untreated, childhood anxiety can lead to personal/social and academic problems (Feehan, McGee, & Williams, 1993; King & Ollendick, 1989; Mychailyszyn, Mendez, & Kendall, 2010; Van Amerigen et al., 2003) that impede a child's ability to be successful in school and beyond. For these reasons, the U.S. federal government (Mental Health Commission, 2003) is calling on schools as the primary source of mental health interventions for children and adolescents (Miller, 2008).

Professional school counselors must remain diligent in their leadership and advocacy roles for creating and implementing effective prevention and intervention strategies in the school environment for students experiencing anxiety. Through comprehensive developmental programs, school counselors can implement responsive services that address the needs of students who experience anxiety and its deleterious effects. This includes advocating and collaborating with student support personnel, parents, and mental health professionals in the community. Parent and teacher education on the affects of anxiety disorders on student learning can facilitate the development of classroom and home modifications conducive to alleviating overwhelming anxiety. Also, it is imperative that school counselors assess the degree of debilitation experienced by a student due to anxiety issues and conduct internal and external referral procedures for more intense, long-term treatment services as needed (ASCA, 2009). School counselors who are knowledgeable of the research on best practices that have relevance to the profession will be better able to facilitate the removal of barriers to student learning while creating opportunities for healthy growth and development for all students.

REFERENCES

Altiero, J. (2006). *No more stinking thinking: A workbook for teaching children positive thinking.* Philadelphia, PA: Jessica Kinglsey Publishing.

American Academy of Child and Adolescent Psychiatry. (2007). Practice parameter for the assessment and treatment of children and adolescents with anxiety disorders. *Journal of the American Academy of Child and Adolescent Psychiatry, 46*, 267–283.

American Psychiatric Association. (2000). *Diagnostic and statistical manual of mental disorders* (4th ed., text rev.). Washington, DC: Author.

American School Counselor Association. (2005). *The professional school counselor and comprehensive school counseling programs.* Retrieved from http://www.schoolcounselor.org/files/PS_ComprehensivePrograms.pdf

American School Counselor Association. (2008). *The professional school counselor and group counseling.* Retrieved from http://www. schoolcounselor.org/files/PS_Group%20 Counseling.pdf

American School Counselor Association. (2009). *The professional school counselor and student mental health.* Retrieved from http://www. schoolcounselor.org/files/PS_ StudentMentalHealth.pdf

Baggerly, J., & Jenkins, W. W. (2009). The effectiveness of child-centered play therapy on developmental and diagnostic factors in children who are homeless. *International Journal of Play Therapy, 18*(1), 45–55. doi:10.1037/a0013878

Barrett, P., & Turner, C. (2001). Prevention of anxiety symptoms in primary school children: Preliminary results from a universal school-based trial. *British Journal of Clinical Psychology, 40*, 399–410. doi:10.1348/014466501163887

Barrett, P. M. (1998). Evaluation of cognitive-behavioral group treatments for childhood anxiety disorder. *Journal of Clinical and Child Psychology, 27*(4), 459–68. doi:10.1207/s15374424jccp2704_10

Barrett, P. M., Lowry-Webster, H. M., & Turner, C. M. (1999). *FRIENDS program social validity and treatment integrity scales.* Brisbane, Australia: Australian Academic Press.

Barrett, P. M., & Pahl, K. M. (2006). School-based intervention: Examining a universal approach to anxiety management. *Australian Journal of Guidance and Counselling, 16*, 55–75. doi:10.1375/ajgc.16.1.55

Barrett, P. M., Rapee, R. M., Dadds, M. R., & Ryan, S. M. (1996). Family enhancement of cognitive style in anxious and aggressive children: Threat bias and the FEAR effect. *Journal of Abnormal Child Psychology, 24*, 187–203. doi:10.1007/BF01441484

Barrett, P. M., Webster, H., Turner, C. M., & May, C. (2003). *Introduction to FRIENDS – a program for enhancing life skills promoting psychological resilience.* Retrieved from http://www.friendsinfo.net/downloads/friendsintro.pdf

Barrett, S., & Heubeck, B. G. (2000). Relationships between school hassles and uplifts and anxiety and conduct problems in grades 3 and 4. *Journal of Applied Developmental Psychology, 21*, 537–554. doi:10.1016/S0193-3973(00)00053-8

Beidel, D. C. (1991). Determining the reliability of psycho-physiological assessment in childhood anxiety. *Journal of Anxiety Disorders, 5*, 139–150. doi:10.1016/0887-6185(91)90025-O

Briggs-Gowan, M. J., Carter, A. S., Clark, R., Augustyn, M., McCarthy, K. J., & Ford, J. D. (2010). Exposure to potentially traumatic events in early childhood: Differential links to emergent psychopathology. *Journal of Child Psychology and Psychiatry* 51(10), 1132–1140. doi:10.1111/j.1469-7610.2010.02256x

Buitelaar, J.K., van Andel, H., Duyx, J. H. M., & van Strein, D. C. (1994). Depressive and anxiety disorders in adolescence: A follow-up study of adolescents with school refusal. *Acta Paedopsychiatrica, 56*, 249–253.

Carrion, V. G., Weems, C. F., Ray, R. D., Glasser, B., Hessl, D., & Reiss, A. L. (2002). Diurnal salivary cortisol in pediatric posttraumatic stress disorder. *Biological Psychiatry, 51*, 575–582. doi:10.1016/S0006-3223(01)01310-5

Carthy, T., Horesh, N., Apter, A. & Gross, J. J. (2009). Patterns of emotional reactivity and regulation in children with anxiety disorders. *Journal of Psychopathological Behavior Assessment, 32*, 23–36. doi:10.1007/s10862-009-9167-8

Chorpita, B. F., Yim, L., Moffitt, C., Umemoto, L. A., & Francis, S. E. (2000). Assessment of symptoms of DSM-IV anxiety and depression in children: A revised child anxiety and depression scale. *Behaviour Research and Therapy, 38*, 835–855. doi:10.1016/S00005-7967(99)00130-8

Christophersen, E. R., & Mortweet, S. L. (2001). *Treatments that work with children: Empirically supported for managing childhood problems.* Washington, DC: American Psychological Association.

Clifford, C. A., Murray, R. M., & Fulker, D. W. (1984). Genetic and environmental influences on obsessional traits and symptoms. *Psychological Medicine, 14*, 791–800. doi:10.1017/S0033291700019760

Cobham,V. E., Dadds, M. R., & Spence, S. H. (1998). The role of parental anxiety in the treatment of child anxiety. *Journal of Consulting and Clinical Psychology, 66*, 893–905. doi:10.1037/0022-006X.66.6.893

Costello, E. J., Mustillo, S., Erkanli, A., Keeler, G., & Angold, A. (2003). Prevalence and development of psychiatric disorders in childhood and adolescence. *Archives of General Psychiatry, 60*, 837–844. doi:10/1001/archpsyc.60.8.837

Cunningham, M. J., Rapee, R. M., & Lyneham, H. J. (2006). The Cool Teens CD-ROM: A multimedia self-help program for adolescents with anxiety. *Youth Studies Australia, 25*, 50–56.

Curtis, R. C., Garrett, M. T., Forst, A., & Looney, R. (2006). Revisiting obsessive-compulsive disorder from a transpersonal perspective: A case for using complementary strategies. *The Journal for the Professional Counselor, 21*, 61–72.

Curtis, R. C., Kimball, A., & Stroup, E. (2004). Understanding and treating social phobia. *Journal of Counseling & Development, 82*, 3–9. doi:10/1002/j.1556-6678.2004.tb00279.x

Dadds, M. R., Spence, S. H., Holland, D. E., Barrett, P. M., & Laurens, K. R. (1997). Prevention and early intervention for anxiety disorders: A controlled trial. *Journal of Consulting and Clinical Psychology, 65*, 627–635. doi:10.1037/0022-006X.65.4.627

D'Esposito, S. E., Blake, J., & Riccio, C. A. (2011). Adolescents' vulnerability to peer victimization: Interpersonal and intrapersonal predictors. *Professional School Counseling, 14*(5), 299–309.

Decker, M. L., Turk, C. L., Hess, B., & Murray, C. E. (2008). Emotion regulation among individuals classified with and without generalized anxiety disorder. *Journal of Anxiety Disorders, 22*, 485–494. doi:10.1016/j.janxdis.2007.04.002

Dorn, L. D., Campo, J. C., Thato, S., Dahl, R. E., Lewin, D., Chandra, R., Di Lorenzo, C. (2003). Psychological comorbidity and stress reactivity in children and adolescents with recurrent abdominal pain and anxiety disorders. *Journal of the American Academy of Child and Adolescent Psychiatry, 42*, 66–75. doi:10.1097/00004583-200301000--00012

Edleson, J. L. (1999). Children's witnessing of adult domestic violence. *Journal of Interpersonal Violence, 14*, 839–870. doi:10.1177/088626099014008004

Eley, T. C., & Gregory, A. M. (2004). Behavioral genetics. In T. L. Morris & J. S. March (Eds.), *Anxiety disorders in children and adolescents* (pp. 71–97). New York, NY: Guilford Press.

Eley, T. C., & Stevenson, J. (2000). Specific life events and chronic experiences differentially associated with depression and anxiety in young twins. *Journal of Abnormal Child Psychology, 28*, 383–394. doi:10.1023/A:1005173127117

Ellis, A., & Harper, R. A. (1975). *A new guide to rational living* (3rd ed.). North Hollywood, CA: Wilshire.

Essau, C. A. (2005). Use of mental health services among adolescents with anxiety and depressive disorders. *Depression and Anxiety, 22*, 130–137. doi:10.1002/da.20115

Essau, C. A., Conradt, J., & Petermann, F. (2002). Course and outcome of anxiety disorders in adolescents. *Journal of Anxiety Disorders, 16*, 67–81. doi:10.1016/S0887-6185(01) 00091-3

Essau, C. A., Conradt, J., Sasagawa, S., & Ollendick, T. H. (2011). Prevention of anxiety symptoms in children: Results from a universal school-based trail. *Behavior Therapy, 43*(2), 450–464. doi:10.1016/j.beth.2011.08.003

Eysenck, S. B., & Eysenck, H. J. (1985). A revised version of the psychoticism scale. *Personality and Individual Differences, 6*, 21–29. doi:10.1016/0191-8869(85)90026-1

Feehan, M., McGee, R., & Williams, S. M. (1993). Mental health disorders from age 15 to age 18 years. *Journal of the American Academy of Child and Adolescent Psychiatry, 32*, 1118–1126. doi:10.1097/00004583-199311000-00003

Field, T., Hernandez-Reif, M., & Diego, M. (2006). Intrusive and withdrawn depressed mothers and their infants. *Developmental Review, 26*, 15–30. doi:10.1016/j.dr.2005.04.001

Gelfand, D. M., & Teti, D. M. (1990). The effects of maternal depression on children. *Clinical Psychology Review, 10*, 329–353. doi:10.1016/0272-7358(90)90065-I

Grills, A. E., & Ollendick, T. H. (2002). Peer victimization, global self-worth, and anxiety in middle school children. *Journal of Clinical Child and Adolescent Psychology, 31*, 59–68.

Gross, J. J. (2002). Emotion regulation: Affective, cognitive, and social consequences. *Psychophysiology, 39*, 281–291. doi:0.1017/S0048577201393198

Hawker, D. S. J., & Boulton, M. J. (2000). Twenty years' research on peer victimization and psychosocialmaladjustment: A meta-analytic review of cross-sectional studies. *Journal of Child Psychology and Psychiatry and Allied Disciplines, 41*, 441–455.

Henkes, K. (2000). *Wemberly worried.* New York, NY: HarperCollins.

Hibbett, A., & Fogelman, K. (1990). Future lives of truants: Family formation and health-related behavior. *British Journal of Educational Psychology, 60*, 171–179.

Hirshfeld-Becker, D. R., Masek, B., Henin, A., Blakely, L. R., Rettew, D. C., Dufton, L., ... Biederman, J. (2008). Cognitive-behavioral intervention with young anxious children. *Harvard Review of Psychiatry, 16*(2), 113–125. doi:10.1080/10673220802073956

Hughes, A. A., Lourea-Waddell, B., & Kendall, P. C. (2008). Somatic complaints in children with anxiety disorders and their unique prediction of poorer academic performance. *Child Psychiatry and Human Development, 39*, 211–220. doi:10.1007/s10578-007-0082-5

Kagan, J., Reznick, J. S., & Snidman, N. (1988). Biological bases of childhood shyness. *Science, 240*, 167–171. doi:10.1126/science.3353713

Keeley, M. L., & Storch, E. A. (2009). Anxiety disorders in youth. *Journal of Pediatric Nursing, 24*, 26–40. doi:10.1016/j.pedn.2007.08.021

Kendall, P. (1994), Treating anxiety disorders in children: Results of a randomized clinical trial. *Journal of Consultation and Clinical Psychology, 62*, 100–110. doi:10.1037/0022-006X.62.1.100

Kendall, P. C., Flannery-Schroeder, E., Panichelli-Mindell, S. M., Southam-Gerow, M., Henin, A., & Warman, M. (1997). Therapy for youths with anxiety disorders: A second randomized clinical trial. *Journal of Consulting and Clinical Psychology, 65*, 366–380. doi:10.1037/0022-006X.65.3.366

Kessler, R. C., Berglund, P., Demler, O., Jin, R., Merikangas, K. R., & Walters, E. E. (2005). Lifetime prevalence and age-of-onset distributions of DSM-IV disorders in the national comorbidity survey replication. *Archives of General Psychiatry, 62*, 593–602. doi:10.1001/archpsyc.62.6.593

Khanna, M. S., & Kendall, P. C. (2010). Computer-assisted cognitive behavioral therapy for child anxiety: Results of a randomized clinical trial. *Journal of Consulting and Clinical Psychology 78*(5), 737–745. doi:10.1037/a0019739

King, N. J., & Ollendick, T. H. (1989). Children's anxiety and phobic disorders in school settings: Classification, assessment, and intervention issues. *Review of Educational Research, 59*, 431–470.

Kochanska, G., Murray, K. T., & Harlan, E. T. (2000). Effortful control in early childhood: Continuity and change, antecedents, and implications for social development. *Developmental Psychology, 36*, 220–232. doi:10.1037/0012-1649.36.2.220

La Greca, A. M., & Harrison, H. (2005). Adolescent peer relations, friendships, and romantic relationships: Do they predict social anxiety and depression? *Journal of Clinical Child and Adolescent Psychology, 34*, 49–61. doi:10.1207/s15374424jccp3401_5

Langley, A. K., Bergman, R. L., McCracken, J., & Piacentini, J. C. (2004). Impairment in childhood anxiety disorders: Preliminary examination of the child anxiety impact scale-parent version. *Journal of Child and Adolescent Psychopharmacology, 14*, 105–114. doi:10.1089/104454604773840544

Legrand, L. N., McGue, M., & Iacono, W. G. (1999). A twin study of state and trait anxiety in childhood and adolescence. *Journal of Child Psychology and Psychiatry, 40*, 953–958. doi:10.1111/1469-7610.00512

Lindsey, E. W., & Colwell, M. J. (2003). Preschoolers' emotional competence: Links to pretend and physical play. *Child Study Journal, 33*, 39–52.

Litrownik, A. J., Newton, R., Hunter, W. M., English, D., & Everson, M. D. (2003). Exposure to family violence in young at-risk children: A longitudinal look at the effects of victimization and witnessed physical and psychological aggression. *Journal of Family Violence, 18*(1), 59–73. doi:10.1023/A:1021405515323

Lowry-Webster, H. M., Barrett, P. M., & Dadds, M. R. (2001). A universal prevention trial of anxiety and depressive symptomatology in childhood: Preliminary data from an Australian study. *Behaviour Change, 18*, 36–50. doi:10.1375/bech.18.1.36

Ma, X. (1999). A meta-analysis of the relationship between anxiety toward mathematics and achievement in mathematics. *Journal for Research in Mathematics Education, 30*(5), 520–40. doi:10.2307/749772

March, S., Spence, S. H., & Donovan, C. L. (2009). The efficacy of an internet-based CBT intervention for child anxiety disorders. *Journal of Pediatric Psychology, 34*(5), 474–487. doi:10.1093/jpepsy/jsn099

Mendlowitz, S., Manassis, K., Bradley, S., Scapillato, D., Miezitis, S., & Shaw, B. (1999). Cognitive behavioral group treatments in childhood anxiety disorders: The role of parental involvement. *Journal of the American Academy of Child and Adolescent Psychiatry, 38*, 1223–1229. doi:10.1097/00004583-19910000-00010

Mennin, D. S., Turk, C. L., Heimberg, R. G., & Carmin, C. N. (2004). Focusing on the regulation of emotion: A new direction for conceptualizing and treating generalized anxiety disorder. In M. A. Reinecke & D. A. Clark (Eds.), *Cognitive therapy over the lifespan: Theory, research and practice* (pp. 60–89). New York, NY: Wiley.

Mental Health Commission, Subcommittee on Children and Family. (2003). *Promoting, preserving, and restoring children's mental health.* Retrieved from http://www. mentalhealthcommission.gov/ subcommittee/children_family020703. doc

Mian, N. D., Wainwright, L., Briggs-Gowan, M. J., & Carter, A. S. (2011). An ecological risk model for early childhood anxiety: The importance of early child symptoms and temperament. *Journal of Abnormal Child Psychology, 39*(4), 501–512. doi:10.1007/s10802-010-9476-0

Miller, L. D. (2008). Facing fears: The feasibility of anxiety universal prevention efforts with children and adolescents. *Journal of Cognitive and Behavior Practice, 15*(1), 25–28.

Muris, P., & Broeren, S. (2009). Twenty-five years of research on childhood anxiety disorders: Publication trends between 1982 and 2006 and a selective review of the literature. *Journal of Child and Family Studies, 18*, 388–395. doi:10.1007/s10826-008-9242-x

Muris, P., Meesters, C., & Rompelberg, L. (2006). Attention control in middle childhood: Relations to psychopathological symptoms and threat perception distortions. *Behaviour Research and Therapy, 45*, 997–1010. doi:10.1016/j.brat.2006.07.010

Muris, P., Merckelbach, H., Mayer, B., & Prins, E. (2000). How serious are common childhood fears? *Behaviour Research and Therapy, 38*, 217–228. doi:10.1016/S0005-7967(98)00204-6

Muris, P., Steerneman, P., Merckelbach, H., & Meesters, C. (1996). The role of parental fearfulness and modeling in children's fear. *Behaviour Research and Therapy, 34*, 265–268. doi:10.1016/0005-7967(95)00067-4

Mychailyszyn, M. P., Mendez, J. L., & Kendall, P. C. (2010). Anxiety disorders and school functioning in youth: Comparisons by diagnosis and comorbidity. *School Psychology Review, 39*(1), 106–121.

Neil, A. L., & Christensen, H. (2009). Efficacy and effectiveness of school-based prevention and early intervention programs for anxiety. *Clinical Psychology Review, 29*, 208–215. doi:10.1016/j.cpr.2009.01.002

Ost, L. G. & Treffers, P. D. A. (2000). Onset, course and outcome for anxiety disorders in children. In W. K. Silverman & P. D. A. Treffers (Eds.), *Anxiety disorders in children and ado-*

lescents: research, assessment, and intervention (pp. 293–312). Cambridge, England: Cambridge University Press.

Pelaez, M., Field, T., Pickens, J. N., & Hart, S. (2008). Disengaged and authoritarian parenting behavior of depressed mothers with their toddlers. *Infant Behavior and Development, 31*, 145–148. doi:10.1016/j.infbeh.2007.06.002

Piper, W. (1930). *The little engine that could.* New York, NY: Platt & Munk.

Podell, J. L., Mychailyszyn, M., Edmunds, J., Puleo, C. M. & Kendall, P. C. (2010). The Coping Cat program for anxious youth: The FEAR plan comes to life. *Cognitive and Behavioral Practice, 17*, 132–141. doi:10.1016/j.cbpra.2009.11.001

Ramirez, G., & Beilock, S. L. (2011). Writing about testing worries boosts exam performance in the classroom. *Science, 331*, 211–213. doi:10.1126/science.1199427

Rapee, R. M. (2001). The development of generalized anxiety. In M. W. Vasey & M. R. Dadds (Eds.), *The developmental psychopathology of anxiety* (pp. 481–503). New York, NY: Oxford University Press.

Rapee, R. M., Schniering, C. A., & Hudson, J. L. (2009). Anxiety disorders during childhood and adolescence: Origins and treatment. *Annual Review of Clinical Psychology, 1*, 311–341. doi:10.1146/annurev. clinpsy.032408.153628

Rueda, M. R., Posner, M. I., & Rothbart, M. K. (2004). Attentional control and self-regulation. In R. F. Baumeister & K. D. Vohs (Eds.), *Handbook of self-regulation: Research, theory, and applications* (pp. 283–300). New York, NY: Guilford Press.

Russ, S. W., & Schafer, E. D. (2006). Affect in fantasy play, emotion in memories, and divergent thinking. *Creativity Research Journal, 18*, 347–354. doi:10.1207/s15326934crj1803_9

Sanson, A., Hemphill, S. A., & Smart, D. (2004). Connections between temperament and social development: A review. *Social Development, 13*(1), 142–170. doi:10.1046.j.1467-9507.2004.00261.x

Shaw, D. S., Keenan, K., Vondra, J. I., Delliquadri, E., & Giovannelli, J. (1997). Antecedents of preschool children's internalizing problems: A longitudinal study of low-income families. *Journal of the American Academy of Child & Adolescent Psychiatry, 36*(12), 1760– 1767. doi:10.1097/00004583-199712000-00025

Shen, Y. (2002). Short-term group play therapy with Chinese earthquake victims: Effects on anxiety, depression, and adjustment. *International Journal of Play Therapy, 11*(1), 43–63. doi:10.1037/h0088856

Silverman, W. K., Kurtines, W. M., Ginsburg, G. S., Weems, C. F., Lumpkin, P. W., & Carmichael, D. H. (1999). Treating anxiety disorders in children with group cognitive-behavioral therapy: A randomized clinical trial. *Journal of Consulting & Clinical Psychology, 67*(6), 995–1003. doi:10.1037/0022-006X.67.6.995

Simpson, D., Suarez, L., & Connolly, S. (2012). Treatment and outcomes for anxiety disorders among children and adolescents: A review of coping strategies and parental behaviors. *Current Psychiatry Reports, 14*(2), 87–95. doi:10.1007/s11920-012-0254-2

Spence, S. H., Holmes, J. M., March, S., & Lipp, O. V. (2006). The feasibility and outcome of clinic plus internet delivery of cognitive-behavior therapy for childhood anxiety. *Journal of Consulting and Clinical Psychology, 74*(3), 614–621. doi:10.1037/0022-006X74.3.614

Stevenson, J., Batten, N., & Cherner, M. (1992). Fears and fearfulness in children and adolescents: A genetic analysis of twin data. *Journal of Child Psychology and Psychiatry, 33*, 977–985. doi:10.1111/j.1469-7810.1992.tb00919.x

Storch, E. A., & Masia-Warner, C. (2004). The relationship of peer victimization to social anxiety and loneliness in adolescent females. *Journal of Adolescence, 27*, 351–362. doi:10.1016/j.adolescence.2004.03.003

Suveg, C., & Zeman, J. (2004). Emotion regulation in children with anxiety disorders. *Journal of Clinical Child and Adolescent Psychology, 33*, 750–759. doi:10.1207/s15374424jccp3304_10

Thapar, A., & McGuffin, P. (1995). Are anxiety symptoms in childhood heritable? *Journal of Child Psychology and Psychiatry, 36*, 439–447. doi:10.1111/j.1469-7610.1995.tb01301.x

Thomas, K. M., Drevets, W. C., Dahl, R. E., Ryan, N. D., Birmaher, B., Eccard, C. H., ... Casey, B. J. (2001). Amygdala response to fearful faces in anxious and depressed children. *Archives of GeneralPsychiatry, 58*, 1057–1063. doi:10.1001/archpsyc.58.11.1057

Turner, S. M., Beidel, D. C., & Costello, A. (1987). Psychopathology in the offspring of anxiety disorders patients. *Journal of Consulting and Clinical Psychology, 55*, 229–235. doi:10.1037/0022-006X.55.2.229

Van Ameringen, M., Mancini, C., & Farvolden, P. (2003). The impact of anxiety disorders on educational achievement. *Journal of Anxiety Disorders, 17*, 561–571. doi:10.1016/S0887-6185(02)00228-1

van Brakel, A. M. L., Muris, P., Bogels, S. M., & Thomassen, C. (2006). A multifactorial model for the etiology of anxiety in non-clinical adolescents: Main and interactive effects of behavioral inhibition, attachment, and parental rearing. *Journal of Child and Family Studies, 15*, 569–579.

Van Horne, J. (2012, April 17). *Breathing techniques* [personal communication]. Copy in possession of author.

Vasey, M. W., & MacLeod, C. (2001). Information-processing factors in childhood anxiety: A review and developmental perspective. In M. W. Vasey & M. R. Dadds (Eds.), *The developmental psychopathology of anxiety* (pp. 253–277). New York, NY: Oxford University Press.

Warren, S. L., Schmitz, S., & Emde, R. N. (1999). Behavioral genetic analyses of self-reported anxiety at 7 years of age. *Journal of the American Academy of Child and Adolescent Psychiatry, 38*, 1403–1408. doi:10.1097/00004583-19911000-00015

Weems, C. F., Zakem, A., Costa, N. M., Cannon, M. F., & Watts, S. E. (2005). Physiological response and childhood anxiety: Association with symptoms of anxiety disorders and cognitive bias. *Journal of Clinical Child and Adolescent Psychology, 34*, 712–723. doi:10.1207/s15374424jccp3404_13

Wettig, H. H., Coleman, A. R., & Geider, F. J. (2011). Evaluating the effectiveness of Theraplay in treating shy, socially withdrawn children. *International Journal of Play Therapy, 20*(1), 26–37. doi:10.1037/a0022666

Wood, J. (2006). Effect of anxiety reduction on children's school performance and social adjustment. *Developmental Psychology, 42*(2), 345–349. doi:10.1037/0012-1649.42.2.345

Wood, J. J., McLeod, B. D., Sigman, M., Hwang, W., & Chu, B. C. (2003). Parenting behavior and childhood anxiety: Theory, empirical findings, and future directions. *Journal of Child Psychology and Psychiatry, 44*, 134–151. doi:10.111/1469-7610.00106

World Health Organization. (2004). *Prevention of mental disorders: Effective interventions and policy options.* Geneva, Switzerland: Author.

Wuthrich, V. M., Rapee, R. M., Cunningham, M. J., Lyneham, H. J., Hudson, J. L., & Schniering, C. A., (2006). A randomized controlled trial of the Cool Teens CD-ROM computerized program for adolescent anxiety. *Academy of Child and Adolescent Psychiatry, 51*(3), 261–70. doi:10.1016/j.jaac.2011.12.002

CHAPTER 12

The Sustained Reduction of Youth Suicidal Behavior in an Urban Multicultural School District

Frank J. Zenere and Philip J. Lazarus

ABSTRACT

An 18-year longitudinal case study of the suicide rates of students attending a large, urban, multicultural school district between 1989 and 2006 is described. The high rate of suicide (5.5 per 100,000 students ages 5–19) in the district during the period 1980–1988 led to the development and implementation of a district-wide Youth Suicide Prevention and Intervention Program. The program is based on a three-tier suicide prevention model incorporating universal, selected, and indicated prevention/intervention strategies. Suicide and suicide attempt data were collected from crisis hotline reports. Since implementation of the program, a significant decrease in the suicide rate (1.4 per 100,000) was observed from 1989 to 2006. There also was a steady decline in the suicide attempt rate during this same period. This study is among the first to provide longitudinal evidence that youth suicidal behavior can be reduced potentially through school-based suicide prevention programs.

Youth suicidal behavior, particularly its most extreme forms (i.e., suicide attempts; suicide), is a continuing national problem (Miller & Eckert, 2009). The issue of youth suicidal behavior is a critical one for our nations schools, and has led to increased calls for school-based suicide prevention (e.g., Kalafat, 2003; Lazarus & Kalafat, 2001; Mazza, 1997; Mazza & Reynolds, 2008; Miller & DuPaul, 1996) and intervention (e.g.,Lieberman & Davis, 2002; Lieberman, Poland, & Cassel, 2008; Sandoval & Zadeh, 2008) efforts. In response to the growing need for suicide prevention programs in the schools, the Miami-Dade County Public Schools in Miami, Florida, developed a comprehensive, multitier suicide prevention and intervention program after 18 students took their own lives in 1988. In this case study, the components of the program and its effect on youth suicide and suicide attempts over an 18-year span are described. This study is significant for being among the first to demonstrate the potential utility of comprehensive school-based prevention programs for reducing youth suicidal behavior over sustained periods.

Although other studies examining the effectiveness of school-based suicide prevention programs have been evaluated, to date these have largely focused on measuring changes in students' knowledge and attitudes regarding suicide rather than suicidal behavior (Berman, Jobes, & Silverman, 2006). In contrast, Zenere and Lazarus (1997) conducted a study in which they examined program effects on various aspects of suicidal behavior, including suicidal ideation, suicide attempts, and suicide. Further, this suicide prevention program deviated significantly from others reported in the professional literature, in that a district-wide program was developed, implemented, and evaluated over a 5-year period. Although no significant reductions were observed in suicidal ideation, both the number of student suicide attempts and suicides decreased substantially following program implementation. This case study provided one of the first clear documentations that school-based suicide prevention programs can potentially reduce suicidal behavior, including its most severe forms (i.e., suicide and suicide attempts). The study was also notable for being the only 1 among 13 school-based suicide prevention programs to be classified as exhibiting promising evidence for educational/clinical significance (Miller, Eckert, & Mazza, 2009) according to the Task Force on Evidence-Based Interventions in

School Psychology Procedural and Coding Manual (Kratochwill & Stoiber, 2002). The present study was designed as a longitudinal extension of this earlier work.

METHOD

Miami-Dade County Public Schools is the nation's fourth largest school district, serving over 350,000 students in 392 school sites. The district provides educational services to a multilingual and culturally diverse student community. The student population is 61.3% Hispanic, 26.8 African American, 9.4% Caucasian, and 2.5% nonspecified. Because of an alarming increase in youth suicidal behavior in the Miami-Dade County Public Schools, the Youth Suicide Prevention and Intervention Program was created by the Division of Student Services and the Guidance Counselor Coordinator in 1989. The program is managed by the Administrative Director of the Division of Student Services and is staffed by members of the Student Services Crisis Team, which is presently composed of a school psychologist and school social worker, and has ranged in size from two to four professionals.

The Youth Suicide Prevention and Intervention Program was implemented in all existing school sites. Additional schools have received services from the Youth Suicide Prevention and Intervention Program as they opened. The program is consistent with recommended best practices in the professional literature. According to many researchers (e.g., Kalafat, 2003; King, 2001; Mazza & Reynolds, 2008), universal prevention programs should (a) focus on developing a district-wide school policy concerning suicide; (b) educate school professionals about suicide warning signs and risk factors; (c) encourage collaboration among teachers, nurses, and counselors; (d) include suicide prevention education in the classroom curriculum; (e) develop peer assistance programs; and (f) implement activities aimed at increasing school connectedness. Programs should also support school and family partnerships and establish a school crisis team. In addition, an effective school-based suicide prevention program should incorporate prevention, intervention, and postintervention procedures (Mazza, 1997, 2006; Miller & DuPaul, 1996).

UNIVERSAL INTERVENTIONS

To Reach Ultimate Success Together. Universal strategies are implemented through the To Reach Ultimate Success Together curriculum (Miami-Dade County Public Schools, 1985) in a series of skill development lessons. The curriculum (http://studentservices.dadeschools.net/trust/curriculum.asp) is focused on the delivery of prevention education and intervention strategies across grade levels. Lessons emphasize skill building in the areas of self-awareness, communication, problem solving, coping, decision making, relationship building, stress management, and knowledge of health issues and resources. The program attempts to mitigate student risk factors and promote protective factors. It was in place at the inception of the Youth Suicide Prevention and Intervention Program, and was initially created as a part of a substance abuse prevention and intervention initiative. The program is currently providing prevention education and intervention services in all middle and senior high schools and six elementary schools.

Life Management Skills curriculum. Historically, suicide prevention in Miami-Dade County Public Schools was formally addressed in 10th grade through the state-mandated Life Management Skills curriculum (Miami-Dade County Public Schools, 1979). Within this curriculum (http://www.dadeschools.net/students/cbc/famconsume.asp), a unit of study is devoted to teaching students the possible warning signs of suicidal behavior and the development of help-seeking behaviors. Students are taught to identify signs and behaviors associated with potential suicide risks in themselves and others and to take appropriate action in gaining adult assistance.

Training school staff. Training school administrators, faculty, and support staff to recognize risk factors and warning signs related to potential youth suicidal behavior is a critical component of universal prevention efforts. All Miami-Dade County Public Schools staff members receive training on the recognition of risk factors and warning signs associated with potential suicidal behavior and are given information regarding the supervision and referral of at-risk students. The training emphasizes to staff that students who commit suicide most often have predisposing mental health problems (e.g., depression, bipolar disorder), a finding that has been well documented in the literature (Fleischmann, Bertolote, Belfer, & Beautrais, 2005). School mental health professionals receive additional training in suicide risk assessment, parental notification, referral to community-based mental health resources, and postintervention practices. This training has been delivered via a variety of methods over the years, including staff presentations, video inservice, and written materials. On-site training is approximately 1 hr in length and is provided by members of the Student Services Crisis Team annually by school-based mental health professionals, as well as upon request. Informed and vigilant staff members have successfully intervened with suicidal youth with considerable success. Since the inception of the Youth Suicide Prevention and Intervention Program in 1989, the authors can identify only two occasions when a Miami-Dade County Public Schools student, previously identified by staff as a potential risk for suicidal behavior, has eventually taken his or her life. In contrast to these two tragic losses, thousands of additional potentially suicidal students identified by staff have been directed to helping resources where they have received needed intervention and support.

The Good Samaritan Communities of Caring Program. The Good Samaritan Communities of Caring Program (Miami-Dade County Public Schools, 2004) was created to address student knowledge of plans to self-harm or harm other students. Because research has demonstrated that students are more likely to express their suicidal thoughts and plans to peers than to adults in their environment (Kalafat & Lazarus, 2002; Mazza, 2006), it seems logical to equip youth with the ability to recognize risk situations in their peers and to seek immediate adult assistance. Specifically, students are taught by student services counseling professionals and instructed in the classroom setting to recognize warning signs associated with suicidal behavior and to make immediate contact with an adult on campus or to call a confidential hotline. The program is reinforced by numerous on-campus posters.

SELECTED INTERVENTIONS

The Student Intervention Profile. The Student Intervention Profile is a means of identifying students who may potentially represent a suicide risk. At the end of each grading period, counselors receive a printout on each student that reviews seven major areas of concern, including academic performance, effort, conduct, attendance, negative report card comments, Code of Student Conduct violations, and involvement with school police. Classroom teachers and other school professionals are responsible for rating student performance in the aforementioned areas. Students demonstrating difficulty in three or more of these areas are referred to a school counselor. A counselor then meets with the student to assess specific needs and works with other school staff to help the student succeed in school and cope more effectively with particular emotional and/or behavioral difficulties, including possible suicidal behavior.

Student Support Team. Once a student has been identified as potentially being at risk, a Student Support Team meeting may be held to determine the best course of action to assist the student. Miami-Dade County Public Schools mental health professionals offer a wide array of individual and group counseling services to support students. Possible issues addressed in counseling sessions include alcoholism in the family; bereavement; self-esteem enhancement; gay, lesbian, bisexual, and transgender youth issues; anger management; conflict resolution; social skills development; and dropout prevention.

Health Connect in Our Schools. The introduction of the Health Connect in Our Schools initiative (Miami-Dade County Public Schools, Children's Trust of Miami-Dade County, and Miami-Dade County Health Department, 2006) provides an opportunity to address the health needs of school-age children by uniting fragmented prevention and intervention services from around the county. The goal of this initiative is to improve health outcomes of children and adolescents through health promotion, education, and care. This collaborative effort has created school-based health teams consisting of one nurse, two health aides, and a clinical social worker. Each team is assigned to cover two school sites. The initiative is now in place in 165 schools and is projected to be fully implemented in all Miami-Dade County Public Schools by 2011, pending district budget approval.

On-site mental health services. When a student's needs exceed the capacity of Miami-Dade County Public Schools staff to resolve a problem effectively, it is imperative that timely connections to community-based services are provided. In some cases, agencies have been given clearance to offer mental health services on campus as part of full-service school (Dryfoos, 1994) initiatives. These supplemental mental health services provide students with expert assistance they would otherwise be unable to typically access.

INDICATED INTERVENTIONS

Assess imminent risk. Indicated intervention services are initiated when a member of a school's staff learns of a student who presents as possible or imminent risk for suicide, based on communications and/or behavior. Once identified, the student is escorted by a staff member to the office of a school mental health professional (e.g., school psychologist or counselor). The school mental health professional interviews the student to assess the level of suicidal risk and then contacts the parent or guardian. In situations in which risk for suicide is considered moderate or high, parents are requested to retrieve their child and are given recommendations for seeking community-based mental health services. The parent is asked to sign a release of information form allowing the school mental health professional the opportunity to collaborate with the student's community-based therapist or agency contacts (if present), thereby enhancing the continuity of care. In the event a student presents as an imminent risk for suicidal behavior and is judged to be a threat to his or her own safety, school police are also notified. The student remains under the constant supervision of professional staff until the parent or guardian or a community-based authority (e.g., police, child protection agency) retrieves the student. In such cases, a law enforcement professional may transport the student to a local hospital or crisis stabilization unit for additional assessment.

Crisis Hotline. Miami-Dade County Public School's policy stipulates that the school mental health professional responding to a student's suicidal behavior call the district's Crisis Hotline to report the event to a member of the Student Services Crisis Team. This procedure is designed to gather pertinent student information, along with a description of the incident and actions undertaken to address suicidal risk. This approach affords the caller an opportunity to review cases with highly trained district colleagues who are experienced in suicide risk assessment and intervention. The reporting of the event also provides valuable data that can be used in determining the prevalence of suicidal behavior and trends that may affect the delivery of prevention and intervention services.

Returning to school after treatment. After a student returns to school following hospitalization or receiving community-based mental health services, a Miami-Dade County Public Schools mental health professional meets with the student and his or her parents to provide support services. Such support may include an adjustment in the student's class schedule, length of school day, or quantity of homework required. It always includes the assignment of a key staff person to serve as an immediate support resource.

POSTINTERVENTION

Following a student suicide, it is paramount that schools implement crisis postintervention plans (Brock, 2002). At this stage, an emphasis is placed on addressing feelings of loss, preventing possible contagion effects, and expanding prevention efforts by maintaining a safe, secure, and positive school climate. The reestablishment of coping and the removal and/or lessening of stigmatization for help seeking are two of the major goals of the postintervention period (Brock, 2002). In the aftermath of a student suicide, the Miami-Dade County Public Schools Student Services Crisis Team assists school administrators, faculty, mental health professionals, and parents/guardians in responding to student and staff needs. Consultation, student advocacy, psychoeducation, psychological first aid, and suicide prevention training may be provided as part of this response.

DATA COLLECTION

According to available records, Miami-Dade County Public Schools did not institute any formal suicide prevention programming prior to the Youth Suicide Prevention and Intervention Program initiative; however, the district did compile student suicide data from 1980 to 1988. Student data, used to determine postintervention change, were retrieved from Crisis Hotline reports maintained by the Student Services Crisis Team. The reports provide a detailed account of student suicidal behaviors, including suicide attempts and suicides. The reports also provide additional information, including student demographic data, description of the behavior or incident, and response interventions. All student deaths presumably resulting from suicide are crosschecked and confirmed through the Miami-Dade County Office of the Medical Examiner. National and Florida youth suicidal behavior data used in the study were obtained from the Centers for Disease Control and Prevention (CDC, 1990–2005). Miami-Dade County Public Schools student population reports provided information for statistical comparison.

RESULTS

Student suicide data have been gathered since 1980 by Miami-Dade County Public Schools. An analysis of the data from 1980 to 1988 (preintervention period) shows a district average suicide rate of 5.5 per 100,000 for students aged 5–19 years. Since the implementation of the Youth Suicide Prevention and Intervention Program in 1989, the student suicide rates demonstrated a downward trend through the last data collection period in 2006 (see Figure 7.1), with the average student suicide rate declining to 1.4 per 100,000 for students aged 5–19 years (1989–2006). The student suicide rate reduction is further magnified by organizing the data into 6-year intervals beginning with the program's inception. This grouping of data yields the following student suicide rates: 1989–1994, 1.97 per 100,000; 1995–2000, 1.45 per 100,000; and 2001– 2006, 0.73 per 100,000 (see Figure 7.1). An analysis of variance was conducted to evaluate the relationship between pre-and postintervention suicide rates. The analysis of variance was significant, $F(3, 23) = 14.01$, $p < .0001$. Post hoc tests were conducted to evaluate pairwise differences among the suicide rates. There were statistically significant mean differences between the preintervention period and all three postintervention periods (Tukey's honestly significant difference [HSD], $p < .001$ for periods 1989–1994, 1995–2000, 2001–2006). No statistically significant mean differences were found between the postintervention periods (Tukey's HSD, $p = 1.00$ for periods 1989–1994 and 1995–2000; Tukey's HSD, $p = .74$ for 1989–1994 and 2001–2006; Tukey's HSD, $p = .69$ for 1995–2006 and 2001–2006).

Student suicide attempt data also revealed a pattern of general reduction throughout the implementation period (see Figure 7.2). Suicide attempt data were not collected prior to 1989 when the program began. During the first year of program implementation, the number of suicide attempts was 88 per 100,000. This was reduced to 52 per 100,000 in the second year, and 39 per 100,000 in the third year. Again, suicide attempt data are grouped by 6-year intervals beginning with the program's inception. For the first 6-year interval (1989 –1994), the number of suicide attempts was 45.5 per 100,000 and for the second 6-year interval (1995–2000) the rate was 17.2. For the latest 6-year period from 2001 to 2006, the number of suicide attempts declined to 9.0 per 100,000 (Figure 7.2).

To further compare the Miami-Dade County Public Schools data with state and national suicide rates, a comparison was made beginning with data collected in 1990 and ending in 2005. During this period, the suicide rate of Miami-Dade County Public Schools students' ages 5–19 years was 1.3 per 100,000 students. This rate is

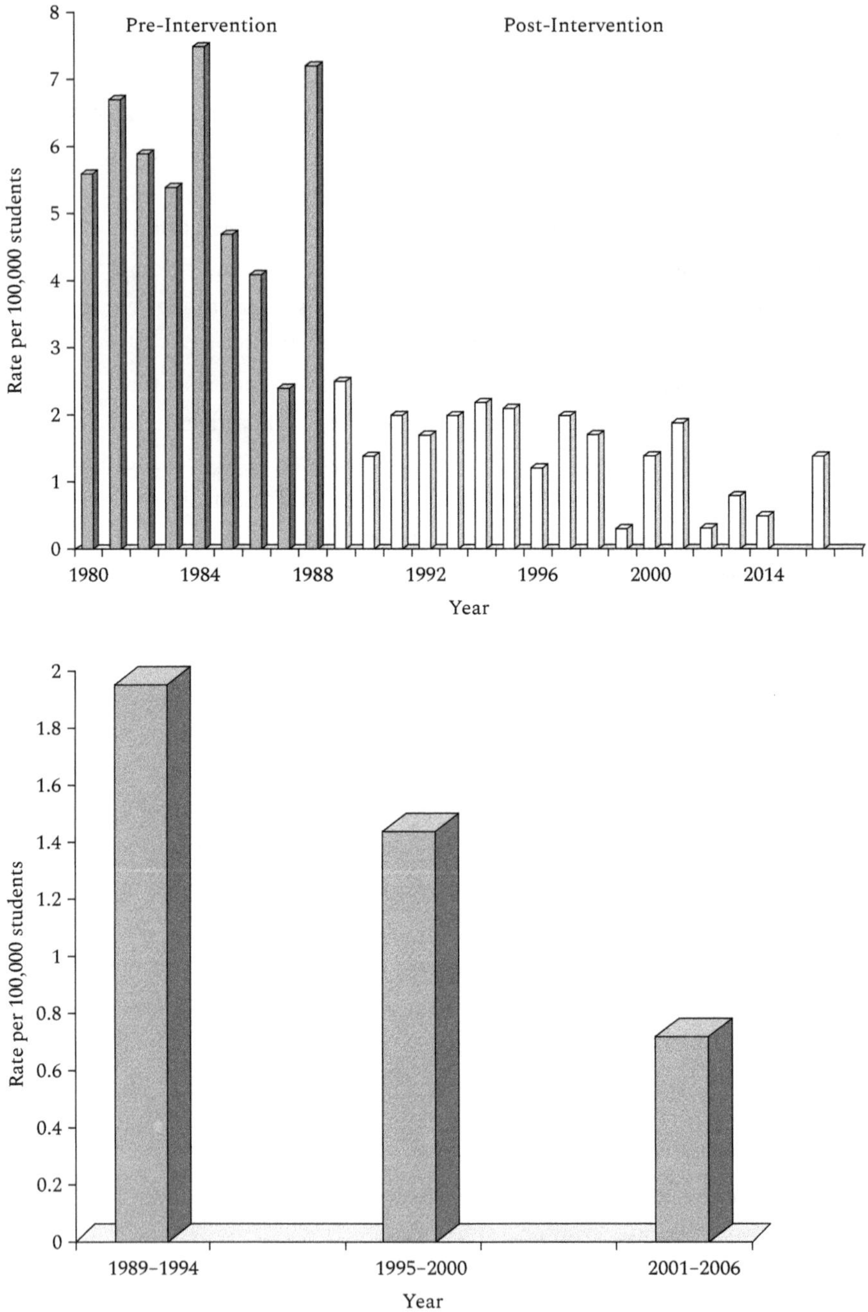

FIGURE 7.1. Top panel: Miami-Dade County Public Schools student suicide rate per 100,000 students, ages 5–19 years, 1980 –2006. Bottom panel: Miami-Dade County Public Schools postintervention suicide rate per 100,000 students, ages 5–19 years, 1989–1994, 1995–2000, 2001–2006.

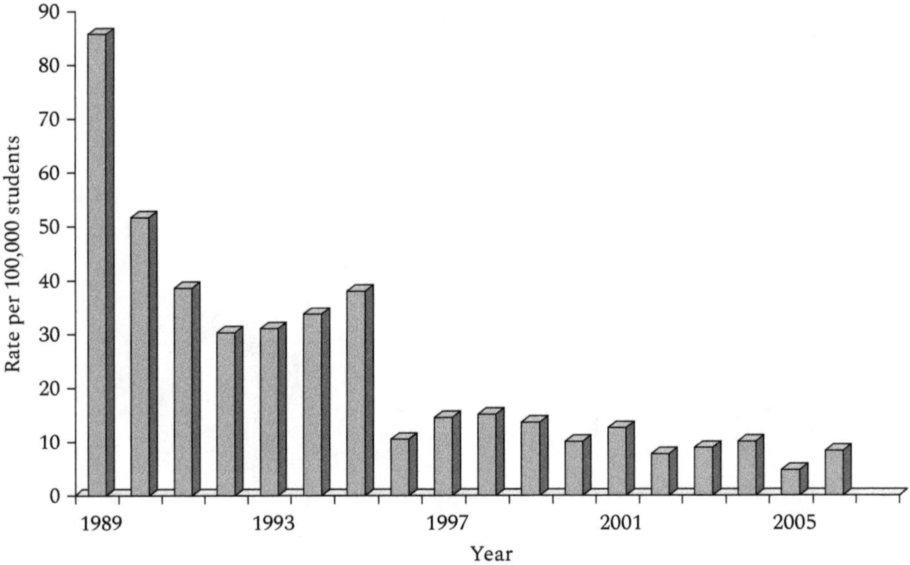

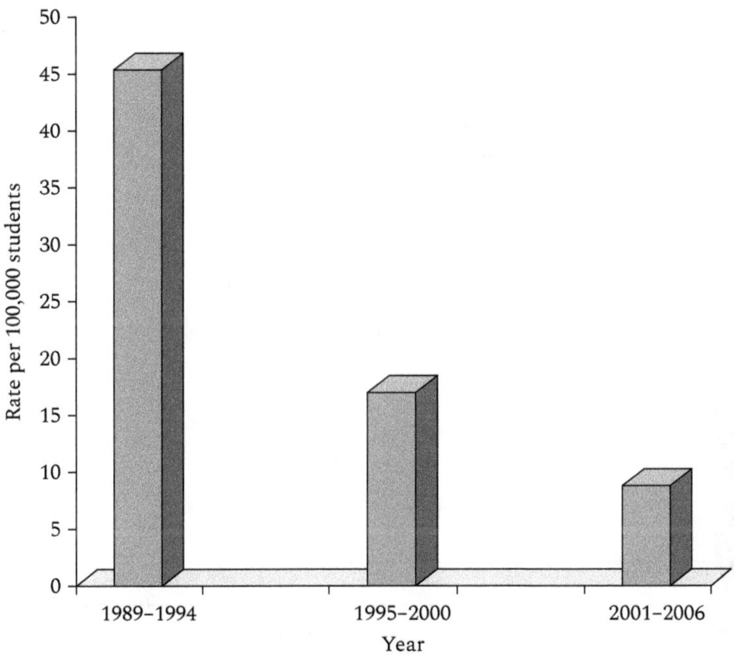

FIGURE 7.2. Top panel: Miami-Dade County Public Schools student suicide attempt rate per 100,000 students, ages 5–19 years, 1989–2006. Bottom panel: Miami-Dade County Public Schools student suicide attempt rate per 100,000 students, ages 5–19 years, 1989–1994, 1995–2000, 2001–2006.

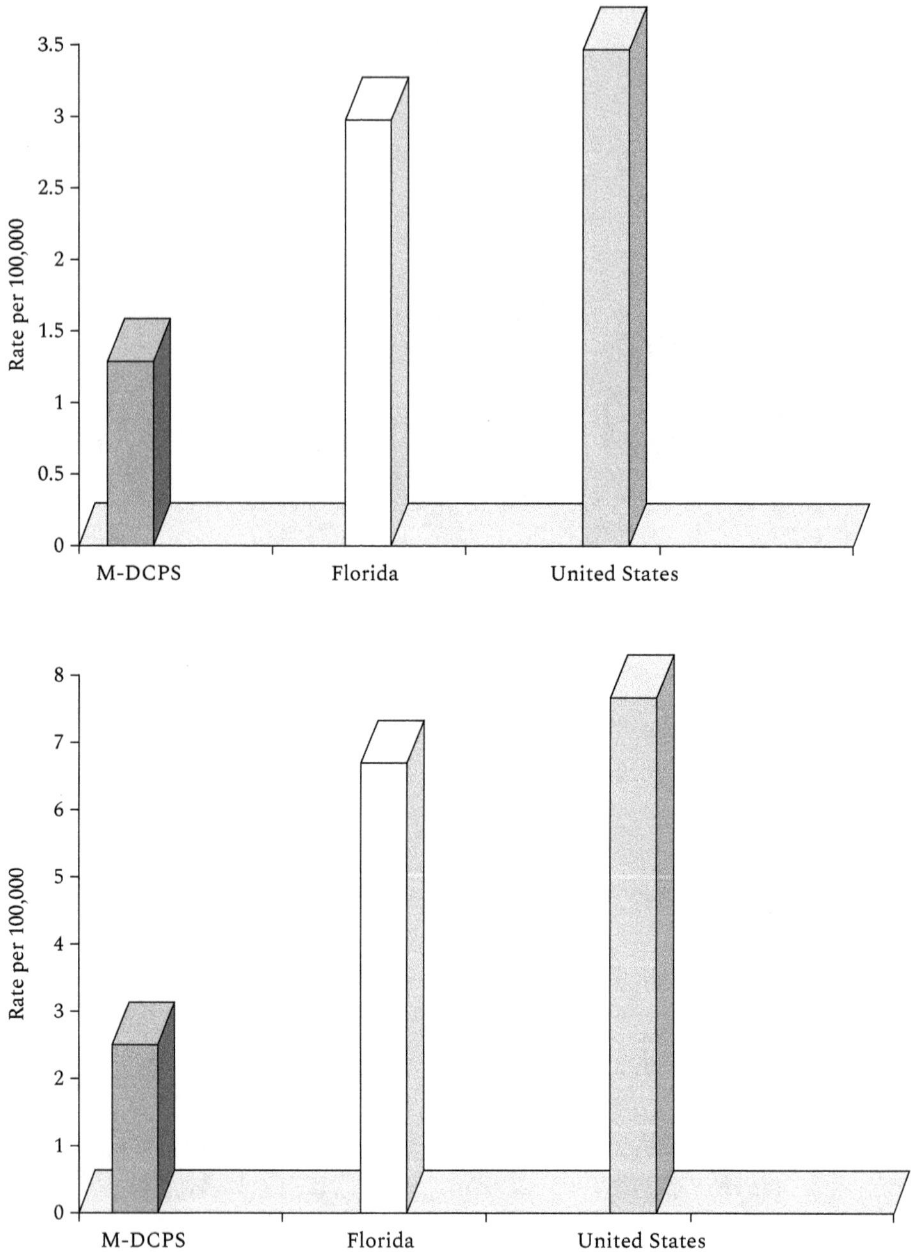

FIGURE 7.3. Top panel: Comparative youth suicide rate per 100,000 students, ages 5–19 years, in Miami-Dade County Public Schools (M-DCPS), Florida, United States, 1990–2005. Bottom panel: Comparative youth suicide rate per 100,000 students, ages 15–19 years, in Miami-Dade County Public Schools (M-DCPS), Florida, United States, 2001–2005.

lower than age-equivalent groups from Florida (3.0 per 100,000; Centers for Disease Control and Prevention, 1990–2005) and the United States (3.5 per 100,000; Centers for Disease Control and Prevention, 1990–2005; see Figure 7.3). A more dramatic difference is observed when contrasting the suicide rates of Miami-Dade County Public Schools students ages 15–19 years (2.5 per 100,000) with other age-equivalent groups from Florida (6.7 per 100,000), and the United States (7.7 per 100,000; Centers for Disease Control and Prevention, 2001–2005; see Figure 7.3).

DISCUSSION

This case study is among the first to suggest that comprehensive school-based suicide prevention programs can reduce youth suicidal behavior and sustain this reduction over time. A frequent criticism of many school-based suicide prevention programs is that most of them to date have been largely focused on changing knowledge and attitudes about suicide rather than actual rates of suicide and suicide attempts (Berman et al., 2006; Mazza, 1997; Mazza & Reynolds, 2008; Miller & DuPaul, 1996). A longitudinal extension of an earlier demonstration (Zenere & Lazarus, 1997), this comprehensive prevention program resulted in sustained reductions in both suicide and suicide attempts among students in the district. The study is also unique for being the only one of which the authors are aware that has collected longitudinal data on a district-wide suicide prevention program over an extended (i.e., 18-year) period. There are several limitations of this case study, however, which are described in the next section.

LIMITATIONS OF THE STUDY

Although great effort has been directed at gathering student suicidal behavior data, youth suicidal behavior is not always reported to the district office. As such, district data likely reflects an underestimation of actual incidents, although the extent to which this occurs in unknown. There is high confidence in the validity of student suicide data, however, as it is confirmed through officials at the Miami-Dade County Office of the Medical Examiner. Nevertheless, potential suicide deaths are possibly classified as accidents because of a lack of available evidence. In addition, state and national comparison data related to suicide attempts and suicide were obtained differently than data obtained by Miami-Dade County Public Schools. For instance, the Youth Risk Behavior Surveillance System (2007) administered by the Centers for Disease Control often obtains state and national rates of suicidal ideation and attempts via self-report surveys of large representative samples of youth in schools; this random form of sampling yields anonymous/confidential reports of suicidality that are likely to result in a larger estimate (rate) of suicidality than would be obtained only from youth whose suicide attempts are detected by others or self-reported (i.e., the method used to track rates of suicidality within Miami-Dade County Public Schools). Thus, methods of obtaining rates were not equivalent.

It should therefore be understood that comparative findings referenced in this study may approximate but not reflect actual levels of *nonfatal* suicidal behavior. Parents and caregivers frequently are unaware of their child's suicidal behavior, including suicide attempts (Kashani, Goddard, & Reid, 1989; Mazza, 2006). If suicide attempts go unreported by parents or peers (e.g., because of a lack of knowledge or a reluctance to report this behavior to the school system), then it would be expected that the number of suicide attempts would be higher, but by precisely how much cannot be determined.

Further, it is difficult to determine the degree of student exposure to suicide prevention curricula and services, because students enter and exit Miami-Dade County Public Schools at different stages and because some components were introduced later than others. Moreover, the suicide prevention program reviewed in this article has not been subjected to a rigorous evaluation, including treatment integrity checks, and the relative effect of each component cannot be determined. Finally, although it appears that this district-wide program may be an effective approach to school-based suicide prevention, given the lack of controlled experimental or quasi-experimental research evaluating this program, its effectiveness still needs to be demonstrated (Miller et al., 2009). Nevertheless, like case study demonstrations of reductions of student antisocial behavior using school-wide positive behavior support procedures (McCurdy, Mannella, & Eldridge, 2003), the results of this case study are promising and can form the basis for more comprehensive attempts at school-based suicide prevention program evaluation.

Despite these and other limitations (e.g., overall youth suicide rates in the United States generally declined during parts of the period in this study), the data suggest that the program has effectively reduced the rate of youth suicide over a long-term (18-year) period. As such, it appears there is now increasing evidence that school-based suicide prevention programs can potentially reduce youth suicidal behavior, and that school psychologists and other school personnel can play a prominent role in this process.

REFERENCES

Berman, A. L., Jobes, D. A., & Silverman, M. M. (2006). *Adolescent suicide: Assessment and intervention.* Washington, DC: American Psychological Association.

Brock, S. E. (2002). School suicide postvention. In S. E. Brock, P. J. Lazarus, & S. R. Jimerson (Eds.), *Best practices in school crisis prevention and intervention* (pp. 553–575). Bethesda, MD: National Association of School Psychologists Press.

Centers for Disease Control and Prevention. (1990 –2005). *Suicide death rates by age, WISQARS.* Retrieved July 9, 2008, from http://webappa.cdc.gov/sasweb/ncipc/mortrate.html

Centers for Disease Control and Prevention. (2007). *Youth Risk Behavior Survey, Division of Adolescent and School Health.* Retrieved July 1, 2008, from http:// apps.nccd.cdc.gov/yrbss/

Dryfoos, J. G. (1994). *Full-service schools: A revolution in health and social services for children, youth, and families.* San Francisco, CA: Jossey-Bass.

Fleischmann, A., Bertolote, J. M., Belfer, M., & Beautrais, A. (2005). Completed suicide and psychiatric diagnoses in young people: Examination of the evidence. *American Journal of Orthopsychiatry, 75,* 676 – 683.

Kalafat, J. (2003). School approaches to youth suicide prevention. *American Behavioral Scientist, 46,* 1211– 1223.

Kalafat, J., & Lazarus, P. J. (2002). Suicide prevention in schools. In S. E. Brock, P. J. Lazarus, & S. R. Jimerson (Eds.), *Best practices in school crisis prevention and intervention* (pp. 211–223). Bethesda, MD: National Association of School Psychologists Press.

Kashani, J. H., Goddard, P., & Reid, J. C. (1989). Correlates of suicidal ideation in a community sample of children and adolescents. *Journal of the American Academy of Child and Adolescent Psychiatry, 28,* 912–917.

King, K. (2001). Developing a comprehensive school suicide prevention program. *Journal of School Health, 71,* 132–137.

Kratochwill, T. R., & Stoiber, K. C. (2002). Evidence-based interventions in school psychology. Conceptual foundations of the Procedural and Coding Manual of Division 16 and the Society for the Study of School Psychology. *School Psychology Quarterly, 17,* 341–389.

Lazarus, P. J., & Kalafat, J. (2001). Suicide prevention and youth: Recommendations for public policy. *International Journal of Sociology and Social Policy, 21,* 22–37.

Lieberman, R. A., & Davis, J. M. (2002). Suicide intervention. In S. E. Brock, P. J. Lazarus, & S. R. Jimerson, (Eds.), *Best practices in school crisis prevention and intervention* (pp. 531–551). Bethesda, MD: National Association of School Psychologists.

Lieberman, R. A., Poland, S., & Cassel, R. (2008). Best practices in suicide intervention. In A. Thomas & J. Grimes (Eds.), *Best practices in school psychology V* (pp. 1457–1473). Bethesda, MD: National Association of School Psychologists.

Mazza, J. J. (1997). School-based suicide prevention programs: Are they effective? *School Psychology Review, 26,* 382–396.

Mazza, J. J. (2006). Youth suicidal behavior: A crisis in need of attention. In F. A. Villarruel & T. Luster (Eds.), *Adolescent mental health* (pp. 156–177). Westport, CT: Greenwood Publishing Group.

Mazza, J. J., & Reynolds, W. M. (2008). School-wide approaches to prevention of and treatment for depression and suicidal behaviors. In B. Doll & J. A. Cummings (Eds.), *Transforming school mental health services* (pp. 213–241). Thousand Oaks, CA: Corwin.

McCurdy, B. L., Mannella, M. C., & Eldridge, N. (2003). Positive behavior support in urban schools: Can we prevent the escalation of antisocial behavior? *Journal of Positive Behavior Interventions, 5*, 158–170.

Miami-Dade County Public Schools, Children's Trust of Miami-Dade County, & Miami-Dade County Health Department. (2006). *Health Connect in the Schools.* Miami, FL.

Miami-Dade County Public Schools (1979). *Life Management Skills Curriculum.* Miami, FL.

Miami-Dade County Public Schools (2004). *The Good Samaritan Communities of Caring Program.* Miami, FL.

Miami-Dade County Public Schools (1985). *To Reach Ultimate Success Together* (TRUST) *Program.* Miami, FL.

Miller, D. N., & DuPaul, G. J. (1996). School-based prevention of adolescent suicide: Issues, obstacles, and recommendations for practice. *Journal of Emotional and Behavioral Disorders, 4*, 221–230.

Miller, D. N., & Eckert, T. L. (2009). Youth suicidal behavior: An introduction and overview. *School Psychology Review, 38*, 153–167.

Miller, D. N., Eckert, T. L., & Mazza, J. J. (2009). Suicide prevention programs in the schools: A review and public health perspective. *School Psychology Review, 38*, 168–188.

Sandoval, J., & Zadeh, S. (2008). Principles for intervening with suicide. *School Psychology Forum, 2*, 49–66.

Zenere, F. J., III, & Lazarus, P. J. (1997). The decline of youth suicidal behavior in an urban multicultural school system following the introduction of a suicide prevention and intervention program. *Suicide and Life-Threatening Behavior, 16*, 360–378.

CHAPTER 13
Re-Imagine High School Students' Career Development and the Transition From School to Work

Marie Michelle Rosemond, Ph.D.

This chapter endeavors to offer broad and in-depth information to strengthen career development and the transition process for high school students. Because career development and transition are exclusively their own body of knowledge, the analysis for this section reflects mutual themes within the intersection of career development and transition to inform implications for high school counselors. The results are discoveries and recommendations to support the guiding principles, and helps set the intention for practitioners to be mindful of career access challenges and associated implications in addressing career and college readiness (Stone, 2016).

School counselors tend to become utility specialist who are assigned a host collateral assignments in addition to their loosely connected to primary duties. Fundamentally, school counselors for high school students assist with the transition from high school to postsecondary education, vocational school, or the world of work (Nystul, 2004). Because of this dynamic along with trends in education and a labor market in recovery, this chapter provides school counselors with tools and insights to guide the transition for high school students' career development that leads to world of work.

Transition is multifaceted and complex for all age groups. Therefore, transition out of high school and implications for career counselors is critical because of students' stage in life development. This stage of development highlights the criticality of the services career counselors provide in the 21st century and knowledge economy. Historically, career counselors are essentially teachers who have played a critical role in society and in the lives of high school students. This influence is significant and as with most industries, career counseling in secondary education as a profession will have to reinvent to provide relevant knowledge for emerging adolescents.

Career counselors managing career development and the transition out of high school for emerging adolescents require a transition framework, an understanding of educational and labor market trends, to rethink content area preparation and delivery. This approach positions the career counselor fundamentally rooted in both authoritarian and nonauthoritarian educational theories. The understanding of these theories, which strengthens the proposed approach and theories in contestation, the transition framework is merged with educational theories as a tool to align practices. By aligning theories from education and transition, implications for school counselors working with high school students emerge.

INTENTIONAL AND UNINTENTIONAL BIASES RELATED TO CAREER COUNSELING

Perennialism, essentialism, behaviorism, and positivism are education theories that espouse an authoritarian approach to subject matter, classroom organization, teaching methods, and assessment. "The authoritarian principle ... is that truth and goodness are entities that are best understood by the person with expertise who is in authority" (Pressley, 2007).

Certain components of the authoritarian approach add value to career development. However, to a greater degree it is in contestation with emerging career development trends. Career development and education are interrelated. Because education is in crisis, career development requires a more versatile career counselor practitioner. Those in education face budget cuts, change in student demographics, and a labor market in recovery from the depression and recession. The Trump administration proposes $10.6 billion in cuts to make federal education initiatives (Brown, Strauss, Douglass-Gabriel, 2017).

By 2017, although the economy had recovered from the 2008–2009 recession, the data suggested that certain populations did not benefit equally from the recovery (Rosemond, 2015). Although recovery was a part of workforce participation for high school students, the greater issue has been levels of participation in the labor market. In 2017, unemployment rates varied by racial groups; however, and the total unemployment for high school students fell into the 15–17% range. Higher levels of inclusion for marginalized and underrepresented groups require more mindfulness for students in these populations. Career development and transition practices will require school counselors to understand data and that students should not be viewed from a single lens (Stone, 2016).

These insights affect career development consideration for students transitioning out of high school. Career development is affected by societal shake ups, levels of chaos from the environment, demographics, and labor market data. As a result, authoritarian educational philosophies to some degree are in opposition to the fluid nature needed by school counselors to manage today's educational realities and labor market forces. Career development in the 21st century that is influenced by nonauthoritarian philosophies has a greater ability to be inclusive indicated by shifting demographic data. Progressivism, reconstructionism, humanism, and constructivism espouse nonauthoritarian approaches (Johnson, 2002). With these approaches, there are multiple truths (Johnson, 2012). This notion is very important, because for these adolescents, technology is ubiquitous (Nesi, Widman, Choukas-Bradley, & Prinstein, 2017). Adolescents are part of the generational cohort of remaining millennials and generation Z. The approximate birth dates for millennials fall between 1982 and 2004 (Niesen, et. al 2014) and generation Z, consist of those born in 1995 or later (Beall, 2016). The two groups differ; however, the constant theme to their development is their relationship with technology. This influence and steady dose of technology infiltrates all aspects of the lives of generation Z and millennials. Two studies reported adolescence frequency rates for the use of technology. In the longitudinal study by, "Adolescents are currently the defining users of the Internet. They spend more time online than adults do, and they use the Internet for social interaction more often than adults do" (Valkenburg & Peter, 2009).

In nonauthoritarian philosophies, teachers are learners and vice versa (Johnson, 2002). This constructivist approach supports the changes affecting career development for high school students and the career counselors offering career development in today's economic landscape. A constructivist pedagogy is central to career counselors. Career counselors are invited to think about and raise questions about changes in student demographics, the labor market, globalization, learning styles, technology, and so on. This positionality endeavors to offer support for career counselors to foster learning that "occurs through the construction of new insight and the emergence of new ways of thinking" (Johnson, 2002).

SPECIAL POPULATIONS

The period from adolescence through young adulthood is one of extraordinary promise and vulnerability (Santrock, 2010). This paradox is critical because during adolescents, knowledge, skills, and habits of a lifetime are often established at this time of life and they have disproportionate influence on the later economic productivity and health of individuals (Reyna & Farley, 2006). This outcome stresses the need for creating specialization of the school counselor role and functions. To manage this extraordinary promise and vulnerability (Santrock, 2010), a clear function of the school counselor role is the design a series of related activities, school curriculum, and individual student planning to help students manage career development (Nystul, 2004). Further, these trends "require a paradigm for respecting students' and families' values, beliefs, sexual orientation, gender identification/expression and cultural background" (Stone, 2016).

ADOLESCENTS AND CAREER DEVELOPMENT

ADOLESCENT BRAIN LEARNING AND CAREER DEVELOPMENT

Adolescence roughly encompasses the second decade of life, which would include the proverbial college sophomore and the "emerging adults (Arnett, 2000). Numerous development theories have emerged that can be used for counselors to adjust their approach to the unique and emerging needs of their students (Nystul, 2004) and to promote higher levels of adjustment. Unique to today's adolescence is research by psychologists and economists that have cited humans' adaptive edge in negotiating the real world seems to be surprisingly absent among adolescents and young adults (Reyna, et. al 2012). This body of research demonstrates that career development for students transitioning out of high school must not only explore the link between career and adolescent development, but include information about learning, reasoning, and decision making.

The examination of this intersection helps highlight specific general activities during this transition to create appropriate career development strategies, learning objectives, and curricula. During adolescence Erikson's eight stages indicate that adolescents experience identity versus role confusion (Erikson, 1985). During the latter stage, adolescents face pressures and expectations. Therefore, school counselors, are charged with the task to keep students motivated.

IDENTITY AND ROLE CONFUSION

Although the key to motivation lies in understanding how to shift abstract concepts within career development with concrete activities (Blair & Schwartz, 2012), adolescent motivation is also influenced by microsystems and macrosystems. Microsystems and macrosystems are forces that operate simultaneously and interactively (Bronfenbrenner, 1979, 1989). Bronfenbrenner contends that proximal environments (i.e., the microsystems of community, school, church/synagogue/mosque, immediate family) have great impact on children. Distant environmental factors and cultural forces are macrosystems that have an influence as well. However, by adolescence microsystems and macrosystems are forces that continue to set the tone for pressures. Adolescence grapple with expectations for values, career aspirations, and academic achievements. Ironically, it is during this phase that academic motivation for some adolescents declines (Pressley, 2007).

By establishing the connection between adolescent pressures, successes, and career development, school counselors have the greatest chance to mitigate barriers to the transition and career development process. Because, this is the period when some adolescents begin to show lack of interest in school or their academics. It is during this time that high school adolescents experience levels of reinforcement and punishments (Pressley, 2007). Reinforcements and punishments have shaped students' perception of their own academic abilities and help students predict future achievement (Bandura, Barbaranelli, Caprara, & Pastorelli 2001).

As a result, fostering self-efficacy during the career development process for students transitioning out of high school is critical. Self-efficacy is a learner's perception of his or her capability of reaching a desired goal or a certain level of performance. The criticality for self-efficacy and career development in high school is critical to the career or work identity. Levels of socialization to career development or orientation to work more generally (Cheney, Zorn, Planalp, & Lair, 2008) must be examined with these youth (Kashefi, 2011).

WAIT—WHAT'S CAREER SOCIALIZATION?

School counselors provide opportunities for all students to develop the mindset and behavior necessary to learn work related skills and resilience—as a part of long-term career success (Barker & Satcher, 2000). However, to unpack this broad directive, school counselors will need a framework to guide career development and transition. The framework includes career identity development, work socialization, orientation to career goals, values, and aspirations. This specialized knowledge helps move the overarching goal referred to in academic, career, and social/emotional development to recognizing distinct issues impacting the delivery of services.

The new roles and responsibilities may create a state of flux for students (Rosemond, 2015). Without expanding this lens, school counselors can expect identity or role confusions as it relates to work. Further, the ambiguity exists because fundamentally, careers are viewed as a "long-term 'bundle' of socialization experiences as they move through various work-related roles over the span of her or his work life" (Hall, 1990). Adolescents are essentially in emerging stages of the career socialization continuum.

Often success requires levels of education about the work culture and climate. When individual's career aspiration is integrated with career development and work socialization additional complexities emerge. School counselors are in a key position to teach career development skills that are central to one's development across the life span. Managing students' career success includes understanding the students' intent for defining career aspiration. Ideally addressing both the prior knowledge and the lack of prior knowledge about career development and workplace socializations is essential for career access and success. Some scholars have proposed that "concrete materials help students connect new ideas to their prior knowledge; and, ensuring that students can successfully engage in problem solving is an important part of enabling them to learn" (Blair & Schwartz, 2012). In addition to problem solving, adolescents use meaning to learn associations.

"Arbitrary associations are rarely retained because to do so requires at least some degree of meaningful relatedness" (McRae, Khalkhali, & Hare 2012). This approach creates consideration of different goals for different students.

Students bring various levels of support or understanding of the career development process. The career development process assumes that one understands various aspects such as crystallization to one's career goals, influences on career aspirations, cognizance of the labor market, factors that affect starting, stopping the search, and accepting a job. Connecting the pieces of this complex social fabric is necessary to transition high school students in their career development process (Rosemond, 2015). As a result, there are multiple consequences for students who may experience higher levels for applying and securing, apprenticeships, internships, or a job. In these cases where the experience results in higher levels of frustration during a more fragile development stage, school counselors, students, and families should anticipate coping resources to help reconcile crises through teachable moments and life skills to move through the transition from school to work.

TRANSITION THEORY AND CAREER DEVELOPMENT

TRANSITION THEORY AND PRACTICE

Finding a solution might not be the answer because "one size fits all" really fits no school or school district (Gouwens, 2009). Offering this framework and knowledge as a tool to increase the understanding of opportunities and challenges for transitioning high school students might be warranted. The Rosemond 2015 Career Development for Emerging Adult Study, explored constructs such as identity development, identity crises, and environmental changes combined with new tasks career developments. Trends from this phenomenon demonstrated that students were not aware how to manage this transition, were formulating a work identity, experienced levels of frustration due to the lack of orientation to the career development process, and needed guidance in the school to work transition.

Schlossberg's (1984) Transition Theory offers insight to discover how high school students shift from school to work. The key concept of transition, expands understanding of the process involved in thriving during the school-to-work post-graduation, not just survival (Rosemond, 2015). Transition involves anticipated and unanticipated events (Schlossberg, 1984).

The theory considers the individual through an integrative model considering coping resources, personal characteristics, duration, assets, and liabilities in the school-to-work experience (Rosemond, 2015; Schlossberg, 1984). The integrative transition process involves three lenses: moving in, moving through, and moving out, as students anticipate exiting school and entering work life. The model factors the various changes in roles and tasks, what occurs during the separation, the period of confusion, duration within the transition, and cycles back to renewal. The final component of Schlossberg's (1984) transition theory is the 4 S system: situation, self, support, and strategies. (Goodman, Schlossberg, & Anderson, 2006). System is seen as the continuum through which college graduates prepare for anticipated and unanticipated events.

CONCLUSION

The breadth and depth of career development and transition require time, resources, and specialized knowledge. The shifting demographics, higher cost to attend college, make rethinking preparation and content for high school career development a viable option for students, parents/guardians, families, and society. A priority for this agenda is the recognition that career counseling education is relevant to the shifting job market demands. The recommendation is to support school counselors with negotiating for resources and collaborate with administration, teachers, staff, and decision makers to create a culture of career readiness (Belasco, 2013).

REFERENCES

Arnett, J. J. (2000). Emerging adulthood: A theory of development from the late teens through the twenties. *American Psychologist, 55*(5), 469–480.

Bandura, A., Barbaranelli, C., Caprara, G. V., and Pastorelli, C. (2001). Self-efficacy beliefs as shapers of children's aspirations and career trajectories. *Child Development, 72*, 187–206. doi:10.1111/1467-8624.00273

Barker, J., & Satcher, J. (2000). School counselors' perceptions of required workplace skills and career development competencies. *Professional School Counseling, 4*, 134 –139.

Belasco, A. S. (2013). Creating college opportunity: School counselors and their influence on postsecondary enrollment. *Research in Higher Education, 54*, 781–804.

Blair, K. P., & Schwartz, D. L. (2012). A value of concrete learning materials in adolescence. In Reyna, V. F., Chapman, S., Dougherty, M., & Confrey, J. (Eds.). *The adolescent brain:*

Learning, reasoning, and decision making (pp. 95–122). Washington, DC: American Psychological Association.

Bronfenbrenner, U. (1979). *The ecology of human development: Experiments by nature and design.* Cambridge, MA: Harvard University Press.

Bronfenbrenner, U. (1989). Ecological systems theory. In R. Vasta (Ed.), *Annals of Child Development: Vol. 6. Six theories of child development: Revised formulations and current issues* (pp. 187–249). Greenwich, CT: JAI Press.

Brown, E., Strauss, V., & Douglass-Gabriel, D. (2017, May 17). Trump's first full education budget. Deep cuts to public school programs in pursuit of school choice. *The Washington Post.*

Bureau of Labor and Statistics. *E-16. Unemployment rates by age, sex, race, and Hispanic or Latino ethnicity report.* Retrieved from https://www.bls.gov/web/empsit/cpsee_e16.htm

Cheney, G., Zorn, T. E., Planalp, S., & Lair, D. J. (2008). Meaningful work and personal/social well being. In C. S. Beck (Ed.), *Communication yearbook* (Vol. 32, pp. 137–185). New York: Routledge.

Erikson, E. H. (1985). *Childhood and society.* New York: Norton.

Goodman, J., Schlossberg, N. K., & Anderson, M. L. (2006). *Counseling adults in transition: Linking practice with theory* (3rd ed.). New York: Springer.

Gouwens, J. (2009). *Education in crisis: A reference handbook.* Santa Barbara, CA.

Hall, D. T. (1990). Promoting work/family balance: An organization change approach. *Organizational Dynamics, 18*(3), 5–18.

Johnson, J. A. (2002). *Introduction to the foundations of American education* (12th ed.). Boston: Allyn & Bacon.

Kashefi, M. (2011). Structure and/or Culture: Explaining Racial Differences in Work Values. *Journal of Black Studies, 42*(4), 638–664. Retrieved from http://www.jstor.org/stable/41151364

Lenhart, A., Smith, A., Anderson, M., Duggan, M., & Perrin, A. (2015). *Teens, technology and friendships. Retrieved from http://www.pewinternet.org/2015/08/06/* teens-technology-and-friendships/

McRae, K., Khalkhali, S., & Hare, M. (2012). Semantic and associative relations: Examining attenuous dichotomy. In V. F. Reyna, S. B. Chapman, M. R. Dougherty, & J. Confrey (Eds.), *The adolescent brain: Learning, reasoning, and decision making* (pp. 39–66). Washington, DC: American Psychological Association.

Nesi, J., Widman, L., Choukas-Bradley, S., & Prinstein, M. J. (2017). Technology-based communication and the development of interpersonal competencies within adolescent romantic relationships: A preliminary investigation. *Journal of Research on Adolescence, 27*, 471–477. doi:10.1111/jora.12274

Nisén, J. et al., 2014. Age-specific fertility by educational level in the Finnish male cohort born 1940–1950. Demographic Research, 31(July), pp.119–136.

Nystul, M. (2004). *Education in the new millennium: not like your grandmother's schoolhouse.* Lanham, MD: University Press of America.

Pressley, M. (2007). *Child and adolescent development for educators.* New York: Guilford Press.

Reyna, V., & Farley, F. (2006). Risk and rationality in adolescent decision making: implications for theory, practice, and public policy. *Psychological Science in the Public Interest, 7*(1), 1–44. Retrieved from http://www.jstor.org.ezproxy.emich.edu/stable/40062377

Reyna, V. F. (2012). A new intuitionism: Meaning, memory, and development in fuzzy trace theory. *Judgment and Decision Making, 7*, 332–359.

Rosemond, M. (2015). *Discoveries from recent college graduates: documenting lived experiences from school to work during a period of economic downturn* (Doctoral dissertation). Eastern Michigan University

Santrock, J. W. (2010). *Educational psychology.* New York: McGraw-Hill.

Schlossberg, N. K. (1984). *Counseling adults in transition: Linking practice with theory.* New York: Springer.

Stone, C. (2016). 2016 ASCA ethical standards school for counselors [PowerPoint slides]. Retrieved from https://www.schoolcounselor.org/asca/media/PDFs/WebinarPowerPoints/WEB100516_Sone.pdf

Valkenburg, P., & Peter, J. (2009). Social consequences of the Internet for adolescents: A decade of research. *Current Directions in Psychological Science, 18*(1), 1–5. Retrieved from http://www.jstor.org/stable/20695984

CHAPTER 14

Improving College Access

A Review of Research on The Role of High School Counselors

Mary E. M. McKillip, Anita Rawls and Carol Barry

ABSTRACT

High school counselors potentially hold a key position to help increase the number of U.S. students receiving post-secondary degrees, particularly to address inequalities that prevent certain students from successfully transitioning to college. Using the model of student success (Perna & Thomas, 2008), this study reviewed the literature to understand how various contexts (social, school, family, student) shape high school counselor interactions with students as they work to improve post-secondary outcomes of college access and enrollment.

Many educational policy makers are calling for an increase in the number of United States students receiving post-secondary education and earning college degrees (Matthews, 2010; Obama, 2009). More jobs than ever before require education beyond high school and estimates suggest that if changes are not made, the U.S. in 2018 will have more available jobs requiring a college degree than qualified people to fill them (Carnevale, Smith, & Strohl, 2010). As the need for college-educated

Mary E. M. McKillip, Anita Rawls, and Carol Barry, "Improving College Access: A Review of the Research on the Role of High School Counselors," *Professional School Counseling*, vol. 16, no. 1, pp. 49-58.

workers grows, the connection between higher education and high wages remains strong (Aud et al., 2010; Danziger & Ratners, 2010). Current economic concerns put the wage gap and need for highly educated workers in stark relief (Clinedinst & Hawkins, 2009).

Regrettably, many high school students do not move successfully from college aspirations, to access, to persistence in college, and, finally, to a degree (Aud et al., 2010). The issue is not a lack of desire on the part of young adults. Most high school students seek postsecondary education; 92% of U.S. high school seniors in 2004 planned to continue their education after high school (Chen, Wu, & Tasoff, 2010). However, in 2009, just 31% of 25- to 29-year-olds had completed a bachelor's degree or higher (Aud et al., 2010).

There is a particular need to find ways to support traditionally under-represented students in their preparation for and pursuit of post-secondary degrees (Bowen, Chingos, & McPherson, 2009). This includes low-income students, first generation college-bound students, and students from Black, Latino/a, and American Indian backgrounds. The lower likelihood of college degrees for these groups is particularly pressing among the current U.S. student population that is increasing in racial and ethnic diversity each year (Aud et al., 2010).

The emphasis on increasing the educational attainment of U.S. students has heightened the need for research on factors that contribute to both college admission and college completion. High school counselors can contribute substantially to reaching the goal of increased college enrollment and persistence. Counselors are school-based representatives who work to deliver programs and services to support all students via "individual planning" in the school (ASCA, n.d.). They are also in a position to address inequalities that prevent certain students from successfully transitioning through high school and into college (Holcomb-McCoy, 2007). A surprising finding was that researchers studying the transition from high school to college often overlook the role of school counselors (Adelman, 1999, 2006) even when school counselors are their targeted audience (Trusty, 2004).

For this literature review, the authors provide a summary of the current research on college preparation in high school and the role of school counselors. Further developing past reviews (McDonough, 2005), the article begins with a conceptual model based on the work of Perna and Thomas (2008) to establish the need for a contextual understanding of the work of high school counselors. The conceptual framework is situated within these contexts: (a) broad social, (b) school, (c) familial, and (d) student internal. The four sections of this research review are organized around these contexts, with a focus on the school counselor-student interactions in high school to improve post-secondary outcomes of college preparation and enrollment. Each section highlights what the research suggests about the role of school counselors within this context and notes potential areas for future research. In addition to providing researchers with suggestions regarding areas in need of deeper study, this article offers some points of guidance to counselors as they work to implement individual student planning as part of the delivery system component of the framework of the ASCA National Model (American School Counselor Association [ASCA] 2005).

CONCEPTUAL FRAMEWORK

Perna (2006) and Perna and Thomas (2008) developed a conceptual model based on various theoretical approaches to student success, including those from the disciplines of psychology, sociology, economics, and education. This approach recognizes that students do not exist in isolation, but rather interact in and with a larger social environment. Student outcomes vary and are influenced by the different contexts within which they live and learn. Furthermore, student success is the result of a longitudinal process throughout the student's preschool, primary, and secondary school experiences.

This model is certainly not the only approach that emphasizes the importance of context or longitudinal processes when studying the high school to college transition (see, e.g., applications of Brofenbrenner's ecological theory of student development [Schultheiss, 2005] or Glen Elder's life-course perspective [Johnson, Crosnoe, & Elder, 2011]). However, the Perna and Thomas model was developed based on a comprehensive, interdisciplinary review of the research on student success in college readiness, enrollment, achievement, and postcollege attainment. Thus, its application to the role of the high school counselor in helping students prepare for college is particularly relevant for the time period of the high school to college transition. Other applications are more expansive in their views of the trajectory of student development. The approach addressed here is also particularly useful as a way to develop a long-term research agenda on the high school counselor's role in the college preparation of students.

Based on the Perna and Thomas conceptual model, the authors propose a framework for research that considers the multiple layers of context within which school counselors interact with students to assist in college readiness and enrollment. Each of the four layers previously mentioned influences the college-preparatory process of the student, including the students' own attitudes and behaviors, leading a student towards or away from college readiness and access. The interactions between a school counselor and student reach across the school context and student internal contexts, and are only a piece of the college preparatory process of the student.

SOCIAL CONTEXT OF HIGH SCHOOL COUNSELING

At one time, college counseling was a high school counselor's primary task, with counselors acting as "gatekeepers" to help a privileged few access college (Rosenbaum, Miller, & Krei, 1996). During the 1970s, counselors took on more visible administrative duties in order to maintain their positions (Lambie & Williamson, 2004). However, as responsibilities were added, none were removed, and high school counselors' professional identities shifted, leading to the expectation that they would be mental health experts as well as administrators and college counselors (McDonough, 2005). Meanwhile, policies have changed, and where once only an elite group of students was expected to attain college credentials, it is now a common expectation that all students attend college after high school (Krei & Rosenbaum, 2001; Rasinski, Ingels, Rock, & Pollack, 1993). As counseling programs and policies changed, the types of colleges expanded to include both those with selective admission criteria and those with open admissions policies (Rosenbaum et al., 1996).

Through all these varying expectations of what tasks counselors are expected to do and how much of their time is to be spent on the tasks, role confusion emerges (Janson, 2009; Lieberman, 2000). When school counselors do not have a clear definition of their job position, other roles and duties can easily get in the way of college counseling, and do (Joyce Ivy Foundation, 2008, 2009). School counselors vary greatly in their reports of day-to-day duties, including student registration and scheduling for classes, crisis counseling, handling disciplinary problems, test administration, and other administrative tasks that help keep the school running smoothly (Burnham & Jackson, 2000; MacAllum, Glover, Queen, & Riggs, 2007; Parsad, Alexander, Farris, & Hudson, 2003). This role confusion likely has an impact on counselors' effectiveness, although these issues have not been sufficiently linked by the research to counselor's abilities to effectively help prepare students for college access and success.

Furthermore, although college counseling is an important responsibility of the expanded job list of high school counselors (Parsad et al., 2003), some evidence suggests that pre-service education programs for school counselors do not emphasize preparation for college counseling (McDonough, 2005; Pérusse & Goodnough, 2005; Pérusse, Goodnough, & Noel, 2001). This lack of training in college counseling often means that counselors must take the initiative once established in high schools to seek out knowledge on how to help students prepare for college (McDonough, 2005).

High school counselors also encounter structural constraints at the district and state level that prevent them from offering adequate college counseling to students. For example, financial constraints at the administrative level prevent schools from hiring more school counselors when there is a need. Case-study research by Perna et al. (2008) in five states demonstrated how district-level commitments to college opportunity, complex financial aid policies at the state level, reliance of schools on state agencies, and involvement of local colleges and universities impact the availability of college counseling at the high school level. State-level mandates for counseling, however, appear to have little impact on the availability of college counseling at the school level.

The results of research on the social context of school counseling offer a few implications for policy and future research. A counselor's ability to work effectively with students could be improved with a more explicit definition of high school counselor roles and duties. Research is needed to test this connection more explicitly by examining alignment between counselors' visions of their job duties in college preparation and their actual daily activities, and between the pre-service training counselors receive and their actual practice when they enter schools. The need also exists for research that expands on the study by Perna et al. (2008) to understand the way the larger social context at the national, state, or district level impacts the high school counselor-student relationship in college preparation.

SCHOOL CONTEXT

Various researchers call for an approach to the study of student access to college that examines the overall college-going culture in a school, or the extent to which staff expect, encourage, and provide practical steps for all students to access what they need for college (Holland & Farmer-Hinton, 2009; Roderick, Coca, & Nagaoka, 2011). Four aspects of a school college-going culture that may impact the school counselor's role with college preparatory help in the school are: (a) organization of the counseling department within the school, (b) college preparation that is early and ongoing, (c) collaboration with other staff and teachers that allow school counselors to work to build and maintain this culture, and (d) resources to help in college preparatory activities. The interaction between school counselors and students fall in this fourth category. Each aspect is described below.

One consideration in terms of school context is the structure of the counseling department within the school, as researchers argue that organizational challenges often limit counselor effectiveness (Farmer-Hinton & Mc-Cullough, 2008). Two organizational components of the department are the number of students for each counselor, and the time allotted for counselors to spend on college counseling. Students (Ceja, 2000; Corwin, Venegas, Oliverez, & Colyar, 2004; González, Stoner, & Jovel, 2003), parents (MacAllum et al., 2007), and counselors themselves (Joyce Ivy Foundation, 2008, 2009) argue that counselors are overburdened and do not have time to give all students in their caseload the college preparatory help they need.

Counselors' lack of time for college preparatory help is due to the combination of two factors: the large numbers of students that counselors tend to have in their caseloads, and the limited amount of time most counselors have during their day to devote to college preparatory activities. Considering these two factors in tandem is important, because research looking only at student-to-counselor ratios has found no relationship between this ratio and college enrollment of students (Engberg & Wolniak, 2009). A low student-to-counselor ratio is not very helpful to address college preparatory issues if the demands on the counselor's time push him or her to focus on other things (Lee, 2005). Similarly, a high student-to-counselor ratio may not be such a burden in schools where the counselor has his or her schedule cleared of other tasks to focus on college counseling. Qualitative research that has considered student-to-counselor ratios within the larger school context has found an association between lower student-to-counselor ratios and more proactive college preparation for students with increases in college attendance of students after high school (McDonough, 1997).

Second, McDonough (1997) found in her study of four high school counseling programs that schools do better preparing students for college if they start with students in the ninth grade. This finding, supported by other research (Cooper & Liou, 2007), connects with theories of college preparation, defined as a process in which students move through stages during the pre-college years (Hossler & Gallegher, 1987). As Tierney and Venegas (2006) concluded in their study of peer advisors and peer groups in high school as a means of sharing college information, "the insertion of one treatment at the end of the process cannot overcome the lack of other necessary treatments along the way" (p. 1698). This early counseling does not appear to be common in high schools, however, as Bell, Rowan-Kenyon, and Perna (2009) found that ninth-graders had much less college counseling exposure than did students in the upper grades of high school.

A third school contextual factor that impacts the school culture is collaboration between counselors and the rest of the school community. The literature often cites the need for collaborative teams in schools between counselors and other staff and teachers (ASCA, n.d.; Breen & Quaglia, 1991). Although researchers have not linked this collaboration directly to student outcomes, some researchers have found that a lack of collaboration impacts the abilities of counselors to serve their students (Corwin et al, 2004; Janson, 2009), while the presence of collaboration improves counselor job satisfaction and retention (Clemens, 2009).

Finally, researchers often find that inadequate college resources are a concern among school staff and educators (Cooper & Liou, 2007; Perna et al., 2008). These resources may be material resources such as brochures and admissions requirements for particular schools, but more often than not, researchers are referring to less-tangible information and knowledge that school staff, including counselors, share with students (Cooper & Liou, 2007).

Results from national surveys of high school students offer support for the importance of school-level resources for college preparations. For instance, Plank and Jordan (2001) used data from the National Educational Longitudinal Survey of 1988 (NELS:88) and found that students whose parents reported using more financial aid resources, including talking with the high school counselor, were more likely to enroll in a four-year institution as compared to enrolling in a two-year institution or never enrolling. Furthermore, students who reported more school-level guidance in terms of the school's assistance in filling out college applications, financial aid forms, writings essays, or days off to visit colleges were more likely to enroll in a four-year institution as compared to enrolling in a two-year institution or never enrolling. The findings of Plank and Jordan (2001) were mirrored in a similar study also using NELS:88 data (Cabrera & Nasa, 2001). More recently, Engberg and Wolniak (2009) used data from the national Education Longitudinal Study of 2002 (ELS:2002) and found that students who reported seeking college entrance information were more likely to enroll in college than students who did not, with counselors included along with many others as possible sources of this college information. These national-level studies, however, do not offer great detail about the resources offered to students, nor do the surveys used ask students explicitly about the role of their counselors in accessing these resources.

A growing number of researchers have found connections between one specific resource—student access to a rigorous curriculum—and college success outcomes. Course-taking paths in high school impact college enrollment (Engberg & Wolniak, 2009) and persistence (Adelman, 2006; Trusty, 2004). Furthermore, the National Association for College Admission Counseling (NACAC) reports that college admissions officers cite students' academic achievements, including grades, course-taking history, and admission test scores as the most important factors in their admission decisions (Clinedinst & Hawkins, 2009). Tracking in high school moves some students on a college path and others elsewhere, often to the detriment of Black, Latino/a, and lower-income students (Deil-Amen & Turley, 2007; Farmer-Hinton, 2008; Mahoney & Merritt, 1993). Counselors can play a role in who goes on which path (Howard, 2003), although research is needed to directly link counselor's activities to student course access and their subsequent success in college.

The research using national surveys of high school students and research investigating the importance of high school course rigor demonstrate the importance of these school-level resources. Although high school counselors can impact student access to these materials, the studies reviewed do not directly address the role of school counselors. Some qualitative researchers have looked more closely at high school counselors and their role in delivering school-level resources. For example, Farmer-Hinton (2008) studied the types of resources and information offered by high school counselors to students through focus group interviews with seniors at one high school with a college-going focus. The seniors spoke of how college materials were readily available, and interactions with counselors and teachers helped them to more critically analyze their choices.

The types of interactions identified by Farmer-Hinton (2008) are similar to those advocated by Rosenbaum et al. (1996) based on interviews with school counselors in Chicago. Rosenbaum et al. advocated for interactions that walk the middle ground between "gatekeeping" and "college-for-all."

Gatekeeping means discouraging certain students from attending college but encouraging others, while the college-for-all approach refers to lukewarmly encouraging all students towards college. The preferred interaction, they argue, is that counselors provide "concrete information about such things as college admissions standards and job characteristics and offer alternatives to plans that are implausible"

(p. 273). Students appear to be much more satisfied with their counselors when they have quality interactions that offer them access to information about colleges and the application process (Farmer-Hinton, 2008; Kimura-Walsh, Yamamura, Griffin, & Allen, 2009).

Research suggests that, unfortunately, meetings between counselors and students all too often focus on exchanging functional information (Deil-Amen & Tevis, 2010), and students much less often get access to more critical information such as identifying colleges, navigating the application process, and making college decisions (Roderick, Nagoka, Coca, & Moeller, 2008). Students are found to lack accurate information about college costs and availability (Gibbons, Borders, Wiles, Stephan, & Davis, 2006), as well as both a developed understanding of the financial aid process and the practical assistance to navigate this process (Luna De La Rosa, 2006; McDonough & Calderone, 2006).

At the school level, given the results of the research presented in this section, staff should consider the organization of the school counseling department and aim for early and ongoing college preparatory help. School staff also should not underestimate the importance of collaboration and adequate resources. However, additional research is needed to more carefully isolate these and other school-level factors. Much of the current research asks about school-level resources without separating counselors from other school staff, or asks about student-counselor interactions without considering context. With a large-scale research study, researchers could gather comprehensive information on the school-level characteristics listed above and follow students in their transitions after high school. On a smaller scale, researchers could focus on school counselors in similar school contexts who have similar time and resources to devote to college counseling. What strategies do the more successful counselors use to make the most effective use of their time and resources?

FAMILY CONTEXT

School counselors and other mentors outside of the home are particularly crucial for students who lack other resources, such as parents and guardians who have already navigated the college-going process themselves (Erickson, McDonald, & Elder, 2009; Levine & Nidiffer, 1996). These ideas have been developed through social capital theory, as introduced by Bourdieu (1977) and further defined and applied to educational settings by Coleman (1988). Social capital is found in the structure of relations between people, such as the close ties among family members, community residents, and religious affiliates. When considering students and schools, Coleman theorized that social capital can be found in the relationships that exist among students' parents and in parents' relationships with their children. The presence of social capital leads to the creation of human capital—defined by Coleman as knowledge or skills acquired through education. For example, parents who are connected with parents of their child's classmates can share information and resources that can improve the educational experiences of their child.

Stanton-Salazar (1995) developed these ideas of social capital further to address the college preparatory process among Mexican-origin high school students. A student, through a relationship with a school staff member such as a school counselor (called school-level "institutional agents"), may receive knowledge-based resources such as information on college admission policies, or may receive help in connecting to other institutional agents, such as college recruiters or college preparatory programs offered outside of school, thereby increasing his or her social capital. Students need social capital to successfully navigate the path through high school and into college, and school-level institutional agents such as school counselors can be essential to developing social capital for students who do not have access to social capital through other means (i.e., family members, friends, neighbors).

Research that explicitly examines social capital finds that relationships are indeed important to predicting college enrollment, although how social capital is operationalized varies across studies (Engberg & Wolniak, 2009; González et al., 2003; Kim & Schneider, 2005; Plank & Jordan, 2001). For example, Engberg and Wolniak (2009) found that as the number of people (including school counselors) sought out by students for college entrance information increased and as the frequency with which students discussed school- and college-related issues with their parents increased, the likelihood that students attended a two- or four-year college also increased.

The research of González et al. (2003) was more specific to school counselors as agents who help to build social capital. They interviewed 20 Latina students from high poverty schools and working class backgrounds: one half attended a selective university; the other half attended community college with the intention of transferring to a four-year college. They found that those who were successful at the selective university had access to high volumes of social capital during their K-12 experience that the community college Latina students did not, including access to very supportive school counselors who devoted a great deal of time to helping the students.

Quantitative research using Chicago public school data collected through the Consortium on Chicago School Research also suggests a benefit to Latino/a students in particular (Roderick et al., 2008). Controlling for student characteristics, Latino/a students were much more likely to apply to a four-year school if they reported that they had strong levels of support from teachers and school counselors in completing tasks such as filling out applications and making decisions about what school to attend. Latino/a students who attended schools where students often reported that their counselors were active in helping them make post-graduation plans were also more likely to follow through on their plans and apply to a four-year college. Strong counselor and teacher support had a large impact on Latino/a students, although their effect on other students' likelihood of applying was modest, and the reasons for this difference are unclear (Roderick et al, 2008).

A national-level quantitative study of school resources and their connection to college enrollment after high school finds that tangible resources are important, but more so is connecting deeply with students and families (Hill, 2008). Hill used the High School Effectiveness Study conducted in conjunction with the NELS:88 and its follow-up study in 1994 and found that schools that initiated outreach to families regarding the college planning process, above and beyond the resources offered within the school walls, seemed to have the more effective strategy for facilitating four-year college enrollment, as compared to schools that only offered resources but no outreach, or schools that offered little to no resources or outreach.

What the research on social capital noted above suggests is that, first and foremost, students rely on their parents and immediate family for any college knowledge and support they can get. Students with parents from higher education levels and from higher socioeconomic status (SES) backgrounds tend to rely more on parents for information and less on high school counselors (MacAllum et al., 2007). But when families do not have the information students need, which is more often the case for lower-income students whose parents did not attend college, school counselors often become the primary source of information to help students access college (Choy, 2001; Deil-Amen & Tevis, 2010; Fallon, 1997; Hurtado & Gauvain, 1997; Kimura-Walsh et al., 2009; Mahoney & Merritt, 1993; McDonough, 1997). This is the case even for students who feel their counselors are not serving them well (Ceja, 2000; Howard, 2003; MacAllum et al., 2007).

At the same time, research suggests that the students who most need the assistance of the school counselor and could benefit most from this assistance in their preparation for college are more likely to have trouble accessing the school counselor

(Erickson et al, 2009). This includes: first-generation, lower income students (Ceja, 2000; Cooper & Liou, 2007; Kim & Schneider, 2005; Lee & Ekstrom, 1987); students who are not in the top 10% of their grade (Kimura-Walsh et al, 2009); students with low post-secondary aspirations in the early years of high school (Roderick et al., 2008); Black or Latino/a students (Ceja, 2000; Lee & Ekstrom, 1987; González, 2003); and students from small schools in rural areas (Lee & Ekstrom, 1987). In these cases, when help from families and counselors is not sufficient, sometimes students are able to access social capital through alternative routes like college preparation programs, teachers, or others (Ceja, 2000; Kimura-Walsh et al., 2009), but in other cases, they leave high school inadequately counseled (Roderick et al., 2008).

The social capital literature is important in furthering an understanding of why some high school students make successful transitions to college and others do not. To better comprehend the role of high school counselors, it is critical to know what college preparation students have received from their families and community outside of the school before and during their time in high school. The social capital research suggests that students without social capital from other sources need substantive, on-going interactions with school-based institutional agents such as school counselors, and benefit from them in ways that other students do not. This research also suggests the value of the interaction between family and school context, since students who have trouble accessing social capital at home are more likely to have trouble accessing social capital at school. Strategies are needed at the school level to help counselors to identify which students may need more support in college preparatory guidance than others. Future research is needed to examine particular ways school counselors can identify students who could benefit from additional resources, and concrete ways school counselors can help these students to understand the college-going process and be successful on the path.

STUDENT CONTEXT

High school counselors can help students on the path to college by offering individualized services that meet each student's needs. This approach was addressed in the above section, in terms of counselors taking the time to identify the academic strengths and weaknesses of students as they move through the college preparatory process. But individualized services go beyond this and require that school counselors address student's attitudes and behaviors in school (Perna &

Thomas, 2008). This is because a lack of student motivation and effort seems to be a significant roadblock to college success (Avery, 2009). Individualized services include helping students to develop coping strategies to address the psychological aspects of transitioning to college when living in communities where college is not the norm (Farmer-Hinton, 2008).

Individualized services also require that school counselors address individual student needs. In other words, counselors should account for the social capital that they are able to access from other sources, and provide additional information and guidance for each student to succeed. Schools with a mission to prepare students for college that have a significant population of students who are lower-income, first generation college-bound, or from Black, Latino/a, and American Indian backgrounds, may need to account for individualized attention in the time their school counselors are allotted to spend on college preparatory activities with these students. Holcomb-McCoy (2007) addressed the distinction between viewing college for all as meaning offering equality of services to all students versus offering equitable access to students. Holcomb-McCoy stated, "At its most fundamental level, equity is an orientation toward doing the right thing by students, which does not mean treating students equally regardless of their different needs" (p. 20).

Changing student motivation and effort in school is not easily impacted by policy. As noted above, Avery (2009) found that more than one-third of the low-income, high-achieving students who received college counseling advice did not follow through on the advice they received. What prevents students from translating advice into action? How can counselors better identify the disconnect that happens and improve the outcomes for their students? Clearly, additional research is needed to extend Avery's findings.

CONCLUSION

This literature review emphasized two research trends: (a) the importance of high school counselors as social agents who can help students along the path toward college, and (b) the need for improvements and expansion of research conducted on school counselors as they work to prepare high school students for college success. Some promising research has suggested ways to improve the school counselor's ability to effectively help students prepare for college. However, to draw stronger conclusions about how counselors can assist high school students to prepare for college success, additional research that sufficiently considers the multiple layers of context surrounding high school counselors is needed.

Of particular importance, future investigations should be designed with a strong conceptual framework such as Perna and Thomas's (2008) model of student success elucidated here. School counselors would benefit from additional information on how the larger social environment (in terms of policy, counselor training, and job descriptions) shapes the counselor's effectiveness in the schools. Subsequent research on school counselors and the college preparatory resources they can provide to students must consider the larger college-going culture of the high school, including how the counseling department is organized, when students begin to access these resources, and how counselors collaborate with each other and with other staff to develop and maintain the culture of the school. Current research suggests that, to help prepare students for college, particularly those who lack the social capital from other sources (e.g., family members), students need ongoing access to and individualized engagement with college preparatory knowledge and information. However, additional studies are needed on specific aspects of which information and what resources can be most beneficial to students and how counselors can best help students to access the materials.

With a stronger appreciation of the environment within which school counselors interact with students to help in college preparation, research can better consider what counselors are doing and if they are effective. Furthermore, a better understanding of the effectiveness of school counselors at preparing students for college success is particularly important as calls for counselor accountability increase (Dimmitt, Carey, McGannon, & Henningson, 2005; Sink, 2009). As secondary school administrators seek ways to increase student academic success within the constraints of their budgets and limited staff, recognizing the role and potential of their school counselors is critical.

An awareness of context will help researchers and educational stakeholders to recognize external factors that impact the ability of school counselors to adequately reach students. For example, Scarborough and Culbreth (2008) found that school counselors prefer to spend their time in accord with best practice, but context affects whether they actually carry out the goals they wish to accomplish. The context may change the approach a counselor will use to ensure student success; it does not make student success impossible or remove responsibility from school counselors to impact the students with whom they work.

FROM RESEARCH TO PRACTICE

What can school counselors do to improve their effectiveness in terms of helping students prepare for college? A strong understanding of the context surrounding their school is important, but a great deal of this is out of the counselor's direct control. School counselors can have an indirect influence on family and student context by making efforts to acknowledge the backgrounds of students and encourage parental involvement in the school, and by working to find ways to motivate students to increase the students' own efforts to succeed.

At the high school level, counselors can analyze the current organization of their school counseling department and determine whether altering its current structure would improve interventions with students, particularly in terms of offering early and ongoing college guidance. School counselors also can take leadership roles to build more collaboration among school staff and to bring more resources to students (one key resource: helping students to access rigorous coursework). Counselors can also work with other staff and the students themselves, and rely on administrative-level data to target students for college preparation (e.g. by first generation status, by achievement records) who might otherwise fall through the cracks. With this approach, school counselors can develop tailored interventions to better reach these students and provide them with concrete steps to improve their chances of college access and success. These suggestions can help school counselors to improve their interactions with students in terms of college preparation, but also can help counselors to increase their visibility as leaders within the school. These suggestions are aligned with the framework of the ASCA National Model (ASCA, 2005), particularly the method of individual student planning whereby school counselors assist students individually through ongoing systematic activities to establish personal goals and develop future plans.

REFERENCES

Adelman, C. (1999). *Answers in the tool box: Academic intensity, attendance patterns, and bachelor's degree attainment.* Washington, DC: U.S. Department of Education.

Adelman, C. (2006). *The toolbox revisited: Paths to degree completion from high school through college.* Washington, DC: U.S. Department of Education.

American School Counselor Association. (2005).*The ASCA National Model: a framework for school counseling programs* (2nd ed.). Alexandria, VA: ASCA.

American School Counselor Association. (n.d.). *Why secondary school counselors?* Retrieved from http://www. schoolcounselor.org/content. asp?contentid=233

Aud, S., Hussar, W., Planty, M., Snyder, T., Bianco, K., Fox, M., ... Drake, L. (2010). *The condition of education 2010 (NCES 2010–028)*. Washington DC: National Center for Education Statistics, Institute of Education Sciences, U.S. Department of Education.

Avery, C. (2010). *The effects of college counseling on high-achieving low-income students* (NBER Working Paper No. 16359). Cambridge, MA: National Bureau of Economic Research.

Bell, A. D., Rowan-Kenyon, H. T., & Perna, L. W. (2009). College knowledge of 9th and 11th grade students: Variation by school and state context. *The Journal of Higher Education, 80*(6), 663–685.

Bourdieu, P., & Passeron, J. C. (1977). *Reproduction in education, society, and culture.* London, UK: Sage.

Bowen, W. G., Chingos, M. M., & McPherson, M. S. (2009). *Crossing the finish line: Completing college at America's public universities.* Princeton, NJ: Princeton University Press.

Breen, D. T., & Quaglia, R. (1991). Raising student aspirations: The need to share a vision. *School Counselor, 38*(3), 221.

Burnham, J. J., & Jackson, C. M. (2000). School counselor roles: Discrepancies between actual practice and existing models. *Professional School Counseling, 4*(1), 41–59.

Cabrera, A. F., & Nasa, S. M. L. (2001). On the path to college: Three critical tasks facing America's disadvantaged. *Research in Higher Education, 42*(2), 119–149.

Carnevale, A. P., Smith, N., & Strohl, J. (2010). *Help wanted: projections of jobs and education requirements through 2018.* Washington, DC: Georgetown University, Center on Education and the Workforce.

Ceja, M. (2000). *Making decisions about college: Understanding the information sources of Chicana students.* Paper presented at the Annual Meeting of the Association for the Study of Higher Education, Sacramento, CA, November 16–19, 2000.

Chen, X., Wu, J., & Tasoff, S. (2010). *Postsecondary expectations and plans for the high school senior class of 2003–04.* Washington, DC: National Center for Educational Statistics.

Choy, S. P. (2001). *Students whose parents did not go to college: Postsecondary access, persistence, and attainment.* Washington, DC: National Center for Educaiton Statistics.

Clemens, E. V., Milsom, A., & Cashwell, C. S. (2009). Using leader-member exchange theory to examine principal-school counselor relationships, school counselors' roles, job satisfaction, and turnover intentions. *Professional School Counseling, 13*(2), 75–85.

Clinedinst, M. E., & Hawkins, D. A. (2009). *2009 State of college admission.* Arlington, VA: National Association for College Admission Counseling.

Coleman, J. S. (1988). Social capital in the creation of human capital. American *Journal of Sociology, Supplement 94*: S95–S120.

Cooper, R., & Liou, D. D. (2007). The structure and culture of information pathways: Rethinking opportunity to learn in urban high schools during the ninth grade transition. *The High School Journal, October/November*, 43–56.

Corwin, Z. B., Venegas, K. M., Oliverez, P. M., & Colyar, J. E. (2004). School counsel: How appropriate guidance affects educational equity. *Urban Education, 39*(4), 442–457.

Danziger, S., & Ratners, D. (2010). Labor market outcomes and the transition to adulthood. *The Future of Children, 20*(1), 133–158.

Deil-Amen, R., & Tevis, T. L. (2010). Circumscribed agency: The relevance of standardized college entrance exams for low SES high school students. *The Review of Higher Education, 33*(2), 141–175.

Deil-Amen, R., & Turley, R. L. (2007). A review of the transition to college literature in sociology. *Teachers College Record, 109*(10), 2324–2366.

Dimmitt, C., Carey, J. C., McGannon, W., & Henningson, I. (2005). Identifying a school counseling research agenda: A Delphi study. *Counselor Education & Supervision, 44*, 214–228.

Engberg, M. E., & Wolniak, G. C. (2009). Examining the effects of high school contexts on postsecondary enrollment. *Research in Higher Education, 51*(2), 132–153.

Erickson, L. D., McDonald, S., & Elder, G. H. (2009). Informal mentors and education: complementary or compensatory resources? *Sociology of Education, 82*, 344–367.

Fallon, M. V. (1997). The school counselor's role in first generation students' college plans. *School Counselor, 44*(5), 384–394.

Farmer-Hinton, R. L. (2008). Social capital and college planning: Students of color using school networks for support and guidance. *Education and Urban Society, 41*(1), 127–157.

Farmer-Hinton, R. L., & McCullough, R. G. (2008). College counseling in charter high schools: examining the opportunities and challenges. *The High School Journal, April/May*, 77–90.

Gibbons, M. M., Borders, L. D., Wiles, M. E., Stephan, J. B., & Davis, P. E. (2006). Career and college planning needs of ninth graders—as reported by ninth graders. *Professional School Counseling, 10*(2), 168–178.

González, K. P., Stoner, C., & Jovel, J. E. (2003). Examining the role of social capital in access to college for Latinas: Toward a college opportunity framework. *Journal of Hispanic Higher Education, 2*(1), 146–170.

Hill, L. D. (2008). School strategies and the "college-linking" process: Reconsidering the effects of high schools on college enrollment. *Sociology of Education, 81*(1), 53–76.

Holcomb-McCoy, C. (2007). *School counseling to close the acheivement gap: A social justice framework for success.*Thousand Oaks, CA: Corwin Press.

Holland, N. E., & Farmer-Hinton, R. L. (2009). Leave no schools behind: The importance of a college culture in urban public schools *The High School Journal, February/March*, 24–43.

Hossler, D., & Gallegher, K. (1987). Studying student college choice: A three-phase model and the implications for policymakers. *College and University, 62*(3), 207–21.

Howard, T. C. (2003). "A tug of war for our minds:" African American high school students' perceptions of their academic identities and college aspirations. *The High School Journal, October/ November*, 4–17.

Hurtado, M. T., & Gauvain, M. (1997). Acculturation and planning for college among youth of Mexican descent. *Hispanic Journal of Behavioral Sciences, 19*(4), 506–512.

Janson, C. (2009). High school counselors' views of their leadership behaviors: A Q methodology study. *Professional School Counseling, 13*(2), 86–97.

Johnson, M., Crosnoe, R., & Elder, G. (2011). Insights on adolescence from a life course perspective. *Journal of Research on Adolescence, 21*(1), 273–280.

Joyce Ivy Foundation. (2008). *The eleven-month challenge: 22 recommendations for improving the transition from high school to college* (Michigan High School Counselor Report). Ann Arbor, MI: The Joyce Ivy Foundation.

Joyce Ivy Foundation. (2009). *Converting high school achievement into adult opportunity: The school counselor role and beyond* (Ohio High School Counselor Report). Ann Arbor, MI: The Joyce Ivy Foundation.

Kim, D. H., & Schneider, B. L. (2005). Social capital in action: Alignment of parental support in adolescents' transition to postsecondary education. *Social Forces, 84*(2), 1181–1206.

Kimura-Walsh, E., Yamamura, E. K., Griffin, K. A., & Allen, W. R. (2009). Achieving the college dream? Examining disparities in access to college information among high achieving and non-high achieving Latina students. *Journal of Hispanic Higher Education, 8*(3), 298–315.

Krei, M. S., & Rosenbaum, J. E. (2001). Career and college advice to the forgotten half: What do counselors and vocational teachers advise? *Teachers College Record, 103*(5), 823–942.

Lambie, G. W., & Williamson, L. L. (2004). The challenge to change from guidance counseling to professional school counseling: A historical proposition. *Professional School Counseling, 8*(2), 124–131.

Lee, C. C. (2005). Urban school counseling: context, characteristics, and competencies. *Professional School Counseling, 8*(3), 184–188.

Lee, V. E., & Ekstrom, R. B. (1987). Student access to guidance counseling in high school. *American Educational Research Journal, 24*(2), 287–310.

Levine, A., & Nidiffer, J. (1996). *Beating the odds: How the poor get to college.* San Francisco, CA: Jossey Bass.

Lieberman, A. (2000). Confusion regarding school counselor functions: School leadership impacts role clarity. *Education, 124*(3), 552–558.

Luna De La Rosa, M. (2006). Is opportunity knocking? Low-income students' perceptions of college and financial aid. *American Behavioral Scientist, 49*(12), 1670–1686.

MacAllum, K., Glover, D. M., Queen, B., & Riggs, A. (2007). *Deciding on postsecondary education: Final report* (NPEC 2008–850). Washington, DC: National Postsecondary Education Cooperative.

Mahoney, J. S., Jr., & Merritt, S. R. (1993). Educational hopes of Black and White high school seniors in Virginia. *Journal of Educational Research, 87*(1), 31–38.

Matthews, D. (2010). *A stronger nation through higher education: How and why Americans must achieve a "big goal" for college attainment.* Indianapolis, IN: Lumina Foundation for Education.

McDonough, P. M. (1997). *Choosing colleges: How social class and schools structure opportunity.* Albany, NY: State University of New York Press.

McDonough, P. M. (2005). *Counseling and college counseling in America's high schools.* Alexandria, VA: National Association for College Admission Counseling.

McDonough, P. M., & Calderone, S. (2006). The meaning of money: perceptual differences between college counselors and low-income families about college costs and financial aid. *American Behavioral Scientist, 49*(12), 1703–1718.

Obama, B. (2009). *Remarks of President Barack Obama – As Prepared for Delivery Address to Joint Session of Congress.* Washington DC. Retrieved from http://www.whitehouse.gov/the_press_office/Remarks-of-PresidentBarack-Obama-Address-to-JointSession-of-Congress

Parsad, B., Alexander, D., Farris, E. & Hudson, L. (2003). *High School Guidance Counseling: E. D. Tabs.* Washington, DC: National Center for Education Statistics.

Perna, L. W. (2006). Studying college choice: A proposed conceptual model. In J. Smart (Ed.), *Higher Education: Handbook of Theory and Research* (Vol. 21, pp. 99-157). Dordrecht, The Netherlands: Springer.

Perna, L. W., Rowan-Kenyon, H. T., Thomas, S. L., Bell, A., Anderson, R., & Li, C. (2008). The role of college counseling in shaping college opportunity: Variations across high schools. *The Review of Higher Education, 31*(2), 131–159.

Perna, L. W., & Thomas, S. L. (2008). *Theoretical Perspectives on Student Success: Understanding the Contributions of the Disciplines* (Vol. 34). San Francisco, CA: Wiley Periodicals.

Pérusse, R., & Goodnough, G. E. (2005). Elementary and secondary school counselors' perceptions of graduate preparation programs: A national study. *Counselor Education & Supervision, 45*(December), 109–118.

Pérusse, R., Goodnough, G. E., & Noel, C. J. (2001). A national survey of school counselor preparation programs: Screening methods, faculty experiences, curricular content, and fieldwork requirements. *Counselor Education & Supervision, 40*(June), 252–262.

Plank, S. B., & Jordan, W. J. (2001). Effects of information, guidance, and actions on postsecondary destinations: A study of talent loss. *American Educational Research Journal, 38*(4), 947–979.

Rasinski, K. A., Ingels, S. J., Rock, D. A., & Pollack, J. M. (1993). *America's high school sophomores: A ten year comparison, 1980-1990*. Washington, DC: National Center for Education Statistics, Office of Educational Research and Improvement, U.S. Department of Education.

Roderick, M., Coca, V., & Nagaoka, J. (2011). Potholes on the road to college: high school effects in shaping urban students' participation in college application, four-year college enrollment, and college match. *Sociology of Education, 84*(3), 178–211.

Roderick, M., Nagaoka, J., Coca, V., & Moeller, E. (2008). From high school to the future: potholes on the road to college. Chicago, IL: Consortium on Chicago School Research, University of Chicago.

Rosenbaum, J. E., Miller, S. R., & Krei, M. S. (1996). Gatekeeping in an era of more open gates: High school counselors' views of their influence on students' college plans. *American Journal of Education, 104*(4), 257–279.

Scarborough, J. L., & Culbreth, J. R. (2008). Examining discrepancies between actual and preferred practice of school counselors. *Journal of Counseling & Development, 86*(4), 446–459.

Sink, C. A. (2009). School counselors as accountability leaders: Another call for action. *Professional School Counseling, 13*(2) 68–74.

Schultheiss, D. (2005). University-urban school collaboration in school counseling. *Professional School Counseling, 8*(4), 330–336.

Stanton-Salazar, R. D., & Dornbusch, S. M. (1995). Social capital and the reproduction of inequality: Information networks among Mexican-origin high school students. *Sociology of Education, 68*(2), 116–135.

Tierney, W. G., & Venegas, K. M. (2006). Fictive kin and social capital: The role of peer groups in applying and paying for college. *American Behavioral Scientist, 49*(12), 1687–1702.

Trusty, J. (2004). *Effects of students' middle-school and high-school experiences on completion of the Bachelor's degree.* Amherst, MA: Center for School Counseling Outcome Research, School of Education, University of Massachusetts.

CHAPTER 15

Social Justice, Multiculturalism, and School Counselors

Christina Woloch and Shanice Lockhart

Professional school counselors have been faced with the immense challenge, yet fruitful opportunity to address the unique needs of their student populations through tailored interventions and practical application. However, research has revealed that today's students are impacted by more complex daily psychological, environmental, and social issues, such financial hardship, family distress, cruelty, and other circumstances occurring outside of schools, thus justifying the call for a continued focus in this facet (Couillard et al., 2006; Flowers & Flowers, 2008). In the past, responding to student needs by only focusing on general curriculum improvements in academia was simply not enough to satisfy the magnitude of systemic changes necessary to enhance student educational outcomes overall (Noguera, 2003; Schmidt, 2014). Although it was observed that some educational reform policies were developed to support the school counselor in this arduous endeavor (Teale & Scott, 2010), as it stands, 64 years after *Brown v. Board of Education*, a holistic understanding of the impact of prejudice, power, and other various forms of oppression within school-based infrastructures remains relatively unexplored (Bisgaard, 2005).

Dahir and Stone (2009), state that "school counselors are ideally situated in schools to serve as social justice advocates to eliminate the achievement gap and to focus their efforts on ensuring success for every underserved and underrepresented student" (p. 12). Therefore, as schools become more demographically diverse, the need to recognize and challenge systemic inequities that exist between these student groups will become more evident (Wilczenski, Cook, & Hayden, 2011). The term *social justice* is based on the belief that all individuals share equivalent, intrinsic values, have identified human rights, and are granted the liberty to experience justice in a democratic society built on equal opportunity (Ratts, DeKruyf, & Chen-Hayes, 2007). For that reason, the goal of social justice is often derived from efforts that consist of the elimination of systems of oppression, inequity, inequality, or exploitation of marginalized populations and communities (Constantine, Hage, Kindaichi, & Bryant, 2007; Sue & Sue, 2016) in the facets of advocacy, prevention, intervention, and psychoeducation (Vera & Speight, 2003). Hence, a school counselor who successfully embodies the role of a social justice advocacy must work diligently to "right injustices, increase access, and improve educational outcomes for all students" (Ratts et al., 2007, p. 90). Whereas, through this dedicated work, educational inequalities and differences in academic achievement can be addressed using a multifaceted lens that is mindful of unique aspects of one's identity, such as race/ethnicity, gender, class, disability status, and sexual orientation (Cox & Lee, 2007).

According to the 2006–2008 American Community Survey, approximately 61 million children were enrolled in K-12 schools nationwide (U.S Census Bureau, n.d.). In 2020, 46% of this school population will be students of color (Pallas, Natriello, & McDill, 1989). Thus, school counselors must be prepared to work collaboratively with student populations that have experienced immense diversification in terms of socioeconomic status, race, and ethnicity, more so than what was required when working with previous generations (Feldwisch & Whiston, 2016; Schmidt, 2014).

In addition, professional organizations, such as the American School Counselor Association (ASCA) have made purposeful calls for counselors to engage in social justice advocacy in educational settings in the past (Bemak & Chung, 2005; Dixon, Tucker, & Clark, 2010; Holcomb-McCoy, 2007; Lee & Hipolito-Delgado, 2007; Lewis, Arnold, House, & Toporek, 2003; Ratts et al., 2007; Schmidt, 2014). The achievement gap in academia was initially addressed by ASCA when they included advocacy as a major theme in a revision of the ASCA National Model (ASCA, 2012a). More specifically, school counselor competencies that aligned with the ASCA National Model included a section (I-B-3), which described advocacy-oriented abilities and skills (ASCA, 2012a). ASCA was also issued social justice-oriented policy statements that urged school counselors to advocate for equity for all students in all life domains (ASCA, 2012b). In addition the American School Counselor Association has put forth a position statement on cultural diversity (ASCA, 2015). Similarly, the Council for Accreditation of Counseling and Related Educational Programs (CACREP) echoed ASCA's call for counselors in addressing injustice in schools and communities by revising its standards in 2009 to include a specific section on the implementation of social justice elements dedicated exclusively to advocacy and diversity (CACREP, 2009; Dixon et al., 2010). Furthermore, it has been observed that CACREP has continued this trend even in its most recent guideline revisions when they incorporated a narrowed focus on the need for graduate programs to properly educate future counselors in "advocacy processes, which address institutional and social barriers that have the potential to impede access, equity, and success for clients" (CACREP, 2016, p. 8). Thus, illustrating the overall importance of a continued integration of social justice advocacy initiatives within counseling domains on, not only a mezzo platform (i.e., CACREP [2016] and ASCA [2012a] revisions), but also on alternative and more introspective levels, which encourage school counselors to adopt their own social justice-oriented attitudes and behaviors as a means to eliminate gaps observed in achievement.

Although the successful execution of a progressive social justice movement within a school system presents itself as a daunting task, it is important to note that initial change must first begin on an individual (micro) level. More specifically, school counselors must first identify their own beliefs, as well as understand how these beliefs could consciously or subconsciously influence behavior and guide their overall judgment making processes when working with students. For example, when school counselors conduct ongoing self-evaluation through an inventory of their own worldviews and biases, they explore their own cultural heritage and identify how it shapes the perceptions of diverse belief systems formed within the context of their current role (Sue & Sue, 2016). Thus, Ratts and colleagues (2007) suggested that counselors who fully comprehend their attitudes and beliefs, as well as possess an accurate assessment of their existing knowledge and skills in social justice based realms were ultimately better equipped to work collaboratively with students in a school system and to create meaningful change. In addition, when examining the intersectionality of school counseling, social justice, and multicultural counseling initiatives, it is also important to assign collective responsibility. This responsibility is shared by counselors and all integral stakeholders operating within a school system alike. Ockerman and Mason (2012) wrote that the promotion of justice, equity, and access for students can be enhanced through the utilization of a collaborative network focus. More specifically, used as a unifying strength for school counselors when faced with resistance, as well as inspire others to become leaders and make strides against injustice and inequality in schools (Ockerman & Mason, 2012).

According to ASCA (2015) school counselors who responded most efficiently to the needs of marginalized student populations also embodied the skills of a social justice advocate. Whereas, an increased appreciation in cultural diversity and understanding through advocacy, resource utilization, and networking was observed in individuals when they operated in these specific roles (ASCA, 2015. However, it is also important to note that potential challenges can emerge when a school counselor attempts to work with student's academic struggles in isolation from knowledge of external factors (Adelman & Taylor, 2002; Griffin & Farris, 2010). Thus, school counselors must address all the needs of students in a manner that builds on the assets of students and their communities through each social justice role that they embrace (Adelman & Taylor, 2002; Griffin & Farris, 2010).

Social justice has been identified as a key component of multicultural counseling competency (MCC) training, as evidenced by the revised Multicultural and Social Justice Counseling Competencies (Ratts, Singh, Nassar-McMillan, Butler, & McCullough, 2016, 2016). Therefore, it can be said that counselors become social justice advocates by working with clients and communities to remove barriers and promote change (Bemak & Chung, 2011). School counselors should establish high and achievable expectations for all students, encourage parent and community involvement, establish support programs, be proactive and data driven (Holcomb-McCoy, 2007). Social justice requires counselors to take action when inequities exist, which in some instances, may require school counselors to speak out against the status quo. School counselors work to advocate for students, especially those who are currently unable to be their own advocates. In doing so, school counselors become leaders as they collaborate with parents, the community, and other school officials to ensure equity and access for all students. With social justice in mind, school counselors use data to develop goal-oriented social action plans. Additionally, school counselors verify the effectiveness of their work by using outcome data to determine academic achievement and program effectiveness.

School counselors serve a vital role in helping children and adolescents progress in the school environment. Even though school counselors work primarily in the school setting, the students they serve are facing problems that stem from external forces of situations outside of the school setting. The need for multicultural competency becomes more evident as the student population grows and becomes more diverse. School counselors must have the competency to work with students of various demographics such as age, ethnicity, gender, and socioeconomic status. With the vast number of students, they serve, being culturally competent is a must.

According to the American School Counselor Association (ASCA), it is recommended that the ratio of students to counselors is 250 to 1, but during the 2014–2015 school year, the United States national average was 482 to 1. These ratios not only show that there is a need for more school counselors, but they support the notion that culturally competent counselors are needed as well. Each student is unique and no student is the same. A child may present with an academic issue, but this could be caused by varies external factors and not necessarily lack of intrinsic motivation. It is necessary for school counselors to have the skills to work in a world that is "globally and culturally interconnected" (Alexander, Kruczek, & Ponterotto, 2005; Sue & Sue, 2016).

Sue, Arredondo, and McDavis (1992), have developed Multicultural Counseling Competencies (MCC) that have served as a guideline for many counseling professionals. After the contribution of the MCC, accreditation standards and professional organizations began to mandate multicultural training. Multicultural competence in school counselors helps them become more aware of their own racial/ethnic identity, in addition to combating any color blind racial attitudes they may hold (Chao, 2013). In a study completed with school counselors, research revealed that people of color had higher MCC scores than their White counterparts when there is minimal training. At higher levels of training, racial/ethnic school counselors and White school counselors had similar MCC scores (Chao, 2013). This study is an indication that multicultural training can make a difference in the competencies of school counselors.

CONCLUSION

Social justice and multicultural competency training is essential early on in counselor education training programs. School counselors who have been practicing prior to the implementation of social justice and MCC standards are urged to seek continuing education. Attending conferences and workshops with a specific emphasis on issues of justice and marginalization of underserved populations is encouraged.

REFERENCES

Alexander, C. M., Kruczek T., & Ponterotto, J. G (2005). Building multicultural competencies in counselor trainees: An international immersion experience. *Counselor Education & Supervision*, 44, 255–269.

Adelman, H. S., & Taylor, L. (2010). *Mental health in schools: Engaging learners, preventing problems, and improving schools*. Thousand Oaks, CA: Corwin Press.

American School Counselor Association. (2012a). ASCA National Model: A framework for school counseling programs (3rd ed.). Alexandria, VA: Author.

American School Counselor Association. (2012b). Position statement: The professional school counselor and equity for all students. Retrieved from http://www.schoolcounselor.org/content. asp?pl=325&sl=127&contentid=178

American School Counselor Association. (2015). Position statement: The school counselor and cultural diversity file. Retrieved from ///C:/Users/dowens1/Desktop/PS_CulturalDiversity.pdf

Bemak, F., & Chung, R. C. Y. (2005). Advocacy as a critical role for urban school counselors: Working toward equity and social justice. *Professional School Counseling*, 8, 196–202.

Bemak, F., & Chung, R. C. Y. (2011). Applications in social justice counselor training: Classroom without walls. *Journal of Humanistic Counseling*, 50, 204–219.

Bisgaard, D. (2005). Diversity [15 years from now] Do we have 2020 vision? *Independent School*, 64, 42–48.

Chao, R. C. (2013). Race/ethnicity and multicultural competence among school counselors: multicultural training, racial/ethnic identity, and color-blind racial attitudes. *Journal of Counseling & Development, 91*(2), 140–151. doi:10.1002/j.1556-6676.2013.00082.x

Constantine, M. G., Hage, S. M., Kindaichi, M. M., & Bryant, R. M. (2007). Social justice and multicultural issues: Implications for the practice and training of counselors and counseling psychologist. *Journal of Counseling and Development*, 85, 24–29.

Couillard, D., Garnett, J., Hutchins, A., Fawcett, M. L., & Maycock, G. (2006). Student risk factors identified by school counselors and student achievement. *Alberta Journal of Educational Research*, 52, 277.

Council for Accreditation of Counseling and Related Educational Programs. (2009). *2009 accreditation manual*. Alexandria, VA: Author.

Council for Accreditation of Counseling and Related Educational Programs. (2016). 2016 CACREP Standards. Retrieved from http://www.cacrep.org/wp-content/uploads/2012/10/2016- CACREP-Standards.pdf

Cox, A. A., & Lee, C. C. (2007). Challenging educational inequities: School counselors as agents of social justice. In C. C. Lee (Ed.), *Counseling for social justice* (2nd ed., pp. 3–14). Alexandria, VA: American Counseling Association.

Dahir, C. A., & Stone, C. B. (2009). School counselor accountability: The path to social justice and systemic change. *Journal of Counseling & Development*, 87, 12–20.

Dixon, A. L., Tucker, C., & Clark, M. A. (2010). Integrating social justice advocacy with national standards for practice: Implications for school counselor education. *Counselor Education and Supervision, 50*, 103–115. doi:10.1002/j.1556-6978.2010.tb00112

Feldwisch, R. P., & Whiston, S. C. (2016). Examining school counselors' commitments to social justice advocacy. *Professional School Counseling, 19*, 166–175.

Flowers, T. A., & Flowers, L. A. (2008). Factors affecting urban African American high school students' achievement in reading. *Urban Education, 43*, 154–171. doi:10.1177/0042085907312351

Griffin, D., & Farris, A. (2010). School counselors and collaboration: Finding resources through community mapping. *Professional School Counseling, 13*, 248–256. doi:10.53330/PSC.n.2010-13.248

Holcomb-McCoy, C. (2007). *School counseling to close the achievement gap: A social justice framework for success*. Thousand Oaks, CA: Sage Publications.

Lee, C., & Hipolito-Delgado, C. P. (2007). Introduction: Counselors as agents of social justice. In C. C. Lee (Ed.), *Counseling for social justice* (2nd ed.). Alexandria, VA: American Counseling Association.

Lewis, J., Arnold, M. S., House, R., & Toporek, R. (2003). *Advocacy competencies*. Retrieved from http://www.counseling.org/Publications

Noguera, P. A. (2003). The trouble with Black boys: The role and influence of environmental and cultural factors on the academic performance of African American males. *Urban Education, 38*, 431–459.

Ockerman, M. S., & Mason, E. (2012). Developing school counseling students' social justice orientation through service learning. *Journal of School Counseling, 10*(5), 1–26.

Pallas, A. M., Natriello, G., & McDill, E. L. (1989). The changing nature of the disadvantaged population current dimensions and future trends. *Educational Researcher, 18*, 16–22.

Ratts, M., DeKruyf, L., & Chen-Hayes, S. (2007). The ACA advocacy competencies: A social justice advocacy framework for professional school counselors. *Professional School Counseling, 11*, 90–97.

Ratts, M. J., Singh, A. A., Nassar-McMillan, S., Butler, S. K., & McCullough, J. R. (2016). Multicultural and social justice counseling competencies: Guidelines for the counseling profession. *Journal of Multicultural Counseling and Development, 44*, 28–48.

Schmidt, J. J. (2014). *Counseling in schools: Essential services and comprehensive programs* (4th ed.). Needham Heights, MA: Allyn & Bacon.

Sue, D. W., Arredondo, P., & McDavis, R. J. (1992). Multicultural counseling competencies and standards: A call to the profession. *Journal of Multicultural Counseling and Development, 20*, 64–88.

Sue, D. W., & Sue, D. (2016). *Counseling the culturally diverse: Theory and practice* (7th ed.). Hoboken, NJ: Wiley.

Teale, W. H., & Scott, J. L. (2010). Making urban schools better places for students, teachers, and families: An interview with Charles Payne. *The Reading Teacher, 63*, 701–704.

U.S. Census Bureau. (n.d.). *ACS demographic and housing estimates: 2006–2008*. Retrieved from http://factfinder.census.gov/servlet/ADPTable?_bm=y&-geo_id=01000US&-qr_name=ACS_2008_3YR_GOO_DP3YR5&-ds_name=&-_lang=en&-redoLog=false

Vera, E. M., & Speight, S. L. (2003). Multicultural competence, social justice, and counseling psychology: Expanding our roles. *Counseling Psychologist, 31*, 253–272.

Wilczenski, F. L., Cook, A. L., & Hayden, L. A. (2011). Conceptual and curricular frameworks for infusing social justice in urban school counselor education. *Journal of Counselor Preparation and Supervision, 3*(1). 6–17.

CHAPTER 16

School Shootings and Counselor Leadership

Four Lessons from the Field

Albert H. Fein, Cynthia S. Carlisle and Nancy S. Isaacson

ABSTRACT

This article discusses four lessons for school counselors responding to any serious crisis: (a) School counselors can expect to take on leadership roles in times of crisis due to their expertise. (b) Crisis teams are temporary organizations within a school structure. Membership in two organizations can create role conflict. (c) Effective school counselors have found subtle ways to support and counsel formal leaders. And, (d) school counselors must be vigilant in their own care, especially during a crisis.

The Virginia Tech shootings in Blacksburg, Virginia, in April 2007 set a new "record ... for campus carnage" (Thomas, 2007, p. 24), almost doubling the number of fatalities of the 1966 University of Texas shooting incident. Six months prior to Virginia Tech, in October 2006, the nation watched in horror as children's bodies were recovered in the small Amish

Albert H. Fein, Cynthia S. Carlisle, and Nancy S. Isaacson, "School Shootings and Counselor Leadership: Four Lessons from the Field," *Professional School Counseling*, vol. 11, no. 4, pp. 246-252.

schoolhouse of Nickel Mines, Pennsylvania. Until the massacre at Virginia Tech, the shootings at Columbine High School in Littleton, Colorado, were the most widely known case of school violence in the United States. These incidents of rage and violence have become a wake-up call that our campuses not only are vulnerable to attack, but that our children can be murdered as well.

Recent campus violence probably also conjures memories of other shooting events: Frontier Middle School in Moses Lake, Washington (1996); Pearl High School in Pearl, Mississippi (1997); Heath High School in West Paducah, Kentucky (1997); Westside Middle School in Jonesboro, Arkansas (1998); Thurston High School in Springfield, Oregon (1998); and Santana High School and Granite Hills High School in suburban San Diego (2001), to name only a few. These school shootings still register on the public radar in the form of lawsuits, insurance settlements, and ongoing community mental health services for victims and families (Breen, 2001; Flaherty, 2001; Pitman, Sparr, Saunders, & McFarlane, 1996).

Campus mass killings and the terrorist strategies employed by both rage-filled students and adults have forced American educators, including teachers, school administrators, and school counselors, to prepare for and deal with assault situations (Auger, Seymour, & Roberts, 2004; Carlisle & Frare, 2003). Public school personnel have recently become conversant in such terminology as "lockdown drills," "search-and-rescue duties," and "triage sites"—a vernacular that did not previously exist in school policy books just a few years ago. The demand for trained crisis leadership on campuses has forced new roles for administrators, and not surprisingly, for school counselors.

Fein (2001) interviewed leaders at four North American school shooting sites to understand the leaders' experience of responding to these incidents. Formal leaders such as superintendents, principals, and other administrators were the anticipated participant pool. However, these formal leaders often named other informal leaders, including school counselors, as key contributors in the aftermath of the shooting incident. Consequently, Fein's study also included school counselors and other mental health practitioners who assumed leadership roles during the crises. This article will draw on the results of this study to present some general lessons for school counselors who may be faced with disaster situations.

School counselors who responded to a major school incident or disaster have voiced feelings of inadequate preparation (Lovre, 2003; Shen & Sink, 2002). One school counselor stated, "We had nothing. We started at zero. Nothing" (Fein, 2003, p. 147). Although school districts attempt to keep training updated and drills current, school counselor preparedness is frequently overlooked (Auger et al., 2004). Fein found that professional school counselors played significant leadership roles in the aftermath of some school shootings—especially in the immediate aftermath. Debriefings of counselors and other leaders from high-profile shootings revealed that many school counselors performed duties that were not part of their formal preparation or training. However, the gap between the knowledge and skills required for effective leadership in crisis response and actual counselor preparation is significant (Allen et al., 2002). Demands placed upon school counselors in crisis response situations continue to increase as the scope of school and community critical incidents broadens. We argue that these disturbing trends present school counselors, and those who professionally support them, with four lessons.

LESSON 1: BE PREPARED TO LEAD

When a disaster occurs, school counselors often must often respond to the needs and demands of students, staff, and administrators. Student safety and accountability, staff needs, law enforcement communications, fire and rescue squad requirements, administrative directives—all these functions can (and in some instances, did) converge on the shoulders of the school counselor.

When one is overseeing the needs of children and adults during a crisis response, tensions can run high among those seeking support (Chibbaro & Jackson, 2006; Luna, 2000). Responding to a disaster or emergency situation distresses everyone, especially those in leadership roles. School administrators who have responded to shootings attempted to contain and control further harm. They were called upon to address the media and perform duties they never dreamed possible. Unanticipated demands on school administrators made them unavailable to make many other decisions. Often school counselors were asked to perform duties that included executive decision-making about issues of student safety or security, or triage needs following the shootings (Fein, 2001, 2003; Riley & McDaniel, 2000).

In the days immediately following the campus shootings, some school counselors, largely due to their training and expertise, became extremely influential, sometimes emerging as a kind of "CEO" of post-shooting events (Fein, 2001). At one site, the superintendent announced that he planned to close the schools the day after the shooting occurred, but a school counselor advised against the decision, explaining that many children might be left in situations where no adults would be available to help them cope, arguing that the children would be cared for and be safer at school. The superintendent took her advice and district schools remained open the day after the shooting.

In another setting, a school counselor refused to allow the district maintenance department to patch up the bullet holes in walls immediately after the shooting, which the department had been directed to do by a central office administrator. The counselor reasoned, "We left the bullet holes there for students. Some put their fingers in saying, 'I was here,' or 'That one came close.' Those kids needed to do that. I told maintenance when it was time to patch them up" (Fein, 2003, p. 140). In another situation, a school counselor, reflecting on the scope of his role, stated that he bore a lot of the weight of what was going on in the school and the entire school district (Fein). Shootings caused school counselors to be thrust into positions of responsibility (Fein, 2003). Wiger and Harowski (2003) found that during crises, school counselors took on administrative tasks without incident command training or formal role assignment. One counselor in Fein's study described how he was selected to head the incident response team:

> I arrived right after the shooting. There were still bodies on the ground. We got everything under control and got the children home and I went up to the superintendent and said, "You have got to put someone in charge of this." He pointed his finger at me and said, "You're in charge." (Fein, pp. 135–136)

According to Fein, both administrators and counselor leaders worried about making mistakes; they felt the "weight of leadership" (p. 147). One "counselor CEO" said, "I never felt so alone in my life" (p. 147). This feeling of isolation was a frequent finding for leaders, including school counselor leaders, in similar situations.

During a school crisis, a disproportionate transfer of intense emotions from traumatized individuals to school counselors often occurs. One counselor described what he referred to as the "boy-on-a-bike syndrome" (Fein, 2003, p. 99) to characterize the weight that came with crisis intervention and the need for a team approach under circumstances such as a school shooting:

> A boy is riding his bike and he falls and scrapes his knee. He gets up and sees three or four people looking at him; but he won't cry. He will get on his bike and peddle home as fast as he can, and when he sees his mother at the door, then he cries. So the boy-on-the-bike syndrome is what happens in schools.

> Teachers will often hold it together. Students even will hold it together, if they are being informed that the counselors and the crisis response team are on their way. But once we enter into the school, then, like the boy-on-the-bike, there is this invisible, yet tangible transfer of power from the teachers onto our shoulders, in relation to the emotional wellbeing of the students—and at some level, of the staff. Typically only one or two of us go into a school, but how can one or two handle that emotional transfer of power for [so many] students [for an event of the magnitude of a school shooting]? So an entire team went in and worked collaboratively. (pp. 99–100)

What this counselor did not state directly, but which no doubt also occurred, was that this same transfer of power onto the shoulders of school counselors also occurs from formal organizational leaders who feel absolutely in new territory in violence or disaster situations.

LESSON 2: SERVING TWO ORGANIZATIONS CREATES ROLE CONFLICT

The crisis response team for an event of the magnitude of a school shooting has as its primary mission the management of both the event and post-event counseling needs of students, staff, and the community. This "organization" remains in place as long as immediate and long-term post-event counseling needs remain to be addressed by the crisis team.

The school counselor's role has historically varied from district to district, from campus to campus, and from day to day. Especially in smaller districts, school counselors have traditionally been assigned quasi-administrative duties such as student supervision or responding to parent or visitor emergencies (Allen et al., 2002). At some school shooting sites, administrators were absent or unavailable when shootings erupted. Therefore, when a school is subjected to such a horrific event, leaders arise not only from those who are well versed in crisis situations, but also from those who do not have classroom responsibilities (Lovre, 2003). In essence, school counselors constitute "slack" resources in the system—available resources beyond the minimum necessary to conduct daily operations (DeMarco, 2001).

School shootings are such an overwhelming disaster that many organizational adaptations are needed in response. In the aftermath of the shootings, counselors could not simply continue to perform the same tasks for which they were normally responsible (Auger et al., 2004). Scheduling, testing, and guidance took a back seat to the needs of traumatized students, teachers, and support staff. School counselors carried out their normal counseling functions, but the scope of their work quantitatively and qualitatively went well beyond their usual routine. Also, counseling needs often exceeded the school districts' capacity to provide it, so public and private agencies offered to assist (Fein, 2001, 2003). Although the membership and structures of these outside agencies did not change, their role and their relationship to the public schools changed dramatically.

As often occurs in response to a crisis or disaster, new "organic" structures emerge (Dynes, 1970), and this occurred at some school shooting sites with "counselor CEOs" in the lead. Freed up to manage some aspects of the chaos (such as coordination of response efforts and/or channeling of communications), school counselors took on administrative roles that forced them to make hundreds of decisions they would not normally have made in more ordinary times (Fein, 2001, 2003). However, there were very few, if any, structures in place to address issues such as determining licensing qualifications for outside counselors and monitoring their counseling activities. Some non-school counselor volunteers had no experience with children. Some clergy volunteers had no counseling credentials and/or insinuated their particular religious perspectives onto victims. One crisis team leader described having no protocols and no policies or guidelines to consult (Fein, 2003).

One counselor, who served as a kind of lieutenant on the crisis response team, described the organization that emerged at her site:

> I describe it as a kind of octopus with [name of school counselor] at the center—not as a negative characterization, but structurally. There were several people who were like the tentacles. I was one of those people. We basically did the planning process. They [formal leaders] relied on our expertise. Those of us who were the arms of the octopus were not directly involved in facilitating groups, rather, we just kind of moved around to make sure things were getting done. Quality control. I did very little direct service. (Fein, 2001)

Even in non-crisis times there is much confusion about the role of professional school counselors (Beesley, 2004; House, 2002; Lieberman, 2004; Paisley, 2001), with role confusion exacerbated by the changing needs of schools, by differing administrative views about the role of the school counselor, and by assignments to multiple campuses. The onset of a crisis also contributes to role confusion because crisis response teams became an "organization within an organization" (Fein, 2001, 2003). School counselors who led the crisis response teams had to set aside one role for another. The goals of the school or district and the goals of the crisis response team certainly overlapped, but they were not identical.

School counselors who find themselves in these circumstances must understand the inherent role conflicts in serving two different organizations simultaneously. As leaders in the emergent crisis team organization, school counselors had authority and responsibility, often based on their expertise, that they did not have in the larger organization of the school or district. In the immediate aftermath of the crisis, they sometimes "outranked" their principal or superintendent, due to the unusually compelling circumstances brought upon them. The same school counselors seen as heroic during a crisis sometimes became the target of post-crisis criticism for having overstepped their authority. This type of harsh judgment underscores the tension inherent in serving two organizations simultaneously.

LESSON 3: EMPLOY SUBTLE COUNSELING

Typically, formal leaders (i.e., superintendents and principals) refused to attend debriefing sessions, and if they did attend, they participated only perfunctorily, or they left early (Fein, 2003). A typical response from school leaders regarding their participation in critical incident debriefings was they "didn't have time" (Fein, p. 65). One principal stated,

> You felt like you had to protect the children that were still here and had to be concerned about the teachers and the community and you didn't have time to be concerned about yourself. You are kind of forced in a position of leadership where everyone is looking for you for an example, so you just had to set the example that you wanted everyone else to follow. (Fein, 2001)

The professional culture of school leaders has promoted care for others over care for oneself. School counselors, sensitive to these leadership norms, often used informal conversations as an effective method of "counseling" despite administrators' refusals or reluctance to attend formal debriefings. Counselor training and expertise proved invaluable to formal leaders, both organizationally and personally, because district and building administrators were overwhelmed with unfamiliar and threatening issues they had never before faced (Fein, 2001, 2003; Lerner, Volpe, & Lindell, 2003). According to Fein, formal leaders were poorly equipped to make sense of their own normal responses to traumatic events as they tried to maintain what they viewed as proper leader demeanor.

Because of their training, school counselors had a clearer vision of what was needed to address basic human needs than did many school district administrators. One counselor stated that his role and that of the team was to try to mitigate the trauma response by allowing victims "to ventilate some of their feelings in a safe environment" (Fein, 2003, p. 89). Another explained that he saw his role as "mega-family therapy… . I applied system principles from the family and broadened it to the school and to the community at large" (Fein, p. 158). Often what some principals, superintendents, and other central office administrators did not realize was that they did have opportunities to talk about their own experiences when fortunate enough to dialogue with school counselors who practiced "subtle" counseling (Lerner et al., 2003). Skilled school counselors employed stress-debriefing strategies and counseling techniques that appeared to school leaders to be just another conversation (Fein, 2001, 2003).

Even when debriefings were set up exclusively for school and district managers, school leaders tended not to participate fully. One superintendent's comment was representative of the attitude toward counseling and debriefing expressed by formal school leaders:

> We [the administrative team] thought, "We're tough," you know. We can do this [critical incident debriefing] in a half an hour or two hours in an afternoon and be done. Probably we didn't do that very well. It would be something to learn. Because you need to allow time to debrief. (Fein, 2003, p. 65)

School counselors who understand the school leader culture can address individual leader needs and help leaders to make sense of their own experiences in a crisis. Many school counselors understand their role as serving and supporting others; by doing so in times of crisis they provided much-needed support to students, parents, and staff, including administrators.

LESSON 4: MINISTER TO THYSELF

School counselors were as impacted by the shootings as the formal leaders. Investigations into the depth and scope of mental health issues following campus murders reveal long-term health impacts on a broad population, including school administrators, school counselors, teachers, support staff, and any direct witnesses to the event (Lerner et al., 2003; Riley & McDaniel, 2000). Fein (2001, 2003) found the most commonly reported physiological response to the shootings by all participants was disordered sleep. Sleep disturbances are a major marker of both short- and long-term traumatization (Wiger & Harowski, 2003). One school counselor who headed the crisis team in his school district described his lack of sleep during the first few days after the shooting: "My sleep was four hours max a night, for that week—interrupted sleep. I would wake up, you know, a half-hour after falling asleep, panicking over something I forgot to do. Literally, I was hyper-aroused for seven days" (Fein, 2003, pp. 52–53). Hyper-vigilance is one of many fallout phenomena that can occur for even the most prepared crisis responders. Other physiological responses to trauma may include a heightened startle reflex, loss of appetite, general nervousness, increased fatigue, and listlessness (van der Kolk, 1987; Wigert & Harowski).

Emergency personnel are trained to prevent themselves from experiencing secondary trauma exposure and to limit their periods of trench-level work (Lerner et al., 2003). Law enforcement officers, fire department personnel, hospital staff, and other emergency responders are usually trained in the Mitchell model of critical incident stress debriefing (Lerner et al.; Wiger & Harowski, 2003). However, in educational settings, neither school counselors nor administrators are routinely trained for crisis response or formal stress debriefing (Chibbaro & Jackson, 2006).

It is unthinkable for major government organizations that respond to emergencies, such as police and fire departments, to set up work shifts without scheduling incident stress debriefings (Lerner et al., 2003). Without these debriefings, emergency responders may be vulnerable to secondary trauma due to either direct exposure to the traumatic event or to interactions with traumatized victims. Disordered sleep, irritability, and impaired judgment are all symptoms of secondary trauma (Figley, 1995). In times of extreme crisis, school counselors and administrators are especially vulnerable to secondary trauma.

In Fein's (2001) study, one school counselor acknowledged the effects of secondary trauma on the counseling team: "We were all impacted. We were all traumatized, but at a much lighter rate than the kids" (p. 121). Counselors reported that they were aware of their own susceptibility to secondary trauma—a result of contact with individuals who were traumatized—but that their desire to help victims trumped the personal risk. Often they did not seek counseling for themselves. One stated, "We did not debrief as much as we should have" (Fein, p. 121). Therefore, school counselors, like many of the formal leaders of schools where shootings occurred, carry scars from these incidents. One counselor reported, "Emotionally, I am fine" (p. 110), but then described an experience that suggested otherwise:

> There's a memorial case in the school. I walk in there and see some of the things in there. That bothers me, so I don't look at it, even now. When I get in the front door, I just avert my head because it bothers me. I don't know why, but it does. (p. 110)

When they were able to draw upon their knowledge and expertise, counselors could access resources that were not available to formal leaders. One school counselor crisis team leader described looking at himself as his own private science experiment. As he experienced several days of hyper-arousal, he was able to look at his own experience and to make sense of it:

> Is this happening to me because I am weak or because I am going nuts? Or is this just a normal human reaction? The crux of crisis intervening is to try to normalize some of what victims experience. I was able to naturalize my own experience as well. At that time I realized that I was probably under more pressure than most folks, so I knew I was okay. (Fein, 2003, p. 173)

CONCLUSION

We are indebted to voices from the field, the men and women who shared their experiences with us, sometimes at considerable personal cost. They did so because they wanted something good to come out of a horrific event they had experienced. Their experiences and the continued leadership trends in crisis response needs in our society led to the four lessons presented here. Based on these lessons, we offer the following recommendations.

BE PREPARED TO LEAD

Care-giving is central to the role of school counselors and is what is most needed in a crisis event. Most school district policy and procedure books are woefully lacking descriptions or directions for the school counselor's role in emergencies (Wiger & Harowski, 2003). Critical incident tasks are either unaddressed or omitted entirely in these policy records. Whether or not they are trained, and despite ongoing ambiguities about their role, school counselors will likely emerge as leaders during crises. School districts must identify and prepare all leaders for multiple role responsibilities during and after a crisis event. Formal training can only enhance their effectiveness. School counselors and administrators must be certified in critical incident stress debrief methods in order to promote and model self-care, and to better serve their constituencies. Counselor educators should be able to network at state and national levels to regularly review certification procedures. Changes in certification standards also must be conveyed to school administrators on an annual basis.

SERVING TWO ORGANIZATIONS CREATES ROLE CONFLICT

Crisis teams are organizations that temporarily emerge within an organization, but few recognize them as such. During a crisis, school counselors may find that their roles and duties expand to meet needs and demands that did not exist in pre-crisis times. As reported in Fein (2001, 2003), the weight of such expanded leadership was stressful. To reduce stress, much of it caused by the extreme ambiguity engendered by major crises, crisis teams should have coleaders so that responsibilities can be shared. Finally, all school counselors, along with administration, should review incident response roles and duties and understand the inherent role conflicts during crises.

EMPLOY SUBTLE COUNSELING

The culture of school leadership places high value on caring for others over care of oneself. A major crisis is a time when both the school district community and its leaders are most vulnerable. The needs of others will always trump personal needs. Denial is no substitute for the pain of gnawing self-doubt, deep sorrow, guilt, or shame. Leaders are just people, regardless of their assumptions—and sometimes our own—that they are super-human. Leaders who were reluctant to attend critical incident debriefing sessions were willing to spend a few moments checking in with the crisis team leader. One superintendent described how he casually mentioned that he wasn't sleeping well and his appetite was diminished. The school counselor's response reassured him that not feeling that way would be worrisome. In a crisis, leaders experience substantial anxiety about events over which they have little or no control. Subtle counseling helps reduce some of the anxiety that leaders may have about themselves.

MINISTER TO THYSELF

Care-givers or other responders should not become casualties in incident response because they are overburdened. Despite their knowledge and training about secondary trauma (Figley, 1995), care-givers in the Fein (2001) study did not take the time to debrief as often as they should have. One rule of thumb for responders is to serve only 3 to 4 hours or less on a critical incidence response shift and then be immediately allowed to debrief with trained personnel (Lerner et al., 2003). Like the instructions recited by flight attendants before takeoff, crisis responders must put on their own oxygen masks first.

One school counselor's words, responding to the question "What if you had it all to do over again?" captured what may have been true for many of the mental health professionals who provided assistance in the days following school shootings. His words capture both the horror of counseling work under crisis circumstances and the tremendous contribution that counselors made: "That was the worst three weeks of my life, but it was rewarding. We sure did a lot out there" (Fein, 2003, p. 165). Whatever scars these school counselors suffered from their experiences were seen as preferable to the scars they might have carried if they perceived themselves as not having done all they could have done in such situations. In other words, living with a traumatic injury was seen as preferable to living with personal and professional shame of not serving students—albeit in ways never even imagined when choosing the school counseling profession.

REFERENCES

Allen, M., Burt, K., Bryan, E., Carter, D., Orsi, R., & Durkan, L. (2002). School counselors' preparation for and participation in crisis intervention. *Professional School Counseling*, 6, 96–102.

Auger, R., Seymour, J., & Roberts, W. (2004). Responding to terror: The impact of September 11 on K-12 schools and schools' responses. *Professional School Counseling*, 7, 222–230.

Beesley, D. (2004). Teachers' perceptions of school counselor effectiveness: Collaborating for student success. *Education*, 125, 259–270.

Breen, M. (2001). Duty to foresee, forewarn, and protect against violent behavior: A plaintiff attorney's perspective. In M. Shafii & S. Shafii (Eds.), *School violence: Assessment, management, prevention* (pp. 189–200). Washington, DC: American Psychiatric Publishing.

Carlisle, C., & Frare, S. (2003). Resiliency in the wake of crisis. *ASCA School Counselor*, 41, 28–32.

Chibbaro, J., & Jackson, C. (2006). Helping students cope in an age of terrorism: Strategies for school counselors. *Professional School Counseling*, 9, 314–326.

DeMarco, T. (2001). *Slack: Getting past burnout, busywork, and the myth of total efficiency*. New York: Broadway Books.

Dynes, R. R. (1970). *Organized behavior in disaster*. Lexington, MA: D. C. Heath.

Fein, A. H. (2001). *There and back again: A phenomenological inquiry of school shootings as experienced by school leaders* (Doctoral dissertation, Gonzaga University, 2001). Proquest, AAT3010147.

Fein, A. (2003). *There and back again: School shootings as experienced by school leaders*. Lanham, MD: Scarecrow Education.

Figley, C. R. (1995). Compassion fatigue: Toward a new understanding of the cost of caring. In B. H. Stamm (Ed.), *Secondary traumatic stress* (pp. 3–28). Lutherville, MD: Sidran Press.

Flaherty, L. (2001). School violence and the school environment. In M. Shafii & S. Shafii (Eds.), *School violence* (pp. 25–51). Washington, DC: American Psychiatric Publishing.

House, R. (2002). School counselors: Becoming key players in school reform [Electronic version]. *Professional School Counseling*, 5, 261–267.

Lerner, M., Volpe, J., & Lindell, B. (2003). *A practical guide for crisis response in our schools: Acute traumatic stress management, empowering educators during traumatic events*. Commack, NY: American Academy of Experts in Traumatic Stress.

Lieberman, A. (2004). Confusion regarding school counselor functions: School leadership impacts role clarity [Electronic version]. *Education*, 124, 552–560.

Lovre, C. (2003). Collaborating with the community. *ASCA School Counselor*, 41(2), 8–11.

Luna, J. (2000). The counselor as leader: Critical incident stress management in the Long Beach schools. In D. Sandhu & C. Aspy (Eds.), *Violence in American schools*. Alexandria, VA: American Counseling Association.

Paisley, P. (2001). School counseling for the 21st century: Challenges and opportunities [Electronic version]. *Professional School Counseling*, 5, 106–115.

Pitman, R., Sparr, L., Saunders, L., & McFarlane, A. (1996). Legal issues in post-traumatic stress disorder. In B. van der Kolk, A. McFarlane, & L. Weisaethal (Eds.), *Traumatic stress: The effects of overwhelming experience on mind, body, and society* (pp. 378–397). New York: Guilford Press.

Riley, P., & McDaniel, J. (2000). School violence, prevention, intervention, and crisis response. *Professional School Counseling*, 4, 120–125.

Shen, Y., & Sink, C. (2002). Helping elementary-age children cope with disasters. *Professional School Counseling*, 5, 322–330.

Thomas, E. (2007, April 30). Making of a massacre. *Newsweek*, 22–31.
van der Kolk, B. (1987). *Psychological trauma*. Washington, DC: American Psychiatric Publishing.
Wiger, D., & Harowski, K. (2003). *Essentials of crisis counseling and intervention*. Hoboken, NJ: John Wiley & Sons.

CHAPTER 17
School Violence

Anne Gregory and Elise Cappella

INTRODUCTION

In the past 10 years, many communities were shaken by well-publicized shootings that resulted in multiple student deaths. Discussions about the problem of school violence increased. Fears of students as "super predators" were on the rise. While the events were certainly tragic, heightened concerns have not been grounded in the reality of declining violent crime in school settings over the past decade (National Center for Education Statistics [NCES], 2004). The chances of serious violent crime occurring in school are statistically quite low. During the school year 1999–2000, 16 of the 2,124 homicide victims who were school-aged children occurred in the school setting (NCES).

While violent crime may be rare, low-level aggression in schools is not uncommon. Thus, this chapter addresses prevalent behavior, to which many school staff are faced with on a daily basis. We define *aggression* as an intent or action to harm through verbal or physical force. A broad definition of aggression allows for a consideration of how delinquency in adolescents and young adults unfolds. For a group of serious offenders, aggressive actions begin early in life, gain momentum across the school years, and take on multiple and increasingly serious forms (Loeber, Burke, Lahey,

Winters, & Zera, 2000). A preventive approach is called for in light of the escalation of aggressive behaviors across the school years.

VIOLENCE AND AGGRESSION IN SCHOOLS

Rates of violence vary by the characteristics of the school. Violent crimes, including those against teachers, are more likely to happen in high schools than elementary or middle schools (NCES, 2004). Overall, urban schools have higher rates of violence than suburban and rural communities (NCES). Teachers in urban schools are more likely to be victims than those teaching in rural or suburban schools (NCES). Negative gang activities are particularly common in city schools, such that, in 1999, one third of city schools reported this as a problem (NCES, 1999). While urban schools have a particular confluence of poverty and violence, some evidence is suggestive that rural schools also have contextually specific patterns of violence. In 2003, students from rural areas, compared with urban and suburban areas, reported higher rates of bullying (NCES, 2004). A more in-depth study of three rural schools with students in grades three to eight also found high rates of bullying (Dulmus, Theriot, & Sowers, 2004). With greater residential stability and smaller populations in rural settings (Osgood & Chambers, 2003), perhaps rural students are more likely to attend years of schooling as a stable cohort leaving little room for reputations as victims or bullies to shift across the years.

Even with the variation in rates of violence across schools, there has been an overall downward trend in violence. A recent report issued by the U.S. Department of Education declared that school-based violent crimes against adolescents from 1992 to 2002 dropped by half (NCES, 2004). By 2003, 13% of high school students reported having been in a fight on school grounds—down from 16% in 2003. Similarly, students' reports of carrying weapons to school within the past month dropped from 12% to 6%.

Serious violent crime might be an infrequent occurrence, but low-level aggression appears to be more prevalent. The 1999 national school survey on crime and safety found that almost 30% of schools reported frequent bullying and almost 20% of schools reported frequent student acts of disrespect for teachers (NCES, 1999). In 2000, 3 million suspensions and 97,000 expulsions were reported. In some states, such as Delaware and South Carolina, between 14% and 19% of the male students had been suspended (NCES, 2000). A study of 1992–1993 data from a random sample of disciplined 6th through 12th graders in 67 Florida school districts found that 47% of in-and out-of-school suspensions, corporal punishment, and expulsions were given for disruptive behavior in class, defiance of authority, or disrespectful behavior. The next largest offense, fighting, accounted for 9.5% of the disciplinary consequences (Florida Department of Education [DOE], 1995). The frequency of suspensions and expulsions and the reasons for such sanctions suggest that schools and counselors are faced with a serious problem of aggressive behavior.

CURRENT DEVELOPMENTS

"Get tough approach." Sociopolitical and historical developments affect how school violence and aggression is conceptualized and addressed. School counselors may have to navigate the tensions between a punishment orientation and a support orientation toward aggressive behavior. In response to increased public fear of school violence, many schools have taken an increasingly punitive, "get tough" approach. In the 1990s, zero tolerance policies were implemented across the states with a federal mandate passed in 1994, which called for a minimum 1-year expulsion for bringing a weapon to school (Gun-Free Schools Act). Critics of such policies argue that a mandate for expulsions does not take into account extenuating or contextual circumstances, which results in superfluous and overly punitive sanctions. The Harvard Civil Rights project (2000) compiled case examples of children suspended or expelled for carrying sparklers, a Boy Scout pocketknife, a toenail clipper, and a toy ax for Halloween. They argued that punitive approaches to discipline may differentially affect African American and Latino students, who are overrepresented in suspensions and expulsions. In 1999, a survey showed that in grades 7 to 12, 20% of Hispanic students, 35% of African American students, and 15% of White students had ever been suspended or expelled (NCES, 2003). In light of the increasing numbers of students, particularly African American students, being suspended or expelled and with heightened fears of school violence, educational researchers (e.g., Devine, 1996) have documented the prison-like school environments that rely on video surveillance, metal detectors, and harsh sanctions.

Recognition of the complex needs of students provides a counterweight to the popularity of increased surveillance and harsh sanctions to reduce school violence. Some states and school districts are acknowledging the importance of addressing social and emotional development in school (Shriver & Weissberg, 2005), with states in every region across the United States mandating the teaching of social and emotional development alongside academic learning (National Association of State Boards of Education, 2005). In the mid-1990s, federal school safety funds spawned preventive interventions. Antibullying programs (e.g., Olweus, 1999), conflict mediation interventions (Johnson & Johnson, 1996), and on-campus suspension programs have become widespread. Concerns about the punitive approach of zero tolerance policies have generated new programs, such as a systematic school-based threat assessment to lower overreaction to a *perception* of student threat (Cornell et al., 2004). This may be helpful in addressing the problem of criminalizing youth, particularly youth of color.

Research-based interventions. Increasingly, school counselors may be asked to show the results of their interventions with evidence of decreased aggressive behavior and increased prosocial behavior. At the same time, counselors may be faced with the pressure to continue programs that are familiar to school staff, despite a lack of rigorous evidence that suggests they are helping. Currently, there is a federal push toward the use of evidence-based practice in schools, as seen in the establishment of the Institute for Education Sciences whose mission is to understand the effectiveness of education programs and improve academic achievement and access to educational opportunities for students. Efficacy and effectiveness research that utilizes experimental designs—randomly assigning schools, classrooms, or students to interventions—is prioritized in funding.

Faced with the pressure to show results, counselors may be called upon to ask critical questions of the research on interventions. This chapter aims to provide counselors with a knowledge base from which to raise such questions. It begins with an outline of the current research on the predictors of child and adolescent aggression. A theoretical understanding of how environmental factors interact with individual student characteristics to predict aggressive behavior will help counselors target risk factors specific to developmental stage and identify the reasons the intervention may help reduce aggressive behavior. With its focus on the prevention of serious school violence, the chapter then describes a range of research-based interventions. Several of the interventions focus on supporting students already identified as aggressive; others involve supporting individuals in the students' lives, namely teachers, parents, and peers. Also described are multilevel programs that intervene systematically across a range of settings and with different types of participants. Finally, the chapter provides counselors with concrete strategies to consider when selecting and developing interventions.

AGGRESSIVE BEHAVIOR IN SCHOOL

INDIVIDUAL STUDENT CHARACTERISTICS

Individual students differ in many ways—in their approach to social situations, in their struggles or successes with academic schoolwork, and in the ways their bodies are made up. These differences have been hypothesized to contribute to the behaviors students are likely to use in school. Researchers have isolated each of these individual characteristics to examine their relative contribution to the development and use of overt aggression in school settings. However, none of these factors operates separately from one another or outside the contexts of family, school, and community. We will outline the theory and evidence for the biological, cognitive, and academic differences associated with overt aggression, while keeping in mind the complex and interactive pathways through which aggression develops in students in school.

Biological factors. possible biological contributors to overt aggression include genetic inheritance, temperament differences, neurotransmitter effects, and hormonal influences. This literature has been reviewed thoroughly elsewhere and will be summarized only briefly here (see Berman, Kavoussi, & Coccaro, 1997; Brain & Susman, 1997; Coie & Dodge, 1998).

Behavior-geneticists have postulated that a *tendency* toward aggressive behavior can be inherited, but aggressive behavior itself cannot (see Coie & Dodge, 1998). For example, biological genotypes passed down from parent to child may affect physiological processes, which influence a child's behavioral or cognitive style, which then interact with environmental factors to lead to behaviors. Twin and adoption studies from around the world support the theory. Genetic factors influence individual characteristics such as impulsivity and reactivity, and these may lead to a *disposition* toward externalizing behavior (e.g., Matheny, 1989), but there appears to be no relationship between genes and *actual* physical aggression or violence (Mednick, Gabrielli, & Hutchings, 1984; Raine, 1993).

Children's temperament has been hypothesized to relate to future behavior, in part through the stability of personality characteristics and in part through an interaction with environmental influences such as relationships with parents and peers. Early demonstrations of emotional regulation—for example, ability to inhibit inappropriate behaviors, cope with arousal, and organize for goal-oriented behavior when experiencing strong emotions—have been thought critical to children's later use of aggression (Dishion & patterson, 1997). Research has demonstrated qualified support for these hypotheses: temperamental characteristics in preschool are stable over time (Bates, Bayles, Bennett, Ridge, & Brown, 1991), but a "difficult" temperament does not necessarily predict future delinquency (Caspi, Henry, McGee, Moffitt, & Silva, 1995; Earls & Jung, 1987). In addition, associations between early temperament and later aggression tend to be weak, confounded by use of maternal reports, and linked with parent–child attachment (Bates, Maslin, & Frankel, 1985) and the home environment (Earls & Jung). That said, *connections* between disposition and cognition (discussed next) may help to explain *some* children's aggressive responses to environmental stimuli (Dodge, 1991).

The framework for understanding the role of neurotransmitters in aggressive behavior is Gray's (1987) theory of brain function; in particular, his description of the behavioral facilitation and behavioral inhibition systems within the brain that launch or halt interactions with the environment. Although engagement or inhibition of activity is related to multiple neurotransmitters, concentration of *serotonin* metabolites in the cerebrospinal fluid is critical, such that low concentrations may lead to an increase in stress reactivity (Berman et al., 1997; Spoont, 1992). Studies of serotonin in children indicate that lower concentrations are, in fact, related to conduct disorder in adolescents (Pliszka, Rogeness, Renner, Sherman, & Broussard, 1988) and disruptive behavior disorders among children (Kruesi et al., 1992). However, investigators and theorists postulate a reciprocal transaction, such that the levels of neurotransmitters not only are genetically determined, but also respond to early environmental influences and socialization (see Rogeness, Javors, & Pliszka, 1992).

Finally, testosterone has been suggested to play an organizing or activating role in physically aggressive behavior, the former occurring during the perinatal period and the latter occurring during puberty (Brain & Susman, 1997). Study results have been conflicting (Inoff-Germain et al., 1988; Olweus, Mattsson, Schalling, & Low, 1988; Susman et al., 1987), and Archer (1994) attempted to explain the differences in theory and research in a dynamic model that posits early gender differences due to hormonally driven activity levels that lead boys and girls toward different play subcultures with a different need for physical aggression. These subcultures then interact with broader societal influences, individual temperaments, and baseline levels of testosterone. Later in adolescence, when testosterone levels are rising, a child's established patterns of aggression interact with hormones to produce more or less aggression, which fuels future testosterone if the aggression induces feelings of dominance and success. Although not empirically tested, this model is a compelling explanation of the role of testosterone as an *interacting* agent across time influencing children's aggression.

Social cognition. Beyond biological factors, individuals bring particular cognitive styles to social interactions (Dishion & patterson, 1997). One of the most studied cognitive theories, social information processing, suggests that a social situation triggers a succession of cognitive and emotional operations that first represent, then interpret, the situation (Dodge & Schwartz, 1997). When these operations are effective and accurate, the social behavior is adaptive; when the operations are biased, the behavior is often maladaptive. A set of conscious and unconscious steps are hypothesized to occur repeatedly; however, children may develop patterns that simplify the steps and create relatively stable behavioral responses to situations over time (Huesmann, 1988; Schneider, 1991).

Researchers have used correlational studies with hypothetical social scenarios to examine the links between different aspects of the social cognitive processing model and children's aggressive behavior. For the most part, these studies have verified the connection between social information processing skills—for example, attending to and recalling social cues, requesting additional information, interpreting others' intentions, generating responses to the situation—and aggressive behavior (see Dodge & Frame, 1982; Dodge, Pettit, McClaskey, & Brown, 1986; Guerra & Slaby, 1989; Quiggle, Garber, Panak, & Dodge, 1992; Slaby & Guerra, 1988; Spivak & Shure, 1980). In addition, several studies indicate that aggressive children evaluate aggressive actions in a more positive light than do their nonaggressive peers (Guerra & Slaby), value the results of aggression more highly (Boldizar, Perry, & Perry, 1989), and have positive efficacy beliefs for the use of aggression (Crick & Dodge, 1989). However, the deficits in social information processing have been shown to differ based on the child's use of a particular subtype of aggression, in particular, reactive aggression (retaliation based in anger and frustration) and proactive aggression (unprovoked and goal-directed behavior; Dodge & Coie, 1987). Use of reactive aggression has been linked with hostile attributional biases, whereas use of proactive aggression is related to positive evaluations of aggressive behaviors and instrumental goals for social situations (Crick & Dodge, 1996).

Academic skills. An extensive body of research demonstrates a strong relationship between externalizing behavior problems and academic underachievement, with comorbidity up to 50% when including a broad set of externalizing syndromes and indications of school failure (Barkley, Fischer, Edelbrock, & Smallish, 1990; Hinshaw, 1992). A recent meta-analysis demonstrated that students with emotional behavior disorders (EBD) performed significantly worse across settings and subject areas than their nondiagnosed peers (R. Reid, Gonzalez, Nordness, Trout, & Epstein, 2004). A meta-analysis of the link between underachievement and delinquency revealed that academic difficulties were related to the onset, level, frequency, and persistence of delinquency in both males and females (Maguin & Loeber, 1996). Early in schooling, the link can be explained primarily by inattention and hyperactivity (Frick et al., 1991); in adolescence, the association grows increasingly robust (Hinshaw).

Paths between underachievement and delinquency have been hypothesized to be unidirectional (problems in one domain cause problems in the other; e.g., Hirschi, 1969; Rutter & Giller, 1983) or cyclical (bidirectional influences between domains). Deficits in academic skills may lead to aggressive behavior through task frustration, lack of motivation, low academic self-concept, and school disengagement (see Arnold et al., 1999). For example, continued academic problems may produce a negative association with schooling, thus increasing the likelihood of hostility, disobedience, and aggression in school (McEvoy & Welker, 2000). High levels of externalizing, on the other hand, have been thought to lead to academic problems through reduced time on task related to social skills deficits, inattention, or noncompliance (Arnold et al., 1999; McEvoy & Welker). Acting out in the classroom may help an underperforming student avoid academic tasks or may distract the teacher from the student's academic problems (Carr, Taylor, & Robinson, 1991).

Despite methodological problems, studies have provided some evidence of predictive, if not causal, pathways between academic skills and aggression. A subset of children with reading failure but no behavior problems in childhood has been shown to grow into adolescents with antisocial tendencies (Maughan, Gray, & Rutter, 1985). A delay in the onset of reading relates to later externalizing problems (e.g., McGee & Share, 1988), and aggression in middle childhood predicts low academic achievement in adulthood after controlling for early intelligence test scores (Huesmann & Eron, 1986). Finally, through such mechanisms as speech delay, familial adversity, and neurodevelopmental immaturity (e.g., Howlin & Rutter, 1987; Richman, Stevenson, & Graham, 1982; Tallal, Dukette, & Curtiss, 1989), aggression and learning are linked even before a child begins school (see Hinshaw, 1992). This provides additional support that the connection between aggression and achievement is complex and multifaceted, beginning early in development and interacting across contexts and domains to reinforce the relationship.

Final issues. The research summarized briefly provides theory and evidence of individual student factors within the biological, social–cognitive, and academic domains related to the use of aggression in schools. This extensive body of research has limitations. First, male students tend to be overrepresented and female students underrepresented in the study samples. This leads to a lack of complete knowledge about possible gender differences in the development of aggression, particularly as related to hormonal influences (e.g., Inoff-Germain et al., 1988; Susman et al., 1987) and links to achievement. A second and related limitation is that studies define aggression as overt or direct, rather than covert or indirect. An emerging area of interest among researchers and school personnel alike is the development and use of subtle forms of aggression in schools (see Crick, 1996; Underwood, 2003), but the pathways toward the use of social or relational aggression are less understood (see Kaukianinen et al., 1999; Xie, Swift, Cairns, & Cairns, 2002). Finally, although researchers have isolated these areas to study the development of aggression, most models are dynamic and comprehensive, linking biological, social–cognitive, and academic domains, as well as the multiple social contexts in which students live, work, and play.

CHARACTERISTICS OF THE SOCIAL CONTEXT

Children traverse multiple social contexts as they develop across their years of schooling. The primacy of the home context shifts as they enter schooling and interact with peers. They encounter new adults in classrooms and are asked to abide by the structures of the daily school routines and rules. They draw on multiple communities outside of school and the home while being exposed to mass media and entertainment. In interaction with a child's attitudes and attributes, these social contexts provide key experiences that shape development, including acerbating or escalating aggressive or violent behavior. A review of the literature suggests that family, peers, neighborhoods, mass media, schools, and classrooms should be considered when examining the ecology of the developing child.

Family. Children can transfer negative behaviors learned with family members into the school setting (e.g., Earls, 1981). Family research has identified two areas of the home context that have been linked to children's and adolescents' aggressive and violent behavior: (a) parent–child interactions and (b) parenting practices. Focused on the patterned exchanges between parents and their children, patterson and his colleagues have investigated a social interactional theory of the development of aggressive behavior (J. B. Reid, Patterson, & Snyder, 2002). Drawing on principles of operant conditioning, they have documented coercive cycles between parents and young children whereby a child's whining or tantrums are rewarded when a parent gives in to the child's request. These interlocking reinforcement patterns repeat themselves daily and children learn that aggressive behavior ushers in positive results. Investigators have also studied how children learn from adult modeling of aggression (Bandura, 1973), especially related to parents' discipline practices. From a social learning theory perspective, if an adult expresses anger by physically punishing the child, then the child may learn to do the same. Longitudinal studies have linked physical punishment to later aggression and delinquency (Eron, Huesmann, & Zelli, 1991; Farrington & Hawkins, 1991). Supervision during adolescence has also been studied as a parenting practice linked to aggression. providing structure and adult guidance for adolescents has been posited as developmentally appropriate, even during a stage when needs for autonomy increase (Connell, 1990). Several longitudinal studies have shown that a lack of parent supervision is one of the strongest predictors of adolescent conduct disorder and delinquency (e.g., Hawkins, Herrenkohl, & Farrington, 1998).

Increasingly, scholars recognize that parenting practices should be considered within cultural context (Baumrind, 1991). Generalizations about the detrimental effects of particular parenting practices can be hard to make when for some families in certain neighborhood contexts such practices may be protective. For instance, Lansford, Deater-Deckard, Dodge, Bates, and Pettit (2004) showed that for African Americans, unlike for White adolescents, physical discipline such as spanking was linked to lower externalizing problems. A similar cultural specificity may be considered when examining the role of parental supervision and adolescent aggression. While some evidence shows that authoritative parenting may be linked to positive outcomes for adolescents from diverse groups (Gregory & Weinstein, 2004), culturally specific findings (Gonzales, Cauce, & Friedman, 1996; Steinberg, Lamborn, & Darling, 1994) present a more complex picture. Strict monitoring was adaptive for adolescents living in high-crime neighborhoods

(Eamon, 2001; Gonzales et al., 1996), suggestive of the benefits of an authoritarian parenting style.

Peers. As early as 1939, Sutherland theorized that peers make up a crucial social context in which aggressive and violent norms are transmitted. Since then, empirical research has firmly established the reciprocal relationship between friendship networks and behavior (e.g., Dishion, French, & patterson, 1995). Negative peer experiences (both peer rejection and "deviant" peer affiliation) have been cited as "on-ramps" to adolescent aggression (Laird, Jordan, Dodge, pettit, & Bates, 2001). Aggressive children are more likely to be rejected by their classmates, which then increases the risk for later antisocial behavior (Asher & Coie, 1990). In fact, research has shown that the link between peer rejection and antisocial behavior is mediated by affiliation among aggressive peers (Dishion, patterson, Stoolmiller, & Skinner, 1991). In the early years of schooling, a pattern of negative interactions with peers can become relatively stable across the school year for aggressive children (Snyder, 2002). These children are reinforced for their behavior, but often rejected by other peers. Seeking social niches that will hold them in high regard, they develop relationships with other aggressive children (Thornberry & Krohn, 1997). Longitudinal studies have shown that affiliation with an aggressive peer group is a powerful predictor of the persistence and progression of antisocial behavior (Moffit & Caspi, 2001; Patterson, Dishion, & yoerger, 2000).

Within peer networks, friends may support and encourage each other's aggressive behavior through positive reinforcement and modeling. In observational studies of adolescents, researchers have shown that peers reinforce each other's aggressive talk and behavior through both verbal and nonverbal behavior (Buehler, Patterson, & Furniss, 1966; Dishion, Andrews, & Crosby, 1995; Dishion, Spracklen, Andrews, & Patterson, 1996). Moreover, displays of toughness and power can help an adolescent gain status and, for males, reinforce a type of masculine identity (Fagan & Wilkson, 1998). The processes of impression management, peer reinforced aggressive behavior, and expected gender roles need further examination. That said, research has firmly established that it is important to consider a teenager's friendship group to understand heightened aggression, especially during the adolescent years.

Neighborhood and media influences. A review of studies showed that differences in neighborhoods have a small to moderate effect on delinquency and violence (Leventhal & Brooks-Gunn, 2000). The mechanisms through which neighborhoods affect children's development include institutional resources, relationships, and the norms and collective efficacy in neighborhoods (Jencks & Mayer, 1990; Leventhal & Brooks-Gunn). For instance, access to high-quality childcare, with low adult-to-child ratios, is limited in poor neighborhoods (Fuller, Coonerty, Kipnis, & Choong, 1997); this resource is linked to positive behavioral outcomes (e.g., Benasich, Brooks-Gunn, & Clewell, 1992). protective relationships may also be lacking or compromised in low-income communities. Economic hardship has been thought to increase parents' social isolation, stress, and depression, which then compromises their ability to provide monitoring (Conger et al., 2002). Lower monitoring predicts higher rates of delinquency (Hawkins, Herrenkohl, & Farrington, 1998). The benefits of watchful community members may also be compromised in low-income neighborhoods with high residential turnover. These neighborhoods have been shown to have weak norms to control aggressive behavior and low collective efficacy to change the neighborhood (Sampson, Morenoff, & Earls, 1999). Cut out from mainstream economic opportunities, key pathways out of poverty may be lost, which leaves generations trapped in poverty and exposed to violent neighborhoods (Hill, Fernando, Chen, & LaFrombois, 1994). Such exposure has been prospectively linked to greater aggressive behavior (Gorman-Smith & Tolan, 1998).

Increasing evidence has established a link between exposure to media violence and aggressive behavior (Anderson & Bushman, 2001). The link is robust and replicable, although not statistically large (Huesmann, Moise, & podoloski, 1997). Experimental conditions in the lab have shown that exposure to violent media increases the likelihood of physical assault (see Anderson, Berkowitz, & Donnerstein, 2003, for a review). Longitudinal studies support the laboratory findings. For instance, in a study spanning over 25 years, Huesmann (1988) found that criminal convictions at age 30 were linked with preference for violent television in the third grade. Substantial evidence supports theories of observational learning of behaviors and cognitions to help explain why media exposure predicts aggression. Children replicate the behavior of admired television characters (Huesmann & Eron, 1986) who receive rewards for their acts of violence (Bandura, 1973). Via the media, children learn cognitive scripts for aggressive behavior and develop beliefs about the acceptability of aggression as a means to a goal (Huesmann et al., 1997).

Schools. Schools have been shown to differ in their rates of aggression and violence even when taking into account the characteristics of the enrolled students (Rutter,

Maughan, Mortiore, & Ouston, 1979). Such differences have prompted inquiry into school policies, procedures, and structures that distinguish low from high aggressive schools. Three underlying theoretical approaches differentiate research in this area. The first approach implies that there is a developmental mismatch between students and the way schooling is organized such that the school either lacks appropriate monitoring or lacks appropriate autonomy. Said differently, schools are seen as under or over-controlling. The second approach posits that students are not given the opportunity to bond with school whereby they do not become personally invested in the rules and in the community. The third approach suggests that schools' organization of students results in reinforcing maladaptive behavior. Research with these approaches has been conducted primarily at the elementary school level, yet evidence is suggestive that they may be helpful in understanding middle and high school effects on aggression.

Mismatched with young children's developmental needs, some schools may lack consistent, schoolwide expectations for behavior (Horner, Sugai, Lewis-Palmer, & Todd, 2001) or adequate supervision throughout the school grounds. Specific settings in the school may be particularly conducive to aggressive behavior. Using naturalistic observations of elementary students, Craig, Pepler, and Atlas (2000) found that, compared with behavior in classroom settings, children exhibited more aggression on the playground, where very little teacher intervention occurred. J. B. Reid and colleagues (1999) also showed that less supervision during recess was linked with higher levels of aggression. Additional settings such as hallways and lunchrooms may also need to be examined for their lack of appropriate supervision. Behavioral regulation, while underemployed in certain settings in the elementary school grades, may be implemented in a counterproductive manner in later grades without consideration for adolescents' increasing need for autonomy. Hyman and perone (1998) argued that police presence, metal detectors, and locker searchers are displays of control and disrespect. Zero-tolerance and punitive suspension policies may also contribute to a culture of threat and control (Ayers, Dohrn, & Ayers, 2001). In repressive school environments, students may respond with moral indignation and active resistance (Giroux, 1983). Correlational research has shown that students' perceptions of feeling respected and perceiving clear and fair rules are linked to lower rates of discipline (Gottfredson, Gottfredson, & Hybl, 1993; Hollingsworth, Lufler, & Clune, 1984). Additional research on students' responses to school cultures of threat and surveillance is needed.

Schools may vary in the degree to which they offer the conditions that promote school bonding, which has been theorized as a factor that can lower aggression and violence. Combining social control theory (Hirschi, 1969) and developmental theory, Hawkins, Smith, and Catalano, (2004) have conceptualized school bonding as a commitment to doing well in school and an attachment to those at school, characterized by close emotional relationships. They posit that a strong social bond asserts an informal control on a student's behavior. Evidence to support their theory has accrued. Lowered school bonding has been linked to escalating aggression during the teen years (Hawkins, Guo, & Hill 2001). Relatedly, Battistich, Solomon, Watson, & Schaps (1997), in a longitudinal study across elementary grades, found that students' sense of community predicted lower delinquency.

School policies on tracking and ability grouping may also be linked to the problem of aggression. The drawbacks of homogenous grouping have been examined from the perspective of operant conditioning principles such that students who behave similarly reinforce each other's behavior and, by doing so, strengthen it. Some evidence is suggestive that classroom placement can have long-term effects on the escalation of aggression. Kellam, Ling, and Merisca (1998) found that first graders perceived as high in aggression had higher rates of aggression in sixth grade if they were placed in first-grade classrooms with high mean levels of aggression. They concluded that tracking aggressive children with similar children can have detrimental effects. Similarly, grouping lower achieving students together has been linked to increasing behavior difficulties over time (Werthamer-Larsson, Kellam, & Wheeler, 1991). In fact, some scholars have described the sorting of students as "structural violence." They argue that the monitoring of African American students as "behavior disordered" in special education serves to colonize and control this population of students, which leads to stigmatizing labels (Watts & Erevelles, 2004).

Classrooms. Classrooms in the early grades and the later grades have been shown to differ in levels of discipline problems (Baerveldt, 1992; Gregory, Nygreen, & Moran, 2006). Inquiry into what differentiates classrooms with higher levels of aggression and disruptive behavior can be grouped into three approaches. The first approach emphasizes the teachers' abilities to manage the classroom as a whole. Of importance are teachers' skills in engaging the students in academic tasks without being sidetracked by disruption. The second approach emphasizes the quality of teachers' relationships and interactions with individual students. The third approach focuses on teachers' attitudes and expectations that are brought into the classroom.

While most of this research has been conducted at the elementary school level in single classrooms, some middle- and high-school-level research has sought to understand divergent behavior across classrooms (e.g., Gregory & Weinstein, 2008).

The findings of Jacob Kounin (1970) are relevant today in understanding the importance of group management for well-run classrooms. Kounin found that more important than their specific discipline techniques, teachers with less aggression in their rooms were skilled at keeping the whole classroom on task and, thus, prevented escalating problems with aggression. Using systematic coding of videotaped elementary schools classrooms, Kounin found five skills that were linked with lower disruptions. "Withitness" is a teacher's preemptive actions and heightened awareness of behavior in the classroom. With quick and subtle interventions, a skilled teacher intervenes early to keep students engaged in the academic tasks. "Overlapping" is a teacher's ability to multitask with a focus on keeping the academic lesson going. He or she is able to address off-task behavior without derailing the lesson. "Momentum" helps transitions occur quickly with little time for losing students' motivation. "Smoothness" keeps the lessons focused with minimal deviations from the task at hand. "Group alerting" uses skills to keep each student engaged without letting some drift off. Overall, these teachers are able to anticipate problems with a focus on the antecedents of misbehavior (Emmer, Evertson, & Worsham, 2003; Evertson, Emmer, & Worhsam, 2003).

Indicators of well-run classrooms include how teachers interact with individual students. Reviews of research on classroom discipline have shown consistently that frequency of positive reinforcement is linked with orderly classrooms and low levels of misbehavior (see Doyle, 1985). The importance of positive feedback supports theories of operant conditioning, whereby behavior is strengthened when it is reinforced. The quality of interactions has also been examined from a relational standpoint. Close teacher relationships have been shown to serve as protective factors for young children at risk of negative discipline trajectories (Pianta, 1999). Evidence suggests that students' experience of teachers as nurturing with high academic expectations are linked to positive social and behavioral outcomes for middle school (Wentzel, 2002) and high school students (Gregory, 2004). Teachers, like parents, may help establish positive emotional climates with children (Davis, 2002). Within this climate, teachers may develop trust with students that enables them to effectively prevent or de-escalate aggressive behavior (Gregory, 2004). Or, teachers may develop effective regulatory processes with their students (via the relationship) to help students identify and control their emotions (Pianta & Weinstein, 2008).

Teacher attitudes and expectations may exacerbate or prevent escalating aggression in the classroom. Research in this area asserts that teachers enter classrooms with preconceived notions of students, which affect their teaching practices. Though conducted mostly at the elementary school grade levels, research on teacher perceptions suggests that, on average, teachers are more likely to hold negative judgments of students of color than of White students (Weinstein, 2002). For instance, compared with teachers of color, White kindergarten teachers were more likely to report having conflict with their students of color (Saft & pianta, 2001) and report overall higher rates of student difficulty in following directions (Rimm-Kaufman, Pianta, & Cox, 2000). From her ethnographic study of an elementary school, Ferguson (2000) argued that White teachers draw on stereotypes and their own fears of difference when they perceive "defiance" in African American students. In their large study of urban middle schools in the Midwest, Skiba and colleagues (2002) identified reasons for suspension given to African American students as more subjective compared with reasons for suspensions given to White students. In a path analysis explaining the disproportionate sanctioning of Black students, McCarthy and Hoge (1987) found that, despite Black and White students' similar self-reports of misconduct, teachers' evaluation of the students' demeanor explained a significant amount of the association between race and sanctions received. Additional research is needed to examine students' behavioral response to differential treatment.

Final issues. The social contextual effects on aggression often have small to moderate effect sizes, with meaningful implications for the escalation of aggressive behavior across schooling. That said, limitations of the empirical understanding of social contextual effects need to be highlighted. While it is helpful to pinpoint a given setting's particular effects on aggression, the reality of interacting settings is far more complex. Ecologically grounded research that accounts for the interacting influences encountered in a given day and across developmental stages is needed. The field is only beginning to address the generalizability and the cultural specificity of particular processes. Differences related to gender, social class, race and ethnicity, and region may influence how and why some social forces have more or less impact on some children's behavior.

CONTINUOUS AND RECIPROCAL INTERACTIONS BETWEEN INDIVIDUALS AND CONTEXTS

Individual attitudes and attributes interact with social contextual influences in a dynamic and reinforcing fashion (Rutter & Sroufe, 2000). Thus, across a child's life, genetic, neural, behavioral, and environmental systems likely interplay in a bidirectional manner (Gottlieb & Halpern, 2002). A life-course developmental model of aggressive behavior points to critical windows when particular risk factors play a greater or lesser role (J. B. Reid & Eddy, 1997). Longitudinal research has helped to identify when such risk factors set in motion negative developmental trajectories within particular subgroups of children. Confirmed by other studies, Patterson (1995) and Moffitt and Caspi (2001) delineated between early childhood onset of aggression, which is more likely to be life-course persistent, and adolescent onset of aggression, which is more likely to desist in early adulthood. These early-onset children often exhibit aggressive behavior outside the normative developmental levels before they start formal schooling. An interplay between individual factors (e.g., attentional problems, low verbal IQ, or irritable temperament) and family factors (e.g., disrupted inconsistent parenting, parents with a history of antisocial behavior, or coercive parenting) has been shown to be a strong predictor of such early onset. Thus, in these early years between infancy and 5 years of age, family and individual risks factors are particularly salient (J. B. Reid & Eddy).

When the "early-onset" children enter formal schooling, another set of risk factors exacerbate the aggressive behavior. School and peer factors such as a lack of positive teacher attention, academic underachievement, and rejection by peers, contribute to the "snowballing" of the problem. In high school, these children with histories of aggressive behavior are matched by another subgroup of later onset youth (Moffit and Caspi, 2001). For both groups of teens, a lack of adequate monitoring by parents accompanied by affiliation with high-risk peers exacerbates the aggressive behavior. Equipped with a developmental perspective that considers multiple pathways and risk factors that co-occur between individuals and their social contexts, school counselors can better understand how aggressive behaviors can become more wide-ranging in scope and seriousness across children's years in schooling.

COUNSELING PRACTICE TO REDUCE SCHOOL VIOLENCE

CURRENT PRACTICE IN SCHOOLS

Recent efforts abound to study the effectiveness of school-based interventions to prevent violence and aggression (see Durlak & Wells, 1997; Henrich, Brown, & Aber, 1999; Johnson & Johnson, 1996; Leff, Power, Manz, Costigan, & Nabors, 2001; Wilson, Lipsey, & Derzon, 2003). Based in theory and research, most programs with evidence of effectiveness have been designed and evaluated by university researchers. These demonstration programs focus on building competence and/or addressing deficits within the individual student (e.g., cognitive processing skills, academic achievement), supporting and/or changing one or more social contexts (e.g., playground, classroom), or both. prevention programs have been found to have the largest effects on the highest risk populations (Wilson, Gottfredson, & Najaka, 2001). Unlike demonstration programs, "routine practice programs"—those that currently exist in schools—generally have not been studied, have been shown to be minimally effective, or are evidence-based programs being inadequately implemented (see Wilson et al., 2003). In the following sections, we will outline some common routine practice programs and several effective demonstration programs to prevent and/or reduce aggression and violence in schools.

Routine practice programs. One common practice to reduce school violence involves the removal of disruptive students from the situation (e.g., detention or suspension) either alone or in combination with a parent–teacher conference (Gottfredson et al., 1993; Tolan & Guerra, 1994). Although research has demonstrated the importance of consistent consequences for violation of clear school rules (e.g., Colvin, Sugai, Good, & Lee, 1997), the long-term effectiveness of punitive disciplinary measures in reducing or preventing violence is not evident (see Skiba, peterson, & Williams, 1997; Mayer, 1995). Similarly, when parent– teacher conferences are oriented toward problem solving and establishing consistent policies and communication across home and school, they may be helpful. However, when they occur only after negative events and emphasize punishment, their helpfulness in reducing the problem behavior is questionable.

A second widespread practice involves providing psychological testing and/or supportive counseling for individual students. Although an educational and psychological assessment may be a reasonable first step for the most disruptive students, it is not a realistic preventive or treatment solution given the tremendous resources needed to carry out this approach for all whose behavior and achievement may suggest it. In addition, supportive counseling (noncognitive behavioral therapy) has not been demonstrated to be effective in reducing aggression in the contexts in which disruptive children and youth act out (Wilson et al., 2001). Finally, even when school personnel try to implement evidence-based demonstration programs, for many reasons, the implementation of these interventions is often inadequate, thus reducing the likelihood of effectiveness. In a recent review, Gottfredson and colleagues (2004) found that only 57% of delinquency prevention activities in schools were implemented to a satisfactory level in terms of duration, intensity, and frequency of activities; content of programming; method of delivery; and participation among staff and students.

Demonstration programs. Many preventive and treatment programs designed and supported by a university-based research team have been the subject of rigorous examination documenting at least moderate effectiveness within particular school–community contexts when implemented with fidelity. The intervention programs are based in theory and research, and focus on the students (e.g., as individuals or groups), the social context (e.g., classroom, playground), or both (e.g., multilevel and whole school). A recent meta-analysis of school-based intervention effects on aggressive behavior indicates that well-implemented, intensive, teacher-administrated, behavioral/academic/social competence programs can have a sizeable impact on student aggression (Wilson et al., 2003). We will discuss several of these programs next. In addition, we will describe some well-studied multimodal programs that may have smaller effects on aggressive behavior (see Wilson et al., 2003) but may have an impact *across* domains of student development such as social competence and academic learning. Given the differences in program effectiveness when programs are supported by a research team versus implemented without support, recommendations will be provided to counselors interested in utilizing an evidence-based approach in their schools to maximize the possibility of a positive impact on student aggression and violence.

INDICATED OR TREATMENT PROGRAMS

Typically, counselors intervene with individual students who already have demonstrated aggressive behavior with the aim of preventing the unfolding of a full-scale disorder. A recent meta-analysis showed that school-based programs that aim to prevent the escalation of aggression are most effective with students who already have exhibited aggressive behavior (Wilson et al., 2003). School interventions may be individual, parent, or group focused; however, the configuration of interventions with identified students is under strict scrutiny. With cost effectiveness a priority, schools often place aggressive children in group interventions, where students with similar difficulties interact in weekly meetings. Recent research on the negative peer influences in groups has raised questions about the unintended iatrogenic effects of group-format interventions at the elementary and middle schools (Boxer, Guerra, Huesmann, & Morales, 2005) and the high school level (Cho, Hallfors, & Sanchez, 2005). At this point, additional research is needed to understand whether mixed student groups are more or less beneficial than homogenous groups and whether high-aggressive or low-aggressive peers undermine or enhance intervention goals (Dishion & Dodge, 2005). With caution in mind, a well-studied group-based intervention follows. Then, we will describe a school-based parenting intervention, followed by a well-established individually focused intervention.

Anger Coping Program. The Anger Coping program was designed as an 18-session, small–group format intervention with aggressive children (Lochman, Barry, & Pardini, 2003). The program draws on a social–cognitive approach, which emphasizes that children's perceptions of conflicts, encoding of relevant details, and interpretation of others' intentions are linked with their behavioral response (Crick & Dodge, 1996). Using a curriculum, group leaders address the following topics: anger management, perspective taking, socials skills training, goal setting, coping with peer pressure, emotional identification, problem solving, and relaxation training (Lochman et al., 2003). Sessions vary with a range of interactive tasks such as practicing calming self-talk while being teased, role-playing conflicts from different perspectives, and videotaping the negative consequences of an aggressive action.

The Anger Coping program has been administered primarily in middle schools for boys identified as exhibiting aggressive behavior. It has been run as a single intervention (e.g., Lochman, 1992) and in combination with a parenting intervention (e.g., Lochman & Wells, 2004). Chorpita and his colleagues (2002) concluded in their review of three relevant studies that the intervention has a modest effect size in reducing aggressive behavior. In one study, only those who received a booster intervention the next school year showed significant reductions in classroom, off-task behavior (Lochman, 1992). The most recent published evaluation showed more promising results. The program was aimed at fifth- and sixth-grade boys who had relatively high aggressive ratings by parents and teachers (Lochman & Wells). Small groups of 4 to 6 boys participated in 32 sessions across 2 school years. The year after the intervention was completed, teachers rated the boys as improved in behavioral problems, anger management, and problem solving. No moderating effects of race were found such that the intervention effects held for the sample of White and African American boys. While the Anger Coping program is a promising intervention, as mentioned previously, care should be taken when grouping aggressive children and adolescents in sustained "pull-out" programs (Dishion & Dodge, 2005).

Functional behavioral assessment and intervention. The 1997 and 2004 reauthorizations of the Individuals with Disabilities Education Act require schools to address discipline problems with students in special education using functional behavioral assessment and intervention. Grounded in behaviorist and social learning theory, functional analysis and intervention is frequently conducted with students exhibiting aggressive or disruptive behavior (Quinn et al., 2001). Crone and Horner (2003) described the procedures in detail. A teacher and counselor gather data about environmental factors that precede and follow the behavior. Hypotheses about the predictors and function of the behavior are developed. For instance, students may engage in problematic behaviors to obtain or escape something in the classroom (Ervin et al., 2001). Once hypotheses are formed about what drives the behavior, interventions are then designed to make the behavior irrelevant, inefficient, and ineffective (Crone & Horner, 2003). Interventions can include teaching a child an appropriate replacement behavior to obtain the desired goals or eliminating the reinforcers that strengthen the negative behavior (Ervin et al., 2001).

The functional approach to changing individual behavior in the classroom seems to be ahead of the research supporting its widespread use. While examination of 100 studies using functional behavioral assessment and intervention with 278 students showed positive short-term gains, most of the studies have been conducted with preschool and elementary students with disabilities (Ervin et al., 2001). Research with older students and those without disabilities is scarce. Moreover, long-term follow up to ascertain if the gains are sustained is rare. In addition, this approach can be quite time intensive and requires anywhere from 1 week to 30 days (Quinn et al., 2001). Thus, whether it is a cost-effective use of teacher and counselor time in comparison with classroom-wide interventions remains open to question. That said, a recent meta-analysis concluded that interventions based on learning principles and behavioral theory are most effective compared with other interventions such as mentoring or supportive counseling (Wilson et al., 2001). Thus, despite the fact the research on functional behavioral assessment and intervention is lagging, it is a promising approach that has become expected professional practice.

Parenting—The incredible years. For the past 20 years, Carolyn Webster-Stratton and her colleagues at the University of Washington Clinic have been developing interventions with young children to prevent the onset and escalation of conduct problems. After fine-tuning a parenting intervention, they developed child and teacher components (Webster-Stratton, 2005). Their program theory uses cognitive social learning principles with a focus on relationships. Using Patterson's interactional model (1982), they aimed to interrupt the coercive patterns that can become established between children and parents, which have been predictive of aggressive behavior. They also emphasized the importance of the emotional climate between parents and children with the goal of reducing harsh and inconsistent parenting and increasing warmth and positive interactions. Their programs relied heavily on videotaped parenting vignettes to model effective and ineffective parenting (see Webster-Stratton). The BASIC training program has 13 to 14 weekly 2-hour sessions and teaches parents of 2-to 7-year-olds how to positively engage, use praise and rewards effectively, set limits, and deal with noncompliance. The ADVANCE program aims to maintain treatment effects by lowering the detrimental effects of relationship distress and divorce, which were found to be predictors of treatment relapse. The program attempts to strengthen interpersonal skills in coping, communication, problem solving, social support, and self-care. They also offer four to six additional sessions that address how parents can promote their children's learning.

The BASIC parenting intervention has been studied extensively and summarized in more detail elsewhere (Webster-Stratton, 2005). The bulk of the research was with White middle-class families and children aged 2 to 6 years. However, they have extended their scope to include more diverse populations and children up to 10 years old. In brief, six randomized controlled trials have shown that the intervention improves parent–child interaction and reduces child conduct problems. The intervention has resulted in sustained gains for half to three quarters of the participants. A 3-year follow-up study showed that children with single parents or parents with relationship difficulties or negative life stress were less likely to sustain benefits. The intervention has also been successfully implemented with a low-income, Head

Start population (M. J. Reid, Webster-Stratton, & Baydar, 2004). Children and their mothers with more difficulties benefited the most. The parent training has shown that behavioral improvements can generalize to the school setting. A recent study showed that the children of the parents in the intervention sustained improved classroom behavior across one school year, as rated by teachers (Webster-Stratton, Reid, & Hammond, 2004).

UNIVERSAL OR SINGLE CONTEXT PROGRAMS

Beyond programs focused on students who already have demonstrated some aggressive behaviors, several setting-wide programs have evidence of effectiveness. Some of these are curricula with the primary goal of building skills and competencies within individual children, such as the promoting Alternative THinking Strategies (pATHS) curriculum or classwide peer tutoring. These programs have the potential benefit of impacting both those students who may be at risk of developing aggressive tendencies, as well as those who already use aggression in school. Others are interventions whose primary goal is to alter the functioning of a setting, such as teacher consultation and playground restructuring. In this case, addressing environmental or structural characteristics related to the promotion of aggression may be especially critical, particularly for children in elementary school (e.g., J. B. Reid, Eddy, & Fetrow, 1999).

PATHS. The promoting Alternative THinking Strategies program is a 60-lesson curriculum taught by the elementary school classroom teacher over one school year and integrated into the classroom curriculum with an emphasis on both changing the environment and educating the child (Greenberg, Kusche, & Mihalic, 1998). In particular, the program is designed to increase student self-control, emotion understanding, positive communication, prosocial behavior, and interpersonal problem solving. This theory-based program derives from the ABCD model of development (affective–behavioral–cognitive–dynamic) in which children's internal and external coping arises from their combined emotion awareness, cognitive understanding, and behavioral skills, with the affective component preceding the cognitive and behavioral functions (see Greenberg et al., 1998). Teaching methods for the 20- to 30-minute lessons include direct instruction, discussion, role plays, modeling, and reinforcement. Lessons focus on labeling and managing feelings, delaying gratification and controlling impulses, reading and interpreting social cues, using a procedure for problem solving and decision making, and developing nonverbal and verbal communication skills. Teachers are trained in a 3-day workshop at the beginning of the year, with ongoing support and consultation.

The PATHS curriculum is unusual in the rigor of the research base and its demonstrated effectiveness in both regular and special education classrooms (Greenberg & Kusche, 1993; Greenberg, Kusche, Cook, & Quamma, 1995). It has been tested in randomized, longitudinal studies with classroom observation components in Seattle-area first-to third-grade classrooms with approximately 60% White and 40% African American students and mainly low-to middle-income families. positive outcomes include increased fluency and comfort in discussing basic feelings, as well as positive efficacy beliefs around managing and changing feelings. Among students at behavioral risk, teachers noted significant improvements in frustration, tolerance, social skills, task orientation, peer relations, and internalizing behaviors. Investigators mentioned significant variation regarding the level at which the teacher modeled cognitive and behavioral skills, shared emotions, and established an atmosphere of respect for varying beliefs and feelings (Greenberg et al., 1998). However, no outcomes were reported regarding differences by teacher ability or ways in which support staff attempted to bolster teacher skills. Finally, although the program includes generalization activities to be used outside the classroom and materials for families, outcomes generally have not been reported on the impact of nonclassroom and parent materials.

Peer tutoring. Peer tutoring, also called peer-assisted learning, has been used as a classroom-wide intervention aimed at raising achievement and increasing prosocial behaviors. Students are paired in fixed or reciprocal tutor–tutee roles. Primarily implemented in the elementary and middle schools, programs have addressed reading (Fuchs, Fuchs, & Burish, 2000) and mathematics (Fantuzzo, King, & Heller, 1992). Student tutors are trained to structure the tutoring time and use immediate corrective feedback with their tutee. Goals and rewards are built into the tutoring time to help the pair work efficiently and foster mutual motivation. The theoretical basis of peer tutoring is derived from research on the influence of classroom peers on behavior and motivation. It has been argued that in successful tutoring programs, students teach academic skills, model on-task behavior (Topping & Ehly, 2001), and foster academic and social motivation for learning (Rohrbeck, Gins-burg-Block, Fantuzzo, & Miller, 2003).

Given that academically targeted programs have been shown to reduce aggressive behavior (Wilson et al., 2003), the effectiveness of peer tutoring at raising academic outcomes shows promise for improving overall classroom behavior. A meta-analytic review that looked across effect sizes in 90 studies found that, on average, students in peer tutoring made moderate achievement gains (Rohrbeck et al., 2003). The programs were particularly beneficial for younger elementary students, low-income students, and urban students. While much of the research has focused on achievement gains, several studies have shown that peer tutoring is linked with improved behavior (Pigott, Fantuzzo, & Clement, 1986; Wolfe, Fantuzzo, & Wolfe, 1986). For instance, in a study with urban African American peer tutors, groups that were given rewards contingent on academic success were perceived by the teacher as showing lower negative classroom conduct (Fantuzzo et al., 1992).

Teacher consultation (Good behavior game). It has been argued that school counselors' roles should be expanded to include teacher consultation with the aim of increasing teacher capacity in classroom management (e.g., Adelman & Taylor, 2002). Drawing on behavioral consultation models, a counselor identifies the teacher's concern, gathers information about antecedents and consequences of the concern, develops a plan of intervention with the teacher, and determines the outcome of the intervention (Sladeczek, Kratochwill, Steinback, Kumke, & Hagermoser, 2003). A counselor may consult with a teacher to help implement specific programmatic interventions designed to improve classroom behavior. One such program is the Good Behavior Game (Barrish, Saunders, & Wolf, 1969), which draws on the premise that group-based rewards increase the likelihood that peers will be motivated to inhibit negative behavior. To implement the program, the teacher identifies a specific block of time when the game likely will have initial success. Then, the teacher, in consultation with the students, selects negative behaviors to decrease and chooses "activity rewards," such as extra time for free-choice reading. The teacher divides the students into teams, which receive points when they exhibit the predetermined negative behaviors. All the teams can win if they have fewer than the predetermined number of points (Embry & Straatemeier, 2001). The intervention has been found to be well liked by teachers (Tingstrom, 1994).

Embry (2002) offered a thorough review of the Good Behavior Game and its proven effectiveness in diverse classrooms. In short, implementation of the game lowered a range of negative behaviors across grades levels, in multiple settings in the school, and with at-risk populations. For instance, the program was associated with lowered disruptions with fourth graders (Barrish et al., 1969), elementary-age special education students (Darveaux, 1984; Grandy, Madsen, & De Mersseman, 1973), and adolescents (Salend, Reynolds, & Coyle, 1989). In a randomized trial in Baltimore with first graders, the game had the largest effect in reducing the aggressive behavior of students rated as high on aggression prior to the intervention (Dolan, Kellam, & Brown, 1993). Long-term effects of the classroom-centered intervention found that by sixth grade, the first graders who had played the game, relative to the control group, had fewer conduct problems and fewer suspensions (Ialongo, poduska, Werthamer, & Kellam, 2001). A key ingredient appears to be peer pressure, such that positive peer norms are set and disruptive behavior is discouraged (see Hegerle, Kesecker, & Couch, 1979).

Playground interventions. Aggressive behavior in schools occurs most frequently in unstructured settings such as the lunchroom and playground (Craig & Pepler, 2000; Craig et al., 2000). Recent attention has been paid to the characteristics of safe and productive playgrounds, and programs targeting these characteristics have been shown to reduce aggression and violence among elementary school students. The characteristics include access to structured activities and an organized space (Bay-Hinitz, peterson, & Quilitch, 1994), clear communication of rules and expectations (Colvin et al., 1997), sufficient and active supervision (Olweus, 1999), and incentives and consequences for positive and negative behavior (Eddy, Reid, & Fetrow, 2000). Although playground interventions may be imbedded in more comprehensive programs, research demonstrates that targeting these characteristics can reduce aggressive behavior. In one low-income, predominantly African American, urban elementary school, structured and organized games on the playground were associated with higher cooperative play and lower rough physical play over the school year, while active supervision by parent volunteers was associated with higher intercultural interaction (Leff, Costigan, & Power, 2004).

Another research team included a playground intervention in a multicomponent program (Linking the Interests of Families and Teachers; LIFT) in high juvenile crime neighborhoods within a small and majority Caucasian city. Researchers modified the Good Behavior Game (previously described) so students earned armbands from playground staff for clearly identified positive behaviors (toward a whole class reward) and negative behaviors were logged and subtracted from "good faith" points (adding to small group rewards; Eddy et al., 2000). The comprehensive program had a 3-year positive effect on elementary school children with high initial levels of aggression. Younger students had reduced playground aggression and hyperactive/inattentive behaviors, and older students had reduced arrests, delinquency, and drug use (J. B. Reid et al., 1999).

Finally, related to the peer tutoring program previously described, older peers have been trained to mediate conflicts on the playground as a supplement to the supervision by adults. In one well-implemented and evaluated program, older peers received 15 hours of training in recognizing and resolving conflicts, as well as ongoing support from a mediation team and playground supervisors. When eight trained and supported peer mediators were present on elementary school playgrounds in a middle-income, suburban community, there was an abrupt and sustained reduction in physical aggression that lasted for 2 years (Cunningham et al., 1998). Taken together, these intervention studies indicate the effectiveness of a strategy to target the *contexts* in which aggressive behaviors occur, not only the aggressive *individuals*.

MULTILEVEL PROGRAMS

Programs designed to target multiple levels at which aggression develops and is impacted have been shown to be somewhat effective in preventing and reducing aggressive behavior in schools. These generally require more resources to implement, as well as more "buy-in" among school personnel, but the trade-off may be benefits across domains of development (e.g., reducing aggression and enhancing achievement).

Fast track. Based on research indicating that externalizing problems are multiply determined, the Conduct problems prevention Research Group (1999a, 1999b) designed, implemented, and studied a comprehensive school-based program to target risk and protective factors across universal and high-risk groups of first-grade students. The universal aspect of the program included the classroom-based PATHS curriculum addressing emotions, social behaviors, and social problem solving (described earlier), along with basic parent education and skills groups. The targeted program included student social skills groups, academic tutoring, parent–child pair work, peer pair work, and home visits for students identified as behaviorally disruptive (Conduct problems prevention Research Group). The universal program was delivered mainly by teachers after an intensive workshop and with regular consultation; the selective program was delivered by family/educational coordinators and paraprofessionals who received extensive and ongoing training and supervision.

This intervention study was unique in its scope and rigor. Researchers matched and randomly assigned 54 schools in diverse communities across the United States to intervention or control conditions, and studied the impact of the universal and high-risk components with classroom observations, as well as teacher, student, and parent reports, over a 3-year period. Initial positive effects were found for classroom climate, on-task behavior, and rule following among the universal population of students, and among parenting, aggressive behavior at school, coping skills, language arts grades, and peer acceptance for high-risk students across four sites (Conduct problems prevention Research Group, 1999a, 1999b). Differences were not found by site or student background (gender or race). Limitations to this intervention study include a lack of knowledge of program sustainability over time, the dosage necessary for a positive effect, the reasons why some students do not respond, and the role of school/classroom context in intervention impact. In addition, recent studies indicate that the long-term consequences for school behavior of this intensive and comprehensive program were less strong than anticipated (Conduct problems prevention Research Group, 2004).

Child Development Project. The Child Development project aims to build "caring communities of learners" in elementary schools (Battistich, Schaps, Watson, & Solomon, 1996). Like the programs just described, the Child Development project includes activities across multiple levels: (a) the school—principal leadership, schoolwide activities; (b) the classroom—developmental discipline; cooperative learning; values-rich, literature-based reading and language arts curricula, and a phonics-based reading program for struggling readers and, (c) the family—home activities to build home–school communication as well as understanding of family culture. Unlike these programs, however, the Child Development project is designed not only to address the problem of aggressive behavior in school, but also to create a school *community* that more generally enhances student learning, cooperation, and respect.

Quasi-experimental studies with video observation of implementation quality and a range of student sociodemographic characteristics (ethnicity, income) showed short-and long-term positive results. In high implementation elementary schools, third-to sixth-grade students had lower rates of truancy, theft, substance use, and weapon carrying, and reported more sense of positive school community (Battistich et al., 1996). Follow-up studies indicated that when students in high-implementation elementary schools attend middle school, they had higher achievement and educational expectations, as well as lower misconduct and delinquent behavior than comparison students (Solomon, Battistich, Watson, Schaps, & Lewis, 2000). In addition, the phonics-based reading curriculum alone increased reading achievement for all students, but particularly for non-native English speakers (Battistich, 2000). A significant limitation of this program was that less than half of the schools that implemented the program did so to a high degree of fidelity. However, when implemented well, results indicated the potential importance of a universal emphasis on both academic learning and classroom/school culture as a means toward reducing behavioral problems among all students.

Positive Behavioral Interventions and Supports. Based on a public health model, positive Behavioral Interventions and Supports (pBIS) emphasizes a three-tiered approach to preventing and addressing disruptive behaviors (Lewis & Sugai, 1999). The first tier (universal) targets all children and adults across the school setting with the idea that that every student needs clear instruction, support, and reinforcement regarding appropriate and inappropriate behaviors in and around the school building (Horner et al., 2001). The second tier (targeted) is geared toward children at risk for disruptive behavior, meaning they have engaged in problem behaviors in the past and have minimal access to protective supports. They are seen as unlikely to respond to universal interventions and in need of secondary-level interventions (e.g., daily report card, functional behavioral assessment) to move them in a more positive direction (Hawken & Horner, 2003; March & Horner, 2002). The third tier (intensive) is designed to provide team-based individualized and comprehensive services for those children with more severe behavioral problems who respond to neither universal nor targeted interventions (see Eber & Nelson, 1997). Across the three tiers, PBIS emphasizes the importance of measuring outcomes and using data for decision making, using practices with evidence of effectiveness, and attending to systems within the school to sustain the program.

The implementation and research data on PBIS is promising. Elementary and middle schools in primarily suburban, middle-income communities have been able to incorporate PBIS into their schools to high standards (e.g., Lewis, Sugai, & Colvin, 1998; Taylor-Greene & Kartub, 2000). Research studies with a pre/post design indicate a 20% to 60% reduction in discipline referrals and suspensions between the year before and the year after full implementation of pBIS (Lohrman-O'Rourke et al., 2000; Luiselli, putnam, & Sunderland, 2002). These effects have been sustained over 6 years in schools that have continued to implement the program (Taylor-Greene & Kartub). Observational methods demonstrate that lower rates of discipline referrals are related to changes in disruptive behaviors in unstructured school settings such as the playground and hallway (Cushing, in press). What is not known is the ability of PBIS to be implemented to the same degree of fidelity and with the same effectiveness in urban low-income schools where the behavioral issues and school systems may be both qualitatively and quantitatively different from their suburban counterparts.

FINAL ISSUES

Although this section demonstrates the range of evidence-based interventions to prevent and reduce aggression in schools, there are several final issues to consider. First, intervention research tends to focus on overt forms of aggression and boys, rather than more subtle forms of aggression or girls. Recent efforts have been made to address the problem of relational or social aggression among girls (see Cappella & Weinstein, 2006; Leff, 2005), but these efforts are preliminary and must be linked with more comprehensive programs. Second, demonstration programs—in particular, those that operate at multiple levels—demand considerable resources. There is conflicting evidence regarding the importance of single- versus multiple-level approaches to addressing violence in schools, but research is clear regarding the importance of quality implementation. That said, few intervention studies describe implementation efforts, leaving gaps in understanding of methods for increasing implementation quality with school and community resources. Third, demonstration programs are developed and implemented most frequently in elementary schools, with middle and high schools receiving minimal attention. Although prevention with younger students is critical, given that aggression continues to develop through adolescence, older students deserve systematic efforts to create classroom and school environments in which pro-social behaviors are the norm. Fourth, with some exceptions, these interventions are largely a-contextual without consideration for peer and cultural norms—which may be critical to the effectiveness of a program. Finally, the evidence-based practice movement relies on a process that moves from highly controlled trials to wider dissemination within schools. A more ecologically valid approach to developing an understanding of what works may be an iterative process of research and development based not only in theory and research, but also within the school and community context in which the efforts exist.

RECOMMENDATIONS

The school counselor can play an integral role in assisting the school to prevent or address the problem of school violence by providing information and support around the use of evidence-based practices in their schools. However, given the multiple and complex realities of different school communities, there are several steps to consider prior to and during the process of implementing one of the previously discussed programs to maximize the potential benefit. From the research and theory on the development, prevention, and management of aggression in schools, we recommend the following guidelines when attempting to address school violence:

1. Collect and analyze data to understand where, when, and with whom aggression occurs.
   - Use existing datasets (e.g., discipline referrals) or gather new data (e.g., conversations or surveys with school staff).
   - Assess multiple forms of aggression, including physical, verbal, and relational aggression (Leff et al., 2001).
2. Coalesce key personnel and the school organization around the need for intervention within particular settings and/or groups of students.
   - promote a supportive school climate around the prevention and reduction of aggression (Gottfredson et al., 2004).
   - Build school capacity to initiate and sustain an innovation (e.g., infrastructure and support, resources, and leadership; Sherman et al., 1997).
   - prepare to integrate elements of the intervention into the structure of the school or setting (e.g., classroom, playground; Heller, 1990; Gottfredson et al., 2004).
3. Help school personnel select empirically supported activities with particular attention to the population with which and context within which the services have been tested.
   - Consider interventions designed to promote change within the individual child, as well as within the social context (e.g., universal, targeted, and indicated levels; Weissberg & Green-berg, 1998).

- Multiple level programs accompanied by a clarification and communication of norms about behaviors are promising; however, it is more important to implement a less-resource heavy program well than a more-resource heavy program poorly (Durlak & Wells, 1997; Gottfredson et al., 2004; Sherman et al., 1997).
- Intervene at the appropriate stage of development (e.g., early in the onset of problems for a student or setting) and during sensitive periods, such as transitions during the school day (Tolan, Guerra, & Kendall, 1995; Weissberg & Greenberg, 1998).

4. Monitor the implementation and/or adaptation of those programs or practices.
    - Adapt program content to ethnic and sociodemographic characteristics of students to maximize the potential that it has meaning in their lives, in particular if the program was tested in a demographically different school community than the one in which it will be implemented (Heller, 1990).
    - provide extensive, quality training of personnel who deliver services, and provide supervision and support for ongoing delivery of services (Gottfredson et al., 2004).
5. Collect data to evaluate the progress of the intervention strategies and make adjustments as needed.
    - Think about the multiple outcomes that may be important to the school and collect data on those outcomes (e.g., different types of aggression, academic achievement, attendance) from multiple sources (e.g., teachers, students, school data).
    - Allow sufficient time for the activities to work before making major adjustments to the intervention strategies; anticipate that the strongest results will be for the students and settings exhibiting the most problems at the start.

REFERENCES

Adelman, H. S., & Taylor, L. (2002). School counselors and school reform: New directions. *Professional School Counseling, 5*(4), 235–248.

Anderson, C. A., & Bushman, B. J. (2001). Effects of violent video games on aggressive behavior, aggressive cognition, aggressive affect, physiological arousal, and pro-social behavior: A meta-analytic review of the scientific literature. *Psychological Science, 12*(5), 353–359.

Anderson, C. A., Berkowitz, L., & Donnerstein, E. (2003). The influence of media violence on youth. *Psychological Science in the Public Interest, 4*(3), 81–110.

Archer, J. (1994). Testosterone and aggression: A theoretical review. *Journal of Offender Rehabilitation, 21*, 3–39.

Arnold, D. H., Ortiz, C., Curry, J. C., Stowe, R. M., Goldstein, N. E., Fisher, P. H., et al. (1999). promoting academic success and preventing disruptive behavior disorders through community partnership. *Journal of Community Psychology, 27*(5), 589–598.

Asher, S. R., & Coie, J. D. (1990). *Peer rejection in childhood.* New York: Cambridge University Press.

Ayers, W., Dohrn, B., & Ayers, R. (2001). *Zero tolerance: Resisting the drive for punishment in schools.* New York: The New Press.

Baerveldt, C. (1992). Schools and the prevention of petty crime: Search for a missing link. *Journal of Quantitative Criminology, 8*, 79–94.

Bandura, A. (1973). *Aggression: A social learning analysis*. Englewood Cliffs, NJ: Prentice Hall.

Barkley, R. A., Fischer, M., Edelbrock, C. S., & Smallish, L. (1990). The adolescent outcome of hyperactive children diagnosed by research criteria: An 8-year prospective follow-up study. *Journal of the American Academy of Child and Adolescent Psychiatry, 29*, 546–557.

Barrish, H. H., Saunders, M., & Wolf, M. M. (1969). Good behavior game: Effects of individual contingencies for group consequences on disruptive behavior in a classroom. *Journal of Applied Behavior Analysis, 2*, 119–124.

Bates, J. E., Bayles, K., Bennett, D. S., Ridge, B., & Brown, N. M. (1991). Origins of externalizing behavior problems at eight years of age. In D. J. Pepler & K. H. Rugin (Eds.), *The development and treatment of childhood aggression* (pp. 93–120). Hillsdale, NJ: Erlbaum.

Bates, J. E.; Maslin, C. A., & Frankel, K. A. (1985). Attachment security, mother–child interaction, and temperament as predictors of behavior-problem ratings at age three years. *Monographs of the Society for Research in Child Development, Vol. 50*, 167–193.

Battistich, V. (2000). *Summary of evaluation findings on the Child Development Project*. Oakland, CA: Developmental Studies Center.

Battistich, V., Schaps, E., Watson, M., & Solomon, D. (1996). Prevention effects of the Child Development project: Early findings from an ongoing multisite demonstration trial. *Journal of Adolescent Research, 11*, 12–35.

Battistich, V., Solomon, V., Watson, M., & Schaps, E. (1997). Caring school communities. *Educational Psychologist, 32*(3), 137–151.

Baumrind, D. (1991). The influence of parenting style on adolescent competence and substance use. *Journal of Early Adolescence, 11*(1), 56–95.

Bay-Hinitz, A. K., Peterson, R. F., & Quilitch, H. R. (1994). Cooperative games: A way to modify aggressive and cooperative behaviors in young children. *Journal of Applied Behavior Analysis, 27*, 435–446.

Benasich, A. A., Brooks-Gunn, J., & Clewell, B. C. (1992). How do mothers benefit from early intervention programs? *Journal of Applied Developmental Psychology, 13*, 311–362.

Berman, M. E., Kavoussi, R. J., & Coccaro, E. F. (1997). Neurotransmitter correlates of human aggression. In D. M. Stoff, J. Breiling, & J. D. Maser (Eds.), *Handbook of antisocial behavior* (pp. 305–313). New york: John Wiley & Sons, Inc.

Boldizar, J. P., Perry, D. G., & Perry, L. C. (1989). Outcome values and aggression. *Child Development, 60*, 571–579.

Boxer, P., Guerra, N. G., Huesmann, L. R., & Morales, J. (2005). Proximal peer-level effects of a small-group selected prevention on aggression in elementary school children: An investigation of the peer contagion hypothesis. *Journal of Abnormal Child Psychology, 33*(3), 325–338.

Brain, P. F., & Susman, E. J. (1997). Hormonal aspects of aggression and violence. In D. M. Stoff, J. Breiling, & J. D. Maser (Eds.), *Handbook of antisocial behavior* (pp. 314–323). New York: John Wiley & Sons, Inc.

Buehler, R. E., patterson, G. R., & Furniss, J. M. (1966). The reinforcement of behavior in institutional settings. *Behaviour Research and Therapy, 4*, 157–167.

Cappella, E., & Weinstein, R. S. (2006). The prevention of social aggression among girls. *Social Development*, 15: 434-462.

Carr, E. G., Taylor, J. G., & Robinson, S. (1991). The effects of severe behavior problems in children on the teaching behavior of adults. *Journal of Applied Behavior Analysis, 24*, 523–535.

Caspi, A., Henry, B., McGee, R. O., Moffitt, T. E., & Silva, p. A. (1995). Temperamental origins of child and adolescent behavior problems: From age 3 to age 15. *Child Development, 66*, 55–68.

Cho, H., Hallfors, D. D., & Sanchez, V. (2005). Evaluation of a high school peer group intervention for at-risk youth. *Journal of Abnormal Psychology, 33*(3), 363–374.

Chorpita, B. F., yim, L. M., Donkervoet, J. C., Arensdorf, A., Amundsen, M. J., McGee, C., et al. (2002). Toward large-scale implementation of empirically supported treatments for children: A review and observations by the Hawaii Empirical Basis to Services Task Force. *Clinical Psychology: Science & Practice*, 9(2), 165–190.

Coie, J. D., & Dodge, K. A. (1998). Aggression and antisocial behavior. In W. Damon & N. Eisenberg (Eds.), *Handbook of child psychology: Vol. 3: Social, emotional, and personality development* (5th ed., pp. 779–862). New York: John Wiley & Sons, Inc.

Colvin, G., Sugai, G., Good, R. H., III., & Lee, y. (1997). Using active supervision and precorrection to improve transition behaviors in an elementary school. *School Psychology Quarterly, 12*, 344–363.

Conduct problems prevention Research Group. (1999a). Initial impact of the Fast Track prevention trial for conduct problems: I. The high-risk sample. *Journal of Consulting and Clinical Psychology, 67*, 631–647.

Conduct problems prevention Research Group. (1999b). Initial impact of the Fast Track prevention trial for conduct problems: II. *Classroom effects. Journal of Consulting and Clinical Psychology, 67*, 648–657.

Conduct problems prevention Research Group (2004). The effects of the Fast Track program on serious problem outcomes at the end of elementary school. *Journal of Clinical Child and Adolescent Psychology, 33*, 650–661.

Conger, R. D., Wallace, L. E., Sun, y., Simons, R. L., McLoyd, V. C., & Brody, H. H. (2002). Economic pressure in African American families: A replication and extension of the family stress model. *Developmental Psychology, 38*(2), 179–193.

Connell, J. P. (1990). Context, self, and action: A motivational analysis of self-system processes across the life-span. In D. C. M. Beeghly (Ed.), *The self in transaction: Infancy to childhood* (pp. 61–97). Chicago: University of Chicago Press.

Cornell, D. G., Sheras, P. L., Kaplan, S., McConville, D., Douglass, J., Elkon, A., et al. (2004). Guidelines for student threat assessment: Field-test findings. *School Psychology Review, 33*(4), 527–546.

Craig, W. M., & Pepler, D. (2000). Observations of bullying and victimization in the school yard. In W. Craig (Ed.), *Childhood social development: The essential readings* (pp. 116–138). Malden, MA: Blackwell publishers Inc.

Craig, W. M., pepler, D., & Atlas, R. (2000). Observations of bullying in the playground and in the classroom. *School Psychology International, 21*(1), 22–36.

Crick, N. R. (1996). The role of overt aggression, relational aggression, and prosocial behavior in the prediction of children's future social adjustment. *Child Development, 67*, 2317–2327.

Crick, N. R., & Dodge, K. A. (1989). Children's evaluations of peer entry and conflict situations: Social strategies, goals, and outcome expectations. In B. Schneider, J. Nadel, G. Attili, & R. Weissberg (Eds.), *Social competence in developmental perspective* (pp. 396–399). Dordrecht, The Netherlands: Kluwer.

Crick, N. R., & Dodge, K. A. (1996). Social information processing mechanisms in reactive and proactive aggression. *Child Development, 67*, 993–1002.

Crone, D. A., & Horner, R. H. (2003). *Building positive behavior support systems in schools: Functional behavioral assessment*. New York: Guilford Press.

Cunningham, C. E., Cunningham, L. J., Martorelli, V., Tran, A., young, J., & Zacharias, R. (1998). The effects of primary division, student-mediated conflict resolution programs on playground aggression. *Journal of Child Psychology & Psychiatry, 39*(5), 653–662.

Cushing, L. S. (in press). Validation and congruent validity of a direct observation tool to assess student social climate at school. *Journal of Positive Interventions.*

Darveaux, D. X. (1984). The Good Behavior Game plus merit: Controlling disruptive behavior and improving student motivation. *School Psychology Review, 13*, 510–514.

Davis, H. A. (2002). Conceptualizing the role and influence of student-teacher relationships on children's social and cognitive development. *Educational Psychologist, 38*(4), 207–234.

Devine, J. (1996). Maximum security: *The culture of violence in inner-city schools.* Chicago: University of Chicago Press.

Dishion, T. J., Andrews, D. W., & Crosby, L. (1995). Antisocial boys and their friends in early adolescence: Relationship characteristics, quality, and interactional process. *Child Development, 66*, 139–151.

Dishion, T. J., & Dodge, K. A. (2005). peer contagion in interventions for children and adolescents: Moving towards an understanding of the ecology and dynamics of change. *Journal of Abnormal Child Psychology, 33*(3), 395–400.

Dishion, T. J., French, D. C., & Patterson, G. R. (1995). The development and ecology of antisocial behavior. In D. Cicchetti & D. Cohen (Eds.), *Manual of developmental psychopathology: Vol 2: Risk, disorder, and adaptation* (pp. 421–471). New York: Wiley.

Dishion, T. J., & Patterson, G. R. (1997). The timing and severity of antisocial behavior: Three hypotheses within an ecological framework. In D. M. Stoff, J. Breiling, & J. D. Maser (Eds.), *Handbook of antisocial behavior* (pp. 205–217). New York: John Wiley & Sons, Inc.

Dishion, T. J., Patterson, G. R., Stoolmiller, M., & Skinner, M. S. (1991). Family, school, and behavioral antecedents to early adolescent involvement with antisocial peers. *Developmental psychology, 27*, 172–180.

Dishion, T. J., Spracklen, K. M., Andrews, D. W., & Patterson, G. R. (1996) Deviancy training in male adolescent friendships. *Behavior Therapy, 27*, 373–390.

Dodge, K. A. (1991). The structure and function of proactive and reactive aggression. In D. J. Pepler & K. H. Rubin (Eds.), *The development and treatment of childhood aggression* (pp. 201–218). Hillsdale, NJ: Erlbaum.

Dodge, K. A., & Coie, J. D. (1987). Social information-processing factors in reactive and proactive aggression in children's playgroups. *Journal of Personality and Social Psychology, 53*, 1146–1158.

Dodge, K. A., & Frame, C. L. (1982). Social-cognitive biases and deficits in aggressive boys. *Child Development, 53*, 620–635.

Dodge, K. A., Pettit, G. S., McClaskey, C. L., & Brown, M. M. (1986). Social competence in children. *Monographs of the Society for Research in Child Development, 51*(2, Serial No. 213), 1–85.

Dodge, K. A., & Schwartz, D. (1997). Social information processing mechanisms in aggressive behavior. In D. M. Stoff, J. Breiling, & J. D. Maser (Eds.), *Handbook of antisocial behavior* (pp. 171–180). New York: John Wiley & Sons.

Dolan, L. J., Kellam, S. G., & Brown, C. H. (1993). The short-term impact of two classroom-based preventive interventions on aggressive and shy behaviors and poor achievement. *Journal of Applied Developmental Psychology, 14*(3), 317–345.

Doyle, W. (1985). Classroom organization and management. In M. C. Wittrock (Ed.), *Handbook of research on teaching* (3rd ed., pp. 392–431). New York: MacMillan.

Dulmus, K., Theriot, M. T., & Sowers, K. M. (2004). Student report of peer bullying victimization in a rural school. *Stress, Trauma, and Crisis: An International Journal, 7*(1), 1–16.

Durlak, J. A., & Wells, A. M. (1997). primary prevention mental health programs for children and adolescents: A meta-analytic review. *American Journal of Community Psychology, 25*(2), 115–152.

Eamon, M. K. (2001). poverty, parenting, peer, and neighborhood influences on young adolescent antisocial behavior. *Journal of Social Service Research, 28*(1), 1–23.

Earls, F. (1981). Epidemiological child psychiatry: An American perspective. In. E. F. Purcell (Ed.), *Psychopathology of children and youth: A cross cultural perspective* (pp. 3–28). New York: Josial Macy Jr. Foundation.

Earls, F., & Jung, K. G. (1987). Temperament and home environment characteristics as causal factors in the early development of childhood psychopathology. *Journal of the American Academy of Child and Adolescent Psychiatry, 26*, 491–498.

Eber, L., & Nelson, C. M. (1997). School-based wraparound planning: Integrating services for students with emotional and behavioral needs. *American Journal of Orthopsychiatry, 67*, 385–395.

Eddy, M. J., Reid, J. B., & Fetrow, R. A. (2000). An elementary school-based prevention program targeting modifiable antecedents of youth delinquency and violence: Linking the interests of families and teachers (LIFT). *Journal of Emotional & Behavioral Disorders, 8*(3), 165–176.

Embry, D. D. (2002). The Good Behavior Game: A best practice candidate as a universal behavioral vaccine. *Clinical Child and Family Psychology Review, 5*(4), 273–297.

Embry, D. D., & Straatemeier, G. (2001). *The Pax acts game manual: How to apply the Good Behavior Game.* Tuscon, AZ: PAXIS Institute.

Emmer, E. T., Evertson, C. M., & Worsham, M. E. (2003). *Classroom management for secondary teachers* (6th ed.). Boston: Allyn and Bacon.

Eron, L. D., Huesmann, L. R., & Zelli, A. (1991). The role of parental variables in the learning of aggression. In D. J. pepler & K. H Rubin (Eds.), *Development and treatment of childhood aggression* (pp. 169–188). Hillsdale, NJ, England: Lawrence Erlbaum Associates.

Ervin, R. A., Radford, p. M., Bertsch, K., piper, A. L., Ehrhardt, K. E., & Poling, A. (2001). A descriptive analysis and critique of the empirical literature on school-based functional assessment. *School Psychology Review, 30*(2), 193–210.

Evertson, C. M., Emmer, E. T., & Worhsam, M. E. (2003). *Classroom management for elementary teachers* (6th ed.). Boston: Allyn and Bacon.

Fagan, J., & Wilkson, D. L. (1998). Social contexts and functions of adolescent violence. In D. S. Elliott, B. A. Hambrug, & K. R. Williams (Eds.), *Violence in American schools* (pp. 55–93). Cambridge, UK: Cambridge University Press.

Fantuzzo, J. W., King, J. A., & Heller, L. R. (1992). Effects of reciprocal tutoring on mathematics and school adjustment: A component analysis. *Journal of Educational Psychology, 84*(3), 331–339.

Farrington, D. P., & Hawkins, J. D. (1991). predicting participation, early onset, and later persistence in officially recorded offending. *Criminal Behaviour & Mental Health, 1*(1), 1–33.

Ferguson, A. A. (2000). *Bad boys: Public school and the making of black masculinity.* Ann Arbor: University of Michigan Press.
Florida Department of Education. (1995). *Florida school discipline study.* Tallahassee, FL: Office of Policy Research. (ED384981)
Frick, P., Kamphaus, R. W., Lahey, B. B., Loeber, R., Christ, M. G., Hart, E., et al. (1991). Academic underachievement and the disruptive behavior disorders. *Journal of Consulting and Clinical Psychology, 59,* 289–294.
Fuchs, D., Fuchs, L. S., & Burish, p. (2000). peer-assisted learning strategies: An evidence-based practice to promote reading achievement. *Learning Disabilities Research and Practice, 15*(2), 85–91.
Fuller, B., Coonerty, C., Kipnis, F. M., & Choong, y. (1997). An unfair headstart: California families face gaps in preschool and child care availability. Berkeley, CA: Berkeley-Stanford pACE Center, yale University, and the California Child Care Resource and Referral Network's Growing Up in Poverty Project.
Giroux, H. A. (1983). Theories of reproduction and resistance in the new sociology of education: A critical analysis. *Harvard Educational Review, 53*(3), 257–293.
Gonzales, N. A., Cauce, A. M., & Friedman, R. J. (1996). Family, peer, and neighborhood influences on academic achievement among African-American adolescents: One-year prospective effects. *American Journal of Community Psychology, 24*(3), 365–387.
Gorman-Smith, D., & Tolan, p. (1998). The role of exposure to community violence and developmental problems among inner-city youth. *Development & Psychopathology, 10*(1), 101–116.
Gottfredson, D. G., Gottfredson, D. C., Czeh, E. R., Cantor, D., Crosse, S. B., & Hantman, I. (2004) Toward safe and orderly schools: National study of delinquency prevention in schools. *U.S. Department of Justice.* September 15, 2005, from http://www.ncjrs.gov/pdffiles1/nij/205005.pdf
Gottfredson, D. C., Gottfredson, G. D., & Hybl, L. G. (1993). Managing adolescent behavior: A multiyear, multischool study. *American Educational Research Journal, 30*(1), 179–215.
Gottlieb, G., & Halpern, C. T. (2002). A relational view of causality in normal and abnormal development. *Development and Psychopathology, 14,* 421–435.
Grandy, G. S., Madsen, C. H., & De Mersseman, L. M. (1973). The effects of individual and interdependent contingencies on inappropriate classroom behavior. *Psychology in the Schools, 10,* 488–493.
Gray, J. A. (1987). *The psychology of fear and stress.* Cambridge, UK: Cambridge University Press.
Greenberg, M. T., & Kusche, C. A. (1993). *Promoting social and emotional development in deaf children: The PATHS project.* Seattle, WA: University of Washington Press.
Greenberg, M. T., Kusche, C. A., Cook, E. T., & Quamma, J. P. (1995). Promoting emotional competence in school-aged children: The effects of the PATHS curriculum. *Development and Psychopathology, 7,* 117–136.
Greenberg, M. T., Kusche, C., & Mihalic, S. F. (1998). *Blueprints for violence prevention, book ten: Promoting alternative thinking strategies (PATHS).* Boulder, CO: Center for the Study and prevention of Violence.
Gregory, A. (2004). *A window on the discipline gap: Cooperation or defiance in the high school classroom.* Doctoral dissertation, University of California, Berkeley.
Gregory, A., & Weinstein, S. R. (2008). A window on the discipline gap: Defiance or cooperation in the high school classroom. *Journal of School Psychology.*46, 455-475

Gregory, A., & Weinstein, R. S. (2004). Connection and regulation at home and in school: predicting growth in achievement for adolescents. *Journal of Adolescent Research, 19*(4), 405–427.

Gregory, A., Nygreen, K., & Moran, D. (2006). The Discipline gap and the normalization of failure. In p. Noguera and J. Wing, (Eds.). *Unfinished business; Closing the racial achievement gap in our schools.* (pp. 121–150) John Wiley & Sons: CA.

Guerra, N. G., & Slaby, R. C. (1989). Evaluative factors in social problem solving by aggressive boys. *Journal of Abnormal Child Psychology, 17*, 277–289.

Gun–Free Schools Act of 1990, Crime Control Act of 1990, pub. L. 101–647, 18 U.S.C. ¶ 922.

Harvard Civil Rights Project. (2000). *Opportunity suspended: The devastating consequence of zero-tolerance and school discipline policy.* Retrieved September 10, 2005, from http://www.civilrightsproject.harvard.edu/convenings/zerotolerance/synopsis.php

Hawken, L. S., & Horner, R. H. (2003). Evaluation of a targeted intervention within a schoolwide system of behavior support. *Journal of Behavioral Education, 12*(3), 225–240.

Hawkins, J. D., Guo, J., & Hill, K. G. (2001). Long-term effects of the Seattle Social Development Intervention on school bonding trajectories. *Applied Developmental Science, 5*, 225–236.

Hawkins, J. D., Herrenkohl, T., & Farrington, D. P. (1998). A review of predictors of youth violence. In R. Loeber & D. P. Farrington (Eds.), *Serious & violent juvenile offenders: Risk factors and successful interventions* (pp. 106– 146). Thousand Oaks, CA: Sage publications, Inc.

Hawkins, J. D., Smith, B. H., & Catalano, R. F. (2004). Social development and social and emotional learning. In J. E. Zins, R. p. Weissberg, M. C. Wang, & H. J. Walberg (Eds.), *Building academic success on social and emotional learning: What does the research say?* (pp. 135–150). New York: Teachers College press.

Hegerle, D. R., Kesecker, M. P., & Couch, J. V. (1979). A behavior game for the reduction of inappropriate classroom behaviors. *School Psychology Review, 8*, 339–343.

Heller, K. (1990). Social and community intervention. *Annual Review of Psychology, 41*, 141–168.

Henrich, C. C., Brown, J. L., & Aber, J. L. (1999). Evaluating the effectiveness of school-based violence prevention: Developmental approaches. *Social Policy Report, 13*, 1–16.

Hill, H. M., Fernando, I. S., Chen, S. A., & LaFrombois, T. D. (1994). Sociocultural factors in the etiology and prevention of violence among ethnic minority. In L. D. Eron, J. H. Gentry, P. Schlegel (Eds.), *Reason to hope. A psychosocial perspective on violence and youth* (pp. 59–98). Washington, DC: American psychological Association.

Hinshaw, S. P. (1992). Academic underachievement, attention deficits, and aggression: Comorbidity and implications for intervention. *Journal of Consulting and Clinical Psychology, 60*(6), 893–903.

Hirschi, T. (1969). *Causes of delinquency*. Berkeley: University of California Press.

Hollingsworth, E. J., Lufler, H. S., & Clune, W. H. (1984). *School discipline: Order and autonomy*. New York: Praeger.

Horner, R. H., Sugai, G., Lewis-palmer, T., & Todd, A. W. (2001). Teaching school-wide behavioral expectations. *Report on Emotional & Behavioral Disorders in Youth, 1*(4), 77–79.

Howlin,)., & Rutter, M. (1987). The consequences of language delay for other aspects of development. In W. Yule & M. Rutter (Eds.), *Language development and disorders* (pp. 271–294). Oxford, UK: MacKeith.

Huesmann, L. R. (1988). An information processing model for the development of aggression. *Aggressive Behavior, 14*, 13–24.

Huesmann, L. R. & Eron, L. D (1984). Cognitive processes and the persistence of aggressive behavior. *Aggressive Behavior, 10*, 243–251.

Huesmann, L. R., & Eron, L. D. (Eds.). (1986). *Television and the aggressive child: A cross-national comparison*. Hills-dale, NJ: Erlbaum.

Huesmann, L. R., Moise, J. F., & podoloski, C. (1997). The effects of media violence on the development of antisocial behavior. In D. M. Stoff, J. Breiling, & J. D. Maser (Eds.), *Handbook of antisocial behavior* (pp. 181–193). New York: John Wiley & Sons, Inc.

Hyman, I. A., & perone, D. C. (1998). The other side of school violence: Educator policies and practices that may contribute to student misbehavior. *Journal of School Psychology, 36*(1), 7–27.

Ialongo, N., poduska, J., Werthamer, L., & Kellam, S. (2001). The distal impact of two first-grade preventive interventions on conduct problems and disorder in early adolescence. *Journal of Emotional & Behavioral Disorders, 9*(3), 146–160.

Inoff-Germain, G., Arnold, G. S., Nottelmann, E. D., Susman, E. J., Cutler, G. B., & Chrousos, G. p. (1988). Relations between hormone levels and observational measures of aggressive behavior of young adolescents in family interactions. *Developmental Psychology, 24*, 129–139.

Jencks, C., & Mayer, S. (1990). The social consequence of growing up in a poor neighborhood. In L. E. Lynn & M. F. H. McGeary (Eds.), *Inner-city poverty in the United States* (pp. 111–186). Washington, DC: National Academy Press.

Johnson, D. W., & Johnson, R. T. (1996). Conflict resolution and peer mediation programs in elementary and secondary schools: A review of the research. *Review of Educational Research, 66*(4), 459–506.

Kaukianinen, A., Bjorkqvist, K., Lagerspetz, K., Osterman, K., Salmivalli, C., Rothberg, S., et al. (1999). The relationships between social intelligence, empathy, and three types of aggression. *Aggressive Behavior, 25*, 81–89.

Kellam, S. G., Ling, X., & Merisca, R. (1998). The effect of the level of aggression in the first grade classroom on the course and malleability of aggressive behavior into middle school. *Development & Psychopathology, 10*(2), 165–185.

Kounin, J. S. (1970). *Discipline and group management in classrooms*. Oxford, UK: Holt, Rinehart, & Winston.

Kruesi, M. J. p., Hibbs, E. D., Zahn, T. p., Keysor, C. S., Hamburger, S. D., Bartko, F. F., et al. (1992). A 2-year prospective follow-up study of children and adolescents with disruptive behavior disorders. *Archives of General Psychiatry, 49*, 429–435.

Laird, R. D., Jordan, K. y., Dodge, K. A., pettit, G. S., & Bates, J. E. (2001) peer rejection in childhood, involvement with antisocial peers in early adolescence, and the development of externalizing problems. *Development and Psychopathology, 13*, 337–354.

Lansford, J. E., Deater-Deckard, K., Dodge, K. A., Bates, J. E., & Pettit, G. S. (2004). Ethnic differences in the link between physical discipline and later adolescent externalizing behaviors. *Journal of Child Psychology and Psychiatry, 45*(4), 801–812.

Leff, S. S. (2005, July). *Joining with stakeholders to design a relational aggression program*. Poster presented at the Eighteenth NIMH Conference on Mental Health Services Research, Bethesda, MD.

Leff, S. S., Costigan, T., & power, T. J. (2004). Using participatory research to develop a playground-based prevention program. *Journal of School Psychology, 42*(1), 3–21.

Leff, S. S., power, T. J., Manz, p. H., Costigan, T. E., & Nabors, L. A. (2001). School-based aggression prevention programs for young children: Current status and implications for violence prevention. *School Psychology Review, 30*, 343–360.

Leventhal, T., & Brooks-Gunn, J. (2000). The neighborhood could live in: The effects of neighborhood residents on child and adolescent outcomes. *Psychological Bulletin, 126* (2), 309–337.

Lewis, T. J., & Sugai, G. (1999). Effective behavior support: A systems approach to proactive school-wide management. *Effective School Practices, 17*(4), 47–53.

Lewis, T. J., Sugai, G., & Colvin, G. (1998). Reducing problem behavior through a school-wide system of effective behavioral support: Investigation of a school-wide social skills training program and contextual interventions. *School Psychology Review, 27*, 446–459.

Lochman, J. E. (1992). Cognitive-behavioral intervention with aggressive boys: Three-year follow-up and preventive effects. *Journal of Consulting and Clinical Psychology, 60*(3), 426–432.

Lochman, J. E., Barry, T. D., & Pardini, D. A. (2003). Anger control training for aggressive youth. In A. E. Kazdin & J. R. Weisz (Eds.), *Evidence-based psychotherapies for children and adolescents* (pp. 263–281). New York: Guilford Press.

Lochman, J. E., & Wells, K. C. (2004). The Coping power program for preadolescent aggressive boys and their parents: Outcome effects at the 1-year follow-up. *Journal of Consulting & Clinical Psychology, 72*(4), 571–578.

Loeber, R., Burke, J. D., Lahey, B. B., Winters, A., & Zera, M. (2000). Oppositional defiant and conduct disorder: A review of the past 10 years, part I. *Journal of the American Academy of Child & Adolescent Psychiatry, 39*(12), 1468–1484.

Lohrman-O'Rourke, S., Knoster, T., Sabatine, K., Smith, D., Horvath, B., & Llewellyn, G. (2000). School-wide application of positive behavior support in the Bangor Area School District. *Journal of Positive Behavior Interventions, 2*, 238–240.

Luiselli, J. K., putnam, R. F., & Sunderland, M. (2002). Longitudinal evaluation of behavior support intervention in a public middle school. *Journal of Positive Behavioral Interventions, 4*(3), 182–188.

Maguin, E., & Loeber, R. (1996). Academic performance and delinquency. In M. Tonry (Ed.), *Crime and justice: A review of research* (Vol. 20, pp. 145–264). Chicago: University of Chicago Press.

March, R. E., & Horner, R. H. (2002). Feasibility and contributions of functional behavior assessment in schools. *Journal of Emotional and Behavioral Disorders, 10*(3), 158–170.

Matheny, A. p. (1989). Children's behavioral inhibition over age and across situations: Genetic similarity for a trait during change. *Journal of Personality, 57*, 215–226.

Maughan, B., Gray, G., & Rutter, M. (1985). Reading retardation and antisocial behavior: A follow-up into employment. *Journal of Child Psychology and Psychiatry, 26*, 741–758.

Mayer, G. R. (1995). Preventing antisocial behavior in the schools. *Journal of Applied Behavior Analysis, 28*, 467–478.

McCarthy, J. D., & Hoge, D. R. (1987). Social construction of school punishment. *Social Forces, 65*(4), 1101–1120.

McEvoy, A., & Welker, R. (2000). Antisocial behavior, academic failure, and school climate: A critical review. *Journal of Emotional and Behavioral Disorders, 8*(3), 130–140.

McGee, R., & Share, D. L. (1988). Attention deficit disorder hyperactivity and academic failure: Which comes first and which should be treated? *Journal of the American Academy of Child and Adolescent Psychiatry, 27*, 318–325.

Mednick, S. A., Gabrielli, W. F., Jr., & Hutchings, B. (1984). Genetic influences in criminal convictions: Evidence from an adoption cohort. *Science, 224*, 891–894.

Moffitt, T. E., & Caspi, A. (2001). Childhood predictors differentiate life-course persistent and adolescence-limited antisocial pathways among males and females. *Development & Psychopathology, 13*(2), 355–375.

National Association of State Boards of Education. (2005). *State-by-state emotional and social health education.* Retrieved October 1, 2005, from http://www.nasbe.org/

National Center for Education Statistics. (1999). *School survey on crime and safety.* Retrieved October 1, 2005, from http://www.nces.ed.gov/

National Center for Education Statistics. (2000). *OCR Elementary and Secondary Survey.* Retrieved October 1, 2005, from http://www.nces.ed.gov/

National Center for Education Statistics (2003). *Status and trends in the education of Hispanic students.* Retrieved October 1, 2005, from http"//www.nces.ed.gov/

National Center for Education Statistics. (2004). *Indicators of school crime and safety.* Retrieved October 1, 2005, from http://www.nces.ed.gov/

Olweus, D. (1999). Sweden. In p. K. Smith, y. Morita, J. Junger-Tas, D. Olweus, R. Catalano, & P. Slee (Eds.), *The nature of school bullying: A cross-national perspective* (pp. 7–27). London: Routledge.

Olweus, D., Mattsson, A., Schalling, D., & Low, H. (1988). Circulating testosterone levels and aggression in adolescent males: A causal analysis. *Psychosomatic Medicine, 50*, 261–272.

Osgood, D. W., & Chambers, J. M. (2003). *Community correlates of rural youth violence.* Washington DC: U.S. Department of Justice, Juvenile Justice Bulletin. patterson, G. R. (1982). Coercive family process. Eugene, OR: Castalia.

Patterson, G. R. (1995). Coercion as a basis for early age of onset for arrest. (pp. 81–105). In J. McCord (Ed.) *Coercion and punishment in long-term perspectives.* New York: Cambridge University Press.

Patterson, G. R., Dishion, T. J., & Yoerger, K. (2000). Adolescent growth in new forms of problem behavior: Macro- and micro-peer dynamics. *Prevention Science, 1*(1), 3–13.

Pianta, R. C. (1999). *Enhancing relationships between children and teachers.* Washington, DC: American Psychological Association.

Pigott, H. E., Fantuzzo, J. W., & Clement, p. (1986). The effects of reciprocal peer tutoring and group contingencies on the academic performance of elementary school children. *Journal of Applied Behavior Analysis, 19*, 93–98.

Pliszka, S. R., Rogeness, G. A., Renner, p., Sherman, J., & Broussard, T. (1988). plasma neurochemistry in juvenile offenders. *Journal of the American Academy of Child and Adolescent Psychiatry, 27*, 588–594.

Quiggle, N., Garber, J., panak, W. F., & Dodge, K. A. (1992). Social-information processing in aggressive and depressed children. *Child Development, 63*, 1305–1320.

Quinn, M. M., Gable, R. A., Fox, J., Rutherford, R. B., Jr., Van Acker, R., Conroy, M., et al. (2001). Putting quality functional assessment into practice in schools: A research agenda on behalf of E/BD students. *Education & Treatment of Children, 24*(3), 261–275.

Raine, A. (1993). *The psychopathology of crime: Criminal behavior as a clinical disorder.* New York: Academic Press.

Reid, J. B., & Eddy, J. M. (1997). The prevention of antisocial behavior; Some considerations in the search for effective interventions. In D. M. Stoff, J. Breiling, & J. D. Maser (Eds.), *Handbook of antisocial behavior* (pp. 343–355). New York: John Wiley & Sons.

Reid, J. B., Eddy, J. M. & Fetrow, R. A. (1999). Description and immediate impacts of a preventive intervention for conduct problems. *American Journal of Community Psychology, 27*(4), 483–517.

Reid, R., Gonzalez, J. E., Nordness, p. D., Trout, A., & Epstein, M. H. (2004). A meta-analysis of the academic status of students with emotional/behavioral disturbance. *The Journal of Special Education, 38*(3), 130–143.

Reid, J. B., Patterson, G. R., & Snyder, J. (2002). *Antisocial behavior in children and adolescents: A developmental analysis and model for intervention.* Washington, DC: American psychological Association.

Reid, M. J., Webster-Stratton, C., & Baydar, N. (2004). Halting the development of conduct problems in Head Start children: The effects of parent training. *Journal of Clinical Child & Adolescent Psychology, 33*(2), 279–291.

Richman, N., Stevenson, J., & Graham, p. (1982). *Preschool to school: A behavioral study*. San Diego, CA: Academic Press.

Rimm-Kaufman, S. E., Pianta, R. C., & Cox, M. J. (2000). Teachers' judgments of problems in the transition to kindergarten. *Early Childhood Research Quarterly, 15*(2), 147–166.

Rogeness, G. A., Javors, M. A., & pliszka, S. R. (1992). Neurochemistry and child and adolescent psychiatry. *Journal of the American Academic of Child and Adolescent Psychiatry, 31*, 765–781.

Rohrbeck, C. A., Ginsburg-Block, M. D., Fantuzzo, J. W., & Miller, T. R. (2003). Peer-assisted learning interventions with elementary school students: A meta-analytic review. *Journal of Educational Psychology, 95*(2), 240–257.

Rutter, M., & Giller, H. (1983). *Juvenile delinquency: Trends and perspectives*. Harmondsworth, U.K.: Penguin Books.

Rutter, M., Maughan, B., Mortiore, P., & Ouston, J. (1979). *Fifteen thousand hours*. Cambridge, MA: Harvard University Press.

Rutter, M., & Sroufe, L. A. (2000). Developmental psychopathology: Concepts and challenges. *Development and Psychopathology, 12*, 265–296.

Saft, E. W., & Pianta, R. C. (2001). Teachers' perceptions of their relationships with students: Effects of child age, gender, and ethnicity of teachers and students. *School Psychology Quarterly, 16*(7), 125–140.

Salend, S. J., Reynolds, C. J., & Coyle, E. M. (1989). Individualizing the good behavior game across type and frequency of behavior with emotionally disturbed adolescents. *Behavior Modification, 13*(1), 108–126.

Sampson, R. J., Morenoff, J. D., & Earls, F. (1999). Beyond social capital: Spatial dynamics of collective efficacy for children. *American Sociological Review, 64*(5), 633–660.

Schneider, D. J. (1991). Social cognition. *Annual Review of Psychology, 42*, 527–561.

Sherman, L. W., Gottfredson, D., MacKenzie, D., Eck, J., Reuter, P., & Bushway, S. (1997). *Preventing crime: What works, what doesn't, what's promising. A report to the United States Congress.* Washington, DC: National Institute of Justice.

Shriver, T. P., & Weissberg, R. P. (2005, August 16). No emotion left behind. *New York Times*, p. A15.

Slaby, R. C., & Guerra, N. G. (1988). Cognitive mediators of aggression in adolescent offenders: I. Assessment. *Developmental Psychology, 24*, 580–588.

Sladeczek, I., Kratochwill, T. R., Steinback, C. L., Kumke, p., & Hagermoser, L. (2003). problem-solving consultation in the new millennium. In E. Cole, J. A. Ester, Siegel, & A. Jane (Eds.), *Effective consultation in school psychology* (pp. 60–86). Ashland, OH: Hogrefe & Huber Publishers.

Skiba, R., Michael, R. S., Nardo, A. C., & peterson, R. (2002). The color of discipline: Sources of racial and gender disproportionality in school punishment. *The Urban Review, 34*(4), 317–342.

Skiba, R. J., Peterson, R. L., & Williams, T. (1997). Office referrals and suspension: Disciplinary intervention in middle schools. *Education & Treatment of Children, 20*(3), 295–313.

Snyder, J. (2002). Reinforcement and coercion mechanisms in the development of antisocial behavior: peer relationships. In J. B Reid, G. R. patterson, & J. Snyder (Eds.), *Antisocial behavior and children in adolescence: The developmental analysis on model for intervention* (pp. 101–122). Washington, DC: American Psychological Association.

Solomon, D., Battistich, V., Watson, M., Schaps, E., & Lewis, C. (2000). A six-district study of educational change: Direct and mediated effects of the Child Development project. *Social Psychology of Education, 4*, 3–51.

Spivak, G., & Shure, M. B. (1980). Interpersonal problem-solving as a mediator of behavioral adjustment in preschool and kindergarten children. *Journal of Developmental Psychology, 1*, 29–44.

Spoont, M. R. (1992). Modulatory role of serotonin in neural information processing: Implications for human psychopathology. *Psychological Bulletin, 112*, 330–350.

Steinberg, L., Lamborn, S. D., & Darling, N. (1994). Over-time changes in adjustment and competence among adolescents from authoritative, authoritarian, indulgent, and neglectful families. *Child Development, 65*(3), 754–770.

Susman, E. J., Inoff-Germain, G., Nottelmann, E. D., Loriaux, L., Cutler, G. B., & Chrousos, G. p. (1987). Hormones, emotional dispositions, and aggressive attributes in young adolescents. *Child Development, 58*, 1114–1134.

Sutherland, E. H. (1939). *Principles of criminology* (3rd ed.). Philadelphia: Lippincott. Reid, Eddy, & Fetrow, 1999.

Tallal, p., Dukette, D., & Curtiss, S. (1989). Behavioral/emotional profiles of preschool language-impaired children. *Development and Psychopathology, 1*, 51–67.

Taylor-Greene, S. J., & Kartub, D. T. (2000). Durable implementation of school-wide behavior support: The high five program. *Journal of Positive Behavior Interventions, 2*, 233–245.

Thornberrry, T. p., & Krohn, M. D. (1997). Peers, drug use, and delinquency. In D. M. Stoff, J. Breiling, & J. D. Maser (Eds.), *Handbook of antisocial behavior* (pp. 218–233). New York: John Wiley & Sons.

Tingstrom, D. H. (1994) The good behavior game: An investigation of teachers' acceptance. *Psychology in the Schools, 31*, 57–65.

Tolan, P. H., & Guerra, N. G. (1994). prevention of delinquency: Current status and issues. *Applied & Preventive Psychology, 3*(4), 251–273.

Tolan, P. H., Guerra, N. G., & Kendall, p. C. (1995). A developmental-ecological perspective on antisocial behavior in children and adolescents: Toward a unified risk and intervention framework. *Journal of Consulting and Clinical Psychology, 63*(4), 579–584.

Topping, K. J., & Ehly, S. W. (2001). Peer assisted learning: A framework for consultations. *Journal of Educational and Psychological Consultation, 12*(2), 113–132.

Underwood, M. K. (2003). *Social aggression among girls*. New York: Guilford Press.

Watts, I. E., & Erevelles, N. (2004). These deadly times: Reconceptualizing school violence. *American Educational Research Journal, 41*(2), 271–299.

Webster-Stratton, C. (2005). The incredible years: A training series for the prevention and treatment of conduct problems in young children. In E. D. Hibbs & P. S. Jensen (Eds.), *Psychosocial treatments for child and adolescent disorders: Empirically based strategies for clinical practice* (2nd ed., pp. 507–555). Washington, DC: American Psychological Association.

Webster-Stratton, C., Reid, M. J., & Hammond, M. (2004). Treating children with early onset conduct problems: Intervention outcomes for parent, child, teacher training. *Journal of Clinical Child and Adolescent Psychology, 33*(1), 105–124.

Weinstein, R. S. (2002). *Reaching higher: The power of expectations in schooling*. Cambridge, MA: Harvard University press.

Weissberg, R. P., & Greenberg, M. T. (1998). School and community competence-enhancement and prevention programs. In W. Damon, I. E. Sigel, & K. A. Renninger (Eds.), *Handbook of child psychology: Vol. 4: Child psychology in practice* (5th ed., pp. 877–954). New York: John Wiley & Sons,.

Wentzel, K. R. (2002). Are effective teachers like good parents? Teaching styles and student adjustment in early adolescence. *Child Development, 73*(1), 287–301.

Werthamer-Larsson, L., Kellam, S. G., & Wheeler, L. (1991). Effect of first-grade classroom environment on shy behavior, aggressive behavior, and concentration problems. *American Journal of Community Psychology, 19*(4), 585–602.

Wilson, D. B., Gottfredson, D. C., & Najaka, S. S. (2001). School-based prevention of problem behaviors: A metaanalysis. *Journal of Quantitative Criminology, 17*(3), 247–272.

Wilson, S. J., Lipsey, M. W., & Derzon, J. H. (2003). The effects of school-based intervention programs on aggressive behavior: A meta-analysis. *Journal of Consulting & Clinical Psychology, 71*(1), 136–149.

Wolfe, J. A., Fantuzzo, J. W., & Wolfe, p. K. (1986). The effects of reciprocal peer management on the arithmetic proficiency of underachieving students. *Behavior Therapy, 17*, 253–265.

Xie, H., Swift, D. J., Cairns, B., & Cairns, R. B. (2002). Aggressive behaviors in social interaction and developmental adaptation: A narrative analysis of interpersonal conflicts during early adolescence. *Social Development, 11*(2), 205–224.

Printed in the USA
CPSIA information can be obtained
at www.ICGtesting.com
LVHW010818030923
757072LV00010B/244

9 781516 527960